Meanings and Values of Water in Russian Culture

Bringing together a team of scholars from the diverse fields of geography, literary studies, and history, this is the first volume to study water as a cultural phenomenon within the Russian/Soviet context. Water in this context is both a cognitive and cultural construct and a geographical and physical phenomenon, representing particular rivers (the Volga, the Chusovaia in the Urals, the Neva) and bodies of water (from Baikal to sacred springs and the flowing water of nineteenth-century estates), but also powerful systems of meaning from traditional cultures and those forged in the radical restructuring undertaken in the 1930s. Individual chapters explore the polyvalence and contestation of meanings, dimensions, and values given to water in various times and spaces in Russian history. The reservoir of symbolic association is tapped by poets and film-makers but also by policy-makers, the popular press, and advertisers seeking to incite reaction or drive sales. The volume's emphasis on the cultural dimensions of water links material that is often widely disparate in time and space; it serves as the methodological framework for the analysis undertaken both within chapters and in the editors' introduction.

Jane Costlow is the Clark A. Griffiths Professor of Environmental Studies at Bates College in Lewiston, Maine, USA. Her scholarly work has focused primarily on nineteenth-century Russian literature and visual culture, ranging from the novels of Ivan Turgenev to writing by Russian women writers and representations of the bear in late Imperial culture. Recent publications include *Heart-Pine Russia: Walking and Writing the Nineteenth-Century Forest* (Cornell University Press, 2013) and, with Amy Nelson, *Other Animals: Beyond the Human in Russian Culture and History* (University of Pittsburgh Press, 2010). At Bates she teaches courses in Environmental Humanities and Russian Literature, interests reflected in recent papers and conference presentations on disaster narratives in film and oral history. Her translation of Lydia Zinovieva-Annibal's *The Tragic Menagerie* received the AATSEEL prize for best translation in 1999.

Arja Rosenholm is Professor of Russian Language and Culture at the University of Tampere, Finland. Her research interests include the history of Russian literature and culture, gender studies, Russian popular culture and mass media, ecocriticism, space, and culture. She is currently heading the Academy of Finland-funded project "Water as Cultural Space: Changing Values and Representations" (2012–2016). Rosenholm has edited several scholarly volumes in English, Russian, and Finnish and published numerous peer-reviewed articles in international and national journals. Recent books include *Women in Russian Cultural History* (in Finnish), with Suvi Salmenniemi and Marja Sorvari (Gaudeamus, 2014), and *Topografii populiarnoi kul'tury* with Irina Savkina (NLO, 2015).

Routledge Studies in Modern European History
For a full list of titles in this series, please visit www.routledge.com

23 History, Memory, and Trans-European Identity
Unifying divisions
Aline Sierp

24 Constructing a German Diaspora
The "greater German empire," 1871–1914
Stefan Manz

25 Violence, Memory, and History
Western perceptions of kristallnacht
Edited by Colin McCullough and Nathan Wilson

26 Turkey and the Rescue of European Jews
I. Izzet Bahar

27 Antifascism After Hitler
East German youth and socialist memory, 1949–1989
Catherine Plum

28 Fascism and Ideology
Italy, Britain, and Norway
Salvatore Garau

29 Hitler's Brudervolk
The dutch and the colonization of occupied eastern Europe, 1939–1945
Geraldien von Frijtag Drabbe Künzel

30 Alan S. Milward and Contemporary European History
Collected academic reviews
Edited by Fernando Guirao and Frances M.B. Lynch

31 Ireland's Great Famine and Popular Politics
Edited by Enda Delaney and Breandán Mac Suibhne

32 Legacies of Violence in Contemporary Spain
Exhuming the past, understanding the present
Edited by Ofelia Ferrán and Lisa Hilbink

33 The Problem of Democracy in Postwar Europe
Political actors and the formation of the postwar model of democracy in France, west Germany and Italy
Pepijn Corduwener

34 Meanings and Values of Water in Russian Culture
Edited by Jane Costlow and Arja Rosenholm

Meanings and Values of Water in Russian Culture

Edited by
Jane Costlow
Bates College

and

Arja Rosenholm
University of Tampere

LONDON AND NEW YORK

First published 2017
by Routledge
2 Park Square, Milton Park, Abingdon, Oxon OX14 4RN

and by Routledge
711 Third Avenue, New York, NY 10017

First issued in paperback 2018

Routledge is an imprint of the Taylor & Francis Group, an informa business

© 2017 selection and editorial matter, Jane Costlow and Arja Rosenholm; individual chapters, the contributors.

The right of Jane Costlow and Arja Rosenholm to be identified as the authors of the editorial material, and of the authors for their individual chapters, has been asserted in accordance with sections 77 and 78 of the Copyright, Designs and Patents Act 1988.

All rights reserved. No part of this book may be reprinted or reproduced or utilised in any form or by any electronic, mechanical, or other means, now known or hereafter invented, including photocopying and recording, or in any information storage or retrieval system, without permission in writing from the publishers.

Trademark notice: Product or corporate names may be trademarks or registered trademarks, and are used only for identification and explanation without intent to infringe.

British Library Cataloguing in Publication Data
A catalogue record for this book is available from the British Library

Library of Congress Cataloguing in Publication Data
Names: Costlow, Jane T. (Jane Tussey), 1955– editor of compilaton. | Rosenholm, Arja, editor of compilaton.
Title: Meanings and values of water in Russian culture / edited by Jane Costlow and Arja Rosenholm.
Description: Milton Park, Abingdon, Oxon; New York, NY: Routledge, 2017. | Series: Routledge studies in modern European history; 34
Identifiers: LCCN 2016021353| ISBN 9781472447500 (hardback : alkaline paper) | ISBN 9781315594378 (ebook)
Subjects: LCSH: Russia–Civilization. | Soviet Union–Social life and customs. | Water and civilization. | Water–Social aspects–Russia–History. | Water–Social aspects–Soviet Union–History. | Water–Symbolic aspects–Russia–History. | Water–Symbolic aspects–Soviet Union–History. | Bodies of water–Social aspects–Russia–History. | Bodies of water–Social aspects–Soviet Union–History.
Classification: LCC DK32 .M465 2017 | DDC 333.9100947–dc23
LC record available at https://lccn.loc.gov/2016021353

ISBN 13: 978-1-138-32993-5 (pbk)
ISBN 13: 978-1-4724-4750-0 (hbk)

Typeset in Sabon
by Out of House Publishing

Contents

List of figures	vii
Notes on contributors	ix
Acknowledgments	xiv
Note on transliteration	xv
Introduction JANE COSTLOW AND ARJA ROSENHOLM	1

SECTION I
Language and myths of water   13

1 The cultural semantics of water idioms in
   Russian dialects   15
   IVAN PODIUKOV

2 Sacred waters: The spiritual world of Lake Baikal   32
   NICHOLAS BREYFOGLE

3 On the veneration of springs in the nineteenth century:
   Models of behavior and decision-making practices   51
   EVGENII PLATONOV

4 *Daemon loci*: The formation of river images
   in Russian mental worlds   65
   DMITRY ZAMYATIN

SECTION II
Socio-cultural identities of water   79

5 "Mother Volga" and "Mother Russia": On the role
   of the river in gendering Russianness   81
   OLEG RIABOV

6 Main street of the Urals: Creating the "Chusovaia" metanarrative 98
MARIA LITOVSKAIA

7 A cup of tundra: Ethnography of water and thirst in the Bering Strait 117
SVETA YAMIN-PASTERNAK, PETER SCHWEITZER, IGOR PASTERNAK, ANDREW KLISKEY, AND LILIAN ALESSA

SECTION III
Water rebuilding landscapes 137

8 Water on the Russian gentry estate 139
E.G. MILIUGINA AND M.V. STROGANOV

9 Celebrating the return of the flood 158
POLINA BARSKOVA

10 Water and power: The Moscow Canal and the "Port of Five Seas" 175
CYNTHIA RUDER

SECTION IV
Aesthetics and poetics of water 189

11 A woman in nature/A WOMAN IS NATURE: The eternal feminine as a conceptual blend of human and liquescent ontologies in Russian Symbolist poetics 191
ANASTASIA KOSTETSKAYA

12 Parched: Water and its absence in the films of Larisa Shepit'ko 207
JANE COSTLOW

13 "Water flows and teaches": Marietta Shaginian's novel *Hydrocentral* 222
ARJA ROSENHOLM

14 Spatriotism: Water recycling in literary polemics (late eighteenth- to early nineteenth-century Russia) 245
GITTA HAMMARBERG

Index 262

List of figures

2.1 Cape Burkhan, also known as the Shaman's Rock or Shamanka, on Ol'khon Island, Lake Baikal — 39
2.2 Offerings of colored cloth and prayer flags, cigarettes, candy, drinks, and money at the sacred site of Cape Khoboi at the northern point of Ol'khon Island, Lake Baikal — 41
2.3 A sign erected as visitors arrive at the base of the Shaman's Rock (Ol'khon Island, Lake Baikal) in an effort to prevent tourists from walking on the sacred rocks. The sign says "Stop. This is a Specially Protected Territory! Entrance is Forbidden!" — 44
2.4 "Julia, I love you." Graffiti painted on the Shaman's Rock (Ol'khon Island, Lake Baikal), reflecting different understandings of the sacredness of the site — 45
5.1 Shaposhnikov, Sergei and Malashkina, Vera. "Mother Volga" (1953) — 86
5.2 A Russian stamp depicting Lyudmila Zykina (1929–2009), a Soviet and Russian singer, and the badge of the Order of St. Andrew — 87
7.1 Municipal water delivery truck – *vodovozka* – operating in Sireniki in 2009 — 119
7.2 Third-grade students and teacher in a Chukotkan village, having a *chaepitie* — 121
7.3 Tea on the tundra — 121
7.4 Newer approaches to winter teatime — 122
7.5 Municipal village bakery, with the marked vessels storing the drinking water and utility water — 127
7.6 A spring catchment on a rocky slope near the old Yupik settlement of Imtuk, Chukotka, photographed in late August — 129
7.7 Resident of Gambell, Alaska, harvests from the village's preferred source of drinking water, photographed in February — 130
7.8 Welcoming a harvested seal with fresh water — 131

7.9	Handcrafted potholder in a Koyukon Athabascan household in Galena, Alaska	133
7.10	Youth from Alaska and Chukotka, and the accompanying staff, heading out for teatime in the tundra near the village of New Chaplino, summer 2010	134
8.1	The Chertov Bridge on the Vasilevo estate	149
8.2	Boulder bridge in the park of the Mitino estate	150
8.3	A system of ponds on the Znamenskoe-Raek estate	151
9.1	Leningraders examine the memorial plaque of the 1824 flood during the flood of 1924	162
9.2	Preservation of the monuments in the Summer Garden after the flood of 1924	170
10.1	"Port of Five Seas" map	183
11.1	Viktor Elpidiforovich Borisov-Musatov. *Apparitions* (1903)	199

Notes on contributors

Lilian Alessa is President's Professor of Resilient Landscapes at the University of Idaho and heads the Center for Resilient Communities at the University of Alaska Anchorage. She is Director of the Alaska Experimental Program to Stimulate Competitive Research, and co-lead for the Arctic Domain Awareness Center at the University of Alaska Anchorage. Professor Alessa currently conducts extensive research on human adaptation to environmental change, community-based observing networks, and Arctic early warning systems funded by the National Science Foundation. She is the lead author and co-author of several book chapters and numerous research articles, including those featured in *Sustainability Science* and *Washington Journal of Environmental Law and Policy*.

Polina Barskova is Associate Professor of Russian Literature at Hampshire College (MA), received her BA from St. Petersburg State University and her MA and PhD from the University of California at Berkeley. Her scholarly publications include articles on Nabokov, the Bakhtin brothers, and early Soviet film. Recently, she published articles in English, Russian, and German on the culture of Petersburg-Petrograd-Leningrad during moments of historical upheaval. She has also authored ten books of poetry in Russian and in translation. Professor Barskova is currently working on a project entitled "The Ruin Screams: The Urban Image and Representation during the Siege of Leningrad (1941–44)."

Nicholas Breyfogle is Associate Professor of History at The Ohio State University. Supported by fellowships from NEH, ACLS, NCEEER, American Philosophical Society, Kennan Institute, Davis Center, Mershon Center, and the Ohio State University, he is currently completing the book: *Baikal: the Great Lake and its People*. He is the author of *Heretics and Colonizers: Forging Russia's Empire in the South Caucasus* (Cornell University Press, 2005, pbk 2011). He is editor or co-editor of *Peopling the Russian Periphery: Borderland Colonization in Eurasian History* (Routledge, 2007, pbk and ebook 2009); *Health, Disease, and Environment in Global History*, Guest Co-Editor of *Journal of World*

History (volume 24, issue 4 (December 2013)); and the online magazine *Origins: Current Events in Historical Perspective* http://origins.osu.edu.

Jane Costlow is the Clark A. Griffiths Professor of Environmental Studies at Bates College in Lewiston, Maine, USA. Her scholarly work has focused primarily on nineteenth-century Russian literature and visual culture, ranging from the novels of Ivan Turgenev to writing by Russian women writers and representations of the bear in late Imperial culture. Recent publications include *Heart-Pine Russia: Walking and Writing the Nineteenth-Century Forest* (Cornell University Press, 2013) and, with Amy Nelson, *Other Animals: Beyond the Human in Russian Culture and History* (University of Pittsburgh Press, 2010). At Bates she teaches courses in Environmental Humanities and Russian Literature, interests reflected in recent papers and conference presentations on disaster narratives in film and oral history. Her translation of Lydia Zinovieva-Annibal's *The Tragic Menagerie* received the AATSEEL prize for best translation in 1999.

Gitta Hammarberg is Professor Emerita at Macalester College, St Paul, Minnesota, USA. Her expertise is in late eighteenth- and early nineteenth-century Russian literature. Her publications include a book on Sentimentalist theory, *From the Idyll to the Novel: Karamzin's Sentimentalist Prose* (Cambridge University Press, 1991) and numerous articles on minor literary genres (album verse, bouts-rimés), the earliest Russian women's journals, the inception of literary criticism, Karamzin's epigones, spa culture, and Gogol's dandyism. Among her forthcoming articles are: "Karamzinolatry & Epigonism" (in *Russian Literature*, Amsterdam) and "Karamzin and France: Travel Discourse and Double Deixis" (in a French Karamzin conference collection).

Andrew Kliskey is a Professor of Landscape Social-Ecology and Co-Director of the Center for Resilient Communities at the University of Idaho. Since 2000, he has been collaborating with the communities of diverse social-ecological adaptations, including the New Zealand Maori, indigenous communities of Hawaii, Inupiat and Denai'na in Alaska, and most recently with the rural communities in Idaho, examining community perception and response to landscape and hydrologic change. He is co-PI of the Community-based Observing Network for Adaptation and Security in the Bering Sea and the author and co-author of research articles featured in *Sustainability Science*, *Global Environmental Change*, *Arctic*, and several other journals.

Anastasia Kostetskaya is Assistant Professor of Russian at the University of Hawai'i, Manoa. Her PhD dissertation, "The Water of Life and the Life of Water: The Metaphor of World Liquescence in the Poetry, Painting and Film of the Russian Silver Age," explores the cultural implications of conceptual metaphor and blending theories from the field of cognitive linguistics. Recent work includes "Symbolism in Flux: the Conceptual Metaphor of World Liquescence across Media, Genre and Realities" (*SEEJ*, 2015), and "Crime is in the Eye of the Beholder: Petr Petrovich Luzhin as a Distorting 'Puddle-Mirror' in Dostoevsky's Crime and Punishment" (*Names*, 2010).

Maria Litovskaia is Professor of Philology at the Ural Federal University, Ekaterinburg, and Professor of the Slavic Department at National Chengchi University (Taiwan). She has edited several volumes in the area of Russian literature and culture. Her publications are on Soviet and post-Soviet culture and include *Massovaia literatura segodnia* (*Mass Literature Today*, 2009, repr. 2011), and the co-edited volume *Obraz dostoinoi zhizni v soveremennykh rossiskikh SMI* (*Images of the Good Life in Contemporary Russian Mass Media*, 2008).

Elena Georgievna Miliugina is Professor at the State University of Tver', Russia. Her research interests focus on the Russian provinces, Russian estate culture, travelogues, artistic experiments in Russian culture, and local texts. She has published several books and articles. Among them are the monograph *Russkaia reka* (Russian River, 2012), the edited book *Voskresnyi den' (Russkaia traditsiia*, 2012), the book *Obgoniaiushchii vremia: Nikolai Aleksandrovich L'vov – poet, arkhitektor, iskusstvoved, istorik Moskvy* (2009), and she has edited (together with M.V. Stroganov) the volume *Tver' v zapiskakh puteshestvennikov XVI–XIX vekov* (2012).

Igor Pasternak holds an MFA degree in Studio Art from American University and teaches fine arts and ethnomycology at the University of Alaska Fairbanks. He is a Co-PI on several collaborative projects supported by the National Science Foundation at the UAF Institute of Northern Engineering. He broadly applies his art practice to explore questions that reach across diverse areas of humanities and science. Pasternak conducts field research in the regions of the Bering Strait and interior Alaska, investigating the aesthetic practices connected with domestic production, preparation, storage, and consumption of traditional foods. The participatory installation he created in 2014, together with Ukrainian and Russian settlers who practice extensive foraging and horticulture in the Subarctic, was shown at the Anchorage International Gallery of Contemporary Art.

Evgenii Platonov completed his PhD in 2005, with a dissertation on rural shrines and natural holy places in northwest Russia. Since then he has completed numerous expeditions in northwest Russia, along with research in local archives on the history of rural shrines in Russia. He organized the Seventh International Conference "Complexity and Regional Aspects of Natural Holy Places" in St. Petersburg in May 2013. He works at the Library of the State Hermitage Museum in St. Petersburg. His main publications include a monograph on *Chapels of the Tikhvin Region (End* *of 19th/Early 20th Centuries)*; *A Primary Inventory of Chapels in the St. Petersburg Province, 1734–1735*; and *The 1692 Inventory of Chapels as an Ethnographic Source*.

Ivan Podiukov is on the faculty of the Perm' State Humanities Pedagogical University, in the Department of Philology. He holds his doctorate, with a dissertation on "Cultural-semiotic aspects of popular phraseology." His scholarly interests include ethnolinguistics, Russian dialectical lexicon and phraseology, occupational languages, and the language of folklore. His publications include articles on Russian dialectical phraseology, folklore of the Collective Farms of the Kama River region, and the Fishing Lexicon of the Kama River Region.

Oleg Riabov is a Professor at St. Petersburg State University. His primary fields of interest are Nationalism Studies, Gender Studies, Cold War Studies, and the History of Russian Philosophy. Recent publications include *"Mother Russia": Nationalism, Gender, and War in the XX Century Russia* (Ibidem, 2007 [in Russian]); Oleg Riabov and Andrzej de Lazari (eds.) *"Russian Bear": History, Semiotics, and Politics* (Moscow: NLO, 2012 [in Russian]); and Oleg Riabov and Tatiana Riabova, "The Remasculinization of Russia? Gender, Nationalism and Legitimation of Power under Vladimir Putin," *Problems of Post-Communism* (2014, Vol. 61, No. 2, pp. 23–35).

Arja Rosenholm is Professor of Russian Language and Culture at the University of Tampere, Finland. Her research interests include the history of Russian literature and culture, gender studies, Russian popular culture and mass media, ecocriticism, space, and culture. She is currently heading the Academy of Finland-funded project "Water as Cultural Space: Changing Values and Representations" (2012–16). Rosenholm has edited several scholarly volumes in English, Russian, and Finnish, and has published numerous peer-reviewed articles in international and national journals. Recent books include *Women in Russian Cultural History* (in Finnish), with Suvi Salmenniemi and Marja Sorvari (Gaudeamus, 2014), and *Topografii populiarnoi kul'tury* with Irina Savkina (NLO, 2015).

Cynthia Ruder is Associate Professor of Russian at the University of Kentucky. Her interest in the depiction of Stalinist culture and ideology in large-scale Soviet construction projects resulted in the book *Making History for Stalin: The Story of the Belomor Canal*, the first monograph on the Belomor project in English. Her current project is a book-length study about the Moscow Canal and its relationship to the construction of Soviet space. She has served as an on-air expert for the History Channel series "Lost Worlds: Stalin's Supercity" (broadcast in 2007). Her recent articles include a discussion of the 70th anniversary celebration of the Moscow Canal, an examination of collective authorship in Soviet literature of the 1930s, and an analysis of the *Biblioteka "Perekovki"* series produced by the NKVD.

Peter Schweitzer is Professor at the Department of Social and Cultural Anthropology at the University of Vienna and a Professor Emeritus at the University of Alaska Fairbanks. His interests range from kinship and identity politics to human–environmental interactions, including the community effects of global climate change, and his regional focus areas include the circumpolar North and the former Soviet Union. Schweitzer is past president of the International Arctic Social Sciences Association, and past chair of the Social and Human Sciences Working Group of the International Arctic Science Committee (IASC). He is the editor of *Dividends of Kinship* (Routledge, 2000), co-editor of *Hunters and Gatherers in the Modern World* (Berghahn, 2000), and co-author of *Russian Old-Settlers of Siberia* (Novoe izdatel'stvo, 2004; in Russian).

Mikhail Viktorovich Stroganov is Professor and Director of the Research Center for Tver Local History and Ethnography of Tver' State University, and he is Senior Fellow of the State Republican Center of Russian Folklore. His research interests are: the Russian provinces, Russian estate culture, travelogues, local texts, and Russian folklore. His recent publications include the co-edited volume *Tver' v zapiskakh puteshestvennikov XVI–XIX vekov* (2012) as well his edited volume *Voina 1812 goda i konsept 'otechestvo'. Iz istorii osmysleniia gosudarstvennoi i natsional'noi identichnosti v Rossii: issledovanie i materialy* (2012), and the book *Pamiati Gertsena* (2012).

Sveta Yamin-Pasternak is a cultural anthropologist holding faculty appointments at the University of Alaska Fairbanks Institute of Northern Engineering, Department of Anthropology, and Ethnobotany Program. Her ethnographic research focuses on the interconnections of foodways, built environment, climate, and social change. She first began working in the Chukotka and Alaska regions of the Bering Strait in 2001, while writing a PhD dissertation on the beliefs and practices connected with tundra mushrooms. The multi-disciplinary research projects supported by the National Science Foundation, on which she has served as a postdoctoral scholar and PI, engage communities around the Bering Strait and interior Alaska. Her research articles are featured in the journals *Current Anthropology*, *Economic Botany*, *Ethnology*, *Etudes Inuit Studies*, *Fungi Magazine*, and as chapters in edited volumes.

Dmitry Zamyatin is lead researcher at the Higher School of Urban Studies of the Higher School of Economics (Moscow). His research interests include human and cultural geography, cultural anthropology, geopolitics, and geohumanities (particularly imagery of space in Russian culture and literature). He is currently lead scholar on the research project "Laboratory of Complex Geocultural Researches on the Arctic" (Yakutsk, Russia, 2014–2016; funded by the Russian Scientific Fund). He is author of several monographs (in Russian): *Humanitarian Geography* (2003), *Meta-geography* (2004), *Culture and Space* (2005), and *Post-geography* (2014).

Acknowledgments

This volume has been supported by various institutions and individuals, whom we would like to acknowledge here. The Academy of Finland and its Program "Sustainable Governance of Aquatic Resources" (AKVA) made a generous award in 2012 to support a four-year scholarly project focusing on the "Social and Cultural Meanings of Water" (University of Tampere). Their support explicitly acknowledges the importance for thinking not only about the political and infrastructural futures of water, but about histories of value and emotional association. This volume would not be appearing without their support.

Bates College made funds available for translation of our Russian colleagues' papers; we are grateful for that support, and for the exceptional work of Stella Rock, Nora Favorov, and Bradley Gorski, whose excellent scholarly translations broaden academic communication and understanding. We also thank Matthew James (University of Tampere) for language checking.

Research for the chapter by Nicholas Breyfogle was supported by funding from a Leverhulme Trust International Network Grant (for the project "Exploring Russia's Environmental History and Natural Resources"), the National Endowment for the Humanities, National Council for Eurasian and East European Research (NCEEER), under authority of a Title VIII grant from the U.S. Department of State, American Philosophical Society, American Council of Learned Societies, Davis Center for Russian and Eurasian Studies, Kennan Institute for Advanced Russian Studies, Mershon Center for International Security Studies and The Ohio State University. Any views, findings, conclusions or recommendations expressed in this article do not necessarily reflect those of the National Endowment for the Humanities or any of the other funding agencies. An early version of this article was presented at the National Convention of the American Association for the Advancement of Slavic Studies, Boston, November 12, 2009, and I thank the panelists and the audience for their comments and suggestions.

An earlier version of Evgenii Platonov's chapter appeared (in Russian) in Traditsionnaia kul'tura, 2014.

The research for Oleg Riabov's chapter was supported by the Russian Foundation for Humanities, project 15-03- 00010 "The Symbol of the Motherland in Contemporary Russian Symbolic Politics."

Note on transliteration

The Library of Congress transliteration system has been used in reference notes to Russian sources. Place and family names that are likely to be well known to non-specialist readers are given in the most commonly used form (Dostoevsky rather than Dostoevskii, Tchaikovsky rather than Chaikovskii). We have maintained Russian terms for weights, measures, distances, and political administrative units, such as *guberniia*, *uezd*, *arshin*, *sazhen*, with explanations as needed.

Introduction

Jane Costlow and Arja Rosenholm

The great nineteenth-century historian Vasilii Kliuchevskii, in public lectures delivered in Moscow in the 1880s, celebrated Russia's rivers – what Dmitrii Zamyatin calls the "most fully and vividly manifested" archetype of water in Russian culture – as essential and much-beloved companions in the development of Russian culture. Kliuchevskii's expansive prose speculates freely about the connection between material cultures and the psychology and mores of a people. For him, Russia's river systems are part of the troika of geographical features that have deeply shaped the country's history; but unlike the other two – forest and steppe – rivers are, he claims, unequivocally beloved.

> While the forest and in particular the steppe were ambivalent in their impacts on Russians, there was no such ambivalence or miscomprehension when it came to the Russian river. The Russian came alive on the river, and lived with her in deep spiritual concord. He loved his rivers; no other elemental force is the object of such loving terms in folk song as the river – and with good reason. At times of resettlement the river showed the way, and when he ultimately settled she was a faithful neighbor: he held close to her, built his dwelling, hamlet or village on her high banks. For much of the long period of religious fast during the year the river fed him. For the merchant she was a ready summer and then frozen winter road, threatening with neither storm nor hidden rocks: one had only to shift course in timely fashion along the never ending, capricious bends of river, watching out for sand bars and low water. In some sense the river even nurtured a sense of order and communal spirit in the populace. The river itself loves order and regularity. Her great spring floods, coming in due order, have no parallel in western European hydro-geography. Marking out where one shouldn't settle, they turn modest streams into great floatable currents, bringing incalculable benefit to shipping, trade, pasturage and crops. Given the inconsequential drop of Russian rivers, rare floods can in no way be compared with the unexpected and destructive floods of western European mountain

rivers. The Russian river taught the dwellers on her banks common life and its virtues. In ancient Russian the populace moved along the rivers; population centers grew particularly dense along the shores of her lively, navigable rivers, leaving wooded or boggy ground in the areas between rivers. If one could look from above on central Russia in, for example, the fifteenth century, it would appear to the observer like a complicated canvas, with marvelous patterns of narrow bands along water lines and large, dark intervals. The river nourished an enterprising spirit, the inclination to work in common; it made one deliberate and adapt, it brought together far-flung parts of the population, it nurtured a sense of being a member of a community, to communicate with those who weren't neighbors, to observe their customs and interests, to exchange both goods and experience, to know one's way around. The historical role of the Russian river was, indeed, diverse.

(85–86)[1]

Kliuchevskii's account of Russian history and Russians' relationships to rivers is grounded in geography, hydrology, and a history of settlement; it acknowledges seasonality and climate, and shifts in its focus between agriculture, religious tradition, and claims about social psychology. It is clearly informed by an aesthetic sense (the canvas of water lines imagined from above), and by national pride. Kliuchevskii's version of Russian geography, whatever its chauvinism and tendency to the idyllic, also makes an explicit attempt at what we might call environmental cultural history, reading not just the dependence of human society on geography and climate, but the ways in which human identities are intimately and creatively interdependent with natural forces that are also key agents of transformation. It is a notably loco-centric account, imagining communities and settlers rather that distant Moscow and the state's efforts to embrace and ultimately control far-flung waterways and the human communities that settled along them.

The environmental historian Douglas Weiner, much more recently, gives us no such idyllic picture: focusing rather on the history of Moscow and the Russian state, Weiner describes what he calls a "predatory tribute-taking state" that knew little restraint (if any) when it came to amassing the resources of the Eurasian landmass. Kliuchevskii's narrative imagines entrepreneurial and communal spirit, the even flow of Russian rivers that permit commerce and predictability, a kind of east Slavic idyll; Weiner's account is written with bitter knowledge of the legacies of state-sponsored, "militaristic" modernization and its impacts on both human and natural populations (Bruno). These differing visions of Russian and Soviet history remind us of what William Cronon suggests about stories more broadly, and the "dilemma" they pose for historians. Cronon's typology – based on radically different histories of the Dust Bowl of the 1930s – charts what he calls "declensionist" narratives of environmental ruin and "progressive" plots of obstacles overcome and problems resolved ("A Place," 1357, 1352).

Translating a bit for the Russian context, we might say that Weiner's early twenty-first-century version is "declensionist"; Kliuchevskii's is idyllic; and the narrative that Cronon calls "progressive" is embedded in versions of state modernization that have mustered both rhetoric and technology to force Russian and Soviet advancement. However, as Cronon goes on to note, it is not merely the *conclusions* of these histories that differ, it is the very stories they tell. "In [differing narratives], the story is inextricably bound to its conclusion, and the historical analysis derives much of its force from the upward or downward sweep of the plot. So we must eventually ask a more basic question: where did these stories come from?" ("A Place," 1348).

Stories of water participate in what Dmitrii Zamyatin, in this volume, calls the "geocultural imagination," drawing on the fluidity of water, its forms, and material potency, to give birth to and shape mythologies that are both national and local. "Culture," suggests the Russian philosopher Pavel Florenskii, entails activities that "assimilate space."[2] Such assimilation, as this volume's authors so richly demonstrate, occurs in multiple realms, in embedded and evolving practices of language, art, and building. To think with and about water is to consider "waterworlds" and lived contexts (Yamin-Pasternak), the ordinary and the visionary (Zamyatin). It is to consider ambivalence and necessity, circulation and obstruction. It is also to consider, as German historian Guido Hausmann has recently argued, the ways in which Russia's rivers – especially the Volga – have been a complex space and essential medium of imperial and national memory. River narratives as Hausmann reads them entail diverse popular images and symbolic meanings, emerging in the historical alteration of knowledge and ideology building. River narratives, as all these scholars remind us, are essential parts of cultural history; the perception and representation of a river or indeed of any aquatic landscape play culturally key roles in the master narratives of Russian and Soviet history.

The chapters in this volume emerge from a three-year project, funded along with ten others by the Academy of Finland and its program "Sustainable Governance of Aquatic Resources" (AKVA).[3] This particular interdisciplinary project, entitled "Water as Social and Cultural Space: Changing Values and Representations,"[4] sought to understand and emphasize the multiplicity and ambiguity of meanings and values given to water. While the essential life-sustaining role that water plays in multiple environments goes without saying, this project has underscored the importance of the humanities' reflective focus for understanding the history of water in ambitious water-shaping technologies, and in emerging environmental challenges. We have sought to underline the value of interdisciplinary cultural studies for better understanding ecological issues, among which multifaceted global water problems are central.

The past decade has seen the emergence of a rich interdisciplinary literature in the humanities that addresses questions of the role of water in a variety of cultural settings and historical periods (see Goodbody and Wanning;

Eibl *et al.*; also Linton). Driven in part by a sense of urgency at deteriorating water quality and looming crises linked to water (in)availability, commodification and inequitable access, scholars in the humanities have worked to understand the role of water in human symbolic and ritual culture. No area of life, knowledge or human ability exists without some connection to water; it flows in and across human and non-human bodies. This explains in part the heterogeneous materials and cross-disciplinary contexts of humanistic approaches to the study of water, both in this volume and in those that have helped to inspire it. The fluidities of water work against conventional divisions between "nature" and "culture," distinctions which contemporary scholars of the environmental humanities understand to be generated and maintained in specific cultural contexts, often for particular political aims (see Chen *et al.* 9; Cronon "The Trouble"; and Soper). As Hartmut Böhme points out in his classic *Kulturgeschichte des Wassers*, the human is simultaneously a subject and an object in relation to water, both initiator and object/recipient of water circulation and water technologies (11, 16). Humans' affective and material relationship with water expresses itself in proverbial and idiomatic language, in dreams and imagination as symbols, rituals, images, and in psycho-historical modes of thinking – all of which are explored in the current volume. Cultural constructions of self are profoundly linked with water in religious, philosophical, and aesthetic modes. The centrality of water and its tropes shapes, not surprisingly, traditional cultures, but as numerous authors in this volume demonstrate, water's role in shaping modern subjectivities continues, fluidly manifest in a variety of emerging media. The possibilities for speaking and thinking with water seem endless.

Contributors to this volume work in a variety of scholarly traditions, and offer a variety of quite different perspectives on how to "read" water in Russian culture. This diversity of methodology and approach, text and context seem particularly appropriate for an interdisciplinary venture. Individually, these authors offer micro-histories of specific places, particular texts, visual images, and films, which complicate any straightforward declensionist, progressive, or idyllic narrative. The authors do, however, make clear certain key motifs in Russia's history of water: enduring attribution of sacred and transformative properties; an association with the subconscious, the repressed, the ever-returning; and a history of the often violent desire to remake the country's geographies of water, allied to dreams of development and the "overcoming" of the past. The waters that fill these pages are all part of the hydrologic regime of the Eurasian landmass, as it extends from the far northwest (Petersburg) to Siberia (Baikal) and even beyond – across the Bering Straits to Russian Alaska. Although various rivers feature centrally in several authors' accounts, the focus of this book is not rivers alone. The chapters as a whole remind us that one of the properties of water is to *circulate*, both physically and symbolically: emerging from tiny springs (whose vernacular and official sanctification Evgenii Platonov examines), flowing into streams and rivers (the Urals' Chusovaia, discussed here by Maria Litovskaia; or the Armenian river whose damming is the subject of a novel discussed by Arja Rosenholm; or the great Volga, whose identification with Russian identity is the focus of Oleg Riabov's chapter; to the Moscow River, ambitiously promoted as a "Port of Five Seas" in the 1930s, discussed here by Cynthia Ruder), channeled across estate infrastructure, spilling ultimately into lakes and seas and – for Russia at least – more rarely the ocean (the Neva flowing and flooding its way to the Finnish Gulf; the waters of Baikal storming into the Angara on their journey to the Arctic). Human history is a history, among other things, of the *use* of water: from the "taste of tundra" that is a cup of daily water to agricultural and ultimately industrial projects that grow vast in scale, the stories assembled here remind us that without water there is simply no life. While many Russian-Eurasian landscapes have been lavish with water, others have not: the history of water technology in the Soviet era is a story of planners and engineers struggling to provide what nature won't.

The historical focus of the authors in this volume is modern Russia, from the early nineteenth century to the post-Soviet era. Various authors draw on sources that take us into deeper reaches of the past (Breyfogle, Platonov, Podiukov, Zamyatin), but the primary focus of these papers is the two centuries in which Russia, and then the Soviet Union, engaged most profoundly with "Western" Europe and the forces of modernization. While technologies of water arise in discussions of the nineteenth century (the estate designs discussed by Stroganov and Miliugina are predicated on a certain amount of engineering capacity), the ambitions and abilities of the state expand exponentially in the Soviet era. Soviet modernization history is at the heart of many of the chapters in this volume. Gigantic hydraulic projects – power plants, canal and dam building, irrigation systems – were endowed with high prestige value, and became the "laboratories" of Soviet modernization, as Klaus Gestwa has recently argued (14, 16). The building of large-scale dams was especially emblematic in the 1950s, when projects like the Volga–Don canal (1952) served as synonyms for the technological breakthroughs of Soviet hydro-engineering. Water power plants, reservoirs, and mega-dams became an essential feature of the Soviet-Russian river landscape, with each construction site an iconic temple to modernity. What is particularly striking in the papers here that address Soviet-era hydrological engineering is the production not merely of hydro-energy but what Vladislav Todorov has called "the overproduction of symbolic meaning," re-produced and reinforced by Russian literary narratives and films that represented the dams as iconic generators of creative breakthrough, leaving the appalling environmental and human losses unspoken and unseen (10). Stalin-era ambitions to remake both the hydrological regimes of Soviet space, but also the hydrological *dreams* and metaphors of the Soviet people, serves as an important leitmotif in many of the papers here. As numerous historians have noted, the Soviet experience of modernization conjoined unchallenged state power, underdevelopment, and vast natural resources and a willingness to use violence in a way that distinguished it from other trajectories of modernization (Josephson; Weiner; Bruno). Launched as both vast corporeal projects and hyperbolic propaganda, the hyper-reality of mega-dams may well have been, as Mikhail Epstein claims, "neither truthful nor false," but the projects involved ideas that did *become* reality "for millions of people" (Epstein 194, 206). These projects laid claim to the imagination as well as the literal geography of Soviet citizens; "water" was to be colonized both imaginatively and physically by the State. Water circulates not only in the physical world but in the symbolic realms of philosophy, literature, and aesthetic imagination. Estate landscapes and elegant spas, dreams of transience and intimations of apocalyptic change: water cycles in Russian and Soviet history are linked not only to histories of technology but to psychic dynamics and cosmological schemes, where, as Veronica Strang puts it "[…] the hydrological cycle provides a spatio-temporal model of change, transformation and regeneration" (119). The particular cultural inflection of those "spatio-temporal models" in the Russian, Soviet, and post-Soviet experience of the Eurasian land mass serves as focus of this volume. There is, as will become clear, no unified "story" of water in Russia, but rather a series of emerging patterns and principles, motifs and flows. To some extent those flows can be mapped onto existing chronologies and geographies of social and political change; it is our hope that these papers will become generative of more work on the "elemental" in Russian and Soviet cultures, but also that the papers as a whole may be suggestive of what it means to take seriously the dynamics and inter-connections of human and more-than-human elements. Water circulates both materially and symbolically, from springs to streams to oceans, and in embedded yet evolving images and narratives. There are many points of overlap and intersection in this collection, and correspondingly various ways in which the volume could be organized. The organization we have chosen follows a progression from histories of vernacular language and evolving mythologies, through socio-cultural identities, to the various kinds of "work" that humans do with water, "making" that involves both matter and meaning.

The authors in Section I – Language and myths of water – consider the symbolic and archetypal meanings of water embedded in language and place-specific ritual, moving from European Russia's natural springs and northern rivers to the vast waters of Siberia's Lake Baikal. These chapters range across time as well as space, raising questions about how appreciations of water's power and danger are deeply embedded in a given culture's traditions, and how attributions of "primordial energy" linger long into a supposedly post-traditional age. Ivan Podiukov, an ethnographer and linguist, gives a richly detailed account of water idioms and what they suggest about Russian mentalities and material life. It is local versions of Russian, Podiukov suggests, whose "figurative content" most powerfully retains a sense of the mythical, the sense that water is identified with the "power of nature" and bespeaks a sacred primordial realm. Evgenii Platonov's archival work examines nineteenth-century veneration of springs in far northwestern Russia, using official documents and records of the church's ambivalence (and often hostility) toward emergent cults to help establish the practices and mentalities at work in village communities. Like Podiukov, Platonov notes the continuing contemporary vitality of the practices he explores; he puts it bluntly: "the fight against holy springs... produced no tangible results." Nicholas Breyfogle's discussion moves us from unremarked springs to the world's "oldest, deepest and largest lake" in order to examine the ways in which cosmology and practice from multiple sacred traditions (Shamanism, Buddhism, and Orthodox Christianity) have informed narrative traditions and practices of daily life. Breyfogle's is a historian's consideration of the ways "the sacred" has been understood and contested by various ethno-cultural communities inhabiting the shores of Baikal. Finally, Dmitrii Zamyatin draws on archetypal studies of folklore and ancient civilization to argue that Russia's modern "geo-cultural imagination" of water is still deeply informed by senses of danger and possibility, of boundary crossing and shape-shifting. Like Podiukov and Platonov, Zamyatin suggests the continued presence, even in modern Russia, of archaic layers of symbolic meaning associated with water. Podiukov's archaic layers are brought to the surface in Zamyatin's analysis of the tantalizing and difficult prose of the contemporary writer Sasha Sokolov, whose imagination of a northern river links animism, folk vernacular, and the bawdy "genius of place." As a group, these papers make claims about continuity even as they explore historical change and evolving – and contested – claims to the sacred powers of water.

Chapters in Section II – Socio-cultural identities of water – continue to consider the *longue durée* and symbolic associations with water, but these papers consider more explicitly the ways in which representations of particular bodies of water evolve under the varying pressures (political, industrial, economic) of modernization. "Identity" is a key term for these scholars, who explore the relationship between water and cultural traditions at three different levels of scale: Oleg Riabov provides a historical overview of the association of the River Volga – *longest of European Russia's rivers (and the longest in Europe)* – with "Mother Russia"; Maria Litovskaia introduces the reader to a lesser-known river whose role in regional (Urals) identity has evolved with industrialization and the growth of tourism; and finally Sveta Yamin-Pasternak explores how drinking water and the form in which water is imbibed has been constitutive of national identity in a region of far northeast Eurasia and far northwest America where culture crosses over the water boundary of the Bering Strait. These chapters use diverse materials and methods to map what Yamin-Pasternak calls "waterworlds": for Riabov, key links between gender and nationalism are evident throughout the history of literary and visual representations of "Mother Volga," in media that range from folk songs to propaganda posters and postage stamps. Key to his discussion is the exploitation of the image, particularly in the Soviet era, as a vehicle of patriotic identity – closely linked with World War II and commemorations of Volgograd (Stalingrad). Litovskaia traces cultural and political history in guidebooks that shift the Chusovaia River's identity from industrial to aesthetic and touristic. This evolution hinges on a particularly influential literary genre – the "sketch" or *ocherk*, and the legacy of one author (Mamin-Sibiriak). Finally, Yamin-Pasternak and her coauthors start their discussion of tea-drinking and national identity at ground level, demonstrating how the "hydrological landscape" on either side of the Bering Strait is an essential part of local identity – and how something as apparently "natural" as the quenching of thirst has been deeply inflected by political and environmental factors. Their chapter gives us a remarkable perspective on the role of "water worlds" – lived contexts – within an ideologized Cold War landscape: in reading Yamin-Pasternak *et al.*'s narratives of tea-drinking we encounter water less from the standpoint of official media and rhetoric, than from the "lived context" of Chukhotka residents for whom saying "I'm thirsty" implies "I crave tea."

The four chapters in the third section – Water rebuilding landscapes – examine the relations between space, place, and water. Their explorations offer maps to "real-and-imagined" spaces as intertwined; these are spaces geographically, physically, and spiritually connected to water (Soja). Water metaphors and images, these chapters suggest, can be transnational even as they are also characterized by clearly marked cultural identities and spatiotemporal mental maps. Spatial mapping, these chapters suggest, correlates to mental mapping and the cultural production of specific hopes and anxieties expressed in images of water. In order to understand how spaces themselves, as well as real and imaginary *perceptions* of space, change over time, we must attend to the importance of water and spatiality for cultural and political cartography (Tally 5). Elena Miliugina and Mikhail Stroganov's chapter explores the role of water in late eighteenth- and early nineteenth-century Russian estate planning, along with the philosophical meaning attributed to flowing water in descriptive poetry devoted to the estate. Nikolai L'vov and Aleksandr Bakunin, two theoreticians of the gentry estate, are the focus of Miliugina and Stroganov's chapter. L'vov's theories found application in the engineering of gentry estates with underground wooden aquaducts, a drainage system, artificial ponds, and water sources for agriculture, fishing, and bathing; Bakunin's poems manifest a philosophical aesthetic in which images of flowing water repeatedly become an object of intensive reflection. Polina Barskova's chapter on the flood of Petersburg/Leningrad in 1924 shows how water becomes a map-maker of imaginary and literary cartographies, as natural and cultural categories overlap in flood discourse. The chapter is propelled by a paradoxical and yet urgent question: what is the cultural and historical significance of natural disaster? How are representations of natural phenomena governed by political concerns? How did the natural disaster shape the self-identification of Petersburg in 1824 and of Leningrad in 1924 in the mental maps of the citizen? Barskova explores everyday journalism and high culture, discourses that interpreted the connection between the recurrence of an emblematic Petersburg flood and the political, psychologically symptomatic and erotically fraught meanings attributed to the disaster. Cynthia Ruder's chapter examines the construction of the Moscow Canal, illustrating how this waterway celebrated Soviet power through the trope of "Moscow – Port of Five Seas" – emblematizing the Canal's significance not only to Moscow and the USSR, but to the world. Ruder's chapter analyzes Stalinist water culture and the Soviet Union as a "hydraulic" society, reaffirming, as Gestwa (254) has argued, that Soviet ideologies of hydro-technology and the taming of water were the work not only of hydro-technological specialists but of authors, film-makers, journalists, and various propaganda specialists.

Chapters in Section IV – The aesthetics and poetics of water – make clear the interconnection of creative thinking, poetic representation, and fluidity. Water emerges in these discussions of culture both as a topic and as *the* constituent metaphor of change, shift, re-conceptualization, and new beginnings. All of the papers in this section share a utopian idea of freedom allied to water and fluidity, whether imagined as a small spring in Shepit'ko's film or the "impetuous" river Mizinka in Shaginian's novel *Hydrocentral*. Fluidity associated with the transformation of social and individual lives is not merely rhetorical; the discourses of water considered in these chapters entails a utopian promise of freedom and emancipation: water exceeds borders and resists binary opposites; it connotes *becoming* as liberation from petrified norms, styles of life, and frozen traditions of aesthetics. Anastasia Kostetskaya's chapter analyses "liquescent" female apparitions in Russian Symbolist work: Konstantin Bal'mont's poem "Apparitions" and Viktor Borisov-Musatov's painting of the same name. With its emphasis on fluidity and the Eternal feminine, Symbolism recuperates early Romantic notions of Utopian freedom beyond the apparent world (Judex), emphasizing fluid interactions between the verbal, visual, and other sensory modes, and the liquescent synthesis of various art forms. In her study Arja Rosenholm reconsiders Marietta Shaginian's classic novel *Hydrocentral* from the 1930s. Although *Hydrocentral* has been considered an example of Socialist realist "production novels," it is not an unapologetic celebration of human mastery over hydrological systems. On the contrary, water for Shaginian is not to be consigned to merely instrumental value, separate from its other values for human culture. Water generates a powerful interplay of human and non-human energies; it is an active medium of artistic and aesthetic self-reflection. Instead of closed, fixed, or politically univocal meanings, Shaginian's *Hydrocentral* favors process and constant transformation, a heterogeneity of becoming analagous to the fluid circulation of desire, productive of hybrid forms in both aesthetic and socio-political spheres. Insufficiently "socialist" when it comes to taming water, reluctant to channel poetic desire into ideologically pure rhetoric: the ambivalence of Shaginian's novel finds parallels in Larisa Shepit'ko's ambivalent representation of the "master narrative" of Soviet modernization. Jane Costlow suggests that Shepit'ko's film aesthetic has a "different" view of water; Shepit'ko avoids the literary and visual celebrations of dam and channel construction of both pre-war and post-war decades. Costlow looks at Shepit'ko's *Heat* (1963) and *Motherland of Electricity* (1967), films that belong to the period of political and cultural revision known by the water metaphor of "The Thaw." Although their focus is on the *lack* of water, both films emphasize all the more powerfully that water is more than merely utilitarian, that it is generative of poetic reverie and hope. Shepit'ko's films call for a reconsideration of technology's ends and the ethical choices to be made in regard to both the human and non-human environment. Finally, Gitta Hammarberg's chapter takes up a popular spatial leitmotif in Russian nineteenth-century literature, the spa. Hammarberg investigates how spas, dandyism, patriotism, and Westernization intersected in late eighteenth- and early nineteenth-century literary polemics, refining various rhetorical uses of water in the process. Examining Sentimentalist spa texts set at the Lipetsk spa, Hammarberg suggests that the "Lipetsk flood" in Russian spa literature colored all aspects of elite culture in late eighteenth- and early nineteenth-century Russia. While the disputes that Hammarberg discusses precede by over a century some of the materials discussed elsewhere in this volume, the "Lipetsk flood" can be seen as emblematic of the ways in which cultural patterns are constantly recycled.

Because Russia (and the Soviet Union which for a time contained Russia) occupies a vast and diverse land mass, and because the history in this vast region of transition from traditional cultures to something approximating "modernity" has been so radical, this collection must of necessity have an introductory character in considering Russia's water stories and their origin. Water is part of the modern history of violence as an intrinsic part of the construction history of hydro-power, but water is also a potent symbol of creative thinking and poetic imagination. The volume presents the foundational importance of water as investigated here in all its many forms; water nourishing body and soul, individual and polis, imagination and rhetoric, artistic and engineer. The chapters collected here suggest that water is a concern not only of the natural sciences but also a cognitive and cultural medium of social imagination and political power.

Notes

1 Translation by Jane Costlow.
2 Florensky's observation is discussed by Zamyatin in this volume.
3 Program #263417. www.aka.fi/en/research-and-science-policy/academy-programmes/current-programmes/akva/
4 www.uta.fi/ltl/plural/common/projects/aqua/index.html

Bibliography

Böhme, Hartmut. "Umriss einer Kulturgeschichte des Wassers. Eine Einleitung." *Kulturgeschichte des Wassers*. Ed. Hartmut Böhme. Frankfurt am Main: Suhrkamp Verlag, 1988, 7–44. Print.

Brown, Tim. "Why Should Biologists Interested in the Environment Take the Humanities Seriously?" *Yale Environmental Humanities Initiative*, August 18, 2015. https://yaleenvironmentalhumanities.wordpress.com/2015/08/18/environmental-humanities-why-should-biologists-interested-in-the-environment-take-the-humanities-seriously/. Web.

Bruno, Andy. *The Nature of Soviet Power: An Arctic Environmental History*. Cambridge: Cambridge University Press, 2016. Print.

Chandler, Michelle, and Astrida Neimanis. "Water and Gestationality: What Flows beneath Ethics." *Thinking with Water*. Ed. Cecilia Chen, Janine MacLeod, and Astrida Neimanis. Montreal and Kingston: McGill-Queens University Press, 2013, 61–83. Print.

Chen, Cecilia, Janine MacLeod, and Astrida Neimanis. "Introduction." *Thinking with Water*. Ed. Cecilia Chen, Janine MacLeod, and Astrida Neimanis. Montreal and Kingston: McGill-Queens University Press, 2013, 3–22. Print.

Cronon, William. "A Place for Stories: Nature, History, and Narrative." *The Journal of American History* 78.4 (March 1992): 1347–1376.

Cronon, William. "The Trouble with Wilderness, or Getting Back to the Wrong Nature." *Uncommon Ground. Toward Reinventing Nature*. New York: Norton, 1995, 69–90.

Eibl, Doris G., Lorelies Ortner, and Ingo Schneider, eds. *Wasser und Raum. Beiträge zu einer Kulturtheorie des Wassers*. Göttingen: V&R unipress, 2008. Print.

Epstein, Mikhail. *After the Future: The Paradoxes of Postmodernism and Contemporary Russian Culture*. Amherst: The University of Massachusetts Press, 1995. Print.

Florenskii, P.A. *Stat'i i issledovaniia po istorii i filosofii iskusstva i arkheologii*. Ed. A.S. Trubachev. Moscow: Mysl', 2000. Print.

Gestwa, Klaus. *Die Stalinschen Grossbauten des Kommunismus*. München: R. Oldenbourg Verlag, 2010. Print.

Goodbody, Axel, and Berbeli Wanning, eds. *Wasser – Kultur – Ökologie*. Göttingen: V&R unipress, 2008. Print.

Hausmann, Guido. *Mütterchen Volga. Ein Fluss als Erinnerungsort vom 16. bis ins frühe 20. Jahrhundert*. Frankfurt and New York: Campus Verlag, 2009. Print.

Josephson, Paul R. *Industrialized Nature: Brute Force Technology and the Transformation of the Natural World*. Washington, DC: Island Press, 2002. Print.

Judex, Bernhard. "Aspekte einer Poetologie des Wassers. Flüssiges bei Novalis und Hölderlin, Bachmann und Celan." *Wasser – Kultur – Ökologie*. Ed. Axel Goodbody and Berbeli Wanning. Göttingen: V&R unipress, 2008, 195–216.

Kliuchevskii, Vasilii. "Lektsiia IV." *Kurs russkoi istorii. Sochineniia v deviati tomakh*. Vol. 1. Moscow: Mysl', 1987. Print.

Linton, Jamie. *What is Water? The History of a Modern Abstraction*. Vancouver and Toronto: UBC Press, 2010. Print.

Scott, James. *Seeing Like a State: How Certain Schemes to Improve the Human Condition Have Failed*. New Haven, CT: Yale University Press, 1998. Print.

Soja, Edward W. *Thirdspace: Journeys to Los Angeles and Other Real-and-Imagined Places*. Oxford: Blackwell, 1996. Print.

Soper, Kate. *What is Nature? Culture, Politics and the Non-Human*. Oxford: Blackwell, 1995. Print.
Strang, Veronica. *The Meaning of Water*. Oxford: Berg, 2004. Print.
Tally, Robert. *Spatiality*. London and New York: Routledge, 2013.
Todorov, Vladislav. *Red Square, Black Square: Organon for Revolutionary Imagination*. Albany: State University of New York Press, 1995.
Weiner, Douglas. "The Predatory, Tribute-Taking State: A Framework for Understanding Russian Environmental History." *Environment and World History*. Berkeley: University of California Press, 2009.

Section I
Language and myths of water

1 The cultural semantics of water idioms in Russian dialects

Ivan Podiukov

The role of water in symbolizing the world has been extensively studied by scholars throughout history – from Thales, the progenitor of Greek philosophy, who believed that the entire variety of nature is a manifestation of a single and eternal water principle; to Carl Jung, whose theory of archetypes points to such fundamental meanings of water as that of a symbol of fertility, abundance, and the life force of the soul (Iung [Jung] 72). The ancient Athenian belief that water is a first principle, and that it was specifically from water that all being emerged, has over time evolved so that water may be variously endowed with conceptual properties, or laden with elements of a world view, philosophy, aesthetic system or religion (Kostin 24). The water mythologem and the important symbolic role water plays across different cultures has been studied through its representation in ancient philosophical and biblical texts (Romanenko 67–77), as well as in film, photography, the language of advertising, and literature (*Obrazy moria*). Water's significance in Slavic cultures and the variety of ways it is used in rituals to purify, protect, or promote wellbeing has been studied in detail by L.N. Vinogradova, who has observed that for Slavs, water space is most strongly associated with the idea of a border between this world and the world beyond (386–390). A.A. Panchenko has described Russia's highly developed cult of water and water sources. He demonstrates that in the Russian northwest there are many sources and bodies of water that are still used in ceremonies to promote contact with the sacral world, ceremonies rooted in both pre-Christian beliefs and Russian Orthodoxy. In a variety of world cultures, water can represent human fate, the fate of the world, or various existential and psychological states; the medium of water is associated with the space of human thought and emotion, and knowledge of the world of things and ideas, as well as humans' self-knowledge, their spiritual transformation, are described using images of cleansing with water, immersion in water, drinking water, and proximity to a water source.

A number of Russian scholars (V.M. Mokienko, V.N. Teliia, N.I. Tolstoi) have demonstrated that idioms function as ethnocultural mental stereotypes within a language system (Mokienko *Obrazy russkoi rechi*; *Slavianskaia frazeologiia*; Teliia; Tolstoi); they view idioms as an ethnos's functioning system of cultural values. Idioms are created out of figurative visions of reality that reflect not just the everyday experience of a language's speakers, but also their mythological beliefs, cultural traditions, and attitudes. Idioms reveal a system of reference points and moral and ethical norms. Idiomatic language involving images of water – water's symbolic and mythological foundation – are common throughout the world. As T.I. Badmaeva has observed, no fewer than 187 water idioms have been identified in English alone, sufficient evidence that water is a key component and a fundamental concept in English-language culture. The mythological and ethnolinguistic concept of "water," the semantics of water as an element of ritual and magic, and its symbolic potential in Slavic idioms and proverbs (including in Russian, Ukrainian, Polish, Czech, Bulgarian, Slovenian, Slovakian, and Croatian) were the focus of a recent international conference, "Water in Slavic Phraseology and Paremiology" (Budapest, 2013; see *Voda v slavianskoi frazeologii*). Only one paper presented at the conference addressed the symbolism of water and the role of water lexemes in Russian dialects, however it is specifically dialects and folk language, including narrowly local usages and elements shared by multiple dialects (and in a number of cases, elements of vernacular and slang) that best reflect the most archaic state of a language and perception of the world. The idiomatic expressions used in everyday speech reveal the stereotypes of folk culture and traditional consciousness and are valuable not just as linguistic tropes that offer a picture of the outer world and inner life of times past, but forms colored by mythological, religious, and ethical concepts. The richest water connotations from folk culture tend to stem from pagan worship, traces of which are still well preserved in contemporary folk culture.

It is not just the fact that dialect idioms are confined to a specific territory that sets them apart from the idioms of literary language. Dialect idioms feature a figurative content that is more compact than that of the idioms used in a standard, literary language; they are associated with the history and daily life of a people, and with traditions and beliefs that still hold sway. Since the formation of populations within a specific territory involves the mutual influence of various subcultures, and since folk culture itself adapts to local historical, cultural, natural, and geographic conditions, dialect idioms have a distinctly regional character. Because they are a rich source of linguistic and cultural information and are characterized by formal and semantic variability, dialect idioms are actively used in researching ethnolinguistics, etymology, and the history of language in general (Tolstoi 3–7; Mokienko *Slavianskaia frazeologiia*).

The purely linguistic parameters of Russian dialect (folk) idioms have been rather thoroughly explored, including in a number of doctoral dissertations. A.I. Fedorov (*Sibirskaia dialektnaia frazeologiia*) examined the ethnographic aspect of idioms used in Siberian dialects of Russian (he has demonstrated that most Siberian idioms have counterparts – idioms with similar semantics and components – in European Russian dialects). Works by L.A. Ivashko argue that, in comparison with the overall lexicon of dialects, the idioms used in folk dialects are more broadly diffused and exceptionally varied. Our research (Podiukov *Narodnaia*; *Kul'turno-semioticheskie*) examines how dialect idioms incorporate traditional symbols and themes found in folk culture, as well as the ability of many folk idioms to associatively express cognitive, moral, and artistic meanings – meanings that are metalinguistic and common across the culture proper. T.G. Nikitina has demonstrated the importance of folks idioms in reconstructing a holistic linguistic picture of the world in ideographic terms and exposed the original informational value of folk idioms. I.A. Kobeleva has made a detailed study of the parameters and features used by Russian lexicographers in cataloging idiom components in the various types of dictionaries of dialect idioms currently being produced.

Studies of Russian folk dialects conducted during the second half of the twentieth century and the early years of the twenty-first have produced such dictionaries as *Frazeologicheskii slovar' russkikh govorov Sibiri* (Phraseological Dictionary of Russian Dialects of Siberia), A.I. Fedorov, editor; *Frazeologicheskii slovar' permskikh govorov* (Phraseological Dictionary of Perm' Dialects), K.N. Prokosheva; *Materialy k slovariu frazeologizmov i inykh ustoichivykh sochetanii Chitinskoi oblasti* (Materials for a Dictionary of Idioms and Other Collocations of Chita Oblast'), V.A. Pashchenko, five editions; *Slovar' pskovskikh poslovits i pogovorok* (Dictionary of Saying and Proverbs of Pskov), V.M. Mokienko and T.G. Nikitina; *Materialy dlia ideograficheskogo slovaria novgorodskikh frazeologizmov* (Materials for an Ideographic Dictionary of Novgorod Idioms), L.N. Sergeeva; *Frazeologicheskii slovar' russkikh govorov Respubliki Komi* (Phraseological Dictionary of Russian Dialects of the Komi Republic), I.A. Kobeleva; *Frazeologicheskii slovar' russkikh govorov Pribaikal'ia* (Phraseological Dictionary of Russian Dialects of the Baikal Region), S.S. Aksenova, N.G. Bakanova, and N.A. Smoliakova; and *Frazeologicheskii slovar' russkikh govorov Nizhnei Pechory* (Phraseological Dictionary of Russian Dialects of the Lower Pechora Region), N.A. Stavshina. The information compiled in these publications significantly expands our understanding of the features of figurative folk speech.

This article examines the semantics of dialect idioms involving water and the ways in which water – as word and symbol – is used in the idioms of Russian dialects. The scope of this study, which makes use of water-related expressions from the dialect dictionaries listed above, has been expanded to incorporate information about idioms used in Russian dialects spoken in the Kama River region, gathered over the course of many years by its author.[1] The objective of this linguistic and cultural study is to ascertain the mythological and poetic meaning of the idiom components examined and to describe how they are linked to traditional Russian ritual culture and to features of the folk worldview.

Dialect idioms reflecting common symbolic meanings of water

The study of dialects shows that the lexeme *water*, because of its rich cultural associations, is an exceptionally productive component of folk speech idioms; in local folk culture and in any folk (dialect) linguistic consciousness where cultural and linguistic archaisms persist, water is still perceived as a substance that embodies the power of nature and represents the world in its sacred primordiality. In a number of cases, the very name of this element is associated with the idea of abundance, as in the expression from the Pskov region *like water* (*kak vody*), which refers to something of which there is a great quantity; with the idea of a standard, an ideal model, as in the Ural region idiom *a person like water, water through and through* (*chelovek kak voda, voda vodoi*), used to refer to someone very good and endearing or with a pleasant manner, or the Pskov Oblast' expression, *talks like water* (*govorit kak voda*), used for someone well-spoken. Water is conceived as a measure of time in expressions such as one from the Novgorod region, *in that water* (*v tu vodu*) – back then, long ago; a foundation of life, as in the Arkhangelsk region figurative expression *on the waters* (*na vodakh*) – over the course of a life; as a destructive force, as in the Perm' Krai turn of phrase *as if taken by water* (*kak vodoi vziato*) – vanished without a trace; or as a substance defying reason, as in the Perm' Krai saying *from water and from forest* (*s vody i s lesu*) – without any order, pell-mell.

In these and similar cases of figurative uses of the water lexeme, its symbolic meanings are lexicalized. How deeply rooted water's symbolic meaning is can be clearly seen in its predicative uses in Perm' Krai dialects, where it stands in for "good" or "favorable" based on the ancient conception of water as a fundamental life principle (*His life here is water* [*Voda emu zdes' zhit'*; SRNG 4: 331]; see also its assignment of a similar meaning in the enduring Perm' Krai expression *the water doesn't suit* [*voda ne podkhodit*] – the living conditions are not suitable in some place; this meaning is also found in Arkhangelsk Oblast' dialects, where water can refer to "pleasant living conditions" – *the climate here isn't water for you, it seems* [*ne voda vam, vidno, zdes', ne klimat*; AOS 4: 147]).

The folk use of water to characterize something ideal or of good quality (like a fine tool, as in the Ural region expression *a scythe like water* [*kosa-litovka kak voda*], meaning that it cuts well) clearly dates back to the mythological idealization of water. There are also instances where the word *water* has a negative connotation – in particular in criminal jargon, where it can be used to refer to the police or signal danger (Trakhtenberg 14). Here we find the symbolic conceptualization of water as a sign of uncertainty, untrustworthiness, and danger: the ancient association of water with danger still found in folklore is not just a matter of a good rhyme (as in the sayings *expect sorrow from the sea and trouble from water* [*zhdi goria s moria, bedy ot vody*]; *misfortune after misfortune, like wave after wave* [*beda za bedoi, kak volna za volnoi*]). These sayings stem from ambivalent feelings toward water as not just beneficial, but as a destructive principle and dwelling place of demonic forces. A particularly wary attitude toward water is expressed in strictures of etiquette that still hold sway. For example, in folk tradition, one must not waste water to no purpose or go out to draw water or bathe after dark. In the Kama River region, the elderly still believe that, at night, *water sleeps* (*voda spit*), so it must not be ladled out at that time. It is also taboo to "insult" water verbally ("You can't even call bread *khlebushka* [diminutive of *khleb* or bread]. And you can't call water *vodichka* [diminutive of *voda* or water], but it's only a sin for water. You can't use a half-name, or you'll insult it" [Lys'va, Perm' Krai]). On the other hand, in dialects one often encounters respectful and affectionate collocations involving water and a beloved relative: *water-mother, water-sister* (*voda-matushka, voditsa-sestritsa*).

The least figurative water idioms are those in which water is personified. Such expressions have a minimal plot, as in the Perm' Krai expression for people who have drowned or otherwise perished from water, *the water took them* (*voda vziala*), where water is analogous to other common stand-ins for death – *the earth took them* (*zemlia vziala*), *God took them* (*Bog pribral*; compare the contemporary saying, *the mountain took* [*gora vziala*], used in reference to mountain climbers suffering accidents, where death means entering a state of subjugation by some personified higher power). Other examples of idioms involving personification are the Arkhangelsk Oblast' expression, *the water is deep in thought* (*voda zadumalas'*), a reference to a "still wind on a river, lake, or sea," and the Kazan' region's *the Volga is deep in thought*, about the special state of the river when, during flooding, it is at its highest point for a few days before beginning to recede. Endowing phenomena of nature a mind, the power to mentally concentrate on something – human characteristics – is more typical, of course, of poetic language (as in the line from Aleksei Apukhtin's poem "Winter": "The sullen forest has fallen deep in thought" [*Ugriumyi les zadumalsia gluboko*]; here nature's state mirrors the poet's feelings). The folk expression *the water is deep in thought* is not a function of poetic convention and is used to emphasize the instability and uncertainty of a natural state and inaction by a natural phenomenon that follows a great exercise of its elemental force. Such expressions assign natural elements feminine qualities (as in the Perm' Krai expression, *the Kama has taken a breath* [*Kama vzdokhnula*], used to refer to the river's first signs of movement after being encased in ice over the winter – the river embodies the feminine principle in nature, building on the mythologically and grammatically motivated "femininity" of water).

Water is personified as a woman in a term associated with the folk calendar, the expression *water, the name day woman* (*voda imeninnitsa*), which relates to the third day of the Trinity holiday. This idea comes from a more expansive proverb that also ties the Trinity holiday to the earth and the forest: folk tradition considers the Day of the Holy Spirit, the day after Trinity Sunday, to be the name day of the earth and the forest; plowing fields, felling trees, or chopping wood are not allowed on this day. The idea that the earth and forest celebrate their birthdays at the beginning of summer is inspired by the renewal of nature and the appearance of greenery and flowers, while attributing water's birth to the time of the Trinity probably echoes the pagan cult of water's life-giving powers: the Christian holiday of the Trinity coincides with *rusalka* (mermaid) week, a time for fortune-telling and magical rituals. This is why people are not supposed to interact with water on the third day of the Trinity holiday. The most serious taboos were against preparing a steam bath (*bania*) or washing clothes or floors ("A *bania* during Trinity is a sin. Today is water's name day, you shouldn't wash yourself," according to a resident of Medianka, a village in Perm' Krai's Orda District).[2] Since "Trinity water" (*troitskaia voda*) was attributed special properties – "Trinity water is holy, we washed with it, poured it over ourselves. We took the horses into the water," states a resident of Anan'kino, a village in Perm' Krai's Yurla District[3] – it could only be used for ritualistic purposes.

However, Trinity water is only one kind of cultic water within folk traditions, which attribute curative properties to such holy waters as Epiphany water, Thursday water (collected on Holy Thursday before Easter and kept to heal the sick, as a talisman, and for purification), Il'ia's water (gathered from rain falling on St. Il'ia's Day, August 2; in spells this curative water can be referred to as Il'ia's wife, since legend attributes the creation of springs and streams to the prophet Il'ia [Elijiah]). Rain that falls either during the Trinity holiday or on St. Il'ia's Day is considered especially beneficial. But at the same time, Trinity water and Il'ia's water are perceived as dangerous: according to a popular belief in Perm Krai, the Trinity holiday rarely passes without a drowning, and the rains considered "obligatory" on St. Il'ia's Day are heavy and can lead to flooding (which is why mills usually released water through their weirs before St. Il'ia's Day, believing that otherwise the weirs would be breached – a belief held in the Iaroslavl' region [SRNG 4: 331]).

The view of water as animate and the generally positive attitude toward it explain why the spring water that bubbles up from underground is thought of as "living water" (*zhivaia voda*). This designation (heard in dialects of Perm' Krai; compare this to an expression used for springs in the Pskov region – "living springs") is tied to the living and dead water found in magical tales and to a surviving cult of water sources, which folk consciousness assigns curative, purifying, and prophetic properties. Yet another name used in dialects (of Perm' Krai) is – *ródnaia* (a term that can mean native or dear when the stress in on a different syllable, but that here has the meaning of something generative and life-giving and is etymologically close to the Russian word for spring, *rodnik*, which originates out of the idea that springs generate or "give birth to" water). The stagnant water of lakes and swamps, on the other hand, are viewed negatively and symbolize decay, dying, and a lack of vitality, the source of the Perm' Krai expression *stagnant water* (*stoiachaia voda*), used for someone idle and lacking initiative (compare the expression used by the Komi-Permiaki people of Perm' Krai, *va puköl*, which translates literally as "stagnant water" and is used to describe a physically weak child or elderly person).

Traces of the archaic cult of water as a divinity that are seen in its frequent personification have been preserved in the ritual of giving to the river, a common ritual in the Russian North. The idiom *to give to the river* (*darit' reku*), or well, or spring, is used in dialects of Perm Krai on a number of occasions. Most often it is a newlywed bride who is moving in with her husband's family in another village that makes a gift to the river: the morning after the wedding, the bride walks to a source of water and tosses in either a coin or a piece of bread. In some places this action is referred to as *to buy water* (*otkupat' vodu*): "The day after the wedding the bride goes, buys water, tosses a coin in to the spring" (Lobanovo, Perm' District).[4] In the nineteenth century, the historian and explorer Vasilii Berkh observed that, when setting out along the Kama or Pechora Rivers, the people from the village of Cherdyn' in northern Perm' Krai "had the custom of throwing a bun into the river while repeating: 'Mother Kama, here is a present for you, let me reach home safely'" (Berkh 109).[5] In many districts of the Kama River region, the ritual of giving to the river persists to this day, especially the first time someone goes onto the water in a boat every year: "The first time I travel by boat I throw a coin into the water: 'Merciful father, mother-water, preserve and save me from the water'" (Timinskaia, Cherdyn' District).[6] This ritual is also performed on a number of holidays ("Yuri's Day falls in May. Then coins are tossed in the Kama or into a well. They give to the water so it would be kinder" [Kriukovo, Elovo District])[7] and during the *ledokhod*, when the ice begins to break up and flow (people toss coins and bread onto the ice flowing down the river with the words "I am giving to you, water, protect me, water," as they mentally repeat "That I may not drown in the summer," Visim, Dobrianka District).[8] Often, people try to placate the river as they make day-to-day use of it to quench their thirst ("You drink from the stream and give it either bread or a little white rag and say: 'Mother-river, please accept this, don't be angry.' This is so the river won't be offended" [Kupros-Volok, Ius'va District]);[9] they give something to the river, throwing a coin into the water for good luck when they relocate to a new place ("We were moving, so I threw some kopeks into the water; they say you have to make a gift to the water when you move to a new place" [Osintsevo, Ust'-Kishert' District).[10]

This ritual is similar to rituals designed to placate other elements and places deified in ancient times. For example, the expression from Perm' Krai, *to give to the earth* or *to buy the earth* (*darit' zemliu, otkupat' zemliu*) is used to refer to the placing of coins in the corners of a newly built home ("You have to put a little money in the corners or under a beam, as if you're giving the earth a present. You definitely have do this and use silver coins. When you built a home, you have to do this" [Kalinovka, Chernushka District]).[11]

Gifts are also made to the earth by tossing a coin into a grave before lowering the coffin into it (Gainy, Perm' Krai).

The reasoning behind expressions featuring images of personified water is accessible, since many rituals with water are still practiced, including appeals for help to a deified water source that are part of an incantatory tradition. These appeals are often direct: *As you flow, river, into the Kama, carry away my sorrow into a pit* (*Techesh' ty, reka, v Kamu, unesi moiu tosku v iamu* [Urolka, Solikamsk District]). The incantation *Mother Kama, you don't flow straight, turn hexes and evil eyes away from me* (*Matushka Kama, techesh' ty ne priamo, zavoroti ot menia uroki i prizory* [Bol'shie Doldy, Cherdyn' District]) takes into account both the mythological idea of the river as a mediator between worlds and the real nature of the Kama – a winding river. (The Kama is considered a "returning" [*vozvratnaia*] river – one whose channel curves at angles of almost 90 degrees.) Similar requests are addressed to the Ob' in Siberian incantations appealing to the power of one of the largest and most full-flowing rivers of Siberia: *Our mother, River Ob', you do not fear to wash away the yellow sand, and steep banks, and roots. Wash away my grieving grief and crying tears, from my heart of hearts, from my lungs, and from my liver, and from my arms and legs, from my entire human figure* (*Nasha matushka – Ob'-reka, ne boish'sia ty smyvat' zhelty peska, i kruty berega, i korni-koren'ia. I tak smyvai s menia tosku toskuchu i plaku plakuchu, s retivogo serdtsa, i s legkikh, i s pecheni, i s ruk-nog, so vsego stanu chelovech'ego* [Emer 94–99]). A variety of idealizing formulaic phrases expressing reverence and affection can be incorporated into ritualized appeals to water as a higher power that grants success: *mother water* (*matushka voditsa*), *water of God's spring* (*Bozhiia kliucheva voda*), and *water tsaritsa* (*voditsa-tsaritsa*).

Water that was collected in a particular way – referred to in the Kama River region as *silent* (*molchannaia*) water – was used in treating illness and in fortune-telling: "When someone dies, you have to sprinkle silent water. Silent water is taken from a hole in the ice without words, and then you say something over it" (Kalinino, Kungur District);[12] "Fortunes would be told using silent water – a girl would pick it up with her mouth from a melted patch or a hole in the ice, run home, and then release it into a glass and drop a ring into it" (Verkhnee Moshchevo, Solikamsk District).[13] It should be noted that the silent water mythologem is also known in other Slavic cultures (*m"lchana, m"lchashna voda* in Bulgarian and the Czech *mlčavá voda* refer to water brought silently from a source for ritualistic purposes; Vinogradova 387). In addition to silence (symbolizing communication with another world), invocatory words called *shepotki* [from the word for whispers – Trans.] could be said over water to intensify its magical properties.

Further evidence of the active symbolic role water plays in dialects can be found in numerous surviving wordless rituals involving water. For example, before going out for a hunt, hunters wash their weapons with water prepared in a ritualistic manner: "A day in advance, a mug with water is put in the corner where the icons are. Blades of grass are placed over the mug to form a cross. Before going out to hunt, you wash your axe and gun and sprinkle yourself, then you'll get any animal" (Churakovo, Kosa District).[14] If a hunt fails, the hunter is supposed to bathe in the river: "When the hunt isn't lucky, they jump into the water, into a stream. Right with their gun, in their clothes. And the dog goes in with them. They say that after that, an animal is sure to come to you" (Ust'-Urolka, Cherdyn' District).[15] A variety of water rituals in contemporary folk culture create a cultural context that preserves the archaic meanings and mythological connotations of the lexeme *water* in dialects.

The plot elements of water idioms in dialects

In a number of folk idioms, water's symbolism is given physical expression with the help of an implicit storyline. Such storylines, which present water as an overwhelming, neutralizing, and transformative force, feature the motif of falling into water and are used to characterize certain psychological and physiological states (the Pskov Oblast' *as if fallen into water* [*kak v vodu upal*], describing a person who has suddenly fallen asleep; Arkhangelsk Oblast's *as if to plop down into water* [*kak v vodu sest'*], used when someone falls suddenly silent) and disappearance (the Pskov Oblast' expressions *grief into water* [*gore v vodu*], to describe the falling away of troubles and *as if removed by water* [*kak vodoi snialo*], to describe the complete disappearance of tiredness, unpleasant sensations, or pain; the Siberian *as if poured over by water* [*kak vodoi zalilo*], when something has been forgotten; the expression *as if water took it away* [*khot' vodoi ponesi*], recorded in Russian dialects of Karelia, referring to something pointless or done in vain). The immersion in water seen here may have either a positive or negative association due to people's ambivalent feelings toward water. (Compare the characterization of unexpected and incomprehensible loss, the disappearance or pointless loss of something such as in Novgorod Oblast's *as if it fell in the water* [*kak v vodu upalo*] or the Perm' Krai idiom, *floated away down water* [*po vode poshlo*].)

Mythological contact with water, especially immersion in it, echoes the idea of a return to the boundless waters of a primeval ocean, to the mythological source of life and the blissful beginning of mythological time. Tied to this is the idea of water as a symbol of fecundity, the idea behind expressions such as one from the Briansk region, *as if to grow out of water* (*kak iz vody rasti*) – to grow quickly and well (usually said of children). In individual cases an idiom may have to do with water's inability to affect a person who is endowed with special qualities, such as the Perm' Krai expression *water doesn't stick* (*voda ne derzhitsia*) to someone who is "strong, well-built, healthy, and energetic." The expression *brought through the same kind of water* (*po odnoi vode vedeny*), of people who share the same essence (found in Arkhangelsk Oblast' dialects), is also tied to the idea of contact with water and is built on the allegorical symbolism of Christian baptism, which involves contact with water either through pouring, immersion, or passage through it. In terms of meaning and structure, this idiom is analogous to the common expression *anointed with the same chrism* ([*odnim mirom mazany*]; chrism is an aromatic oil used in Christian rituals such as baptism). The idiom *brought through the same kind of water* refers to the common attributes of people who adhere to the same faith (another common analogy refers to similarities between people who grew up in the same place – *a berry from the same field* [*odnogo poliia iagoda*]).

Since water is an intermediary connecting the world of the dead and the world of the living – "this" world and "the other" – death is a symbolic crossing to the other bank. Not only the construction of coffins in the form of a boat and the placing of graveyards on the unpopulated side of a river stem from this idea, but also the prevalence of such expressions as the ones from Perm' Krai *to see the other bank* (*tot bereg vidat'*), said of the very old, and *to go across the river* (*uiti za reku*) or *across the Kama*, meaning "to die." The Kama River region expression *to depart with the spring water* (*uiti s veshnei vodoi*) – to die when the water is melting and ice is disappearing – is also tied to human existence. It is based on the image of spring water, a religious and mystical symbol of a destructive but also purifying element. Overflowing rivers, the spring waters that "open" the vernal awakening of nature, are traditionally seen as unleashing natural forces that are both divine and exceptional. The expression *to depart with the spring water* thus echoes a sort of folk pantheism, an understanding of death as a person's dissolving into nature (according to folk beliefs the period between Easter and the Trinity holiday is holy and the best time to die).

Spring water also enters into the expression, common in folk dialects, *to see off the river* (or ice) (*reku* [*led*] *provozhat'*), referring to the springtime ritual parting with ice as it melts and drifts away. According to ethnographers, in the past, Russians living along the Kama River treated the start of the *ledokhod* and the rising waters as a major holiday. (At the metallurgical plant in Dobrianka, for example, the local celebration on that day was referred to as *Seeing off the Kama* [*Provozhanie Kamy*]: the very first day the ice began to move everyone in Dobrianka went to the banks of the river to "admire" the *ledokhod* and celebrate it with dancing, singing, and bonfires [Bazanov 67–70].) The ritual of parting with the ice included placing old items and straw onto the water: "They would put straw into an old basket, damp straw below and dry on top, then light it and send it floating down the river" (Opalikha, Nytva District).[16] Analogously, people would cast away illness onto the spring (melting) water: "They went to watch the *ledokhod*, they would wash themselves, all their pains would be washed off for the ice to carry them away."[17] People would also do somersaults on the river bank "so their backs wouldn't hurt" (Sypuchi, Krasnovishersk District). Sending something off on the melting (*polaia*) water in the spring with time lost its religious significance and was thought of as a universal means of casting off anything negative. This idea is reflected in the Volga region expression *as if on melting water* (*kak na poluiu vodu*), meaning "without a trace or purpose," the Perm' Krai curse, *damn you onto melting water* (*t'fu tebia na poluiu vodu*), the phrase *to go to melting water* (*uiti na polu vodu*), to be for naught ("I accumulated some goods, but now it's all gone to melting water, I gave it all away for nothing" [Belskikh, Solikamsk District]),[18] as well as the Perm' Krai expression *not rushing to a flood* (*ne v polói neset*; the noun *polói*, flood, is etymologically tied to the word *polyi* found in dialects and meaning "opened up"). The folk belief that the spring floods carry away diseases, everything impure and unneeded in general, is quite widespread and was known not only to the Kama River region's Slavic population: the Tatars of Perm' Krai, for example would refer to seeing off the ice with the expression *chir-chor kitu*, literally "diseases are going away," as well as *zin kitu*, "devils are going away."

Another expression demonstrating that the actively flowing water of spring is seen as a harbinger of life and the renewal of both nature and humans is one long heard in Perm' Krai dialects, *to sail out on high water* (*na bol'shuiu vodu vyplyt'*), used to refer to the attainment of success and the overcoming of misfortune and poverty ("Back then they sailed off on high water, got rich" [Chus, Iurla District]).[19] This idiom ignores the obvious danger involved in being on a wide, overflowing river. The main feature of the thinking underlying it is an association between the end of misfortunes and troubles and the idea of a blissful afterlife.

Flowing water is a common theme in folk idioms. Flowing water, as an immediate manifestation of nature's energy and movement, is used in many rituals. For example, a newly purchased animal is supposed to be led through flowing water so that it will "forget" the way to its former home. To overcome a hex, water is supposed to be taken where three streams merge into a river. Flowing water represents the movement of time while simultaneously reminding humans of the essential aspects of existence that are not under their control. This idea is behind the saying, *year after year it goes just as water flows* (*god za god idet kak voda techet*), referring to the unstoppable, inexorable passage of time, and the expression *in Kama, a lot of water will flow by* (*v Kame mnogo vody ubezhit*) – in other words, something will happen "no time soon."

A curious variation on the image of a flowing river is found in the Perm' Krai expression *here a drunken river flows* (*tut p'ianaia rechka techet*), said of a place where a lot of alcohol is consumed ("These days, a drunken river has been flowing around here, the people have really gone to drink" [Kishert', Suksun District]).[20] The verb *to flow* (*tech'*) signifies a movement resulting from natural causes beyond humans' control; the spontaneous force of a river's flow is used to describe misfortunes that have the same power as the elements. It should be noted that this idea relates to the symbolic play on an image commonly reflected in toponymy – the image of the *drunken river* (*p'ianaia rechka*). According to M. Fasmer, the *drunken river* is a common hydronym in Russian because of rivers' tendency to be winding (Fasmer 3: 422).

Other common examples of flowing water serving as a symbol involve the verb *to pour* (*lit'*). This verb is used to suggest intensive flow and/or forcing a flow. The pouring (*vylivanie*) of water is a common symbolic action in rituals. In idioms, *to pour water* (*lit' vodu*) can have an array of nuances and has been found in long-standing expressions with a wide spectrum of meanings associated with talking, cursing, a bad life, and misfortune. In accordance with the archaic logic of the inseparability of the human and the natural, the verb *lit'* takes on the meaning of "to inspire toward life," "to resist death" ("*pobuzhdat' k zhizni*," "*protivostoiat' smerti*"), since the flow of water represents the movement, intensity, and dynamism of the world's phenomena (in Perm' Krai tradition, water is sprinkled behind a coffin being carried as the deceased is ritually escorted, and water is poured behind someone setting out on a distant journey). This symbolism is involved as well in the practice of dousing oneself with water (in folk culture on St. Ivan's Day, the second day of Easter, Pure Monday [the first day of Lent], and St. Peter's Day; water is also ritually poured over newlyweds on the morning after their wedding night).

The belief that poured water has the capacity to symbolically distinguish between what is near and dear and what is alien, and accordingly to protect and to endow special qualities, is reflected in a number of idioms. In explaining the etymology behind the expression [they] *can't be separated by pouring water* (*vodoi ne razol'esh'*), said of a close friendship or inseparability, V.M. Mokienko (O semanticheskom edinstve 79) comments that, despite what may be commonly believed, this expression does not stem from the idea of pouring water on animals or people engaged in a fight (close friends are unlikely to have a scuffle). The idea of inseparable friends that *can't be separated by pouring water* or that *water doesn't pour apart* (*ne razlei voda*) echoes the archaic motif of water's power to symbolically separate what is akin and what is alien, a power related to its purifying force and fundamental indivisibility. In this sense, water in the expression [they] *can't be separated by pouring water* in regard to a close friendship is related to water in the famous saying *I can dilute other people's misfortunes with water, it's my own I can't figure out* (*chuzhuiu bedu vodoi razvedu, a k svoei uma ne prilozhu*); it plays the symbolic role of a sacral means of separating the alien from what is one's own or correcting something negative (as in the Ural region expression *as if washed away by water* [*kak vodoi umylo*], said of a sudden and miraculous recovery from illness). Cherishing water as an ideal essence is seen as a sign of a person's inner qualities (a belief inspiring the Pskov Oblast' expression, [someone] *won't spill water* [*vody ne prol'et*], said of a modest and upstanding person).

The Perm' Krai expression, [someone] *will say it as if pouring it out* (*skazhet kak vy'let*) – said of a person who not only tells the truth, but is exceptionally perspicacious – reflects an association between the act of pouring and magic (in the Viatka region, *how he poured out* [*kak vylil*] is used for someone who has done something exceptionally skillfully, well, and with ease). The Pskov Oblast' expression *to pour out the truth* (*vylit' pravdu*), to say what is true (related to the well-known *truth poured out* [*vylitaia pravda*], the absolute truth), rests on the idea that what has been said has a force of its own and that the information conveyed was somehow obtained magically, from some higher powers (compare this to the common pouring out or draining away of sorrow, disease, and other ills in magical rituals). The pouring in these rituals imitates the flow of water and symbolically recalls the elemental quality of the world while being a mystical way of drawing on water's natural and ineluctable energy.

Comparisons of speech to flowing water are common in folk cultures (as in the idealizing folk expression *talks like a stream babbles* [*rech'-to govorit, slovno rechen'ka zhurchit*]). This analogy rests on the animistically rooted tendency to refer to the sounds of nature as nature's voice. The idea of words flowing like the water in a stream is further supported by their similarity in folk etymology (bolstered by mythology) between the word for speech (*rech'*) and river (*reka*, or the diminutive *rechka*) and the fact that both speech and flowing water are seen as giving rise to life. Of interest in this regard is a Ural region taboo against remaining silent when fording a river that also links the idea of flowing water and speech: "When you're fording, you'd better talk, otherwise you'll get dizzy and fall" (Sylva, Perm' District).[21] This link is also reflected in an expression used for talkative people that is common in Siberian and Volga region dialects, *pour and overpour* (*lei-perelei*). Deeply underlying this expression is the parallel between speech and flowing water (the same is true of the colloquial use of the verb *to pour too much* or *inundate* [*zalivat'*] to mean to lie, to tell an untruth). The symbolism conveyed in the verb *to pour* (*lit'*) is reflected as well in expressions like the one from Perm' Krai, *to pour but not pour out* (*lit' ne vylit'*) used for people who cannot be told apart (compare the common expression *as if poured out* [*kak vylityi*] used to describe a striking resemblance between people). The imagery underlying this expression couples the process itself (*lit'*) and its result (or rather the inability to achieve it: *ne vylit'*). The idea of a perfect resemblance, of people being absolutely identical, is tied to the impossibility of dividing water into specific parts.

In idioms, the water lexeme, representing an elemental force beyond human control, can thus convey either positive or negative associations. Other lexemes semantically related to water are more narrowly defined in dialect idioms. For example, the image of the sea stands in for space that is alien or dangerous in dialect idioms (as it does generally in Russian folkloric tradition). The expression found in dialects of Perm Krai, *to deliver from the blue sea* (*vynesti iz sinia moria*) means "to save": "Something delivered him from the blue sea; he was, after all, on trial!" (Verkhnee Moshevo, Solikamsk District).[22] This idiom is genetically tied to a proverb about the strength and importance of parental exhortation, *A mother's blessing can deliver* [her child] *from the blue sea* (*Materino blagoslovenie iz sinia moria vyneset*; "A father's or mother's blessing, they say, will deliver [a child] from the blue sea" [Terekhino, Karagai District]).[23] The image of a blue sea beyond the bounds of habitable space is common in folk proverbs (*Whoever has not been in the sea has not seen sorrow* [*Kto v more ne byval, tot goria ne vidal*]; *The farther the sea, the less grief* [*Dal'she moria – men'she goria*]). This image is often found in sayings that refer to a place to which disease and misfortunate are sent (*Send disease to the blue sea, to impenetrable forests, to dark forests, into the dank earth, into the steep mountains*" [*Ponesi bolezn' v sine more, v lesy dremuchi, na temnye lesa, vo syru zemliu, v krutye gory*]; see as well Sveshnikova 121–129).

In dialect idioms, the mythological connotations of words referring not to water itself, but to the forms in which it manifests, such as dew or snow, are less apparent. The idea of water as a first principle, as a giver of life, can nevertheless be discerned in idioms based on these manifestations. For example, the expression heard in Pskov Oblast', *a large snow flake hit* [the target] (*snezhina popala*), referring to pregnancy, may echo the folk attitude toward snow as something magical, as a heavenly and divine embodiment of life potential. Snow is treated as one of life's blessings in a number of folk beliefs, such as *a lot of snow brings a lot of grain* (*mnogo snega – mnogo khleba*), as a symbol of love, as in the old belief *If snow falls during* [the holiday of] *the Intercession, there will be many weddings* (*Esli na Pokrov vypadet sneg, to eto predveshchaet mnogo svadeb*), and as a talisman, as in the ritual throwing of snow in the wake of someone departing on a long journey to wish them well (in Perm' Krai). The symbolic meanings of dew as moisture from heaven is apparent in the context of the expression, well-known in the Viatka region, *to hit dew under oneself* (*bit' pod soboi rosu*) – to be alive. This expression, as well as its Smolensk Oblast' analogue, *to stomp on dew* (*toptat' rosu*), to live in good health, rests on the idea of people acquiring vital powers from the world above (dew as heavenly moisture is present in folk culture in magic rituals to promote strength and health). It is noteworthy that these idioms feature not only the motif of treading on dew, but of actively affecting it (*hitting, stomping*). They therefore suggest not just existence, but the boldness and bravado of a person aware of the fleetingness of life and of the limitations of human power over natural forces (compare the analogous jocular expression of humans' temporary independence from higher forces in the Perm' Krai saying *for now I'm on the earth and it's not on me!* [*poka ia na zemle, a ne ona na mne!*]).

Within Russian folk ritual traditions, water serves as a universal symbol not just of the physical power of nature, but of the primordial energy that can set the world, events, and life phenomena into motion. The idioms found in Russian dialects reflect a variety of archaic beliefs tied, most often, to ritual and magical actions involving water and to various aspects of its mythological perception. Dialect idioms attest to a connection between the idea of water and elevated themes of human existence and time that differ from the figurative motifs found in the water idioms of literary Russian. Dialect idioms offer a window onto the archaic worldview and how folk ways of symbolizing the world are given verbal expression.

Notes

1 For information compiled during field work in Perm' Krai (the contexts in which idioms are used, as well as information about rituals relating to water idioms), we provide geographic information (the name of the village or district where the information was recorded).
2 «Ну, баня в Троицу это грех. Вот сегодня вода-именинница – мыться нельзя».
3 «Троицкая вода святая, мылись, обливались ей. Лошадей в воду заводили».
4 «На другой день свадьбы невеста идёт, откупает воду, бросает монетку в ключ».
5 «Матушка Кама, вот тебе гостинец, дай мне благополучно достигнуть до дома».
6 «Я когда еду на лодке первый раз, бросаю денежку в воду: «Милостивый батюшко, мать-водичка, сохрани и спаси меня от воды».
7 «В мае Егорьев день бывает. Тогда монеты в Каму, в колодец бросают. Дарят воду – чтобы добрее была».
8 «Дарю тебя, вода, храни меня, вода»; «Чтобы летом не утонуть».
9 «Пьешь из речки, и даришь ей или хлеб, или беленькую тряпочку, говоришь: «Матушка-речка, бери, не сердись. Это чтобы речка не обиделась».
10 «Переезжали, дак я в воду копейки бросала, говорят, воду подарить надо, когда переезжаешь на новое место».
11 «Нужно в домах в углы или под матицу положить немного денег, как бы дарить землю. Обязательно надо положить, серебрушками. Когда строят дом, обязательно».
12 «Кто умирает, дак надо молчанной водой прыснуть. Молчанну-то воду брали из проруби без слов, а потом на неё наговаривали».
13 «Гадали с молчанной водой – наберёт девка ртом из полыни либо проруби, бежит домой, потом выпустит изо рта в стакан и в эту воду колечко отпускает».
14 «В угол, где иконы стоят, на сутки ставят кружку с водой. На кружку из травинок делают крест. Когда на охоту пойдешь, водой из кружки промоешь топор, ружье, самого себя сбрызнешь, тогда любого зверя возьмешь».
15 «Не везет если на охоте, в воду, в речку прыгают. Которые прямо с ружьем, в одежде. И собаку с собой. Говорят, потом обязательно зверь на тебя выйдет».
16 «Положат в старое, ненужное лукошко солому, снизу сырую, сверху сухую, зажгут, пустят, чтоб плыло по реке».
17 «Смотреть на ледоход ходили, умываться, умывалися, боли все смывали, чтоб лед уносил».
18 «Собирал добро-то, а сейчас всё на полу воду ушло, все даром отдал».
19 «Они в ту пору на большую воду выплыли, разбогатели».
20 «У нас нонче тут пьяная речка течет, спился народ-то».
21 «Идешь бродом, дак баять, говорить надо, а то голова закружится, упадешь».
22 «Что-то же вынесло его из синя моря, совсем ведь он под судом был»!
23 «Отцовское-материно благословленье, оно ведь, говорят, из синя моря вынесет».

Bibliography

Arkhangel'skii oblastnoi slovar' (AOS), vol. 4. Moscow: Izdatel'stvo Moskovskogo universiteta, 1985. Print.

Badmaeva, T.I. "Kontsept "voda" v angliiskoi lingvokul'ture." Kandidat degree dissertation, Volgogradskii gosudarstvennyi universitet, Volgograd, 2006. Print.
Bazanov, V.A. "'Provozhanie Kamy' kak odin iz obriadov traditsionnoi kul'tury Prikam'ia." *Natsional'naia kul'tura i iazyki narodov Prikam'ia: vozrozhdenie i razvitie*. pt. 2, 66–70. Perm': Permskii gosudarstvennyi universitet, 1997. Print.
Berkh, V. *Puteshestvie v goroda i Solikamsk dlia izyskaniia istoricheskikh drevnostei*. St. Petersburg: Pechatano v voennoi tipografii Glavnogo Shtaba ego imperatorskogo velichestva, 1821. Print.
Emer, Iu.A. "Fol'klornyi kontsept: zhanrovo-diskursivnyi aspekt." *Vestnik Tomskogo gosudarstvennogo universiteta. Filologiia* 1(9). Tomsk: Tomskii gosudarstvennyi universitet, 2010. Print.
Fasmer, M. *Etimologicheskii slovar' russkogo iazyka*, vol. 3. Moscow: Progress Publishers, 1987. Print.
Fedorov, A.I. *Sibirskaia dialektnaia frazeologiia*. Novosibirsk: Nauka, Sibirskoe otdelenie, 1980. Print.
Fedorov, A.I., ed. *Frazeologicheskii slovar' russkikh govorov Sibiri*. Novosibirsk: Izd-vo "Nauka", Sibirskoe otdelenie, 1983. Print.
Iung, Karl Gustav [Carl Gustav Jung]. *Arkhetip i simvol*. Moscow: Renaissance, 1991. Print.
Ivashko, L.A. *Ocherki russkoi dialektnoi frazeologii*. Leningrad: Izdatel'stvo Leningradskogo universiteta, 1981. Print.
Kobeleva, I.A. *Sovremennaia russkaia dialektnaia frazeologiia: leksiko-grammaticheskii i leksikograficheskii aspekty*. Syktyvkar: Syktyvkarskii gosudarstvennyi universitet, 2012. Print.
Kostin, A.V. "Voda."*Antologiia kontseptov*. Ed. V.I. Karasik and I.A. Sternin. Volgograd: Paradigma, 2005, 24–36. Print.
Mokienko, V.M. *Obrazy russkoi rechi. Istoriko-etimologicheskie i etnolingvisticheskie ocherki frazeologii*. Leningrad: Leningradskii gosudarstvennyi universitet, 1986. Print.
Mokienko, V.M. *Slavianskaia frazeologiia: uchebnoe posobie dlia filologicheskikh spets. universitetov*. Moscow: Vysshaia shkola, 1989. Print.
Mokienko, V.M. "O semanticheskom edinstve sinkhronii i diakhronii vo frazeologii (Vodoi ne razol'esh')." *Iazyk, soznanie, kommunikatsiia* 46. Moscow: MAKS Press, 2013, 74–82. Print.
Nikitina, T.G. *Problemy izucheniia etnokul'turnoi spetsifiki frazeologii*. Pskov: PGPI, 1998. Print.
Obrazy moria i motivy vody v kul'ture. St. Petersburg: Izdatel'stvo GUMRF im. Ad. Makarova, 2014. Print.
Panchenko, A.A. *Issledovaniia v oblasti narodnogo pravoslaviia. Derevenskie sviatyni Severo – Zapada Rossii*. St. Petersburg: Izdatel'stvo Aleteiia, 1998. Print.
Pashchenko, V.A. *Materialy k slovar'iu frazeologizmov i inykh ustoichivykh sohetanii Chitinskoi oblasti*. Editions 1–5. Chita: Zabaikalskii gosudarstvennyi pedagogicheskii universitet, 1999–2003. Print.
Podiukov, I.A. *Narodnaia frazeologiia v zerkale narodnoi kul'tury*. Perm': Permskii Gosudarstvennyi Pedagogicheskii universitet, 1991. Print.
Podiukov, I.A. "Kul'turno-semioticheskie aspekty narodnoi frazeologii." Doctor of Philological Sciences dissertation, Permskii gosudarstvennyi universitet, Perm', 1997. Print.

Romanenko, Iu.M. *Voda: mif i real'nost'*. St. Petersburg: Izdatel'stvo S.-Peterburgskogo universiteta, 1992. Print.

Slovar' russkikh narodnykh govorov (SRNG). 4. Leningrad: Nauka, 1969. Print.

Sveshnikova, T.N. "O nekotorykh tipakh zagovornykh formul." *Malye formy fol'klora*. Moscow: Izdatel'skaia firma "Vostochnaia literatura" RAN, 1995. Print.

Teliia, V.N. *Russkaia frazeologiia: Semanticheskii, pragmaticheskii i lingvokul'turologicheskii aspekty*. Moscow: Shkola iazyki russkoi kul'tury, 1996. Print.

Tolstoi, N.I. "K rekonstruktsii praslavianskoi frazeologii." *Slavianskoe iazykoznanie*, VII. Moscow: Nauka, 1973. Print.

Trakhtenberg, V.F. *Blatnaia muzyka: Zhargon tiur'my. Po materialam, sobrannym v peresyl'nykh tiur'makh*. St. Petersburg: Tipografiia Rozena, 1908. Print.

Vinogradova, L.N. "Voda." *Slavianskie drevnosti*, vol. 1. Moscow: Mezhdunarodnye otnosheniia, 1995. Print.

Voda v slavianskoi frazeologii i paremiologii, pts. I–II. Budapest: Izdatel'stvo "Tinta," 2013. Print.

2 Sacred waters
The spiritual world of Lake Baikal

Nicholas Breyfogle

As the Old Rite Archpriest Avvakum came upon Lake Baikal during his exiled travels in seventeenth-century Siberia, he was deeply struck by the beauty and bounty of the lake.

> I have wandered over the face of the earth 20,000 *versts* and more, but never have I seen [high mountains such as these]. On their summit are tents and earthen huts, portals and towers, stone walls and courts, all neatly fashioned. Onions grow on them and garlic, bigger than the Romanov onion, and exceeding sweet to the taste; there also grows wild hemp, and in the gardens fine grass and exceeding fragrant flowers, and there is great quantity of birds – geese and swans that fly over the lake like snow. And there are fishes – sturgeon and trout, starlet and salmon-trout and whiting and many other kinds; it is fresh water and in that mighty ocean lake there are sea-calves and great sea-hares. I saw none such during all the time I was living on the Mezen; and the fish in it are of a great weight, the sturgeon and salmon-trout are exceeding fleshy – they are not for frying, for it would be naught but fat. And all this has been fashioned by our sweet Christ for man, so that, with a mind at last at rest, he might give praise to God.
>
> (Avvakum 96–97)

On one level, it is hard to fault Avvakum his hyperbole. He reached the lake's shores after a "tempest" buffeted his boat and after a long, arduous, and hungry journey from Dauria, only one stage in years of imprisonment and wandering in the far reaches of Russia in spiritual torment from the Nikonian reforms. On another level, one can also find in Avvakum's euphoria a view of nature – and of water in particular – that was characteristic of Christian thought (whatever its denomination). Here, the lake, its mountains, and its flora and fauna were a manifestation of God's sacred power and beneficence. The natural world was crafted by God to fulfill humanity's needs in order that they would then best serve and revere the one and only God – the singular source of divine power in the universe. Here too, the extent of the bounty was a reflection of God's attitudes and moods towards humans: lands of plenty reflected God's goodwill towards humanity; an absence of food, or various natural disasters, were taken as manifestations of God's displeasure with the humans there. The "horizontal plane of geography" and "the vertical plane of God's intervention," as Christopher Ely notes, not only intersected but were mutually constitutive (Avvakum 96–97; Ely 28–29; Oestigaard, *Water, Christianity* 11–36).

Avvakum's Christian vision of Lake Baikal as an Eden forged in God's workshop for the benefit of humanity (as long as they proffered proper thanks and respect to God) was by no means the only way that humans have understood or experienced Baikal in religious or spiritual terms – both historically and more recently. This chapter offers an introductory exploration of the wide spectrum of religious experiences and beliefs surrounding Lake Baikal. Baikal is often called the "Sacred Sea" – "Glorious Sea, sacred Baikal!" as the opening line of the famous song goes (Kharitonov). But what does "sacred" actually mean when used to describe Lake Baikal and how was divinity and holiness manifested to, or experienced by, different peoples at different times? The Baikal region is home to people adhering to three world religions – Shamanism, Buddhism, and Orthodox Christianity – who come from multiple ethno-cultural communities (including Buriat, Evenk, and Russian). In what ways have these different people from these distinct faith communities understood Baikal in spiritual terms (its water and ice, fish and aquatic life, rocks and mountains, fogs and storms, and earthquakes)? In what ways does Baikal act as a portal or connecting point with the transcendent and spiritual worlds? How do these worlds – and spiritual understandings of Baikal – transform, guide, or channel the social, economic, and cultural practices of human life around the lake?

Given the tremendous cultural and ecological valence of Lake Baikal both in the past and present, the story of the spiritual aspects of humanity's relationship to Baikal is essential to a fuller understanding of the intertwining of water and culture in Russia. Baikal is the oldest, deepest, and largest lake in the world (largest in terms of volume of water, with some 20 percent of the surface, liquid freshwater on the planet, approximately 23,000 km^3). The lake is home to more than 2,600 species (of which greater than 1,000 are endemic) and Baikal has a history of human habitation dating back many thousands of years. For generations, the religious views and practices of the people living at Baikal transformed daily human action as well as the lake and its flora and fauna: from how to bathe, to the rituals of fishing and hunting, to nature protection movements. Moreover, the spiritual understandings of nature (and water) became important sites of contestation among the different religious communities who came to make the lake their home. Finally, and no less importantly, these diverse cosmologies also blended and influenced each other through mutual interactions around the lake, at times producing syncretic spiritual understandings of Baikal's water.

The spiritual world of Baikal is a large topic, and my comments in this chapter will by necessity be preliminary.

Water and the sacred

Water plays and has played a central (albeit variegated) role in human religiosity and ritual across time and place.[1] As Mircea Eliade notes in his comparative study of religions:

> To state the case in brief, water symbolizes the whole of potentiality: it is *fons et origo*, the source of all possible existence.... Principle of what is formless and potential, basis of every cosmic manifestation, container of all seeds, water symbolizes the primal substance from which all forms come and to which they will return either by their own regression or in a cataclysm. It existed at the beginning and returns at the end of every cosmic or historical cycle; it will always exists, though never alone, for water is always germinative, containing the potentiality of all forms in their unbroken unity.
>
> (Eliade 188)

For many religious communities across human history, water represents both the origin of reality and the transformer of realities. Through immersion in water, the past can be cast away and dissolved – water is, after all, the universal solvent. Then, through re-emergence, a new person can be (re-)born. And Terje Oestigaard notes:

> Water is a medium which links or changes totally different aspects of humanity and divinities into a coherent unit; it bridges paradoxes, transcends the different human and divine realms, allows interactions with gods, and enables divinities to interfere with humanity. Water is a medium for everything – it has human character because we are humans; it is social matter but also a spiritual substance and divine manifestation with immanent powers; and, still, it belongs to the realm of nature as a fluid liquid.
>
> (Oestigaard, "Water" 38)

Different religious communities have understood the degree and form of sacredness inherent to, or conducted through, water very differently – ranging across a wide spectrum from those who see water as inherently divine to those who do not assign any sacredness to water itself other than as a symbol of the transcendent or an element in specific religious rituals. For instance, in certain religious communities – especially in indigenous, animist faiths and Hindu spirituality, but also in different forms in many Asian religions – water is itself considered a sacred entity, possessing and discharging its own divine power. In other cases, while water is not itself a divine power, it might manifest certain godly powers or be a home or host to divine powers or spirits. By contrast, in the words of Gary Chamberlain, "In the desert-origin, Abrahamic religions of Judaism, Christianity, and Islam, with their strongly monotheistic belief system, water is definitely *not* divine, and to attribute a 'sacred' dimension to water seems like a threat to the absolute divinity of the God of Abraham" (33). That said, water plays significant spiritual roles in each of these three faiths because water can "reflect God's creation and God's mastery," can serve to cleanse (physically and spiritually), symbolizes fertility, and was the foundation upon which the world was made and inherent to all creation stories (Chamberlain 41). Such diverging understandings of water's sacral qualities are found in the distinct perceptions of Orthodox, Shamanists, or Buddhists regarding Baikal as a sacred space.

Emerging from the study of comparative religions, the place of water in spiritual beliefs and practices can be understood in four different categories. And we can see all four of these processes at work in the religious world of Lake Baikal: 1) birth, origin, creation; 2) initiation, immersion; 3) healing, restoration, and connections to life and eternal life; and 4) epiphanies and divinities (Chamberlain 12; Eliade 188–215; Bradley 1–36).

Creation stories: Baikal and the Buriats

The concept of Lake Baikal as a site of conception, birth, and origins is found prominently in Buriat creation stories – for instance, of the Bulagat, Ekhirit, and Khori "tribes". In all the stories – and they vary from community to community and exist also in multiple variants within tribes – we see 1) Lake Baikal as the place of creation, 2) a father figure or first ancestor (usually in the form of *Bukha-noion-babai*, the bull master father – a figure who had both an animal and human form, and could switch back and forth), and 3) a caregiver of children (usually female Shaman sisters). In creation stories, Baikal is seen as either the site of genesis of the Buriat people or of humans in general (especially Ol'khon Island – the largest and only inhabited island in Baikal, just off its western shores – which has particularly important religious meaning for the Buriats). For Buriat communities, often several hundred kilometers from Baikal, the lake remains their place of origins and the waters attract pilgrims and visitors from distant Buriat villages (Zhambalova, *Profannyi* 190–192; Dugarov 91, Volkov 10–15; Tivanenko 204–211; Fridman, *Sacred* 89–98; Fridman, "Buryat" 45–56).

In one origin story of the Bulagat Buriats, a woman living on the shores of Baikal became pregnant from the *Bukha-noion-babai*, and when she revealed this to him, he took the twins from her belly, placed them on his back, and swam across Baikal to the northern side. Considering one child not to be his, he abandoned it on the shoreline, and the second baby he swaddled in a green cradle and let him suckle the wool of his chest. Ultimately, two childless female shamans came upon them, presented a special offering to *Bukha-noion-babai* and were given the boy in exchange. They adopted the lad and named him Bulagat, and from him came that Buriat tribe (Dugarov 89–90; Zhambalova, *Profannyi* 191–192).

In a certain origin tale of the Ekhirit, the water–Baikal connection comes across even more strongly. Here, Bulagat, little more than a teenager, went to play at the shore of the lake. There, he met three other children – two boys and a girl – who emerged from the waters of Lake Baikal where they lived. These were the children, the story goes, of one of the daughters of the inhabitants of the eastern sky who came down to the earth in the form of a goat, gave birth to the three children, and placed them on the shore of Baikal where they grew up in the water. The two female shamans learned of the water children from Bulagat and wanted to adopt them as well. The children didn't want to go with the shamans, who nonetheless lulled the children to sleep and then tried to carry them off. When one of the boys awoke, he cried "take me, milk sea-mother [*molochnoe more-mat'*] and rocky mountain father." The lake responded by sending strong waves that crashed on the shore and almost dragged the shamans under water. The girl then turned into a nerpa (Baikal's endemic freshwater seal) and was received back into the water by the milk-mother-sea. The boy turned into a black squirrel and disappeared off into the mountains. The Shamans kept the third child and gave him the name Ekhirit, and he became the founding ancestor of that tribe. As G.D.R. Phillips relates: "He was called 'Ekhirit-who-was-found-on-the-steep-bank,' and it was said of him 'His mother was a crevice on Baikal's shore, his father was the speckled burbot fish' " (Dugarov 90; Zhambalova, *Profannyi* 190–198; Volkov 10–15; Phillips 23).

Here Lake Baikal and its waters became the milieu for the conception, gestation, and birth of different Buriat peoples. In many of these stories, and especially in the Ekhirit origin tale, Baikal takes on a female role as site of conception. The lake is a fertile body where pregnancy is easily achieved and new tribes and peoples are forged. The children live in or near the water, sustained and protected by it. The three children in the Ekhirit story, for example, emerge from the water as if from a womb. The lake's waters are equated with mother's milk and the nurturing bosom. Notably, this linkage of water with traditionally conceived feminine characteristics of fertility, birth, life-giving, and nurturing bosom/milk (where milk and water are often conflated), is common among many peoples across the planet and across time (Eliade 189; Chamberlain 56; Brummond 72–73; Illich 25–27).

In parallel, shamanist Buriat origin stories about the formation of Lake Baikal itself involve divine intervention (and divine anger). To take one example, the Taisha of Ol'khon Island related to M.G. Minin (in or before 1866) that Lake Baikal was formed through the wrath of the spirits. In what is a common explanation about the origins of the Lake, the Taisha declared that before the appearance of the Lake, the land where Baikal now exists was flat and on it lived Buriat communities. However, at some point long in the past, the spirits lost their patience with these Buriats because "instead of living peacefully, praying to the Gods, tending to their flocks, singing and playing balalaikas, they fell into different pranks, arguments, and bad affairs." The gods decided "to destroy all of the dissolute people." They sent an earthquake, which opened the earth and released a huge flame that scorched the earth. Water followed, which filled up the crack in the ground. Only the people on Ol'khon, who had remained good people, were saved and their land became an island above the purging water (Minin 114–117; Demin 26–27; Sgibnev 16–17; Gurevich and Molchanov 74–75).

Sacred waters and rocks: the water-related cosmologies of Baikal

In different times and for different peoples, humans have assigned a wide range of sacred meanings to Lake Baikal (its waters, flora and fauna, and geological features). Orthodox and other Christians – as Avvakum's story underscores – saw the lake as a place, and water as a substance, that could manifest (or temporarily conduct) God's divinity. But, the lake itself possessed no sacred or divine powers.

The belief that the lake and its actions were mirrors of God's views of humanity (and manifestations of god's sacred power) had important effects on how the people of Lake Baikal acted during a massive earthquake and tsunami in the lake, which took place on New Year's Eve 1861. The natural disaster resulted in the permanent submergence of 220 or so square kilometers of the Tsagan steppe, along with the yurts, property, and livestock of the Buriat communities that formerly lived on the land. The majority of Orthodox survivors identified the shaking landscape and freshwater tsunami as a manifestation of Divine Providence – the "voice of God" offering a moral "sermon" to the people around the lake and castigating them for their "sins" (Breyfogle, "Another" 95–106; Breyfogle, "Confronting"; "Golos").

In contrast to those Orthodox Russians who saw the lake as a materialization of God's divine powers and intent, for many Buriats, Evenks, and other Russians, Lake Baikal was home to sacred spirits – as were the mountains stones, trees, springs, rivers, and other sites surrounding it. These spirits each had their own distinct personalities and their own powers over the waters, flora, and fauna of the lake. As anthropologist Janice Brummond has noted: "It is generally believed that all waters are inhabited by *Usan-Khans*, or spirits who control the resource and *lus*, water spirits that are quick to anger. The chief of these spirits *Uha Loson* lives in Lake Baikal. Rivers, lakes, and streams are also the home of powerful water bird and fish spirits, most importantly the loon and the Golden Eyed duck." While the lake contained multiple spirits, the Master spirit of Baikal – known variously as *Dalai yezhen*, *dalai-khan*, *Uha Loson*, among others – lived in the waters of the lake. He was, at times, a capricious sort, who demanded honor and respect or he would provoke the waves and winds of the lake to drown people and crush boats, crack the ice at inopportune moments, and also slash the fishing and nerpa hunting catches (Brummond 65, 72–73; Dugarov 94).

The lake was also home to many sacred geological sites – contact points at which the spiritual and physical worlds meet. For instance, Cape Burkhan on Ol'khon Island (also known as Shamanka or the Shaman's Rock) possessed (and possesses) important spiritual meaning and was a location of human-spiritual communication (Burkhan meaning God of the Lake). It has for generations been the site of ongoing religious activities, especially *tailgans* (community, ritual sacrifices to honor the spirits and ancestors). The cape includes a large, two-pronged rock formation that juts out into Lake Baikal, leaving a lovely, tight bay on one side and opening out into a long straight beach on the other. Both the rock face and the caves are considered sacred places, with the Ol'khon Master Spirit (who goes by several names, including *Oikhoni yezhyen Khan Khoto babai*) descending into the cave when he appeared on earth. Cape Burkhan is only one (and by far the most important) of several rock outcroppings, cliffs, stones, and islands on or near Ol'khon Island (Zhambalova, *Profannyi* 203; Sergeev 27). Cape Burkhan played a variety of roles in Buriat life. It was a place where Buriats would take oaths and bear witness and where they would go to ask the spirits for assistance in cases of infertility. The fecundity of the site derived from understandings in Buriat culture of the cave in Cape Burkhan as a symbol of the female womb and of water in general as a female essence. And there is ongoing pilgrimage and tourism to the Cape Burkhan sacred site, although it is a highly contested site between those who see it as sacred and those tourists who see it as a beautiful and meaningful rock to climb (Zhambalova, *Profannyi* 203; Bernstein, "Remapping" 27; Brummond 72–73; Gurevich and Molchanov 76–77).

Buriat Shamans and others have often described Cape Burkhan as a "temple" or a "cathedral of stone." They do so in an effort to try to translate for Orthodox and Buddhist visitors the sacral importance of the site. In the process, they underscore a very different approach to religiosity: for Orthodox and many other "world" religions, sacred sites are often those created or built by human hands (churches, cathedrals, temples, mosques) – that is, structures where the forms of nature have been cut apart and reformed to make a sacred space. For the Shamanist Buriats, material objects in the natural world (from rock formations, cliffs, springs, rivers, and lakes) are themselves religiously meaningful because of their connections to the spiritual world. And human intervention and reconfiguration in the natural world is not necessary to make a space sacred. As Anya Bernstein notes in describing the sacralization activities of shaman Valentin Khagdaev on Ol'khon in recent years: "Nature is not 'wild,' it is densely inhabited by a multitude of ancestral spirits and deities of various ranks; it is an object of worship worthy of respect and protection, similarly to man-made sacred spaces in the rest of the world" (Bernstein, "Remapping" 32, 36–37; Volkov 15–23; Tivanenko 204–211).

Buriats attach similar spiritual connectivity to the Shaman's Rock, which sits at the point where the Angara River meets Baikal and begins to

Figure 2.1. Cape Burkhan, also known as the Shaman's Rock or Shamanka, on Ol'khon Island, Lake Baikal. Photo by author, 2011.

empty out. According to Buriat traditions, the rock has spiritual origins. The master spirit of Baikal had 330-odd sons and only one daughter – the beautiful and intelligent Angara – whom he loved very much. She had many suitors, but only the dashing Yenisei captured her heart. When Irkut came to ask for Angara's hand in marriage, the Baikal spirit was much swayed and agreed, despite Angara's objections. Days later, Angara made a run for it to join her loved one, Yenisei.[2] When he realized what was going on, the Baikal spirit hurled a massive rock after her in an effort to block her way, but the rock landed behind her at the edge of Baikal. Angara kept going and married Yenisei, never again to return to Baikal, and the rock remained in place at the mouth of the Angara River. For centuries, the rock served as a sacred site that humans used to judge the guilt/innocence of an individual. Those suspected of a crime were taken out to the barren rock and left overnight above the swirling, rushing water. There, the spirits would judge the accused and, if innocent, he would be found alive on the rock the next day. If guilty, he would be sucked into the river never to be seen again (Sergeev 15, 18–19; Brummond 69–70; Gurevich and Molchanov 77–79; Tivanenko 160–169). Cape Burkhan and the Angara Shaman's Rock are but two of many different important religious sites on Lake Baikal (Tivanenko).

Water, spirits, and human action

Shamanist Buriats and others around Baikal organized both their annual community rituals and their daily life activities around their religious understandings of the intersection of the many spirits of the region with the lake's waters and rocks. The watery environment, the spiritual worlds, and human action were an intricately and intimately linked troika. The people living around Baikal believed that the spirits in the lake's waters needed to be "fed," honored, and respected if they were to ensure that the spirits would treat humans well and allow attainment of their aspirations. The idea of the need to provide offerings and esteem to the spirits combined with the Buriat concept of *Tegsh* – which involves, in the words of Katherine Metzo, "living one's life in balance with the world and preserving the balance in nature and human society" and that "nothing should be taken from nature without providing a gift in return." Together, these ideas affected how both Russians and Buriats approached fishing and nerpa hunting (among many other activities) (Brummond 59–60; Metzo 40–44; Fridman, *Sacred* 89–98, 104–112).

In the late nineteenth century, Buriat fishermen and hunters believed in the decisive authority of the spirit-masters over the outcome of their activities. As a result, they carried out an annual cycle of community rituals designed to pay respect to the water (and other) spirits. For example, the people of Ol'khon organized a regular summer *tailgan* offering of sheep or goat in order to honor Baikal's master spirit (and this practice, restricted during Soviet years, revived after 1991). First, they sprinkled milk, then milk mixed with vodka, and then other milk products into the lake. They then killed and prepared the meat, placed it in a wash tub, and offered it to the water with calls for assistance and protection. Men, women, and children all went together to talk to the lake, asking for mercy and bounty from the lake (especially fish and nerpa). They then took the bones and incinerated them with special rites (Dugarov 92–94; Fridman, *Sacred* 207–209; Curtin 38–104).

In addition to these larger events, fishers and nerpa hunters followed specific practices as they set off to fish and hunt in the waters of Baikal and the many rivers that flow into the lake. As I.P. Basharov writes: "The assistance of the Master Spirit (*Khoziain*) for the hunter or the fisher was absolutely essential; the meeting with an unclean spirit was an unwanted evil event" (92). Each time that fishers or hunters would cross from their villages onto the waters and ice of the lake, they would take special measures to ensure the good favor and advantage of the spirits. For instance, hunters heading onto the Baikal ice for winter nerpa hunting would walk down to the shores of the lake with their families and proceed onto the ice. There, they would stop as a group, take out alcohol, pour some onto the ice as an offering, drink a toast to the master spirit of Baikal, and ask him for safe passage on their journey and also success in their

Figure 2.2. Offerings of colored cloth and prayer flags, cigarettes, candy, drinks, and money at the sacred site of Cape Khoboi at the northern point of Ol'khon Island, Lake Baikal. Photo by author, 2015.

hunting venture. Here, they showed respect to the Baikal spirit and also, by sharing their alcohol, they offered the appropriate exchange to maintain balance as they extracted nerpa. Similarly, fishers setting off to fish would pour out alcohol into the rivers and lake or offer food or other gifts to the spirits, entreating the master spirit for success in hunting. Similar rituals accompanied the first catch of any expedition – extending thanks and respect to the spirits for their successful hunt. Throughout their time on the region's waters, fishers and hunters believed that the spirits kept their eyes on them to ensure proper treatment of the animals, waters, and landscape (Basharov 93–98; Zhambalova, *Profannyi* 123–131; Zhambalova, *Traditsionnaia*; Montgomery 66–67; Breyfogle, "Fate" 7–8; Tivanenko 62–72).

Russian fishers and hunters took up certain practices of spirit worship/ respect from the Buriats whom they encountered – one of many examples of how the meeting of different religious traditions in the environmental context of Baikal resulted in spiritual synthesis. Here, Russian migrants to the Baikal area willingly appropriated (in form and in content) local rituals and beliefs if it meant a larger catch, better hunt, or if one avoided the wrath of wavy and stormy Baikal in the process. Russian migrants often went directly to the Buriats and Evenks to gather information about the spirits and ensure their fishing/hunting success and proper spiritual/ritual practice (Basharov 99–100; Tivanenko 22–23).

That said, such syncretism did not mean a wholesale reversal or abandonment of past practice. Working with and placating spirits and little devils had for centuries been part of Russian peasant culture. The shift here was one of degree rather than of kind as traditional practices became reconfigured in the new cultural and geological context of Lake Baikal. Moreover, the appropriation of rituals to feed and honor the water and forest spirits around Baikal did not preclude an active Orthodox life. Many fishers and hunters took with them crosses, icons, and religious books and manuscripts in order to protect and assist them while off on the hunt. Similarly, one author relates how coming to shoot the wild rapids at the Shaman's Rock at the mouth of the Angara, the boat's captain called to his crew "take off your hats" and they kneeled in prayer. "Lord Jesus Christ God, have mercy upon us," he yelled as they approached the rushing water ("Shamanskii" 53–54; Tivanenko 21–22; Heretz 14–41, 102–118; Basharov 113).

In addition, the belief that bodies of waters (whether springs, rivers, or lakes) were contact sites with the spiritual world affected human behavior in other ways for the Buriats, especially in terms of bathing and drinking. Community norms and understandings laid out that an individual should not bathe directly in the water of sacred springs but take out the necessary water for cleanliness and then wash elsewhere. While one could drink directly from a spring with mouth and hands, the hands needed to be washed in advance otherwise the spirit would be angered and cause hardship. The same was true in regards to polluting the waters, which was to be avoided in order to prevent the wrath of the water spirits (Brummond 74). For instance, B.D. Bazarov, a shaman from Ulan-Ude, wrote in 2003 that because Baikal and the lands around it are "controlled" by the "Creator," "everyone should know that polluting Baikal is a sin. Otherwise great misfortunes will come. ... One should not leave trash, sharp objects, or nails on the ice – if you do, you will suffer the deities' punishment" (quoted in Bernstein, "Remapping" 35).

The understanding of Baikal and its surroundings as sacred sites – as homes to spirits and sites of contact between the spiritual and physical worlds – also generated important outcomes in terms of conservation. The sense of Baikal's sacredness has led today's inhabitants to work towards the ecological protection and correct use of the lake and land. For example, the increase in religious activity on Ol'khon Island in the 1990s – tailgans in 1990 and 1993, along with the erection of three tethering posts at Sagaan Khada among many other activities – led to extended efforts to have Ol'khon be designated a sacred park-zapovednik, and also to the creation of a fund to protect the island, "Sacred Ol'khon" (Dugarov 92; Fridman, *Sacred* 200–209). More generally, Katherine Metzo has recently noted how religious values – along with other factors – have helped to create a "Baikal environmental ethic" among Buriats, Russians, and other Slavs in the nearby Tunka region (Metzo 39–54).

Contested waters

The spirits of Lake Baikal and the sacred locations around the lake also became sites of religious and cultural contestation among Russians, Buriats, Evenks, and other inhabitants of Baikal. In one eighteenth-century case, Orthodox monks from the Posol'skii monastery carved crosses into the petroglyphs of Sagan-Zaba in an effort to overlay the old religious importance of those rocks. The Sagan-Zaba petroglyphs date from as early as 4,000 years ago and (although all interpretations of the rock drawings remain highly speculative) appear to have been used as part of hunting rituals by the inhabitants at that time. Sagan-Zaba reflects the very long time that Lake Baikal and its geology have been religiously important for human communities. The petroglyph images include depictions of humans with hands in the air seemingly making prayers to the sky, fighters holding weapons, and many images of domestic and wild animals (bulls, horses, dogs, deer, birds, gooses, swans, and elk). Here, the monks sought to erase or cover over any religious understandings of the flora, fauna, rocks, and water as spiritually infused. Yet, their efforts met with little success as the local population near Sagan-Zaba continued to see its cliffs as a sacred site. And from the earliest times to recent, Buriat communities have carried out prayers with offerings to the spirits – especially the great spirit-master of the cliffs – and the Sagan-Zaba site has have long been a site of pilgrimage (Okladnikov 10–31; Imetkhenov 117–120; "Les gravures"; Tivanenko 170–177).

In the last few years, reflecting the way in which the legacy of the monks carving on the petroglyphs is not entirely so distant, the Shaman Valentin Khagdaev lamented to a tourist group about the ways in which the more secular culture of outsiders was defacing Cape Burkhan and disrupting the shamanist world.

> This is a sacred rock. Russians call it Cape Shamanka. We say, "Ay-Khae," which means "Fear! Tremble! Worship!" In the past, our ancestors were not allowed to live close to it. They could only settle over there. They wrapped their horses' hooves with animal skins and quietly passed by in order not to wake up the Great Spirit. This is His earthly palace. That's why we worship and pray to it. But we only pray from this side now. Because on the other side there are graffiti: "Petia and Vasia were here." I always say to this, "But I'm not writing on a church 'Shaman Valentin was here'." But Westerners like to climb over things and stomp their feet on them. An Eastern person should contemplate and take in the view.
>
> (Quoted in Bernstein, "Remapping" 34)

Figure 2.3. A sign erected as visitors arrive at the base of the Shaman's Rock (Ol'khon Island, Lake Baikal) in an effort to prevent tourists from walking on the sacred rocks. The sign says "Stop. This is a Specially Protected Territory! Entrance is Forbidden!" Photo by author, 2015.

The mineral springs around Baikal also became sites for a very different understanding of water and nature. If for Buriats and Evenks, the springs represented sites of contact between the spiritual and physical worlds, and places in which spirits live, the European medical practitioners and other scientists who arrived to examine the springs looked upon them for their health tourist potential and studied them for their chemical composition and medicinal qualities (Brummond; Rehmann; "Mineral'naia" 144; Shch. 1–20; Tivanenko 256–257).

Baikal's religious sites also became loci of colonial competition between different religious traditions and visions of Lake Baikal's religious meanings and powers. In 1904, traveler Paul Labbé noted this clash of explanatory systems: how Buriats and Russians might explain similar phenomena differently (often seeing the other in derogative terms).

> "There are not only fish in the lake," declared a [Buriat], "there are spirits, each one naughtier than the other. The lord of the waters,

Figure 2.4. "Julia, I love you." Graffiti painted on the Shaman's Rock (Ol'khon Island, Lake Baikal), reflecting different understandings of the sacredness of the site. Photo by author, 2015.

Oulane-Khat, rules them, and when he's angry, it's no joke for the fishermen; he juggles with the boats like a sorcerer with shells."

"Foolish savage," a [Russian] soldier then said to me, "he believes in spirits! Isn't he an idiot!" And the soldier added with conviction: "It's not a spirit, it's a devil who is hidden at the bottom of the lake."

"Who told you?"

"The old people have seen him!"

(Quoted in Matthiessen 49)

Struggles between different religious communities were not the exclusive prevue of Christian-shamanist relations, however, but also Buddhist-shamanist (Fridman, *Sacred* 135–139). According to shaman V.V. Khagdaev, Ol'khon Island – as "one of the most sacred centers of the shamanist world" – served as the place where Mongolian and Buriat Shamans hid themselves "in the epoch of their persecution in the Khalkha region on the part of Zaia-pandity [1599–1662], Pagba-lamy [Drogön Chögyal Phagpa, 1235–1280], and other lamas" (Khagdaev, "Shamanskii" 133; Zhambalova, *Profannyi* 190).

Divine Baikal

Most recently – and in contrast to the Orthodox notions of non-sacred water and Buriat conceptions of sacral water spirits – some inhabitants of the Baikal region have begun to enunciate a view of Baikal as *itself* divine and possessing transcendent powers. In particular, we can discern a growing sacralization of Lake Baikal in which people living near the lake, whatever their faith or ethnicity, have come to see the lake as a spiritual, creative, life-giving, and positive/benevolent force.

We can see these ideas developed clearly in the publications of Siberian writers like Valentin Rasputin and Mark Sergeev (6–7, 37). Rasputin is particularly eloquent in his writings on this theme (notably, his focus on the feminine, fertile powers of Lake Baikal echoes the Buriat creation stories):

> Not everything, as we know, has a name. It's impossible to give a name to the regeneration that occurs in people when they're near Baikal. There's no need to remind anyone that for this to take place a person must have a soul. And here he stands and looks around, is filled with something and carried off somewhere, and can't understand what's happening to him. Like a fetus in its mother's womb, he passes through all the evolutionary stages of human development and, spellbound by the ancient, mighty unfolding of this miracle, he experiences the timeless tidal feeling of the powers that created humankind.
>
> (Rasputin, "Lake Baikal" 127)

And elsewhere:

> Baikal is renowned and sacred for a different reason – for its miraculous, life-giving force and for its spirit, which is a spirit not of olden times, of the past, as with many things today, but of the present, a spirit not subject to time and transformations, a spirit of age-old grandeur and power preserved intact, of irresistible ordeals and inborn will.
>
> (Rasputin, "Baikal" 189)

This sense of the spiritual, creative power of Baikal also comes out in the words of ordinary citizens. A reporter from *Vostochno-Sibirskaia Pravda* interviewed people attending "Baikal Day" in 2005, asking them what Baikal meant to them (Kuznetsov). Their responses – a few of which I include here – reflect the shift in ways of understanding Baikal as sacred.

> Aleksei D'iakov: "Baikal is something unusual that supplies insane happiness when you find yourself there. Some sort of filling up of inexplicable internal energy appears. Baikal it is what gives great happiness."

Larisa Zabrodskaia: "I was born in Buriatiia. I had a great-grand mother, who they say was a shaman. There is a world around us and a world inside us. The internal world is much bigger than the external world. It has always seemed to me that Baikal loves me separately. And when I come to Baikal, it gives to me a revelation, gives me that inner world. It seems to me that Baikal gives me myself, but only in the future: cleaner, stronger, and more open, probably. This is all experienced on a completely different level."

Anatolii Malevskii: "Baikal – it is something holy. It is not simply beautiful, very beautiful, insanely beautiful, but in it there is also something sacred. And I, for one, sense it and clearly feel it."

The religious world of Lake Baikal

The religious world of Lake Baikal reflects the profound ties and mutually constitutive, ever-evolving relations of water and culture – of the physical and the spiritual – in Russian and Buriat culture. The lake was the site of a wide range of sacred practices as well as the focus of cosmologies of creation, causation, and purity and health. The waters of Baikal served as the foundation for Buriat origin stories, explaining the genesis of the Buriat peoples as well as the creation of the lake itself and they helped to explain the violence of earthquakes. They were a site of spiritual practices and beliefs, of religious contestation, and of cultural synthesis. The nexus of water and divinity led to a range of daily life practices – from fishing and hunting, to community festivals, to bathing, drinking, and hand-washing. They also have undergirded political efforts at environmental conservation. And the water–religion interconnection has not only differed from one faith community to the next but evolved and changed over time. Alongside understandings of the lake as a body of water that intersected with sentient deities, producing a wide range of outcomes for Orthodox and Shamanist inhabitants, a more recent conception of the lake has appeared. Baikal is seen as a life-giving, spiritual force all of its own, worthy of human respect and protection not just as a conduit for the divine powers of God and spirits but as a transcendent, creative power.

Acknowledgments

Research for this article was supported by funding from a Leverhulme Trust International Network Grant (for the project "Exploring Russia's Environmental History and Natural Resources"), the National Endowment for the Humanities, National Council for Eurasian and East European Research (NCEEER), under authority of a Title VIII grant from the U.S. Department of State, American Philosophical Society, American Council of Learned Societies, Davis Center for Russian and Eurasian Studies, Kennan Institute for Advanced Russian Studies, Mershon Center for International Security Studies and The Ohio State University. Any views, findings, conclusions or recommendations expressed in this article do not necessarily reflect those of the National Endowment for the Humanities or any of the other funding agencies. An early version of this article was presented at the National Convention of the American Association for the Advancement of Slavic Studies, Boston, November 12, 2009, and I thank the panelists and the audience for their comments and suggestions.

Notes

1 On the relationship of water and religious belief and practice, see Bradley; Altman; Alley; Havrelock; Oestigaard, *Water, Christianity*; Oestigaard, "Water"; Linton; Illich; Tuan; Barnhill and Gottlieb; and Berkes.
2 The Yenisei and Irkut are also the names of rivers. The Irkut joins the Angara in the city of Irkutsk and the Angara later joins the Yenisei on its way to the Arctic Ocean.

Bibliography

Alley, Kelly D. *On the Banks of the Ganga: When Wastewater Meets a Sacred River*. Ann Arbor: University of Michigan Press, 2002. Print.

Altman, Nathaniel. *Sacred Water: The Spiritual Source of Life*. Mahwah, NJ: HiddenSpring, 2002. Print.

Avvakum. *The Life of the Archpriest Avvakum by Himself*, trans. Jane Harrison and Hope Mirrlees. Hamden, CT: Archon Books, 1963. Print.

Barnhill, David Landis, and Roger S. Gottlieb, eds. *Deep Ecology and World Religions: New Essays on Sacred Grounds*. Albany: State University of New York Press, 2001. Print.

Basharov, I.P. *Russkaia promyslovaia kul'tura vostochnogo Pribaikal'ia (konets XIX – nachalo XX v.)*. Ulan-Ude: Izdatel'stvo Buriatskogo nauchnogo tsetra SO RAN, 2005. Print.

Berkes, Fikret. *Sacred Ecologies*, 3rd ed. New York: Routledge, 2012. Print.

Bernstein, Anya. "Remapping Sacred Landscapes: Shamanic Tourism and Cultural Production on the Olkhon Island." *Sibirica: Interdisciplinary Journal of Siberian Studies* 7.2 (2008): 23–46. Print.

Bernstein, Anya. *Religious Bodies Politic: Rituals of Sovereignty in Buryat Buddhism*. Chicago, IL: University of Chicago Press, 2013. Print.

Bradley, Ian. *Water: A Spiritual History*. London: Bloomsbury, 2012. Print.

Breyfogle, Nicholas. "The Fate of Fishing in Tsarist Russia: The Human-Fish Nexus in Lake Baikal." *Sibirica: Interdisciplinary Journal of Siberian Studies* 12.2 (2013): 1–29. Print.

Breyfogle, Nicholas. "'Another Voice from God': An Orthodox Sermon on Christianity, Science, and Natural Disaster." *Orthodox Christianity in Imperial Russia: A Source Book on Lived Religion*. Ed. Heather Coleman. Bloomington: Indiana University Press, 2014, 95–106. Print.

Breyfogle, Nicholas. "Confronting Catastrophe: The 1861–62 Lake Baikal Earthquakes and the Meanings of Nature in Imperial Russia." Unpublished manuscript in progress. Print.

Brummond, Janice. "Sacred Waters of the Mongols: Protecting Natural and Cultural Diversity in the Lake Baikal Region." PhD dissertation, University of Michigan, 2004. Print.

Chamberlain, Gary L. *Troubled Waters: Religion, Ethics, and the Global Water Crisis.* Lanham, MD: Rowman & Littlefield Publishers, 2008. Print.

Curtin, Jeremiah. *A Journey in Southern Siberia: The Mongols, their Religion; and their Myths.* London: Sampson Low, Marsten, and Company, 1909. Print.

Demin, E.V. *Antologiia Provala: Istoricheskie materialy o katastroficheskom Tsaganskom zemletriasenii 1862 g. – Provale na Baikale.* Ulan-Ude: Self Published, 2005. Print.

Dugarov, R.N. "Baikal i Ol'khon v traditsionnom mirovozzrenii Buriat." *Priroda i tsivilizatsiia: reki i kul'tury.* St. Petersburg: Evropeiskii dom, 1997, 88–94. Print.

Eliade, Mircea. *Patterns in Comparative Religion.* New York: New American Library, 1958. Print.

Ely, Christopher. *This Meager Nature: Landscape and National Identity in Imperial Russia.* DeKalb: Northern Illinois University Press, 2002. Print.

Fridman, Eva Jane Neumann. "Buryat Shamanism: Home and Hearth – A Territorialism of the Spirit." *Anthropology of Consciousness* 10.4 (1999): 45–56. Print.

Fridman, Eva Jane Neumann. *Sacred Geography: Shamanism among the Buddhist Peoples of Russia.* Budapest: Akadémiai Kiadó, 2004. Print.

"Golos ot gospoda," *Irkutskie eparkhial'nye Vedomosti,* pribavlenie k no. 5 (January 26, 1863): 42–48. Print.

Gurevich, A.V., and I.I. Molchanov, eds. *Stikhi i legendy o Baikale.* Irkutsk: Irkutskoe oblastnoe izdatel'stvo, 1938. Print.

Havrelock, Rachel. *River Jordan: The Mythology of a Dividing Line.* Chicago, IL: University of Chicago Press, 2011. Print.

Heretz, Leonid. *Russia on the Eve of Modernity: Popular Religion and Traditional Culture Under the Last Tsars.* Cambridge and New York: Cambridge University Press, 2008. Print.

Illich, Ivan. *H$_2$O and the Waters of Forgetfulness.* Dallas, TX: Dallas Institute of Humanities and Culture, 1985. Print.

Imetkhenov, A.B. *Pamiatniki prirody Baikala.* Novosibirsk: Nauka, Sibirskoe otdelenie, 1991. Print.

Khagdaev, V.V. "Shamanskii mir Priol'khon'ia." *Tsentral'no-Aziatskii shamanizm: Filosofskie, istoricheskie, religioznye aspekty (materialy mezhdunarodnogo nauchnogo simpoziuma, 2–16 iiunia, Ulan-Ude, oz. Baikal).* Ulan-Ude: Rossiiskaia Akademiia Nauk Sibirskoe Otedelenie Buriatskii Nauchnyi tsentr, 1996, 129–134. Print.

Khagdaev, V.V. *Shamanizm i mirovye religii: nekotorye voprosy vzaimootnoshenii buriatskogo shamanizma s buddizmom i khristianstvom v Baikal'skom regione: obshchee u shamanizma s buddizmom i khristianstvom i ego otlichie ot mirovykh religii.* Irkutsk: Izd. GP "Irkutskaíà obl. tip.", 1998. Print.

Kharitonov, Leonid. "Glorious Sea – Sacred Baikal," April 4, 2015. www.lkharitonov. com/video/chaikovsky/baikal. Web.

Kuznetsov, Georgii. "V chest' sviashchennogo ozera." *Vostochno-Sibirskaia Pravda* no. 158 (August 30, 2005). Print.

"Les gravures rupestres de sagan Zaba." February 21, 2007. www.baikal-lake.org/culture8.html. Web.

Linton, Jamie. *What is Water? The History of a Modern Abstraction.* Vancouver: UBC Press, 2010. Print.

Lloyd-Sidle, Elena, and Gray Henry-Blakemore, eds. *Water: Its Spiritual Significance.* Louisville, KY: Fons Vitae, 2009. Print.

Matthiessen, Paul. *Baikal: Sacred Sea of Siberia.* San Francisco, CA: Sierra Club Books, 1992. Print.
Metzo, Katherine. "Articulating a Baikal Environmental Ethic." *Anthropology and Humanism* 30.1 (June 2005): 39–54. Print.
"Mineral'naia voda Barguzinskgo okruga." *Izvestiia Sibirskogo imperatorskogo Russkogo geograficheskogo obshchestva* VIII.3–4 (1877): 144. Print.
[Minin, N.G.] "Baikal letom (iz ocherkov Sibiriakov)." *Morskoi sbornik* LXXXVI.9 (1866): 114–117. Print.
Montgomery, Robert Walker. "Buriat Language Policy, 19th c.–1928: A Case Study in Tsarist and Soviet Nationality Practices." PhD dissertation, Indiana University, 1994. Print.
Oestigaard, Terje. "Water." *The Oxford Handbook of the Archaeology of Ritual and Religion.* Ed. Timothy Insoll. New York: Oxford University Press, 2011, 38–50. Print.
Oestigaard, Terje. *Water, Christianity and the Rise of Capitalism.* London and New York: I.B. Taurus, 2013. Print.
Okladnikov, A.P. *Petroglify Baikala: pamiatniki drevnei kul'tury narodov Sibiri.* Novosibirsk: Nauka, Sibirskoe otdelenie, 1974. Print.
Phillips, G.D.R. *Dawn in Siberia; the Mongols of Lake Baikal.* London: F. Muller, 1943. Print.
Rasputin, Valentin. "Baikal (1981)." *Siberia on Fire.* DeKalb: Northern Illinois University Press, 1989, 118–177. Print.
Rasputin, Valentin. "Lake Baikal." *Siberia, Siberia.* Evanston, IL: Northwestern University Press, 1996, 119–178. Print.
Rehmann, Joseph. *Opisanie Turkinskikh mineral'nykh vod na Baikale.* 1808. Print.
Sergeev, Mark. *The Wonders and Problems of Lake Baikal.* Moscow: Novosti Press Agency Publishing House, 1989. Print.
Sgibnev, A.S. "O byvshem v Irkutskoi gubernii i Zabiakal'skoi oblasti zemletriasenii." *Otchet IRGO za 1863 god.* St. Petersburg, 1864, 8–25. Print.
"Shamanskii porog na reke Angare. Iz zapisok puteshestvennika." *Biblioteka dlia chteniia,* t. 89, otd. III (1848): 49–57. Print.
Shch. "Mineral'nye vody vostochnoi sibiri." *Biblioteka dlia chteniia* 89, ch. 3 (1848): 1–20. Print.
Tivanenko, Aleksei Vasil'evich. *Drevnie Bogi Baikala.* Chita: Ekspress, 2012. Print.
Tuan, Yi-Fu. *The Hydrologic Cycle and the Wisdom of God: A Theme in Geoteleology.* Toronto: University of Toronto Department of Geography Research Publications, 1968. Print.
Volkov, Sergei. *Legendy i predaniia ostrova Ol'khon.* Irkutsk: Tip. <<Print Lain>>, 2010. Print.
Zhambalova, S.G. *Traditsionnaia okhta Buriat.* Novosibirsk: Nauka. Sibirskoe otdelenie, 1991. Print.
Zhambalova, S.G. *Profannyi i sakaral'nyi miry Ol'khonskikh Buriat (XIX – XX vv.).* Novosibirsk: "Nauka" Sibirskaia izdatel'skiaia firma RAN, 2000. Print.

3 On the veneration of springs in the nineteenth century
Models of behavior and decision-making practices[1]

Evgenii Platonov

The academic study of holy springs is flourishing in contemporary ethnography, and there is now a substantial bibliography on the topic (Panchenko; Shevarenkova; Poplavskaia; Vinogradov; Geraskin; Inikova; Ermakova, among many others). Such interest is dictated by the role springs play in popular culture: it would be no exaggeration to describe them as the most widespread natural object venerated as holy not only in Russia, but in other countries. Such an exceptional position is connected with the antiquity and universality of perceptions of the properties of water. These perceptions were characteristic of the progenitors of Europeans from the period of Indo-European unity, known in antiquity and the Middle Ages, adapted by the Christian church and, with various mutations, exist too in our times (Gamkrelidze and Ivanov 675–676; Filimonova).

The fight against holy springs, conducted most aggressively in European countries after the Reformation in the sixteenth and seventeenth centuries, did not produce any tangible results. Holy springs remained popular among the educated, as well among the common people who maintained old traditions, despite the repeated prohibitions by secular and ecclesiastical authorities on gathering at springs, praying near them, and using water to which "special" significance was ascribed, and even the physical destruction of such water sources (Johansen; Carroll; Rattue; Bugslag; Walsham; Oestigaard).

Repressive measures against this religious practice among ordinary people were deployed later in Russia, in the course of the struggle with "superstitions" that unfolded in the first decade of the eighteenth century (Lavrov; Smilianskaia). The archival evidence for ecclesiastical attitudes to venerated springs is scant and fragmentary for the eighteenth century, but a large number of investigative files examining individual cases of the appearance of holy springs have come down to us from the nineteenth century.

Throughout the nineteenth century, the spontaneous appearance of holy places was subject to strict investigation by both the secular and the ecclesiastical authorities. T.A. Bernshtam notes that a continuous process of "sanctioning" and "auditing the holiness" of such places was implemented after the Petrine reforms, but the number of holy places accommodated by the church was paltry in comparison to the number of places not recognized by the church authorities (Bernshtam 316–317). There are now multiple sources that narrate the story of natural holy objects, including vitally important ethnographic recordings from the end of the twentieth and the beginning of the twenty-first centuries. However, the tales of elderly residents, in which the venerated object is treated as a *fait accompli*, established in the culture of the rural and urban populations, rarely address the question of how the tradition of veneration arose. Such tales are usually schematic, concisely expressing the essence of events at the holy place by combining the key facts through which it gains special significance. The history of relatively recent healings, which happened within the living memory of the interlocutor or were related to them by old people, is accorded special attention within contemporary tales. The secular and ecclesiastical investigators of the Synodal period were interested in other issues.

The files which were scrutinized in the ecclesiastical consistories and Synod of the nineteenth century do not simply contain references to, or descriptions of, venerated springs. They represent a whole complex of multifaceted and detailed information about the embryonic cult, with detailed description of the actions of peasants, clergy, and the civic authorities. This wealth of detail, and the presence of different points of view, of diverse and occasionally contradictory testimony of peasants, landowners, and priests, allows in-depth understanding of how the village community, the clergy, and authorities reacted to the appearance of a new focus of veneration, or the re-establishment of a formerly venerated object which had been forgotten and discarded. The documents preserved in the archives are an extremely informative and rich source for research in the fields of history, ethnography, and religious studies, and in turning to them we become witnesses of the process by which local holy places take shape.

It is worth stating immediately that the church certainly did not turn its attention to all aspects of the veneration of springs. Ethnographical materials from the end of the nineteenth and the beginning of the twentieth century present more diverse typologies of this sort of cult object: springs are differentiated by the distance pilgrims travel to them, by the extent of their reputation, by their location (from wild, uninhabitable places to sites within monastic complexes), and finally by their origin or the reason why the spring water began to gain repute. In the first half of the nineteenth century, reports were sent to the deans, bishops, and to the Synod only when the appearance of a spring directly entered the spheres of ecclesiastical governance and supervision. This happened when parish clergy served a supplicatory prayer service (*moleben*) at the spring, when an icon kept at the spring was declared to have miraculously appeared, and when the emergence of the spring was accompanied by stories of the appearance of saints in dreams or in reality. As a general rule, all these conditions generated mass pilgrimage, which was followed by the creation and dissemination of rumors about healings, further increasing the spring's popularity. Such occurrences were fraught with the potential to snowball uncontrollably, and efforts were made to curtail the spontaneous veneration of springs.

This article examines the circumstances in which two springs in Saint-Petersburg guberniia began to be venerated, drawing on evidence from the mid-nineteenth century – a period when the veneration of natural holy places was no longer so vigorously suppressed, but the authorities at various levels still maintained continuous control over such places.

In October 1841 the dean [*blagochinnyi*] Feodor Bystreevskii, a priest at the St. Dmitrii Cathedral in Gdov from 1832 to 1864 (*Istoriko-statisticheskie* 131), received a report from the priests of the Resurrection church in Veino village. In it they informed him that a peasant in the hamlet of Zaborov'e, one Feodor Titov, was broadcasting how St. Mitrofan of Voronezh had appeared to him in a dream. Titov was also cleaning up some sort of old well and building the foundations for a chapel over it, in which he intended to put an icon of this saint (TsGIA St P., F.19. Op.113. D. 24, 4). Moreover, Titov had found a fragment of an ancient stone cross at the well,[2] which had given rise to superstition among the common folk. This "superstition" consisted of pilgrims collecting water and using it to cure various illnesses.

According to the interrogation conducted by the zemstvo chief of police, Baron Zal'ts, this spring was venerated because:

> Feodor Titov [...] announced that he had suffered from ill-health for three years, this summer [1841 – E.P.] saw in a dream a man who ordered him to lift a stone from the road and to carry it to the chapel which is located in the hamlet of Zaborov'e and has been there since the olden days, and this he did. After a week he felt an improvement and according to the instruction by this same person in a second dream-vision he cleaned the spring which is located at the foot of the hill near to the aforementioned chapel and around the feast of the Elevation [of the Holy and Life-Giving Cross] washed in the water coming from it. Finally, according to the injunction of the same person, dressed in a chorister's robes, in a third dream-vision, he ordered a peasant in the hamlet of Vyskatka to paint an icon of St. Mitrofan, to hang above the spring, where he was enjoined to erect a chapel.
>
> (Ibid. 29)

This mention of the feast of the Elevation is not a casual one: according to clerical records, the chapel in Zaborov'e village was dedicated to the feast of the Founding of the Church of Christ's Resurrection in Jerusalem, which is celebrated on the eve of the Elevation of the Holy Cross. In other words, the peasant washed himself with water from the curative spring on the village feast day. The altar in Veino's church was consecrated in honor of this same feast, and one of its side-chapels was dedicated to Bishop Mitrofan of Voronezh, canonized ten years before these events unfold. It is clear, then, that the peasant's vision and actions were closely connected with the local, parochial system of feasts.

The dean informed the Consistory about Titov's unauthorized behavior, and the clerical authorities responded with a number of measures: an appeal to the Gdov uezd zemstvo court was prepared, which requested that the peasant be forbidden to build a chapel at the well; it was recommended that the piece of stone cross be carried to the parish church for use under clerical supervision, and the priests were requested to teach and admonish the peasant so that he cease recounting his vision and developing the spring and chapel. The chapel foundations, by then a square measuring 2 × 1¼ arshins (roughly 1.5 × 1 meter), were destroyed by the police. Thereafter, the Gdov ecclesiastical authorities submitted regular reports to the Consistory on how events were developing.

The first report arrived on December 2, 1841. In it, Konstantin Nesvitskii, the second priest at Gdov cathedral, reported that many people had appeared at the spring in Zaborov'e hamlet on November 22, since on November 23 – the feast of St. Mitrofan – they were expecting the consecration of the icon ordered by the peasant Titov and placed in Veino church. This icon was in the church sacristy – not having official authorization, the priests had not permitted it to be displayed alongside the other icons in the church, "however many of the visitors were seeking it and asking [for it] to be carried to the spring in the hamlet of Zaborov'e, four versts from the village of Veino, at which the chapel built without authorization [*samovol'no*] by the peasant is now uprooted, so that an intercessory prayer service [*molebstvie*] should be served there" (ibid. 20). The pilgrims expected a procession of the cross to be organized to the spring, as would be done for accepted foci of veneration. The bureaucrats had also prepared for this day: members of Gdov zemstvo court were present at Veino church, informing people about the false and superstitious divulgence. The people peacefully dispersed "to their settlements," after which the court officials and police officers set off for the spring itself, at which alms of 16 rubles and some kopecks in copper coin were collected. This money was set aside for use by Veino church. Feodor Titov had been sent away from the hamlet for these two days, on some contrived pretext or other, ostensibly at his master's behest.

A similar report was prepared by Simeon Preobrazhenskii, priest of Veino church, on December 14. In addition to a description of the events of November 22 and 23, the report contains some other details. It reveals that the well with the spring was situated in the middle of the hamlet, directly opposite Titov's house, and the spring flowed out in three streams which disappeared into the earth just at that spot. According to the report, conversations were held with Titov without much success: "he is blindly committed to his icon and evidently wants to venerate it alone, is quite embittered, seeing in me [i.e. the parish priest – E.P.] the cause of the initiative having been ruined, and, moreover, of the withholding of his icon. On the matter of his icon being unconsecrated, he declared that the Orthodox world has sanctified it; he talks little, seems mentally deranged, and makes the sign of the cross at every answer" (ibid. 23–24). The residents of Zaborov'e hamlet, meanwhile, struck by the tales of Feodor Titov and by the large number of pilgrims who gathered at the well in summer and autumn, decided to establish a further communal village observance in honor of St. Mitrofan in addition to the village feast of the Founding of the Church.

The course of these events clearly reveals the essence of the behavioral patterns engaged in by all participants, as it does the antagonistic contradictions in the ways that the peasant community, the synodal church, and the state related to the holy spring. Feodor Titov managed to achieve a fair amount before tales of the spring reached the ears of the priests. Interpreting his dream and his healing as the merciful intervention of Mitrofan of Voronezh, Titov confidently began to develop the spring, which should have produced a finished cult complex – the spring and a small, new chapel at the source itself. Having transferred the fragment of stone cross to the old chapel, the peasant gradually began to be healed. In the context of understandings of stone crosses in the western part of Petersburg gubernia, this was also no coincidence: stone crosses feature in the historiography precisely in connection with their healing properties (Trofimov 93), which are considered present in them in no less a degree than in holy water or icons. The creation of a new cult complex came to mean restoring the coherence of a group of venerated objects, thereby strengthening their sacred properties.

The peasant no doubt related the history of his healing to his fellow villagers while undertaking these steps, as a result of which the spring gained renown in the surrounding area and immediately attracted many pilgrims. In October and November 1841, less than a month after Titov's healing, a "crowd of people" gathered at the spring. From the dean's report it can be ascertained that the spring came to the attention of the priests only after widespread pilgrimage had begun, and they then asked for instructions about what to do next. Thus the main events took place beyond the clerical gaze: the holy object was assimilated into the peasant context without the participation of priests and the official church, which did not deprive the spring of its special properties. As the shrine keeper, to use Shchepanskaia's terminology (117), Feodor Titov was the central figure in the initial stage of unfolding events.

Confronted with the spring, the church, in the shape of the Consistory, demonstrated a different attitude. While the documents do not cite the legislation they were operating with in this case, the authorities' actions suggest that the chancellery's higher clergy were directed by article 19 of the 1841 Statute of Ecclesiastical Consistories, passed in the spring of that year. According to this clause, "in the case of superstition actions or divulgences which cause a significant impression amongst the people, especially with indications of malicious fabrication or mercenary aspects" the bishop of the diocese resorted to "measures of instruction and admonition" ("Polnoe sobranie" 224). According to another point of this same Statute, the construction of new chapels was permitted only for the most valid reasons and with the permission of the Holy Synod, but those built without permission ought to be destroyed. Notably, therefore, the foundations of the chapel were destroyed and conversations – the content of which may be guessed at – conducted with Titov.

A third type of behavior was demonstrated by the pilgrims who appeared on the feast of Mitrofan of Voronezh. First and foremost, it is significant that on the eve of the feast, November 22, the pilgrims set off for the spring which, without church recognition and the performance of prayer services, had unstable status. It conveyed rather potential sacrality, confirmed in the eyes of the people by healings. In order to definitively and incontrovertibly legitimize the spring, the pilgrims requested that a procession of the cross be organized to it and that an icon to be put up at it. The clerics' refusal, bolstered by the zemstvo court members' expressed opinion, nevertheless did not seriously shake the pilgrims' attitude to the spring – just as the refusal to bless the icon in church did not alter Feodor Titov's attitude towards it and to all that had happened.

This conflict, in which the main actors were the local parish clergy on one side and the peasant community on the other, demonstrates that when it was necessary to choose between normative religion, regulated by the church, or spontaneous perception of the sacred, peasants opted for the latter. In this they were guided by shared Orthodox tradition, rather than being directed by clerical instruction. This is evidenced by the Zaborov'e peasants' wish to establish an observance in honor of St. Mitrofan despite the clear opposition of the clergy, and also by subsequent events.

In the next report, dated January 25, 1842, priest Simeon Preobrazhenskii stated that there had been some progress in the case. Influenced by sermons, Feodor Titov had given accumulated alms in "copper coins" to the value of 48 rubles over to the church. The flow of pilgrims had dried up little by little, since the icon of the saint was still being kept in the sacristy, hidden from view, and the "well of superstition had frozen completely as a result of shallow water" (TsGIA SPb. F.19. Op.113. D.24 34 rev.).

Rumors of the healing well had already spread far and wide, however. In February 1842 a certain Karl Fridrich from Narva donated a sum of two rubles and 50 kopecks, which was handed over to the priest with the request that two rubles be used for candles and the rest for a supplicatory prayer service to the saint. On March 3, "several dozen individuals appeared from Luga and Revel uezds and remote pogosts of the local [uezd] [i.e. Gdov – E.P.], and it is known that all those who came were at the place of superstition in the hamlet of Zaborov'e" (ibid. 36). The pilgrims gradually incorporated the spring into the system of rural holy places, and visiting it was prioritized over visiting the church, where they went *after* having paid tribute to the spring. As a direct source of miraculous healing in the traditional hierarchy of sacred places, the spring was accorded primary significance.

There were no new developments until the summer of 1842: in winter the spring froze, in spring it was submerged by flood water, but in June "with the paths opening and the warmth, the crippled began to come, most from afar, and no one escaped the spring of superstition. The arms of the law, elected police officials [sotskie], those from the same estate as the peasant Titov and all the inhabitants of the hamlet of Zaborov'e, quite content with the incomers, are trying to keep the visitation of the aforesaid secret from me" (ibid. 40). In July matters intensified. From time to time, "crowds of people" appeared in Veino village church requesting a supplicatory prayer service be served to the saint, and in order to stop pilgrims accessing the source, a police guard was set up at the spring by order of the local authorities. The peasants, frightened by the police, found a means of getting their own way: they got water "in secret from women from Zaborov'e and nearby hamlets, which [...] is not from the spring itself, but is accepted from that hamlet with the same zeal." Sympathy for the "superstition" was mainly shown by inhabitants of the three nearest hamlets, Luzhka, Zales'e and Zaborov'e itself, where incoming pilgrims spent the night (ibid. 41–41 rev.). One of the factors here is that the spring was a source of income for the peasants, allowing them to earn a little money from the wanderers, in addition to a definite pride in the fact that their neighborhood had a miracle-working spring, which attracted a large number of people and the aspiration to make the holy object accessible. As can be gathered from Simeon Preobrazhenskii's next report, decisive measures were finally taken in August 1842: the well was filled in by the police and pilgrimage to it stopped.

Pilgrims played the main role in disseminating information about the spring in the second stage of its lifecycle. The situation in the hamlets nearest to the church can hardly be considered under the control of the parish priest: local residents exercised caution and hid their reverence for the spring. The spring was definitively fixed on the regional map of local shrines by the "crowds of pilgrims" and "people from afar" mentioned in the reports, who were attracted by the stories circulating about the miracle-working spring. That they were grateful to receive water not only from the well itself, but from any other water source on the territory of the hamlet, somewhat widens our perception of the topography of the holy place. In essence, its boundaries might be flexible, subject to particular circumstances.

Events had yet to reach a climax. Feodor Titov, as yet unaware of the fate of his icon (sent from Veino church to St. Petersburg at the request of the St. Petersburg curate Venedikt (Grigorovich) in March 1842), was most disgruntled that he had not been allowed to place his own icon at the spring. Seeking an opportunity to clarify matters, he found it at the village festival of the Founding of the Church, September 13/26. An old, repainted icon of Nicholas the Wonderworker, which "the people revered," had been put up at the chapel by one of the estate's house-serfs. The supplicatory prayer service at the village festival was performed by that same priest,

Simeon Preobrazhenskii, who asked who the icon and crosses hanging on it belonged to. In fairly rude fashion, Titov responded "stolen at your place," thereby alluding to his own icon, and directed further rude words at him. This incident proved to be the last straw: Titov was accused of spending chapel money on his own needs, and was dispatched to prison. Later, however, he was released under the supervision of the local authorities, which is the point at which all traces of him disappear from this story.

As for the icon of St. Mitrofan of Voronezh, after it was delivered to Petersburg Venedikt (Grigorovich) ordered the icon to be put in the Peter and Paul Cathedral or one of the churches of the Alexander Nevsky Lavra (RGIA F.796. Op.122. D.1428 11). According to a peasant Efim Andreev, the icon was kept in one of the Lavra churches' sacristies in the second half of the nineteenth century ("Kratkie istoriko-statisticheskie" 164).

The conflict that flared up between the peasant and clergy reflected a global conflict between two understandings of religiosity – the traditional, embodied by Titov, the peasant community, and the pilgrims, and that of the state, as implemented by the clergy and police. According to the first, the spring – as clearly shown by the saint's appearance in a dream – required an appropriate course of ensuing actions: development, veneration, the conducting of services by it for its complete incorporation into the system of local Christian shrines. The prospect of implementing these unwritten rules was radically ruptured by continual obstruction from the clergy and civil authorities, which was perceived by the peasant community not as the enactment of ecclesiastical or civic legislation but as a direct struggle with a miraculously appeared holy object, the apogee of which was the filling in of the well.

Almost simultaneously with St. Mitrofan of Voronezh's appearance to Feodor Titov in a dream, yet another spring was discovered in St. Petersburg gubernia. This one, however, was in the east, in Novoladozhskii uezd, and it provides a striking contrast with the story that unfolded in the hamlet of Zaborov'e, in terms of attitudes towards it and in the ensuing course of affairs.

The first report made to the Consistory described the exterior aspect of events:

> an icon was found at a hillside stream near the Church of St Nicholas, Terebuzhka pogost, which many residents flocked to in order to venerate [it]. With the arrival of the police superintendent of the first district [*pristav 1-ogo stana*] in the designated pogost, it was found that the place where the holy icon appeared, by the little river or stream below, was no more than 80 *sazhen* [160 meters – E.P.] from the church, this icon is wooden, one and a half *vershki* tall and wide, preserved in the earth, but the face depicted on it is impossible to discern, and a corner of the icon is rotten and damaged. The place itself is fenced off from the hill on three sides with poles, boards have been laid down for people

to walk on and, near to the spring, from which clean water flows, a mug has been put for the collection of money, and a copper cross has been nailed above it and a ladle for scooping up water laid [there]. The clergy of the aforementioned pogost take the money from the mug, and inhabitants of the surrounding areas accept this icon as miraculously appeared.

(TsGIA SPb. F.19. Op.34, D.173 1–1 rev.)

The Petersburg curate Venedikt (Grigorovich) exchanged letters with the civil governor on this case, so that before detailed information was received "through a trustworthy official secret measures on hand for the deterrence of the convergence of the people" were taken (RGIA F.796. Op.123. D.718 1 rev.). A detailed explanation was demanded from the Ecclesiastical board of Novaia Ladoga, and it was then revealed that this well had a firmly established reputation as curative for a year already, even before the appearance of the icon, because the water from this well had healed a certain Evfimiia Il'ina, from the hamlet of Luzha, a peasant woman belonging to the master Prince Meshchersk. As far as can be understood from the context of the report, people also went to it for holy water earlier, before the healings had begun.

In a report by the priest Ioann Miroliubov (d. 1851) of Terebuzhskii pogost, what happened with the peasant woman is described in detail:

> on August 11, 1841 the maiden Evfimiia Il'ina, daughter of Prince Meshchersk's peasant Il'ia Stefanov of the hamlet of Luzha, who formerly worked in the hamlet of Gnori for the peasant Iakov Alekseev, was harvesting oats in a field in the hamlet of Gnori on the right-hand side of the road from Staraia Lagoda. At about three o'clock in the afternoon some sort of strange creature, unseen by anybody, approached her from the woods which encircle the northern side of the field – a woman dressed like a nun, and said to her that she should announce to the people that they should not work on a feast day, because work would bring her terrible suffering, and in order that the people would believe her words, taking from her chest a large, glittering cross, she gave it to the worker to kiss, as a result of which she was struck dumb and lost the use of [her] right arm and leg. Then she told her that if she wanted to be cured she must receive Holy Communion on the feast of the Dormition, have a supplicatory prayer service with a water blessing served at the well which is near the pogost of Terebuzhka [...] on the bank of the little river opposite the burned-down barn. She did not know this well and the residents of Terebuzhka pogost hardly remembered it because none of them had used water from it since long past. Since this maiden was decidedly deprived of speech and extremely weakened, which no one doubted, she was shriven and brought to Holy Communion, and at her request a prayer service with water blessing was served, after

which she recovered. Her recovery convinced the local residents of the water's curative powers, the sick took it and, according to some, recovered [their] health, but we, not having trustworthy evidence, did not report this to Your Blessing.

(TsGIA SPb. F.19. Op.34. D.173 12–12 rev.)[3]

That the parish clergy did not inform the dean about the rumors that were circulating about the healing well was a major omission on their part, since they had been obliged to report such events since the Ecclesiastical Regulation was passed in 1721 (Dukhovnyi Reglament 112). The clergy used the absence of reliable evidence as an excuse, but the instruction to hold the prayer service, after which the peasant woman recovered, and the fact that the parish clergy collected money from the mug by the well, contradicts this claim. They delayed reporting, fearing the unpredictable consequences of the inevitable investigation and the loss of income from pilgrims.

Based on the information in the report, the sequence of events may be reconstructed as follows: the water in the abandoned well, which had formerly been venerated as a holy spring, effected a healing that was clear and obvious to all, which was also followed by other healings. The appearance of the icon completed the logical sequence of events in the assimilation of the holy place, after which the well was developed by local residents.

On the May 25, 1842, several days after the correspondence with the Consistory began, the case took an unexpected turn: the icon disappeared from the spring, and no one could say where it had gone. One may suppose that the icon had been hidden by the peasants, who were afraid that the icon would be taken away – at best, to the parish church. If the parish clergy had taken it, this would probably have been reflected in the correspondence with the Consistory, if – of course – they had not been acting in collaboration with their parishioners. Analysis of similar cases from the nineteenth century shows that priests were extremely keen that there should be a locally venerated shrine near the church or within the parish, since it would become a source of inexhaustible income which could exceed the amount of income generated by performing rites or selling candles.

At the end of June 1842, Ioann Miroliubov conveyed that fewer and fewer people were gathering at the spring, giving rise to the hope that soon they would stop going there altogether.[4] However, in the following report from July, the priest acknowledged that people were still going to the spring, drinking water from the source, washing with it and taking it with them, leaving money in the mug on the post, and ordering supplicatory prayer services in church.

In relation to these events, the Consistory took an uncharacteristic decision – in comparison with similar cases – in August 1842:

> To stop the people in some fashion from taking water from the spring, washing with it and taking it home, would entail generating further folk

fantasies, rather than stopping their convergence at the stream; therefore do not touch the spring and leave the aforesaid as it was until the discovery of the icon at it, but take the mug with the cross and do not sing supplicatory prayer services to the imaginary miraculously-appeared icon in church, but to well-known saints or holy [icons], such as the M[other of] G[od] of Kazan, of Smolensk or other well-known [icons].

(TsGIA SPb. F.19. Op.34. D.173 36)

Thus the venerated spring was accommodated rather than destroyed – in contrast to the spring in Zaborov'e hamlet – and did not vanish from human memory, but was included fairly organically into the parish system of holy places.

After two years the Consistory checked how things were going with the icon and whether people still gathered at the spring, to which the Novoladozhsk ecclesiastical board replied that there was no information about the icon, people did not converge at the place where it was found, and supplicatory prayer services were not being said in church (ibid. 40–40 rev.).

Two of the multitude of examples of the church's relationship with the holy springs which fell within its field of view reveal not only the diverse attitudes representatives of the different estates and functionaries had to venerated natural objects, but also the differentiated approach to them taken by the ecclesiastical authorities. In the first case they strove to curtail the embryonic cult with fairly harsh measures, which aggravated relations between the clergy and the village community. In the second case it was assumed that the spring would gradually be forgotten without interference. In both instances, however, veneration of the springs continued: in his notes of 1865 the peasant Efim Andreev testified that even after the Zaborov'e spring was filled in with earth and stones "the people left in great indignation at the chief, and ever since they go to the feast in the pogost of Veino; they also take water from the spring; believers are cured and bring their gifts in gratitude to the God-pleaser [saint]" ("Kratkie istoriko-statisticheskie" 164). The remark that water was still being taken from the spring, and healings were continuing, shows that the spring continued to fully function as a locally venerated shrine.

As regards the spring in Terebuzhsk pogost, the next news of it dates from the 1880s. This reveals that – contrary to the report of the Ecclesiastical Board – veneration of the spring soon resumed, and probably never stopped. This well is mentioned in the *Istoriko-statisticheskie svedeniia* as particularly venerated by parishioners. According to the stories of a local deacon, Peter Dmitriev, who had already served for around 40 years (making him a former eyewitness of the history outlined above, with the miraculously appeared icon), three people were healed by the water from the well: the aforementioned Efimiia Il'ina – described here as petty bourgeois [*meshchanka*] from Novaya Ladoga rather than a peasant woman; the son of a deacon's widow; and Vera, the daughter of the female landowner Rymleva. The last instance of healing is definitely dated to 1871. Moreover, the local clergy of Terebuzhsk pogost church were asked for permission to walk in a procession of the cross to the spring, and to hold water blessing prayer services at it on the designated days (*Istoriko-statisticheskie* 187).

It is worth noting that a stone church dedicated to the Dormition of the Mother of God was built in Terebuzhsk pogost in 1869 (*Pamiatnaia kniga* 396). Here a direct link with the venerated spring may be discerned: the first significant healing took place on precisely this feast day. If in Zaborov'e the actions of the peasant Feodor Titov were incorporated within the framework of pre-existing parish feasts, then in the second case the venerated spring itself influenced the development of the parochial festive system.

This analysis of the diverse models of behavior displayed at the genesis of a holy spring, as effected in the two given cases unfolding almost simultaneously on the territory of one diocese, suggests the following conclusions.

Holy springs and certain methods for their domestication were so deeply rooted in the culture of the rural population that the appearance of a new object prompted a chain of predictable actions from the peasants, who participated in this process in a variety of roles: as shrine guardians, pilgrims, pilgrim hosts, acting in accordance with traditional understandings of their role in the unfolding events, sidestepping those obstacles which were put in their path.

The process of a holy spring's discovery could unfurl without the participation of the clergy and church; however, ideally it required consummation in the form of specific development (marking with Christian cult objects) and continuous support from the church by way of water blessing services at it. However, the lack of official recognition did not unduly concern pilgrims and the local residents who used the spring water.

At village community level, the implementation of legislation in the eighteenth and nineteenth centuries by officials, including priests, was perceived as a direct attack on miraculously appeared holy items. Measures taken did not lead to the expected results, impacting only on the external facets of the spring's existence: after passions cooled, the spring was firmly incorporated into the existing system of parish holy places and feasts and could, in turn, influence its development.

Notes

1 An earlier version of this essay appeared in the journal *Traditsionnaia kultura* No. 1, 2014.
2 Further on in the document there is a description of this stone fragment, composed jointly by archpriest K.P. Nesvitskii (who served in the Cathedral of St Dmitrii from 1832 to 1845) and the Gdov police chief. It is cited here in an endnote since it does not contain any essential information: "this stone looks like an irregular triangle of natural boulder, ¾ arshin long, 5 vershkas deep,

apparently an engraved mark on one side || and three veins" (TsGIA SPb. F.19. Op.113. D. 24 18).
3 This interesting syncretic female figure represents Paraskeva Piatnitsa, which may be deduced from the description of her appearance and articulated entreaty, and the links between the cult of this saint and the cult of the Mother of God (see Levin 141–142).
4 This point of view was expressed in the Synodal verdict on this case: "since the icon has disappeared, the concourse of people should also stop" (RGIA F.796. Op.123. D. 718 7 rev–8). This is evidence that the members of the Synod underestimated the extent to which natural objects – especially water – were venerated.

Bibliography

Bernshtam, Tatiana. *Prihodskaia zhizn' russkoi derevni: ocherki po tserkovnoi etnografii*. St. Petersburg: Petropolis, 2007. Print.

Bugslag, James. "Local Pilgrimages and Their Shrines in Pre-Modern Europe." *Peregrinations*. International Society for the Study of Pilgrimage Art. 25 August 2015. Web.

Carroll, Michael. *Irish Pilgrimage – Holy Wells and Popular Catholic Devotion*. Baltimore, MD: Johns Hopkins University Press, 1999. Print.

Ermakova, Elena. "Pochitanie Krivankovskogo kolodtsa v Jugrinskom raione Tumenskoi oblasti." *Antropologicheskii forum* 12 (2010): 1–52. Web.

Ermakova, Elena. "Istselenie vodoi: pochitaemie istochniki iuga Tumenskoi oblasti". *Vestnik Tumenskogo gosudarstvennogo universiteta* 2 (2011): 27–32. Print.

Filimonova, Tatiana. "Voda v kalendarnikh obriadakh." *Kalendarnie obychai i obriady v stanakh zarubezhnoi Evropy. Istoricheskie korni i razvitie obychaev*. Moscow: Nauka, 1983, 130–145. Print.

Gamkrelidze, Tamaz, and Viacheslav Ivanov. *Indoevropeiskii iazik i indoevropeitsi*. Part II. Tbilisi: Izdatel'stvo Tbilisskogo Universiteta, 1984. Print.

Geraskin, Juri. "Iz istorii bor'by sovetskoi vlasti s palomnichestvom k sviatim istochnikam." *Rossiiskii nauchnyi zhurnal* 1 (2007): 25–33. Print.

Inikova, Svetlana. "Sviatye istochniki i ozera v religiozno-istoricheskom kontekste." *Russkie Riazanskogo kraia*. Moscow: Indrik, 2009, 293–325. Print.

Istoriko-statisticheskie svedeniia o Sankt-Peterburgskoi eparhii. Vypusk X. St. Petersburg: Sankt-Peterburgskii eparkhialnyi istoriko-statisticheskii komitet, 1885. Print.

Johansen, Jens. "Holy springs and Protestantism in Early Modern Denmark: a Medical Rationale for a Religion Practice." *Medical History* 41 1997: 59–69. Print.

"Kratkie istoriko-statisticheskie svedeniia o tserkvakh i prihodakh Gdovskogo uezda. Iz zapisok krestianina Efima Andreeva." *Istoriko-statisticheskie svedeniia o Sankt-Peterburgskoi eparhii*. Vypusk X. St. Petersburg: Sankt-Peterburgskii eparkhialnyi istoriko-statisticheskii komitet, 1885. Print.

Lavrov, Aleksandr. *Koldovstvo i religiia v Rossii. 1700–1740 gg*. Moscow: Drevlekhranilische, 2000. Print.

Levin, Eve. "Khristianskie istochniki kul'ta sviatoi Paraskevy." *Dvoeverie i narodnaia religiia v istorii Rossii*. Perevod s angliiskogo A.L. Toporkova and Z.N. Isidorovoi. Moscow: Indric, 2004, 141–161. Print.

Oestigaard, Terje. "The Topography of Holy Water in England after the Reformation." *Perceptions of Water in Britain from Early Modern Times to the Present: An Introduction*. Bergen: Bergen University Press, 2010, 15–34. Print.

Pamiatnaia kniga po Sankt-Peterburgskoi eparkhii. St. Petersburg: Tipographiia Otdel'nogo korpusa pogranichnoi strazhi, 1899. Print.

Panchenko, Aleksandr. *Issledovaniia v oblasti narodnogo pravoslaviia. Derevenskie sviatini Severo-Zapada Rossii*. St. Petersburg: Aleteiia, 1998. Print.

Poplavskaia, Kh. "Palomnichestvo, strannopriimstvo i pochitanie sviatin (po materialam Riazanskogo kraia)." *Pravoslavnaia zhizn' russkikh krest'ian XIX – XX vekov: itogi etnograficheskikh issledovanii*. Moscow: Nauka, 2001, 251–300. Print.

"Polnoe sobranie zakonov Rossiiskoi imperii." *Sobranie* II. Tom XVI. Otdelenie I. St. Petersburg: V tipografii II otdeleniia sobstvennoi EIV kantsel'iarii, 1842. Print.

Rattue, James. *The Living Stream: Holy Wells in Historical Context*. Woodbridge: The Boydell Press, 2001. Print.

"Reglament, ili ustav Dukhovony kollegii." Moscow: Synod typography, 1761.

RGIA Fond 796. Opis 122. Delo 1428. *O suevernikh razglasheniiakh krest'ianinom Fedorom Titovim v Gdovskom uezde*. 14.11.1841 – 14.01.1842. Manuscript.

RGIA Fond 796. Opis 123. Delo 718. *O mnimoiavlennoi Novoladozskogo uezda v Terebuzskom pogoste ikone*. 3.06.1842 – 16.07.1842. Manuscript.

Schepanskaia, Tatiana. "Krizisnaia set (traditsii dukhovnogo osvoeniia prostranstva)." *Russkii Sever i problemy lokal'nikh grup*. St. Petersburg: MAE RAN, 1995, 110–176. Print.

Shevarenkova, Iulia. "Legendy o sviatikh istochnikakh (opit sistematizatsii suzhetov na materiale Nizegorodskoi oblasti)." *Vestnik Nizegorodskogo universiteta* 1 (2000): 77–84. Print.

Smilianskaia, Elena. "'Sueverie' i ratsionalizm vlastei i poddanikh v Rossii XVIII v." *Evropeiskoe prosveschenie i tsivilizatsiia Rossii*. Moscow: Nauka, 2004, 204–211. Print.

Smilianskaia, Elena. "O kontsepte "sueverie" v Rossii veka Prosvescheniia". Sny Bogoroditsy. Issledovaniia po antropologii religii. *Studia Ethnologica*. Vypusk 3. St. Petersburg: Izdanie Evropeiskogo Universiteta, 2006, 19–31. Print.

Trofimov, K. "Kamennye kresty Gdovskogo uezda." *Sankt-Peterburgskii zemskoi vestnik* (1911 Iun): 85–98. Print.

TsGIA SPb. Fond 19. Opis 113. Delo 24. *Delo po reportu Gdovskogo Dukhovnogo pravleniia o sueveriakh, razglashaemykh krestianinom Fedorom Titovim v Gdovskom uezde*. 23.10.1841 – 12.10.1843. Manuscript.

TsGIA SPb. Fond 19. Opis 34. Delo 173. *O ikone mnimo-iavlennoi v Terebuzskom pogoste*. 21.05.1842 – 25.06.1844. Manuscript.

Vinogradov, Valentin. "Pochitanie istochnikov v Pskovskoi oblasti: kolodets v bolote." *Traditsionnaia kul'tura* 4 (2006): 33–40. Print.

Walsham, Alexandra. "Sacred Spas? Healing Springs and Religion in Post-Reformation Britain." *The Impact of the European Reformation: Princes, Clergy and People*. Ed. Bridget Heal and Ole Peter Grell. Aldershot: Ashgate, 2008, 209–230. Print.

4 *Daemon loci*
The formation of river images in Russian mental worlds

Dmitry Zamyatin

> I am flying over flatlands, obviously steppe – this must be Russia. I am soaring over a majestic river across which a towering bridge has been built. Underneath the bridge, a brick building juts out into the river; smoke curls from its stack; the grinding of machinery can be heard. It is a factory.
>
> The river curves into a gigantic bend. The banks have become overgrown with forest; the panorama is boundless. The sun has hidden inside the clouds, but everything is permeated with a harsh light that casts no shadow. Greenish, translucent water races headlong through the broad channel, and down deep, shadows flash from time to time over the rocks – huge glimmering fish. I am at peace and filled with trust.
>
> (Ingmar Bergman, *The Magic Lantern*)

River worlds: introduction to the context

The river is a universal image of oblivion, of eternal movement, and of life, transitory yet continuously renewed. The archetype of water, living organically and naturally as seas, lakes, swamps, ponds, and streams, is perhaps most fully and vividly manifested in the image of the river. As an image, the river organizes a multitude of landscapes large and small that give rise, in turn, to clusters of new, developing images.

Ancient cultures saw rivers primarily as a symbol and source of life: river water was potable and was used to irrigate fields and sustain livestock. It provided a source of fish, turned mill wheels, and enabled long-distance travel by boat, thereby opening the door to trade and the exploration of new lands. Rivers often served as obvious natural barriers between tribes, peoples, and states. Crossing a river meant entering a different, alien world, one replete with mortal dangers, but also adventures (Propp 170–171, 185, 208, 221). This border function of rivers made its way into a number of ancient and archaic mythologies: within a variety of very different traditions, it is a river, by whatever name, that serves to divide the earthly, human world and the underworld that awaits us beyond the grave, the realm of the spirits of the dead (Toporov 374–376).

Great rivers were the cradles of the ancient civilizations of Egypt, Mesopotamia, Ancient India, and China; river landscapes determined, in essence, the pathways of ancient humanity's political and cultural development. Lev Mechnikov was the first to typologize this phenomenon, providing a framework for describing the most important features of such civilizations. The pantheons of ancient river civilizations always included river gods, gods of rivers, who played a major role in key myths and were a part of the most important rites and rituals.

Rivers could symbolize both life and death; they could bring life-giving moisture to fields, but they could also destroy houses and roads and kill people during floods; they protected against encroachment by foreign invaders, but in times of drought or low water could commit the "treachery" of letting through enemy attacks. The ancients saw rivers as fickle and two-faced gods, their contradictory images splitting in two and sometimes obscuring one another (Frankfort *et al.* 50, 161; Pavlova 31–41). Both static and dynamic images of rivers have their place.

Images of the river: stasis and dynamism

Static images of the river originate from the fixed, relatively immobile, and stationary position of such images' observers and creators. In most cases, these observers and creators are people who have settled along the banks of a river, who observe its life and make immediate use of its offerings, such as farmers and fishers. For them, the river is primarily an image of a natural, replicating, seasonal force equally capable of bringing benefit and loss, joy and sorrow. The seasonal cycles of the river's life define the cyclical nature of their own lives. In essence, the river for them embodies nature's most important rhythms and serves as a "plenipotentiary" of nature overall.

Any movement down a river or along its banks can generate dynamic images that may be poorer in content yet more rigidly structured and, at times, more expressive.[1] We might include here flight over a river: although flying machines were not known to ancient humans, cliffs, bluffs, and mountain ledges along the banks of rivers offered the opportunity to take a mental snapshot of fluvial panoramas from the air and convert them into something akin to a slideshow of consciousness. No doubt, these "aerial" images of rivers, snaking through broad plains or foaming over mountain rocks, were also available and of interest to those who lived along their shores. But it was among merchants, pilgrims, and soldiers (the most typical river travelers in ancient times) that river panoramas generated the appropriate images most quickly and effectively – majestic or threatening, pleasing or unnerving. Movement promoted the creation of a dynamic picture of river water and its surrounding landscapes, along with the development of a particular mythological or philosophical "scaffolding" for this relentless and seemingly eternal movement.

The dangers and vicissitudes of river travel – rocky rapids and sandy shallows, hostile fortresses and aggressive nomads pursuing travelers by land – and the discovery of heretofore unknown lands at the upper or lower reaches of rivers all left deep impressions that were transformed into images of hostile, hazardous, yet magnetic river landscapes. Perhaps Joseph Conrad's *Heart of Darkness* most vividly portrays the role and significance of the river in the emergence of human characters confronted by wild nature and primitive civilization (Conrad).[2] It is telling that the eras of the Age of Discovery, colonialization, and the carving up of the world by imperial powers gave rise to enduring images of conquistadors, explorers, and Cossacks in which the connection between humans and rivers was vividly manifested. The Amazon and the Mississippi, the Volga and the Ob', the Congo and the Zambezi – all these rivers became symbols of relentless movement into an unknown that promised both gold and new and expanding horizons.[3]

The indigenous communities of humans that formed along the banks of major rivers and adjacent lands developed their own way of life that influenced, in turn, the emergence of fundamental images of countries and peoples. No one will deny that the image of life in the Cossack regions of the Dnieper, the Don, the Kuban, the Ural (Jayiq), the Ob', and the Amur has become an integral part of the ethnocultural image of Russia as a whole. It was only natural for Mikhail Sholokhov to name his outstanding novel about the fate of the Don Cossacks during the tumultuous years of World War I and the Russian Civil War *Tikhii Don* ("Quiet Don," known in English as *And Quiet Flows the Don*).

Daemon loci: the image's genesis

In the ontological sense, any river is an uncertain and changeable place. Furthermore, as a place never clearly seen, one that is constantly flashing past, the ontology of this place is likely to feature *daemons* (demons or spirits). Here, in figurative interpretations of the concept of the *daemon* we follow in the footsteps of the ancient tradition, in which they serve as lower divinities or even uplifted human souls serving as intermediaries between the world of people and the world of the higher gods (Plutarkh 76–81; Trubetskoi 241–245). Typically, daemons are able to bring people both good and evil, depending on the situation. At the same time, the influence they have over people can be very subtle – barely perceptible – "ethereal." All people can have a daemon of their own that whispers advice in difficult situations (Plutarkh, "O daemone Sokrata" 360–363).

The decline of traditional European societies and their gradual desacralization led at first to a revival of the concept of *genius loci* prevalent in ancient mythology, most actively in the Age of Enlightenment and later in the early twentieth century in connection with a growing sense of passéism and a resurgence of a cult of heritage.[4] Modern interpretations of *genius loci*, however different they may look in their culturological, aesthetic, philosophical, literary, or architectural iterations, had and continue to have a positive emotional and rational hermeneutics. This local hermeneutics is ontologically, figuratively, and symbolically tied to a certain geocultural stasis: whether the cult of the home, the estate, the grove, the park, or any other memorable locus that has a personality of its own. The concept of *genius loci* clearly does not fully capture the changeableness, dynamism, ambiguity, ambivalence, and "dark depths" of the local geocultural memory, but here the *daemon loci* comes to the rescue. Within Russian mental worlds, it is the image of the river that seems to most closely correspond to this ontological interpretation, while, perhaps, within the mental worlds of North America it is the ocean or sea that most closely corresponds to a *daemon loci* and its personifications (as seen, for example, in Herman Melville's great *Moby-Dick* or Edgar Allen Poe's *The Narrative of Arthur Gordon Pym of Nantucket*).

The river and image archetypes: the pathways of civilizations

Both static and dynamic images of rivers can unite within themselves, in varying proportions, image archetypes of borders, pathways, and bridges. While a border and a pathway are understandable and natural representations of the image of the river, the bridge can have at least two important image representations that unite and partially sublate other river images.[5] A pontoon, wooden, stone, concrete, or steel bridge built across a river in one way or another signifies a strengthening of the connecting function of a border and enhanced communication and exchange between the people living on a river's opposite sides. At the same time, any bridge across a river is the shortest and often the most fragile path from one means of thinking and imagining the world to another. It is hardly surprising that, during the conflict between Albanians and Serbs in Kosovo in the late twentieth and early twenty-first century, bridges over rivers between ethnically different parts of one and the same city were frequently destroyed; such bridges were at times the sites of ongoing standoffs between warring ethnic communities. If, on the other hand, a river bridge stands within a thriving commercial, military, or administrative city, the capital of a large district or metropolis, it gradually becomes overgrown with shops, tourist attractions, checkpoints, and bridge towers and even becomes a place where shopkeepers and border guards both live and work. A perfect example of such a bridge "for life" is the Charles Bridge across Prague's Vlatava River. In this case, the bridge has become a separate, autonomous world straddling the river to which it owes its origins even as it "surmounts" it, incorporating it into its own broader image of a small, mediative water-air lived-in and cozy space. The combination of the inner, animated panorama of the bridge, bubbling with life, and the outer majestic panorama of the river flowing off into the distance below, of the views of the old city on both banks, gives a feeling of hovering over several landscapes at once, a sense of the diverse fullness of earthly being.

However, the image of the river-as-bridge can take shape over much vaster spaces, becoming a large-scale metaphor for unity among countries and peoples. In this case, the image of the pathway is used as an additional image archetype. The image of the Danube is a classic example: a river of a multitude of heterogeneous ethnic traditions, high and low cultures, a border-river between countries, but at the same time a river pathway enabling mutual understanding between Serbs and Austrians, Hungarians and Roma, Romanians and Bulgarians (Tsiv'ian 167–205).

As one might easily guess, different historical eras and regional and national differences in political, cultural, and economic development "dictate" the differences in rivers' dominant images. When Rome ruled over the Rhine and the Danube, they were exclusively frontier rivers with fortified military camps across the entire Limes line. They have remained largely boundaries even now; however, the image of the river-as-border has become secondary, ceding primacy to the images of the river-as-bridge and the river-as-pathway. At the same time, as if absorbing and transforming all of the historical and cultural events that took place along their banks, many rivers have become national and even sacral symbols, taking on a majority of all the images that were ever predominant. The Rhine for Germany, the Volga for Russia, the Nile for Egypt, the Danube for Hungary, and the Dnieper for Ukraine all fall into this category, of course.

River discourse in Russian culture and literature: key elements

Russian culture and literature are rich in "river" contexts. If culture, as Father Pavel Florenskii famously asserted, is, in essence, the activity of assimilating space, Russian culture has largely unfolded as the activity of assimilating the space of rivers and the lands along their banks – lowlands, naturally. For its part, Russian literature, at least during the nineteenth and twentieth centuries, has often drawn on the stories and lexicon of the river that it carries in its "baggage" (Florenskii 112).

While classical Russian history and later historical geography recognized the importance of the "lowlands-river discourse" as early as the nineteenth century (primarily in the works of the great Russian historians Sergei Solovëv and Vasily Klyuchevsky), Russian literature only gradually, almost imperceptibly began to explore the river as a topic and incorporating it into storylines.[6] Works of note here include Alexander Pushkin's *The Captain's Daughter*, Ivan Turgenev's "Mumu," Nikolai Leskov's "Lady Macbeth of Mtsensk," Melnikov-Pechersky's cycle about Old Believers in the Volga region, and Vladimir Korolenko's "The River Plays," among others.[7] Only in the twentieth century, however, did Russian literature become fully aware of the all-encompassing significance of the river discourse for art and imagery – both from the standpoint of geohistoriosophy (as in Aleksandr Blok's poetic cycle "On Kulikovo Field") and from that of representing a personal, private metageography (the Volga in the prose of Mikhail Kuzmin). It is also important that such processes unfold not only in poetry (Velimir Khlebnikov's "Hadji Tarkhan," about the poet's native Lower Volga region), but also in prose (the stories and memoirs of Maxim Gorky, who at a certain stage of his literary biography could very well have been described as a "Volga writer").

Throughout the entire twentieth century and the early twenty-first, Russian culture and literature have continued to actively use a river discourse. At least three aspects of the geocultural imagining of river spaces can be identified in Russian literature:[8] 1) the incorporation of river images into storylines, either centrally or in the background (such as in the autobiographical story by the contemporary Russian writer and actor Evgenii Grishkovets, *Reki* (Rivers) or in Tatyana Tolstaya's "Okkervil River"; 2) the use of river images as key existential image-archetypes defining a work's overall meaning (as in Sholokhov's *And Quiet Flows the Don* or Valentin Rasputin's *Farewell to Matyora*; 3) the use of river images as, in essence, ontological models of the geocultural imagination, where the river discourse, consciously or unconsciously, is treated as the local essence of the author's writing itself. Here we are interested specifically in this third aspect insofar as it most strikingly represents Russian culture and literature's essential ontological focus on river image archetypes and their associated local mythologies.

In twentieth-century Russian literature we find two very different examples of attempts to conceive the river as an ontological model of imagination. The first is Boris Pasternak's poetry and prose written during the 1910s through the 1940s, writings biographically associated with the upper reaches of the Kama River, as well as with several smaller rivers in the Northwestern Ural region. It is important to understand that in his prose texts – the precursors to *Doctor Zhivago* and the novel itself – the writer never actually gave an integral and truly full-scale (in terms of ontological dimensions) image of the river, however he did manage to provide the first sketches of such an ontological vision that, up to that point, had not been a feature of Russian literature. The second example is a novel by the contemporary Russian writer, Sasha Sokolov (born in 1943), *Between Dog and Wolf*, in which, unlike Pasternak's fragmentary river discourse, a systematically integral and powerful ontology of the river as an autonomous and almost self-sufficient living world is presented, a world that exists in accordance with its own laws, a world that is largely fantastical yet entirely real to the extent that every effective, fully deployed and powerful image gives rise to a corresponding reality.

River and place: the becoming of image

Images of rivers, growing in size and depth, continuously finding new expression in works of culture and art and in the self-awareness of regional communities and peoples, can be seen as content-rich images of places and territories. The toponymy of rivers provides here an important initial key to understanding the image, after which, as a rule, an interpretation of the image is required that inserts the image of the river-as-place, river-as-territory, into the contexts necessary for its development. For example, Boris Pasternak's novel *Doctor Zhivago* describes a made-up river by the name of Ryn'va. Although no such river really exists, the author used what he knew of the toponymy of the Northern Ural region to give the name substantive meaning. Translating it literally from one of the dialects spoken by the Komi people, it means "wide opened river," "river rushing into the future," or, more generally, "river of life" (Pasternak, *Doktor Zhivago* 497). It is noteworthy that when the writer was looking for a name for his novel, one version considered was "Ryn'va" (Pasternak, *Doktor Zhivago* 462–463). Further interpretation is possible with help from an interesting excerpt from "The Beginning of Prose 1936," a prototype for *Doctor Zhivago* (the name "Ryn'va" had already appeared, however, in "Patrick's Notes").

> After we ate our supper and made up, I went to the back part of the grove, up to the cliff high above the river. It's strange that until now I haven't said anything about this daemon of a place that's mentioned in songs and included on maps of any scale.
>
> It was the Ryn'va at its headwaters. It came out of the north all at once as if aware of its river name and right here, where it comes out, a half-verst upstream from our precipice, it holds back in uncertainty, as if casting its gaze over its rightful domain. Each of its vacillations took the shape of a curve. Its contemplation created backwaters. The widest of them was below us. Here, it might be easily taken for a forest lake. On the far side was a different district.
> (Pasternak, *Vozdushnye puti* 295)

In its literary description, the river indivisibly merges with its own name; it seems to be playing the role of this name, justifying it. The river is a living being whose growth and form create an imaginary space; it is a meta-image that grants the right to imagine different slices of time – the past, the present, the future – as specific spaces and places, each with its own set of attributes. The writer evidently intentionally characterizes the Ryn'va's headwaters as the place's daemon (*daemon loci*). Since ancient times, the different ends of a river – its headwaters and lower reaches, its source and mouth – and the different directions of movement along it – upstream or downstream – have more often than not had opposite mythological connotations. A river's headwaters in this binary structure is a world of the mysterious, the dangerous, the daemonic, the as-yet-unrealized, and the secret. Movement toward a river's headwaters signifies a journey toward the source of an unconscious and as yet unborn being, toward taboo secrets, perhaps, of the world beyond.[9] The folklore of many peoples maintains such a dichotomy: for example, *Kaigus'*, a being in Ket mythology and folklore who brings success in hunting and prescribes the laws governing hunting ethics, often resides specifically at the headwaters of a river (*Mify, predaniia, skazki ketov* 120, 127, 169). A river's lower reaches, on the other hand, is the space of a bright future, of vast expanses and full-blooded existence, where cherished desires are realized. A keen sense of the dialectic of the river as the coming into being of a space of existence could also be sensed both in Boris Pasternak's choice of the fateful name of the river and his literary strategies for describing river landscapes. At the upper reaches of his literary journey he wrote such "river" poems as "Ledokhod" (Moving Ice) and "Na parokhode" (On the Steamboat), and at the lower reaches, his novel *Doctor Zhivago*, having literally realized, in essence, the metaphor of "people as rivers."

The river text of Sasha Sokolova: the twilight of daemons

Sasha Sokolov's book, *Between Dog and Wolf*, is a brilliant example of a "river text," one that includes almost all of the main archetypal geographic images of the river and river spaces. The image of the river-as-border – the border between being and nothingness, between life and death – intensified and presented through the culturologically powerful image of twilight, of a certain semi-syncopal, permanent, everlasting, twilight state, is apparently central to this text. At the same time, the meta-space of geographic images of the river (a thinly veiled Upper Volga) serve simultaneously, in the reader's understanding, as a key geographic image of Russian spaces, of a mental and literary micro-model of Russia's meta-geography.

The river – the Volga, the Itil', the Wolf River – seems itself to construct a huge space of image and myth that provides a framework for the intertwining of what seem to be perfectly ordinary, everyday occurrences of the Russian backwaters, described, along the way, from different viewpoints. This is at once a space of sin, miracle and salvation in the Russian orthodox folk tradition, a lupine space of perdition, a space of bustling, finely fractured life that is "grounded" in the river, a space of shore, rapids, hunting lodges, little villages, and the nearest town. It is also the space of Brueghel the Elder, of his spherical perspectives and panoramas, which seem to condense into a single geographic image all the diversity of life's contradictory and tragic episodes, perhaps into a picturesque geographic image of the All.

Sasha Sokolov's river defines both time and space, in fact this is a "coalesced" river-border space-time in which the flow of water models the coming into being and differentiation of the fluvial landscape itself in its temporal stasis and dynamism. The river is "vseobshchaia" [universal, general] (Sokolov 133), "Everywhere is twilight, everywhere is evening, everywhere is Itil'," (Sokolov 85, 106) and the time of year at various points along its banks "depends" directly on it:

Daemon loci 73

But there, where Zimar'-Man carted his spouse to karachun [archaic word for death], the dry leaf rolls itself [as into a cigarette] on the fly; outside Gorodnishe, where they're talking about Egor, about Fëdor, it's December through and through; but on ours, on the Wolf [River] – you wouldn't believe it – there, there's the oriole, there's the black woodpecker. It's steamy, it's sultry for the shellfish in that Gehenna of theirs, they're creaking, I feel for them.

(Sokolov 106)

One character in the book, Il'ia Petrikeich, takes the river-of-time metaphor literally, encouraged by advice from his friend Krylobyl:

Look, Krylobyl, that smarty, he's teaching me, come on and let's take, not time, but ordinary water. Fine. Stop the impressions, he's pestering me; in the backwaters it hardly moves at all, it's all choked up with duckweed, but in midstream, headlong; that's how time functions, he was explaining, in Gorodishche it's full of pep, like the shake of a swift's wing, approximately, in Bydogoshche it's neither here nor there, and in the forests it's nice and quiet. So rest assured that that theft of which you were a victim happened for now just in our beloved town and nowhere else, and on the other side no one's heard anything about it. So all you have to do is cross over to there and it'll all work out. I took this into consideration and went to the day before yesterday on a future dugout.

(Sokolov 152–153)

The river, as an image of time here also forms images of space, even differentiates them, while still remaining a perceived, visual landscape. It is significant that later, in Il'ia Petrikeich's direct speech, such an everyday-existential situation leads as well to geographies of the imagination that are actually different, in which the image of the river serves as a spatial boundary between landscape panoramas and viewpoints that are temporally incompatible in traditional formal logic:

The most important thing is to make it to the mooring stakes. Despite columns and paragraphs of volunteers to help, the lack of means will always mean you're at a crisis point, this is what we've been chosen for. Thus in my odd wanderings the cousins you know, seventh distant and twice removed, have shared with me a cup. I paddled too far and am now dragging myself along the edge any which way, trying to limp my way out of limping, and here you now are, studying this gibberish. They went up onto the terrace for some air and turned their imagination my way: that little rogue of ours, shade yourselves, sure gets around – I behold a knife grinder in Zavolch'e [the place beyond the Wolf River]. No, it is I who see you there, since it's not I who am there, but you. In short, we're both right. We being on different sides, our geography is different: you are beyond the Wolf [River] while I all the more.

(Sokolov 153)

The river's parallel geographies turn out to be translucent, visible to one another and at the same time (or, to be more precise, at the same times) co-spatial to one another – assuming that the concept of co-spatiality implies the coexistence of logical temporal dissonances/contradictions; river worlds "see" one another, contemplate one another, interpenetrate one another, while nevertheless remaining transitory, "twilight," not quite real – the landscape images themselves merge here with the usually more psychologically engrained image of reality, the reality of *Zaitil'shchina* [the world beyond the Itil'] seems a "hazy mirage" of co-spatial visions, perhaps of certain completely hagiographic miracles.

Zaitil'shchina: the optics of twilight landscapes

The space of Zaitil'shchina, while possessing an obvious visual anisotropy (changing in relationship to who travels upon it, and in what direction) and the capacity of mutual transformation has, at the same time, specific optical properties that are clearly associated with the ubiquitous image of twilight and, in essence, represent this image. In one of the book's first sections, "The Trapper's Tale," the words of the painter and poet give twilight a grandiloquent, Old Slavonic intonation that turns it into, within the context of the book as a whole, an image of semi-vision, semi-contemplation, and seems to cast doubt on the visibleness of the space of the river and its landscapes, while at the same time constantly lending it credence through the constant state of affect of its inhabitants and aborigines, including a cast of apparitions and ghosts:

> Lord, in this, the five hundred forty-first year since the invention of the pin, on the last Friday of November, approximately between the hours of five and six, at a great distance from any sort of capital, in the middle of Russia, but also on the banks of a full-flowing river, a certain person is drunkenly beating a tambourine. Twilight has already dragged away the eyes, shaded the perspectives, and abolished darkness.
>
> (Sokolov 24)

Such a space is always teeming with miracles and "transfigurations" in the spirit of Christian traditions, however these miracles and transfigurations themselves transpire in a deliberately degraded "tone" that blends, once again, a certain antiquated, ceremonial solemnity with a squalid ordinariness that frame the miracle of quasi-parodic events. Something of this sort takes place, for example, in the *Notes of a Hunter*, which records the ragpicker's tale, "The Transfiguration of Nikolai Saintov."

> We were wandering and begging house to house,
> Lend a helping hand for Christ's sake to these guests,
> Bring on out your junk and any sort of trash,
> Bits of iron, and your bottles, jars, and bones.
> Twilight fell and then began a heavy snow.
> Don't you yelp, you bitch, you filthy mutt, don't bark.
> We then headed to the tailors for the night,
> And along with us then was Saint Nikolai.
> I'm telling you, with us was the old saint,
> A broken down, and rickety old man.
> We are pilgrims, he's the pilgrim of pilgrims,
> We are cripples, he's a cripple among cripples.
> Kolya-Nikolai has nothing to his name,
> Just his crutches. And the snow comes falling down.
> (Sokolov 81)

The exposition in the spirit of an Orthodox folk tale has, in essence, only one rather important distinction from this tradition: the space (twilight, heavy snow) clearly pretends to be the essential precondition for a future miracle, and, perhaps, one of its causes – not simply the backdrop for an inwardly anticipated sacral event. The story's development supports this supposition:

> Lousy weather. And the ringing din of bells,
> And the jackdaws fly to find their nighttime rest.
> They fly, the hags, off beyond the Itil',
> To Gorodnishche, the town of beggars and of thieves,
> While we are dragging scrap upon a sled,
> Three archangels of secondhand debris.
> The hour between dog and wolf I love:
> It's like a sweet caress mixed up with gloom.
> Don't put it out; I might also have a drag.
> And, I repeat, we hobble off to bed.
> (Sokolov 81)

The key lines here are: "The hour between dog and wolf I love: / It's like a sweet caress mixed up with gloom" – it is these lines that inform us of a coming miracle, that it is conditioned and foretold by Zaitil'shchina; on the other hand, the very existence and ontological status of this twilight space is assured – first here, then there – by the miracles and visions described.

The story's ending is already anticipated and foreseen, and although twilight is no longer mentioned by name (with the exception of night – which happens to be "graying" and reminiscent of that very same twilight), the space of Zaitil'shchina is obviously growing, expanding through the metageographic transfiguration that is taking place:

> Now by candlelight that pip-squeak tailor's working,
> Sewing clothing for the shelter for the blind.
> Open up, come on now, comrade parasite,
> With night falling, welcome in poor vagrant souls.
> Once we settled by the window all as one,
> Night turned gray – like overwashed pants
> Can't recall just where we managed to get wine,
> Just remember that we drank it into shreds.
> Morning came, we look – Kolia-Nikolai is flying:
> Crutches spreading out like two wings overhead.
> The poor devil has transformed into a hawk:
> Overdid the drink. And now he is no more.
> (Sokolov 82)

Meanwhile, the river's twilight landscapes can throughout be called sacrogenic; they are everywhere imbued with their own "genius" of the sort belonging to the Ancient Roman religious tradition: the miracle, the apparition, the vision are also possible on the river's edge, on river islands, and on the glacial space of a frozen river. In an island thicket, during a sunset twilight, amorous encounters take place between the "tough guy" Kaluga-Kostroma and an evil spirit in mermaid form that ends in his death from a wolfberry; during a nighttime twilight a woman, "Eternal Life," appears to Karaban, a man of "invenerable years," in a vision, and he "fiddles around with her a teensy bit"; while ice fishing, again at twilight, the Drunken Hunter encounters the ghost of the Tatar Alladin Batrutdinov, who has long since drowned, "with a lamp and on skates" (Sokolov 110–111, 75–76). And in the end it is as if twilight comes to life and becomes personified through images of the Wolf and the Dog in the hunter's "Valdai Dream":

> When I look out through one window,
> Or look out through the other –
> The pine stands topped in snow
> The glades are in snow too.
> Witches walk to the churchyard,
> Tattling of this and that:
> Freeze, freeze, holy tail,
> Warm yourself, tail of the devil.
> All is blue. And blue as well
> Runs the mica-like Volga,
> Dog rides her on a sled,
> Driving forward the Wolf.
> (74)

The ambivalence and ceaseless becoming of the very images of the river – no one ever steps into the same river twice; no one ever conceives the same image of the river twice – expands the fields of the image's genesis and allows for a redefinition of the concept of the geographic image. One "river interpretation" of the geographic image could see it as a space of spatial possibilities and potentials that are realized and unfold as the maximally numerous and continuous curvilinear forms of earthly topography and earthly landscapes. And if we base our thinking on such a definition, we can assert, using a formally logical but also figurative "boomerang": images of the river are maximally mutable archetypes, signs, and symbols of the water element that are limited by the laws of earth's gravity and the toponymy of being itself.

Notes

1 See, for example, Rozanov 329–409.
2 See especially 61–66. This image was successfully reimagined in Francis Ford Coppola's film *Apocalypse Now*.
3 See, for example, Kofman 57–59, 128–131.
4 See Zamyatin 154–165.
5 See Tsiv'ian 167–205.
6 We do not pretend to offer an exhaustive overview of the treatment of rivers in Russian culture and literature and instead seek to outline a possible basis for further study.
7 A number of Dostoevsky's works also feature an existential river locus (the Neva in particular), especially his Petersburg stories, including *Crime and Punishment*.
8 For now, we will not examine the products of other areas of Russian culture, such as the graphic arts, cinema, video, music, social media, etc. We presume that both the popular and elite strata of Russian culture continue to maintain a certain literaturocentrism.
9 Compare "Going up that river was like traveling back to the earliest beginnings of the world, when vegetation rioted on the earth and the big trees were kings. An empty stream, a great silence, an impenetrable forest. [...] [Y]ou thought yourself bewitched and cut off for ever from everything you had known once – somewhere – far away – in another existence perhaps. There were moments when one's past came back to one, as it will sometimes when you have not a moment to spare for yourself; but it came in the shape of an unrestful and noisy dream, remembered with wonder amongst the overwhelming realities of this strange world of plants, and water, and silence. And this stillness of life did not in the least resemble a peace. It was the stillness of an implacable force brooding over an inscrutable intention. It looked at you with a vengeful aspect" (Conrad 35).

Bibliography

Bergman, Ingmar. *The Magic Lantern*. Trans. Joan Tate. New York: Viking, 1988. Print.
Conrad, J. *Heart of Darkness*. Clayton, DE: Prestwick House, 2014. Print.
Florenskii, P.A. *Stat'i i issledovaniia po istorii i filosofii iskusstva i arkheologii*. Ed. A.S. Trubachev. Moscow: Mysl', 2000. Print.

Frankfort, G., G.A. Frankfort, J. Uilson, and T. Iakobsen. *V preddverii filosofii. Dukhovnye iskaniia drevnego cheloveka*. Moscow: Glavnaia redaktsiia vostochnoi literatury izdatel'stva "Nauka", 1984. Print. [Available in English as: Henri Frankfort, H.A. Frankfort, John A. Wilson, Thorkild Jacobsen, and William A. Irwin, *The Intellectual Adventure of Ancient Man*. Chicago, IL: University of Chicago Press, 1977.]

Kofman, A.F. *Latinoamerikanskii khudozhestvennyi obraz mira*. Moscow: Nasledie, 1997. Print.

Konrad, J. *Serdtse t'my i drugie povesti*. Moscow: Azbuka, 1999. Print.

Mechnikov, L.I. *Tsivilizatsiia i velikie istoricheskie reki; Stat'i*. Moscow: Izdatel'skaia gruppa "Progress", "Pangeia", 1995. Print.

Mify, predaniia, skazki ketov. Comp., introd., comm. and glossary by E.A. Alekseenko. Moscow: Izdatel'skaia firma "Vostochnaia diteratura" RAN, 2001. Print.

Pasternak, B.L. *Vozdushnye puti: Proza raznykh let*. Moscow: Sovetskii pisatel', 1982. Print.

Pasternak, B.L. *Doktor Zhivago*. Moscow: Troika, 1994. Print.

Pavlova, N.L. "Reka i solntse v edinom prostranstvennom iskusstve drevnego Egipta." *Khudozhestvennye modeli mirozdaniia. Vzaimodeistvie iskusstv v istorii mirovoi kul'tury*. Moscow: NII RAKh, 1997. Print.

Plutarkh. "Plutarkh. O like vidimom na diske luny." *Filosofiia prirody v antichnosti i v srednie veka*, pt. 2. Moscow: Institut filosofii RAN, 1999. Print.

Plutarkh. "O daemone Sokrata." *Plutarch, Isida i Osiris*. Moscow: Eksmo, 2007. Print.

Propp, V.I. *Istoricheskie korni volshebnoi skazki*. Moscow: Labirint, 2000. Print.

Rozanov, V.V. *Inaia zemlia, inoe nebo...: Polnoe sobranie putevykh ocherkov, 1899–1913 gg*. Moscow: Tanais, 1994. Print.

Sokolov, S. *Mezhdu sobakoi i volkom*. Moscow: Ogonek–Variant, Sovetsko-britanskaia tvorcheskaia assotsiatsiia, 1990. Print.

Toporov, V.N. *Reka: Mify narodov mira*. Moscow: Izdatel'stvo "Sovetskaia entsiklopediia," 1982. Print.

Trubetskoi, S.N. "Filosofiia Plutarkha." *Plutarkh. Isida i Osiris*. Kiev: UTsIMM-PRESS, 1996. Print.

Tsiv'ian, T.V. *Dvizhenie i put' v balkanskoi modeli mira. Issledovaniia po strukture teksta*. Moscow: Indrik, 1999. Print.

Zamyatin, D.N. "Genii i mesto: uskol'zaiushchaia sovmestnost'." *Obshchestvennye nauki i sovremennost'* 5 (2013): 154–165. Print.

Section II
Socio-cultural identities of water

5 "Mother Volga" and "Mother Russia"

On the role of the river in gendering Russianness

Oleg Riabov

For centuries "Mother Russia" has been one of the most important symbols of Russian culture. This symbol has been formed by various factors, which cannot be considered without analyzing another well-known maternal symbol – "Mother Volga." Just how popular is the symbol of "Mother Volga" in Russian culture? What traits are attributed to it? How are they gendered? What role does it play? How does it influence stereotypes of Russianness? And finally, to what degree are maternal images of river and country correlated?

To answer these questions, I will first characterize ways in which rivers are represented in gendered terms in nationalism. The next section of this chapter will be devoted to the symbol of "Mother Russia" and its influence on stereotypes of Russianness. I will then examine the history of how the Volga has been understood in Russian culture in terms of a maternal essence, and what attributions transform the Volga into a "mother." Finally, I will examine how various discourses (national, imperial, war, political, and ecological) employ the maternal symbol of the river.

My argument here is that the image of the river serves as a substitute for "Mother Russia" and thus adds legitimacy to this construct. In addition, I will argue that, like "Mother Russia," "Mother Volga" is used primarily to emphasize the idea of Russia's specificity, her difference from the West. Using the image of Mother Volga reinforces stereotypes of Russianness using traits juxtaposed to "Western" values: humility, *sobornost'* [communal identity], unselfishness, spirituality, irrationality, spontaneity, unpredictability – all of which have feminine connotations in a Russian cultural context.

Rivers in the discourse of nationalism: gender dimension

Rivers have played key roles in community lives since antiquity: they provide food and energy, serve as traffic arteries and military frontiers. The image of the river is an important part of collective identity, serving as a natural border that separates communities and at the same time connects them. The symbolic border between "us" and "them" is a widely attested, essential element of collective identity (Barth 14).

Rivers occupy a special place in identities of national communities. They are anthropomorphized and represented as autonomous personages in national historical narrative. The river is used not only to mark national boundaries, but also to express the "national spirit."[1] Images of rivers are included in works of art and literature, political rhetoric and war propaganda, advertising and the branding of regions. The importance of such symbols is directly related to claims that national communities are *natural*. Natural phenomena occupy an important place in the symbolic space of nations; portraits of rivers serve as one of the ways this naturalization of nations takes place (Cusack 190).

Rivers are, moreover, associated with fertility and revival, symbolizing life (Zeisler-Vralsted 2), and thus draw maternal metaphor into nations' narratives of identity, as for example with "Mother Ganga" (Cusack 5). Maternal metaphor – and gender discourse in general – plays an essential role in the legitimation of a nation (Smith 22). As Anne McClintock has observed, "nationalism is constituted from the very beginning as a gendered discourse, and cannot be understood without a theory of gender power" (261). The interaction of gender and national discourses facilitates their mutual support and legitimization. Comparing the nation to the family has been an effective way to position a given community as natural and organic. The nation–family comparison is used actively in political mobilization, and in the legitimization and delegitimization of power: political opponents are frequently labeled as internal enemies of the nation, as renegades who have betrayed familial bonds (Tickner 54). It is precisely this that explains the broad dissemination of female, and especially maternal, national personifications ("Britannia," "Mother Svea," "Helvetia," "Hibernia," "Germania," "Marianne," "Mother Latvia," and others) (Mosse; Edmondson; Gailite).

The symbol of "Mother Russia" in Russian nationalism

Among maternal symbols deployed in the service of nationalism, "Mother Russia" is one of the most widely known. The use of the image developed in several stages. The idea can be traced back to the image of Moist Mother Earth, the Russian variant of the Great Mother, retained in popular culture into the Soviet era (Hubbs). Later "Mother Russia" was expressed in imagery of the Russian land: in the literature of ancient Rus earth was represented as a living being, and portrayed in a female – primarily maternal – guise. In the sixteenth century the works of Maxim Grek and Andrei Kurbsky affected the transformation of this image into the figure of Holy Rus. In the eighteenth century the notion of *Fatherland* gained ground, but notwithstanding this "Mother Russia" remained a significant part of Russian Imperial culture, widely used in domestic and international rhetoric. After the October Revolution the Bolsheviks referenced "Mother Russia" largely with negative connotations, as a symbol of backwardness and oppression in Imperial Russia. In the mid-1930s the maternal image of the country underwent revival as the Soviet Motherland and continued to be an essential element of symbolic politics throughout Soviet history. The dissolution of the USSR was accompanied by the deconstruction of Soviet symbols, including the Motherland; in the 1990s "Mother Russia" functioned largely as a part of left-wing and patriotic left rhetoric. "Rehabilitation" of the symbol occurred in 2000s, during Vladimir Putin's presidency; it is now actively employed by high-level Russian officials.[2]

How has this symbol been used in Russian culture? Answering that question involves considering its use in various types of discourse: national, military, imperial, and political. As any other national symbol, the use of "Mother Russia" represents an attempt to make a community out of group of individuals. However, the rhetoric of inclusion is simultaneously connected with the rhetoric of exclusion: "Enemy" is a key part of the discourse of Motherland. Above all, the symbol defines who "we" are and who "they" are in *national discourse*. "We" are sons and daughters of the Motherland. Moreover, the Motherland determines how "we" should treat "them" – above all, the West – thus delineating boundaries within the society.

The symbol also separates "us" from "them" in *military discourse*. "They" are the Enemy – those who threaten the existence of Motherland; "we" are those who defend her and count on her protection. The discourse of "Mother Russia" has tremendous mobilization potential; a person is called to sacrifice his or her own life as well as the lives of others in the name of defending the Motherland. The image plays a significant role in the practices of commemoration; the figure of a mother mourning the loss of sons and daughters occupies a notable place in memories of war.

Besides this, in *imperial discourse* maternal symbolism contributes to representations of Russia as a polyethnic and multiconfessional state: Russia is positioned as the mother of all peoples who live in the territory of the state.

Finally, "Mother Russia" occupies an important place in *political* discourse. Since the native land is a source of strength, fertility, and abundance, feeding all her children, they are in irredeemable debt before her. Thus "Motherland" legitimizes the image of the ruler as Father, one who possesses Russia (according to the mythology of the *hieros gamos*) and speaks on her behalf. The image of sacred marriage has been exploited to legitimize power in Muscovy, in the Russian Empire, in the USSR, and in post-Soviet Russia (Hubbs 188–189; Riabov, "Rossiia" 118–120, 129–130; Riabova, *Pol* 112).

Imagining a country in maternal terms is, as noted above, widespread not only in Russia. Nonetheless, particular factors contribute to the image's popularity in Russian culture. An emphasis on Russia's difference from the West and even juxtaposition to it has played an essential role in Russian constructions of identity; thus Russia is attributed traits that are different from Western individualism, rationality, secularity, hubris. *Russia as woman* and *Russia as mother* serve as symbols of this juxtaposition, embodying traits that are marked as feminine (humility, unselfishness, religiousness, irrationality, *sobornost'*, unpredictability) (Riabov, *Rossiia*).

"Mother Volga": the history of the idea

When and how did the Volga become a "mother"? Several studies focus on how the idea of the Volga's maternal nature developed (Trepavlov; Leskinen; Hausmann). Vadim Trepavlov demonstrates that the cult of river as provider/nourisher was widespread in the traditional cultures of many peoples. For instance, the Tatar "Edigu" epos (seventeenth century) contains the expression "Mother river, full-flowing Itil"; the Nogai called the river "Ana Edel" ("Mother Volga") (43, 46). According to Trepavlov, this doesn't mean that Russians simply adopted the Nogai Turks' image in the process of mastering of the Volga region, because the maternal metaphor had been used by Russians to characterize other rivers (46).[3]

During the process of Russian colonization of the Volga region, accelerated after the fall of the Kazan Khanate in the sixteenth century, maternal imagery became more and more important; the inclusion of "Mother Volga" in the system of poetic images and symbols served as a means of Russian colonization of the Volga region (Trepavlov 41). The Volga entered the culture of the Russian Empire primarily through poetry: Classicist poets Mikhail Lomonosov, Vasily Maikov, Aleksandr Sumarokov, and Gavriil Derzhavin employed the river as a symbol of the state (Ratnikov). In his sentimentalist poems "The Volga" (1793), Nikolai Karamzin emphasized the river's maternal nature, her sacred meaning and high status: "The river, the holiest in the world, / The tsarina of crystal waters, the mother!"

Prominent practitioners of nineteenth-century Russian poetry referred to the maternal nature of the Volga, including Fyodor Glinka ("Dreaming on the Shores of the Volga," 1810), Alexander Pushkin ("When down the wide river Volga ...," 1826), Nikolai Nekrasov ("On the Volga," 1860), Aleksei K. Tolstoy ("My bellflowers," 1862). The appearance of the "Mother Volga" in nineteenth-century Russian musical culture, especially in folk songs (most famously "Yo, Heave, Ho [The Song of Volga Boatmen]" and "Oh You Wide Steppe") confirmed the river's status as a national symbol. In 1838 the government commissioned two landscape painters, brothers Grigorii and Nikanor Chernetsov, to travel down the river (Ely); they produced a significant number of paintings of the river, stressing in their notebooks that "[the Volga] is a fertile vein of Russian land and deserves the name 'Mother provider' in every respect" (Chernetsov and Chernetsov).

A new stage in "Mother Volga's" evolution emerges with the notion of the Volga as *the* Russian river in the mid-nineteenth century, aiming to represent the Volga as the *main* river of Russia (Leskinen, "Volga"; Leskinen, "Problema"). In this period the Volga was also portrayed as both Russian Orthodox and Imperial space, still in need of civilizing (Hausmann 421). Descriptions of the Volga region began to occupy an important place in textbooks and travelogues (Leskinen, "Problema" 91). The genre of "Travelling along the Volga" appeared in Russian literature in the second part of the nineteenth century, including Alexey Potekhin's "Travelling along Volga in 1851" (1851); Sergey Maksimov's "A Sack of Bread and Adventures" (1873); Anna Valueva's "Along the Great Russian River" (1895); and Vasily Nemirovich-Danchenko's "The Great River. Pictures from Life and Nature of Volga" (1902) (Sarbash 158–160). As Christopher Ely points out, many authors admired the river not only for its contribution to state economic prosperity, but as an expression of "Russian soul" (676–678). Tricia Cusack examines the image of the river created in Russian art in the context of cultural nationalism. Analyzing Isaac Levitan's and Ilya Repin's works, she notes that these painters' images of the Volga region's population and scenery marked the river as Russian and, moreover, Christian Orthodox. At the end of the nineteenth and beginning of the twentieth centuries several books under the title "Mother Volga" were published.[4] Of particular significance were a series of stories by Vasily Rozanov entitled "Russian Nile" (1907), about the author's journey along the Volga. Rozanov, who wrote extensively about "Mother Russia" (and even "Grandmother Russia") naturally touched upon the issue of maternal nature of the river.

Finally, it's worth noting sculptures of the Volga in the guise of a woman; the best known example is the sculpture "Volga" (Tolmachëv 595; Golovina 48–49) created by Aleksandr Opekushin together with Mikhail Mikeshin and Dmitry Chichagov for the All-Russian Industrial Art Exhibition of 1882 in Moscow. Remarkably, the great river was portrayed as a female peasant feeding the double-headed eagle, which symbolizes the Empire: the common people are taken to embody Russianness and typical traits of Russian national character.

After the October Revolution many national symbols of the previous epoch – including "Mother Russia" – were desecrated by the Bolsheviks' symbolic politics (Riabov, *Rossiia* 174–179). However, while "Mother Volga" played an important role in pre-revolutionary literary and artistic culture, it was less incorporated in official symbolic politics. It had, moreover, been used as a symbol, on the one hand of the people's suffering, and of popular rebellion on the other. This tradition made the symbol more acceptable to early Soviet symbolization. The defense of Tsaritsyn (on the Volga; later to be renamed Stalingrad) in 1918–1919, as well as the construction activity of the first Five-Year Plan (the Stalingrad Tractor Plant (1926–1930), Gorky Automobile Plant (1929–1932), Moscow–Volga Canal (1932–1937)) also brought the Volga closer to Soviet ideology. Essential to Sovietization of the river was its association with Vladimir Lenin, who was born in the town of Simbirsk on the Volga, a link that was popular throughout the Soviet epoch.[5]

The Soviet cult of the Volga began in the mid-1930s, when the pre-revolutionary image of "Mother Russia" was revived in the guise of Soviet Motherland (Riabov, *Rossiia* 183–187). As Hans Giunter points out, the

Volga became one of the essential symbols of Soviet culture in the second part of the 1930s, when it served as proxy for the Motherland, and was attributed similar traits. The cult is typical for cinema and "mass song" – genres essential to propaganda. Grigory Aleksandrov's musical comedy "Volga-Volga" (1938) as well as "Song of Volga" (Vasily Lebedev-Kumach' lyrics and Isaac Dunaevsky's music) from the film played a prominent role in creating the image of Mother Volga in Soviet culture.

The next phase of the Soviet "Mother Volga" is connected with the Great Patriotic war (World War II). Images of the Soviet Motherland served as essential elements of war mobilization; the maternal image of the river also played a significant role in military propaganda (especially during the Battle of Stalingrad, discussed below). This image was significant also in post-war confrontations with the West, when the Volga was represented as quintessentially Soviet Russian, in opposition to Western warmongers. Construction of the "Mother Volga" monument (by Sergei Shaposhnikov and Vera Malashkina) on the shore of the Volga near the Rybinsk Reservoir, at the height of the Cold War in 1953, indicates the symbol's role in post-war culture. The 28-meter sculpture is an allegory of the river in the guise of a Russian woman.

The Thaw brought new discourses of Russia along with changes in Soviet gender discourse. Emerging new masculinity ("thawed") was reflected in more personal, intimate attitudes to Russia. In songs Russia was frequently depicted as a beloved woman: "trustful," "blushing," and "blue-eyed," compared to Alyonushka, a female character from Russian

Figure 5.1. Shaposhnikov, Sergei and Malashkina, Vera. "Mother Volga" (1953). Photo by author.

Figure 5.2. A Russian stamp depicting Lyudmila Zykina (1929–2009), a Soviet and Russian singer, and the badge of the Order of St. Andrew. Stamp design by A. Drobyshev (1 September 2011, PTC Marka Catalogue No 1508, Michel No 1740).

fairy-tales (Riabov, "Rossiia" 216).[6] Such lyricism was also reflected in songs about the Volga; the river was portrayed as a dear person, rather than a symbol of the state machine – as in "The Volga Flows Into My Heart" (lyrics by Mikhail Pliatskovskii) and "I Just Can't Live Without the Volga" (Andrei Dement'ev's). "The Volga River Flows" (lyrics by Lev Oshanin) became the most popular song about the river. It was first performed by Mark Bernes in 1962, but its real triumph came with Lyudmila Zykina's performance in 1963; the song serves as the singer's "calling card," with the Western media even calling Zykina "Miss Volga (Bespalov). Images of the male character's mother and Mother Volga interflow in the song's lyrics.

In the post-Soviet period the image of the river is employed, on the one hand, as a sign of "genuine Russianness," and on the other as an important symbol of the unity of various ethnic groups within the Russian Federation. Formation of a Russian (Rossiiskii) political nation is interpreted as essential to maintaining the unity of Russia, especially under Vladimir Putin – and is one of the priorities of national politics (reflected in "Russia's National Policy Strategy through to 2025" (O Strategii).[7] Discussion of the river's role in the country's history, held at a special session of the Izborsk Club, an influential conservative think tank, may serve as an example of contemporary rhetoric about the Volga. Aleksandr Prokhanov Head of the Club, is worth quoting in this context: "Thinking about the Volga I feel an almost religious experience. Because the Volga is a goddess who spread her waters... over vast spaces, over the whole continent, and gathered many nations... Turks, and Slavs, and Orthodox Christians, and Moslems, earlier pagans – created the unique Volga civilization. [...] We need to aim at creating a Volga religion."

Gendering semiotics of Volga

Beyond direct portrayal of the Volga as a "mother" in Russian visual culture, separate traits associated with the maternal – giving birth, fertility, feeding, care, mercy, and ambivalence – contribute to such perceptions.

Above all, the Volga is interpreted as life-giving, giving birth both to the people and their living conditions. Rozanov remarked that she had the "sacred name 'mother, Mother Volga'," because "that is how the people felt about their own nascent and dying essence."

The Volga's life-giving ability is so widely assumed that abundance is another well-known characteristic.[8] Vasiliy Tatishchev emphasized in an article from "The Lexicon," the first Russian encyclopedia (mid-eighteenth century) that Volga was called also "Idel', Adel', and Edel': all these names are Tatar and Arabic meaning abundance and gracious. The name is fitting, Tatishchev contends, because the river has an incomparable abundance of fish to catch and fertile pasture lands." Moreover, the Volga does not give birth indifferently, but graciously feeds. Rozanov writes: "We are her children; we feed on her. She is our mother and nurse. [...] Something immeasurable, eternal, and nourishing..." The mother as source of nourishment is a key attribute of "Volga as *the* Russian river" (Leskinen, "Volga" 4). The book "Mother Volga" (1914) reports that "Many people are fed by the Volga [...] Millions work from morning till night on her docks.... There are quantities of factories and mills in her cities and villages! Countless masses of fish are caught in Volga! No wonder the Russian people call the Volga mother and nurse..." (Tarapygin). The river displays maternal care, as well. In Pushkin's poem, noted above, Stenka Razin appeals to Mother Volga: "You have fed me and kept me since childhood, / Rocked me to sleep through long nights / And brought me through storms...".

Another of the Volga's prime characteristics is the ability to display maternal mercy. The tradition of using the dichotomy of "mercy vs. justice" in representing the difference between maternal and paternal treatment of children traces back to the literature of Ancient Rus (Riabova, "Materinskaia"). The author of the book *Mother Volga*, describing how bands of robbers settled along the river's shores in the sixteenth and seventeenth centuries, concludes "Lavish, as always, Volga gave shelter and asylum for everyone..." (Tarapygin 135). "Mother Volga gives refuge to everyone, / She caresses and endows everybody" – so goes the ancient Cossack song (Glazkova 25).

Finally, ambivalence – as Eric Neumann has argued – is a key part of the maternal archetype as ambivalence: the same principle that gives life and takes it away, in what Neumann calls the "negative Anima," the "Terrible

Mother" (Neumann 75, 149). The river not only gives strength but takes it away. One song from a collection of Russian songs published in 1913 contains the words: "Oh, Mother Volga! / Wide and long, / Made us weak, / We don't have strength anymore!" (Hausmann 312). Another folk song begs for mercy: "Volga, my mother, / The Russian river, / Have pity, darling,/ Upon the barge hauler's strength" (Dvoretskova 6). The authors of the earliest works of classic Volga literature – Ivan Dmitriev and especially Karamzin – stressed this dual essence (Zelenkova, "Zhanr" 85–88). Velimir Khlebnikov's poems, written in 1921 during the terrible famine in the Volga region, are devoted to the image of the river as an embodiment of death. These poems juxtapose Volga the nurse to the Volga that takes life away: now she is a she-wolf who devours her children. The river is portrayed as a living, starving creature, embodying savage cruelty and the imminence of death (Zelenkova, "Tema"). The ambivalent nature of the river is apparent in the image of "Stepmother Volga" both in folklore, as in the proverb "the Volga is sometimes a mother and sometimes a stepmother" (Trepavlov 42) and in classic literature, as in Aleksandr Ostrovskii's diary (230).

The functions of "Mother Volga"

At this point we turn to a comparison of "Mother Volga" and "Mother Russia," noting how various discourses (national, imperial, war, political, and ecological) employ the maternal symbol of the river. "Mother Volga" is an essential national symbol with which Russians identify, and which may mobilize them for collective action. There are several aspects of how this symbol is used in *national discourse*.

First, "Mother Volga" is used to symbolize "genuine Russia," serving as an embodiment of Russian character, the quintessence of Russianness. One contemporary author writes, "the Volga is not only a geographical object… but also… the expression of the soul of Russia, embodiment of her essence" (Barminskii). She is credited with traits that play an important role in mythologizing Russianness: strength, "scale" (*razmakh*), naturalness, sincerity, mysteriousness, and broadness of soul (Ely 676; Leskinen, "Volga" 5–6). "Mother Volga" also serves as a substitute for "Mother Russia." Evgeny Chirikov writing in 1923, exclaimed "The Volga! […] … If you want to behold your Motherland and understand the eternal historic instinct that makes you love it […] you can't dispense with the Volga … […] Only then might you feel and understand the mystical secret of love for your motherland – a secret reflected so brightly and vividly by Mother Volga, stretching through Rus' like a big bright road."

Russians are moreover considered the Volga's children; as Evgeny Evtushenko puts it, "We are Russians. We are children of the Volga." As mentioned above, the family metaphor with its assumptions about the organic, "natural" character of bonds among members of a national community, is central. In fact, Russia herself is sometimes declared a daughter of the Volga, thus representing it as the "state-" and "nation-forming" river (Barminski; Prokhanov).

Third, as with any symbol the Volga serves as a tool not only of inclusion, but of exclusion, differentiating "us" from "them" within multinational community of the Russian Empire. In this respect Apollon Korinfskii's poem "The German Heavens" (1903) is indicative; the poet counterposes the Volga Germans' region to "genuine Russia," declaring the "rational German order" alien to Russia, the Russian soul, and Russian scale. Moreover, such rationality is alien to the Volga herself, so that in this "German" region she loses her essential traits: "It's even as if the Volga flows/ more slowly here. / 'Customs here are different!' – / She tells me" (130).

Thus "Mother Volga" functions as a marker of exclusion, arranging ethnic groups within the Empire according to strict hierarchy. At the same time, apart from embodying ethnic Russianness (*russkost'*) in national discourse, the Volga serves as a symbol of political Russianness (*rossiiskost'*) in *imperial discourse*. Many texts written in the second half of nineteenth century stressed that the Volga was a supranational principle, binding the nations of the Russian Empire (Leskinen, "Problema" 94; Leskinen, "Volga" 6). The image of the Volga as a maternal figure worked to legitimate the Empire, for instance, in the poem "Rus' The River" by Mikhail Rosenheim, a nineteenth-century man of letters. He represents the Empire's creation as a process as natural as the river's flow. Rosenheim writes that the Volga had become a mother because of her inclusion and sheltering of numerous large and small rivers, which longed to flow together with her (199, 202). Also like a river, Rus' had included numerous large and small peoples, who joined her voluntarily and thus became the Russian Empire (202). Whereas exclusiveness is the essential trait of a national community (Anderson 19), the essence of an empire is the negation of this exclusiveness, its fundamental boundlessness and constant readiness to expand.

The image of "Mother Volga" also plays a key role in *war* discourse. The maternal image of Russia has, of course, been actively employed in mobilization propaganda, substantiation of war and moral superiority, and practices of commemoration. "Mother Russia" in this context is represented as vulnerable, suffering, calling for help, mighty, and invincible; one notes that the use of such female allegories of nations is widespread in many cultures' war discourse (Riabov, "Rossiia-Matushka" 78–80). However, the phenomenon of the river image in wartime propaganda is uncommon. The Volga is renowned as a place of one of the largest battles in world history, the Battle of Stalingrad, so it is no wonder that discourses of the Great Patriotic War employ the image very actively. For instance, in the essay "Stalingrad," published in September 1942, Ilya Ehrenburg writes: "Stalingrad means the Volga. The meaning of the Volga for Russia cannot be overemphasized. There is no river like it in Europe. It cuts through Russia. It cuts through the heart of every Russian. The people have composed hundreds of songs devoted to Mother Volga. [...] Would despicable Germans bathe their horses in Volga, in the great Russian river?" (2). The motif of the desecration and pollution of the Volga symbolically connotes dishonoring of the native land. The call to protect the honor of the native land serves traditionally as one of the most important tools of war mobilization in Russia, appealing to male gender identity (Chernaia; Sandomirskaia). In war propaganda, besides the cult of heroism, strength and ruthlessness as masculine attributes, representation of the soldier as defender is a crucial discursive practice, rendering war an honorable choice (Tickner 57; Yuval-Davis 15). Images of women's suffering (or the sufferings of the nation, as represented by a female, maternal figure) are therefore widely used in wartime discourse as an appeal to the gender identity of men (Yuval-Davis 94). A distinctive strategy in such representations involves the creation of images of dishonor or sexual violence suffered by women at the Enemy's hands. The enemy as sexual aggressor is constantly evident both in stories about individual women and in representations of the disgraced Motherland.

The association of foreign invasion of Russia with desecration of the Volga finds expression in Soviet folklore. In 1952 a collection of folklore called *Mother Volga* was published, featuring tales recorded in the Kostroma region during the Great Patriotic War. One tale portrays Nazi Germany as a monster, "one-eyed, fanged Evil" who boasts: "I will subdue the Russian land / And dry up the free Volga…" (Khriashchev 31–32). Interpretation of the enemies of the Soviet Motherland as those who threaten the great river had earlier appeared in "The Song of the Volga" (1938): "Let enemies like hungry wolves / Leave tracks at our borders. / They will not see the Volga's beauty / And never will they drink the Volga's water." The Volga is again portrayed as a beauty pursued by a foreign man. Not surprisingly in this cultural context, visual propaganda represented the Battle of Stalingrad as a threat to "Mother Volga" (see, for instance, Vladimir Serov's poster "Let us defend Mother Volga!").

The Volga, like Mother Russia, not only calls for help but is at the same time an undefeatable force. She is first of all an integral part of the Soviet Army's military superiority, sending her sons – Soviet warriors – into battle (Dolmatovskii); beyond that, she herself participates in military operations. "*The Tale of Egorka the Pilot*," from the collection of Soviet folklore noted above, tells of a young pilot who manages to lead a convoy of ships along a stretch of Volga mined by Germans during the Battle of Stalingrad; the river with its fish and birds aid him. Egorka explains how he has accomplished such a difficult mission: "I am a Soviet man. I love my native land and the free Mother Volga more than my own life. She, the mother, hears only our entreaties, and brings death to our worst enemies" (Khriashchev 35). Finally, the river wreaks vengeance on the enemy; the tale represents Soviet victory in the Great Patriotic war in the following way: "We captured the one-eyed Evil, / Put it into fiery traps, / And drowned it in Mother Volga" (Khriashchev 33). Russia is, it seems, protected by the Volga. It's worth noting in this context the popularity of the idea of soteriological mission of the feminine principle in Russian culture: Russia will be saved by a woman, Russia will be saved by a mother (Riabov, *Russkaia*). Finally, contemporary commemoration also stresses the role of the Volga in Russia's military history. "Remarkably, the German fascists were choked exactly at the Volga – the backbone of the German military machine was actually broken in the Battle of Stalingrad …" (Ivankina).

As mentioned above, as an essential symbol of *political discourse*, "Mother Russia" is actively exploited both in the legitimation and delegitimation of power; the maternal image of Volga carries analogous functions. In fact, it is no wonder that the image of Mother Volga became strongly established in Russian culture under Catherine II. The titles "Empress Mother," "Mother of the Russian state," "All-Russian Mother" which were conferred on the ruler by contemporaries, correspond to the legitimation of the term "Mother Russia" (Riabov, *Russkaia* 55–56). As Maria Leskinen points out, Karamzin equated the Volga not simply with Russia but with the Mother Empress herself (Leskinen, *Volga Russkaia reka* 4). It's worth mentioning that traveling down the Volga with members of the ruling family became a means of legitimating power. This tradition started with Catherine's voyage in 1767; as some scholars have pointed out, the purpose of the trip was not only to acquaint her with the Empire but to claim symbolic possession of an important national sacred place.

However, "Mother Volga", like "Mother Russia," is simultaneously exploited in the delegitimation of power. First, the Volga embodies the principle of rebellion, a space of unlimited freedom – *volya*. The history of Russians' colonization of the Volga region was connected with extensive revolt and disobedience. "Mother Volga" and "Free (*vol'naya*) Volga" – these are two inseparable characteristics of the river in the famous song "Oh, You Wide Steppe." A tale from the Soviet folklore collection expresses with still greater clarity: "Volga the Mother" and "Volga the Free" (*voliushka*) (Khriashchev 16). A "free life" in the USSR was equated with the Volga's flow in the "Song of the Volga"; not surprisingly, the song associated the river with images of Stepan Razin and Yemelyan Pugachev who traditionally symbolize Russian rebellion.

Second, the Volga is used to symbolize the suffering of the Russian people under unjust authorities. In particular, nineteenth-century populist *Narodnik* discourse often employed the image of barge haulers (*burlaki*) to illustrate the people's suffering (Hausmann 242–255). In this context the image of Mother Volga itself takes on negative connotations. Nikolai Nekrasov, for example, in an 1860 poem, characterized the Volga as "the river of slavery and melancholy"; this image is further developed in Dmitry Merezhkovsky's poem "On the Volga" (1887). "And in this land, among such nature/ The fatherland sleeps the slavish sleep of darkness…"

Use of the image in delegitimation of contemporary power is often connected with *ecological discourse*, as in discussions of the government's plans to raise the water level in the Cheboksary Reservoir, which started in the mid-1990s. Opponents of these plans use the maternal metaphor of the river in their arguments: they represent the Volga as a living being and mother, as a way of calling to mind human obligations towards her ("U Volgi..."). An article from a conservative newspaper depicts fatal consequences for the river, including inflicting irreversible damage to nature in the Volga region, destruction of cultural artifacts and places sacred to Russian Orthodoxy and, in particular, threats to the effective functioning of military plants concentrated in the region. The author hints that these plans may be supported by pro-Western forces, writing in conclusion, "In Russian songs the Volga justly is endowed with maternal traits. Violence against her and, moreover, actions which lead to her death become symbolic... of a complete rupture between the people and those who rule them" (Barminskii).[9]

Conclusion

"The Volga is more than a river for Russia," wrote Evtushenko. The Volga does indeed play a significant role in Russians' identity. To a considerable degree the Volga's popularity derives from the fact that she is endowed with maternal traits. The image of the Volga as mother is present in various fields of Russian culture (poetry and belles-lettres, cinema and music, folklore and sculpture, graphics and philosophical treatises) and types of discourse (national, war, imperial, political, and ecological). We have examined when, how and why Volga is represented as a mother. Besides direct identification of the river as "mother" there is indirect feminization: the image of the river is invested with maternal traits such as birth-giving, fertility, nursing, care, mercy, and ambivalence. In general, this image corresponds with traits typical for the mother archetype (Neumann; Gimbutas).

Rivers are represented as mothers in many cultures, images that are particularly valuable in the discourse of nationalism, which appeals to nature to legitimate national community. Russian culture has a special interest in labeling the Volga as *mother* because the river serves as a substitute for "Mother Russia," thus adding legitimacy to this symbol. Like "Mother Russia," the image is use largely to emphasize the specialness of Russia, her difference from the West, her alienness to Western values (individualism, rationality, secularity, hubris). Using this image thus contributes to the formation of stereotypes of Russianness containing traits which juxtaposed to Western values – humility, *sobornost'*, unselfishness, religiousness, irrationality, spontaneity, unpredictability – traits which all have feminine connotations.[10]

Notes

1 For instance, on the image of the Rhine as a cradle of the German nation in German nationalism (see Lekan 19).
2 For a detailed history of "Mother Russia," see Riabov, *Rossiia*.
3 The Oka and Kostroma Rivers were also called "mother" (Boborykin 104; Khriashchev 15–17).

4 See, for example, Tarapygin; Blagovidov and Shemiakin.
5 Even the young Evgenii Evtushenko in his poem "Volga" (1958) wrote that the river connected various epochs of the Russian history: that of Razin, and Nekrasov, and Lenin.
6 On codes of masculinity, see Goscilo and Lanoux.
7 «Russian» refers to ethnic Russians, while «Rossiiskii» refers to all citizens of the Russian Federation, regardless of ethnicity.
8 Recall the characteristics of the river in famous songs: "Wide and deep" ("Yo, Heave, Oh / The Song of Volga Boatmen"), "Wide, deep, and strong" ('The Song of Volga") and others.
9 On contemporary ecological problems of the Volga, see Dedikova and Bukharitsin.
10 Some water objects in Russian culture get masculine connotations and are called "father" ("Father Dnieper Slavutich," Rivers Don, Amur, and Yenisei, Lake Baikal. See Kluchevskii 220; Berezovich 50–61). These images occupy an important place in Russian identity; however, unlike the Volga, they are not considered a substitute for Russia. The identity politics during Vladimir Putin's presidency can be defined as involving the "remasculinization of Russia" (Riabov and Riabova); they imply attributing masculine connotations (strength, independence, rationality, etc.) to the image of the country. Perhaps contemporary interest in masculine images of water objects (for instance, the construction of "Father Don" sculptures in Rostov-on-Don and of "Father Yenisei" in Krasnoyarsk) reflects this tendency. This impulse is nonetheless relatively weak; "Mother Volga" remains the primary water symbol of Russia.

Bibliography

Anderson, Benedict. *Imagined Communities: Reflections on the Origin and Spread of Nationalism.* London: Verso, 1983. Print.

Barminskii, Vladimir. "Rok nad Volgoi." *Zavtra*, 13 June 2013. http://zavtra.ru/content/view/rok-nad-volgoj/ [Accessed 15 January 2015]. Web.

Barth, Fredrik, ed. *Ethnic Groups and Boundaries: The Social Organisation of Culture Difference.* Bergen/London: UniversitetsForlaget/George Allen and Unwin, 1969. Print.

Berezovich, Elena L. "V kustakh ruchei tseluetsia s rekoi… ('semeinye'obrazy v leksike rechnogo landshafta)." *Slova. Kontsepty. Mify: K 60-letiiu Anatoliia Fedorovicha Zhuravleva.* Ed. Grigorii Venediktov. Moscow: Indrik, 2011, 50–61. Print.

Bespalov, Iurii A. *Liudmila Zykina. Izdaleka dolgo…* Moscow: Algoritm, 2013. Print.

Bessarabova, Nina V. *Puteshestviia Ekateriny II poRossii.* Moscow: Moscow Humanitarian Institute named after E.R. Dashkova, 2005.

Blagovidov, Nikolai F., and I. Shemiakin. *Volga-matushka.* St. Petersburg: Tipografiia V.V. Komarova, 1895. Print.

Boborykin, Pëtr. "Russkii Sheffild: Ocherk sela Pavlova." *Otechestvennye zapiski* 203 (1877): 76–394. Print.

Chernaia, Liudmila A. "'Chest': Predstavleniia o chesti i beschestii v russkoi literature XI–XVII vekov." *Drevnerusskaia literatura: Izobrazhenie obshchestva.* Ed. Anatolii S. Dëmin. Leningrad: Nauka, 1991. Print.

Chernetsov, Grigorii, and Nikanor Chernetsov. *Puteshteshvie po Volge.* Moscow: Mysl', 1970. Print.

Chirikov, Evgenii N. *Zver' iz bezdny*. www.litmir.net/br/?b=191746&p=51 [Accessed 15 January 2015]. Web.
Cusack, Tricia. *Riverscapes and National Identities*. Syracuse, NY: Syracuse University Press, 2010. Print.
Dedikova, Tatiana N., and Pëtr I. Bukharitsin. "Ėkologicheskoe sostoianie reki Volgi." *Vestnik Astrakhanskogo gosudarstvennogo tekhnicheskogo universiteta* 1 (2010). http://cyberleninka.ru/article/n/ekologicheskoe-sostoyanie-reki-volgi. [Accessed 15 January 2015]. Web.
Dolmatovskii, Evgenii. "Razgovor Volgi s Donom." *Pravda*, 24 November 1942, 2. Print.
Dvoretskova, Klavdiia I. *Volga v pesniakh i skazaniiakh*. Saratov: Saroblgiz, 1937.
Edmondson, Linda. "Gender, mif i natsiia v Evrope: Obraz matushki Rossii v evropeiskom kontekste." *Pol, Gender. Kultura: Nemetskie i russkie issledovaniia*.
Ely, Christopher. "The Origins of Russian Scenery: Volga River Tourism and Russian Landscape Aesthetics." *Slavic Review* 62.4 (2003): 666–682.
Erenburg, Il'ia. "Stalingrad." *Krasnaia zvezda*, 8 September 1942, 2. Print.
Evtushenko, Evgenii. "Volga." www.evtushenko.net/013.html [Accessed 15 January 2015]. Web.
Gailite, Gundega. "'Mother Latvia' in Constructing Self and Other: A Case of Latvian Caricature XIX c. – 1940." *Competing Eyes: Visual Encounters with Alterity in Central and Eastern Europe*. Ed. Dagnoslaw Demski, Ildikó Sz. Kristóf and Kamila Baraniecka-Olszewska. Budapest: l'Harmattan, 2013, 170–189.
Gimbutas, Mariia. *Tsivilizatsiia Velikoi Bogini: mir Drevnei Evropy*. Moscow: ROSSPEN, 2006.
Giunter, Khans. "Poiushchaia Rodina: Sovetskaia massovaia pesnia kak vyrazhenie arkhetipa materi." *Voprosy literatury* 4 (1997): 46–61.
Glazkova, Nonna V. *Volga – matushka, Don – batiushka*. Volgograd: Blank, 2009.
Golovina, Liubov'. "Aleksandr Opekushin. Obretenie natsional'nogo." *Tret'iakovskaia Galereia* 1 (2007): 48–49. Print.
Goscilo, Helena, and Andrea Lanoux. "Introduction: Lost in the Myths." *Gender and National Identity in Twentieth-century Russian Culture*. Ed. H. Goscilo and A. Lanoux. DeKalb: Northern Illinois University Press, 2006.
Hausmann, Guido. *Mütterchen Wolga. Ein Fluss als Erinnerungsort vom 16. bis ins frühe 20. Jahrhundert*. Frankfurt am Main: Campus, 2009.
Hubbs, Joanna. *Mother Russia: The Feminine Myth in Russian Culture*. Bloomington: Indiana University Press, 1988. Print.
Ibneeva, Guzel' V. "Puteshestvie Ekateriny II po Volge v 1767 godu: Uznavanie imperii." *Ab imperio* 2 (2000): 87–104. Print.
Ivankina, Galina. "Reka zhizni." *Zavtra*, 8 January 2014. http://zavtra.ru/content/view/reka-zhizni/ [Accessed 15 January 2015]. Web.
Karamzin, Nikolai. "Volga." www.gumfak.narod.ru/volga.html [Accessed 15 January 2015]. Web.
Khriashchev, Viktor V. *Volga-matushka. Sbornik ustnogo narodnogo tvorchestva Kostromskoi oblasti*. Kostroma: Kostromskoi oblGIZ, 1952.
Kliuchevskii, Vasilii. *Russkaia istoriia. Polnyi kurs lektsii*. Vol. 2. Moscow: AST; Harvest, 2002. Print.
Korinfskii, Apollon A. *Volga: Skazaniia, kartiny i dumy*. Moscow: M.V. Kliukin, 1903.

Lekan, Thomas M. *Imagining the Nation in Nature: Landscape Preservation and German Identity, 1885–1945.* Cambridge: Cambridge University Press, 2004. Print.

Leskinen, Mariia. "Problema assimiliatsii finno-ugorskikh narodov v obosnovanii kontseptsii 'Volga-russkaia reka'." *Ezhegodnik finno-ugorskikh issledovanii* 4 (2013): 91–105.

Leskinen, Mariia. "'Volga–russkaia reka': obrazy i opisaniia glavnoi reki imperii vo vtoroi polovine XIX veka." *Rodina* 12 (2013): 2–7. Print.

McClintock, Anne. "'No Longer in a Future Heaven': Nationalism, Gender, and Race." *Becoming National: A Reader.* Ed. Geoff Eley and Ronald G. Suny. New York and Oxford: Oxford University Press, 1996, 260–285. Print.

Merezhkovskii, Dmitrii. "Na Volge." http://slova.org.ru/merezhkovskiy/na_volge_reka/ [Accessed 15 January 2015]. Web.

Mosse, George L. *Nationalism and Sexuality: Respectability and Abnormal Sexuality in Modern Europe.* New York: Howard Fertig, Inc., 1985.

Nekrasov, Nikolai. "Na Volge." www.nnekrasov.ru/book/581/ [Accessed 15 January 2015]. Web.

Neumann, Erich. *The Great Mother: An Analysis of the Archetype.* Princeton, NJ: Princeton University Press, 1963.

O Strategii gosudarstvennoi natsional'noi politiki Rossiiskoi Federatsii na period do 2025 goda. http://government.ru/docs/3229/ [Accessed 15 January 2015]. Web.

Ostrovskii, Aleksandr N. "Puteshestvie po Volge ot istokov do Nizhnego Novgoroda." *Khudozhestvennye proizvedeniia. Kritika. Dnevniki. Slovar'. 1843–1886.* Vol. 18. Moscow, 1962.

Prokhanov, Aleksandr. "Volga – reka russkogo vremeni." *Zavtra*, 19 June 2014. Print.

Pushkin, Aleksandr S. "Kak po Volge, po shirokoi." www.aspushkin.ru/book/434/ [Accessed 15 January 2015]. Web.

Ratnikov, Kirill. "Russkie reki: Poeziia i politika. Ideologicheskii komponent Gidrotipnykh obrazov v lirike ot Lomonosova do Tiutcheva." *Vestnik Cheliabinskogo universiteta* 1 (2004): 56–66.

Riabov, Oleg. *Russkaia filosofiia zhenstvennosti (XI – XX veka).* Ivanovo: Iunona, IvGU, 1999.

Riabov, Oleg. *"Rossiia-Matushka": Natsionalizm, gender i voina v Rossii XX veka.* Stuttgart and Hanover: Ibidem, 2007.

Riabov, Oleg, and Riabova, Tatiana. "Remasculinization of Russia: Gender, Nationalism and Legitimation of Power under Vladimir Putin." *Problems of Post-Communism* 61 (2014): 23–35. Print.

Riabova, Tat'iana. "Materinskaia i ottsovskaia liubov' v russkoi srednevekovoi traditsii." *Zhenshchina v rossiiskom obshchestve* 1 (1996): 28–32. Print.

Riabova, Tat'iana. *Pol vlasti: Gendernye stereotipy v sovremennoi rossiiskoi politike.* Ivanovo: IvGU, 2008.

Rozanov, Vasilii. "Russkii Nil." http://royallib.com/book/rozanov_vasiliy/russkiy_nil.html [Accessed 15 January 2015]. Web.

Rozengeim, Mikhail P. "Rus'-reka." *Stikhotvoreniia.* St. Petersburg, 1889, vol. 2.

Sandomirskaia, Irina. *Kniga o Rodine: Opyt analiza discursivnykh praktik.* Wien: Wiener Slawistischer Almanach, 2001.

Sarbash, Liudmila N. "'Puteshestvie po Volge v russkoi literature XIX veka: 'Kul' khlebi ego pokhozhdeniia'" S.V. Maksimova." *Filologicheskie nauki. Voprosy teorii i praktiki* 5 (2012): 158–160.
Shore, Elizabet, and Karolin Khayder, eds. *Ekologicheskie problemy reki Volgi. Spravka.* Moscow: RGGU, 2003, 135–162. http://ria.ru/documents/20090714/177327889.html [Accessed 15 January 2015]. Web.
Smith, Anthony D. *National Identity.* Reno: University of Nevada Press, 1991.
Tarapygin, Fedor A. *Volga-matushka: Obrazovatel'noe puteshestvie po Volge: Ocherki i kartiny volzhskoi zhizni ot istoka reki do vpadeniia ee v Kaspiiskoe more.* Petrograd: Novoe vremia, 1914.
Tatishchev, Vasilii N. Leksikon rossiiskoi istoricheskoi, geograficheskoi, politicheskoi i grazhdanskoi. www.encyclopedia.ru/enc/lexicon/ [Accessed 15 January 2015]. Web.
Tickner, J. Ann. *Gendering World Politics: Issues and Approaches in the Post-Cold War Era.* New York: Columbia University Press, 2001. Print.
Tolmachëv, Evgenii. *Aleksandr III i ego vremia.* Moscow: Terra-Knizhnyi klub, 2007. Print.
Trepavlov, Vadim. "'Volga-matushka' –dlia kogo?" *Rodina* 4 (1998): 41–46.
"U Volgi-matushki problemy." http://bellona.ru/russian_import_area/international/ecopravo/37366 [Accessed 15 January 2015]. Web.
Yuval-Davis, Nira. *Gender and Nation.* London: SAGE Publications, 1997.
Zeisler-Vralsted, Dorothy. *Rivers, Memory, and Nation-building: A History of the Volga and Mississippi Rivers.* New York: Berghahn Books, 2015.
Zelenkova, Ekaterina V. "Tema smerti v poslerevoliutsionnoi lirike V. Khlebnikova." *Yaroslavskii pedagogicheskii vestnik* 4 (2012): 227–230.
Zelenkova, Ekaterina V. "Zhanr 'sovetskoi ody' v tvorchestve Lebedeva-Kumacha." *Filologicheskie nauki. Voprosy teorii i praktiki* 6 (2013): 85–88.

6 Main street of the Urals
Creating the "Chusovaia" metanarrative

Maria Litovskaia

> Everyone in the Urals likely knows this river. For us it is more than a name on a map, it is a condition of the soul.
>
> For centuries, the Chusovaia has been the Urals' main street. For almost two hundred years, it served as the main arterial connecting our region to European Russia. This river helped create the unique "alpine-industrial" civilization of the Urals.
>
> Without the Chusovaia, the culture of our region, the specific Ural character would not exist...
>
> ...Much has changed since then. It has been many years since iron caravans traveled along the river, and now tourists come to gaze at the once deadly warrior-cliffs.
>
> But the spirit and the deeds of our ancestors have not disappeared without a trace. The contemporary Urals, with their industrial strength, are that culture's direct inheritors. Today, navigating the Chusovaia, we feel living history, and once again we consider who we are, where we came from, and where we are going.
>
> (Kholmanskikh)

Igor Kholmanskikh, the special representative of the President of the Russian Federation for the Ural Federal District, delivered this grandiloquent proclamation at the river navigation festival "Great Waters" (*Bol'shaia voda*) on June 8, 2013. His words condense an entire system of fixed representations about the Chusovaia River which have come to seem natural to local residents: "main street," "central arterial," progenitor of the "Ural civilization" and the "Ural character," a site of local history and a catalyst of memory for the people of the Urals. Only one definition of the river is missing, but even it is implied throughout the text – "beauty." Denizens of the region take these characteristics as inherent truths, even though their origins can be traced to fairly recent sources.

A particular genre, the descriptive essay, or *ocherk*, consistently accompanied the appearance – and the various subsequent rediscoveries – of the Urals as part of Russian readers' symbolic geography. One of the traditional narrative representations of place, the *ocherk* delineates a system of spatial imagination.

In his book, *Justice, Nature, and the Geography of Difference*, David Harvey (316–317) describes the "formation of place," in which certain geographic "space" transforms into "place" by means of the imaginative investments of several generations. This process arises at the intersection of material, representational, and symbolic practices: the production of "place" occurs by isolating a location's "difference" among adjacent places through economic competition, social differentiation, and discursive encounters.

A feeling of attachment, of sympathy, or of love for a place, that is, the emotional saturation of space, develops, among other things, through the creation, preservation, and dissemination of images in oral and written texts. The formation of place, according to Harvey, follows certain laws: the localized accumulation of values, for instance, and the necessary and regular reappraisal of place. Those who conceptualize a territory, verbalize it, and describe it, transform a geographic object into a textual subject, and by so doing, give it meaning. From this perspective, the history of a place's image can be seen as the struggle for the symbolic status of a space, which contains an unclear but already distinct character. The winner of that struggle gets to dictate the dominant interpretation of the place.

As symbolic construction transforms territories into sites of interest (not least for commerce and tourism), images of both central and regional rivers (Haussman; Cherniaieva and Kropotov) play an essential role in the creation of national (or regional) identity. For the Urals, that river is the Chusovaia.

The aim of the current article is to explore the formation of the Chusovaia's image as a symbol of the region, to trace the history of notions like the "essence," the "meaning," and the "message" of the Chusovaia, and also to expose the sociocultural contexts that influenced each new wave of representations of the river.

The sources of my research are descriptive essays, *ocherki*, written between the end of the nineteenth century to the beginning of the twenty-first, meant to introduce readers to the Chusovaia, and also guidebooks written in an essayistic style between 1930 and 2008. With a single subject and relatively narrow genre variation, each new essay or guide becomes part of a metanarrative about the most famous of Ural rivers; each either follows the dictates of the metanarrative or sets itself against its textual predecessors.

The Chusovaia: the "natural" foundation of a symbolic space

Though much less known than the Volga, the Don, or the Yenisei, the relatively short and shallow Chusovaia is consistently invoked, beginning in the nineteenth century, whenever the Urals are discussed as a discrete integral territory.

Geographically unique, the river takes its source on the eastern slopes of the Ural divide, that is, in Asia, and then crosses westward to flow primarily through the European part of Russia.

The banks of the Chusovaia have been inhabited since the Neolithic era. By the time the first Russian settlements appeared along the Chusovaia in 1568, the territory had been populated for thousands of years by the Mansi, Bashkirs, and Komi-Permiaki. Nevertheless, Ivan the Terrible claimed the entire river basin for the Russian Empire and consigned it to the protection of the Stroganov merchant family. With the support of the state, the Stroganovs, joined by the Demidovs in the eighteenth century, developed a network of iron mills and foundries that would come to characterize the region. By the eighteenth century, the Urals had become one of the world's leading producers of metal, and until the middle of the nineteenth century the region all but monopolized the supply of heavy industrial products to the Russian Empire (Harris 2).

This feverish economic development required new transportation routes to deliver Ural metal to European Russia. Before the completion of the Alpine-Industrial Railway in 1878, the Chusovaia was the main line of industrial transportation.

Every spring, as soon as the waters rose, so-called "iron caravans" – motorless wooden barges, or *barki*, heavily laden with iron – would set off for Perm from docks high up on the Chusovaia. The journey was extremely dangerous: the high spring waters and quick currents often shattered the vessels against riverside rocks; the deck hands, called *burlaki*, and the captains, *splavshchiki*, often perished. Only an experienced captain who knew all the Chusovaia's idiosyncrasies could successfully guide a caravan of *barki* along the entire river route. The skills and knowledge of river navigation were passed from father to son, and the names of successful river captains were well known in the area.

Through the nineteenth century, the river route was adapted to mitigate the hazards of the voyage: the most dangerous "warrior-cliffs" were dynamited, the river's rifts and rapids were cleared of large rocks, and several mooring posts were installed along the route, but the river captains' trade continued to be dangerous even as it was the primary hereditary employment for hundreds of families along the Chusovaia.

Consequently, each voyage became seen as a battle between man and river, and folklore bears witness to attempts to tame the river: the most dangerous rocks and cliffs along the Chusovaia were called "warriors" (*boitsy*), and the name stuck. Up to the present day it is used in both official and colloquial toponymy. Each "warrior" was given a name: "Bandit," "Awl," "Shaitan," "Grave," "Dog's Rib," "Needle," etc. The names give an idea of the dangerous and unpredictable disposition of each cliff and of the river itself. Even the apparently peaceful "Sparrow" gets its name because, as the adjacent current lifts boats and knocks them against the rock, the cliff "pecks" them apart into little pieces (*Predaniia i legendy Urala* 54). Folklore also holds the image of the true and good *splavshchik* – a bold daring river captain, ready to risk his life, who knows the river's "character" and understands its specificities (Blazhes 65–79).

By 1880, the Chusovaia carried up to 8,050,000 poods (132,000 metric tons) of metal each year, but after the completion of the first Alpine-Industrial Railway and then the Trans-Siberian Railway, the river's economic importance began to wane. At the end of the nineteenth century, the river still transported nearly 700,000 poods (11,500 metric tons) of goods annually. But by the beginning of the twentieth century, the Chusovaia carried only a few barges of bread, materials, and other supplies, the last of which completed their voyages in the 1920s.

In the 1930s and 1940s, the river basin was actively forested. Most lumber was loose-floated down the river, an ecologically unsound transportation method that often strands stray logs which then rot, polluting the riverbed. Lumber continued to be loose-floated down the Chusovaia until 1973.

As the river ceased to be an important transportation route, communities along its banks lost their economic foundation and began to move away; by the end of the twentieth century, several population centers had been completely emptied of permanent residents. Some villages were resettled by summer travelers from the Urals' big cities, while others ceased to exist entirely.

From the beginning of the twentieth century the Chusovaia began to be seen as a tourist destination. In a certain way, such a transformation might seem expected, given the river's natural qualities. The Chusovaia has an affecting type of beauty. As the river cuts across the mountain range, sheer cliffs rise up along its banks in natural ornamentation. The river's distinctive topography includes both calm stretches and serious rapids, making it an ideal river for boating, kayaking, and rafting at all levels.

In the 1960s, a rafting route was developed from the town of Sloboda to Chusovoi, which was built to serve the Kourovsky observatory and base camp. From 1960 to 1988, Evgenii Yastrebov developed plans for a national park along the Chusovaia which finally opened in 2004. Many of the riverside cliffs now fall under state protection as natural landmarks. In 1981, the Ethnographic Park of Chusovaia River History was also opened (etnopark.com).

The Chusovaia: literature discovers the river

At the end of the eighteenth century, the river was still seen primarily as a facet of the economy, and was described as such by scholars:

> The river in question is well known for the many mills built upon her tributaries and for delivering the productions of these mills from Siberia. Springtime she carries nearly 400 freighted barges (*kolomenka*), in summer she hasn't the necessary depth for navigation; but when the vessels from Yekaterinburg travel upstream with copper money, all the mills along the tributaries throw open their locks to let the water flow.
> (Primechaniia 752)

But beginning in the 1880s, writers began to describe the Chusovaia aesthetically, marking the river primarily as a visually striking landscape. This fits into a general trend at the time, in which Russian art rediscovered the distinctiveness of provincial Russia and the diversity of Russian landscapes (Sozina 207–209). In particular, authors with biographical connections to the Urals revived and exhibited their homeland for the rest of the world, presenting familiar local sites as worthy of aesthetic representation in their texts.

Dmitrii Mamin-Sibiriak (1852–1912) was one such writer. A journalist and novelist in the tradition of socially conscious realism (Dergachev 139–142), Mamin-Sibiriak played a pivotal role in the transformation of the image of the Chusovaia. Mamin-Sibiriak's few predecessors wrote mostly about the industrial activities of the Ural population: "Our region is rich in characters. All kinds, it seems, live in their own ways – civil servants, merchants, alpine workers, peasants… And how many of the *burlaki*'s secrets are unknown to the world? Why has no one ever described them?," wrote Fedor Reshetnikov (269) in 1862, referring to the river barge-hands, *burlaki*. Mamin-Sibiriak, in large part because of the absence described by Reshetnikov, became an important figure in the history of Russian literature, for he described not only the specificities of the social order of the Ural region, but also its natural environment and the major events of its history.

The son of a priest at the Visimo-Shaitansky mill, Mamin-Sibiriak studied in Yekaterinburg and Perm and lived in Yekaterinburg from 1878 to 1891. He traveled frequently throughout the alpine-industrial Urals, and was a member of UOLE (*Uralskoe obshchestvo liubitelei estestvoznanie*, or The Ural Society of Amateur Naturalists). He is rightly seen as one of the pillars – a discoverer (*pervootkryvatel'*) and singer (*pevets*) – of the Urals in Russian literature: he depicts the Urals from various angles, as a locus all but unknown to a broad audience. Drawing from archeology, statistics, ethnography, and folklore, while also relying on his own travels, Mamin-Sibiriak described the history, environment, and peoples of the region in a series of essays. Because Mamin-Sibiriak's travels in 1868–1870 included several voyages along the Chusovaia with *burlaki*, and because the river is so well known in the region, it served as the setting for several of Mamin-Sibiriak's essays, including "On the River Chusovaia" (1883), "Warriors (Sketches of Springtime Navigation along the Chusovaia River)" (1883), "The Mountain" (1886), "In Stones. From Travels along the Chusovaia" (1898).

Contradictory descriptions of the Chusovaia in Mamin-Sibiriak's work suggest that up through the 1880s, no generally accepted image of the river, or understanding of how best to describe it, had coalesced in the literature.

However, according to Nadezhda Kungurtseva's fine observation, for Mamin-Sibiriak, each kind of landscape carries a specific semantic value: "The mountain depths are associated with mystery and danger; while river landscapes, on the other hand, carry no single meaning, but instead are informed by the characteristics of the surrounding geo-objects, and wooded spaces evoke the modus of 'geo-comfort,' and organicity" (192). But this pattern concerns rivers in general in Mamin-Sibiriak's work: "And then there is the Volga... every time I see that great Russian river, I experience something pleasantly unusual: the sky seems higher and the forest circles around the riverbank..." (Mamin 4: 400). The Iset' river is just as peaceful, if also industrial: "It's such a wonderful river, the most lively artery of the Urals..." (Mamin 4: 379).

In contrast with the peaceful images of other rivers, the area where the Chusovaia flows is described in ominous tones: "In certain places massive cliffs overhung the river, and a chill ran through one's heart as the barge approached these walls which radiated cold and dampness. The water itself went quiet in these places and spun in a silent stream. The smallest sound, drops of water – everything had the hollow sound of a crypt" (Mamin 1: 453).

The Chusovaia is at once a working river and a deadly river. For the inhabitants of the region with its cold climate, the river was the most convenient way to transport lumber. But underwater rocks often tore at the hulls of boats and sunk barges. A mass of cliffs, the cold, a burial ground – these images flow from essay to essay in descriptions of the dangerous, often lethal, and intractable mountain river.

The Chusovaia is cruel to people who try to contain it, as a legend about a sinner who perished on the river attests (see Mamin-Sibiriak's "The Mountain"). Such an understanding of the elements, it seems, appeals to an archaic belief system according to which peaceful coexistence requires propitiation (Kungurtseva, "Etnokul'turnyi" 141–142). But even the contemporary Chusovaia with its actual peculiarities is often painted in negative strokes (Kungurtseva, "Ural'skii" 192).

As Elena Vlasova has noted, in Mamin-Sibiriak's essays, the Chusovaia:

> is set against the mountains as a force of destruction. The river is presented as elemental ('the destructive movement of the water,' 'washed away,' 'blind elemental force'), while the mountains are the firmament and foundation ('the majestic mountain panorama,' 'exposed cliffs,' 'enormous walls of rock, forged as if by the hands of giants'), and the warrior-cliffs [*boitsy*] are the frontlines standing guard, protecting the mountains from the attacking waters. For the writer, the conflict between the mountains and the river reflects the opposition of the elements. The struggle between nature's destructive forces and constructive labor brings together themes of the mountains, the riches of their depths, and of man.
>
> (Vlasova 63)

At the same time, Mamin-Sibiriak poeticizes the life force and dynamism of the river by using a form of personification typical of folklore and literature: the comparison of the river with a willful and beautiful woman:

> Wonderful is the river Chusovaia!... Like all great beauties, her charm is unfading, revealing a new marvel with each new season. In spring, she is a wild, untamable beast, writhing with fury and moans, throwing herself against the narrowing stone giants; in autumn she is an austere and cheerless river flowing strictly along the corridor she has carved through the mountains; in winter she is truly a sleeping beauty, bound under ice and covered in deep snow. Now, in summertime, the Chusovaia rolls along green banks, past *boitsy*, through mountain narrows, and around sharp turns in a lazy flow that rumbles and riots only on the rapids. One feels something lazy and sleepy, gentle and strong...
> (Mamin 4: 501–502)

Highlighting the power of the Chusovaia, Mamin-Sibiriak describes the river's heroic history through a system of images appealing to architecture, folklore, and ancient history.

> The major beauty of the Chusovaia's banks comprises the cliffs [...] several of which rise a perfectly sheer 60 *sazhens* [128 meters], *like colossal walls of some gigantic medieval city; at times extending along the river for several versts.* [...] In places, layers of rock peel off and fall away *like old plaster*. Some cliffs clearly show each separate layer, often revealing a remarkable pattern, *as if they were the work not of elemental forces, but of a thinking being, an enormous display of cyclopean masonry.* The craggy crests of these cliffs complete the illusion. Thousands of years have *crumbled these cornices, arches and towers.* And the obliging imagination fills out reality. Here one sees the remains of strong gates, and here, the foundation of a turret, and here, scattered in refuse, the plinths of columns... After all, these are the very same Riphean mountains to which Alexander the Great forever exiled his errant gnomes.
> (Mamin 5: 246, emphasis added)

Mamin-Sibiriak offers a new way of seeing the Chusovaia landscape: the river's cliffs, rocks and caves cease to belong to the world of geology and economic history and become part of a picturesque canvas. Connections to high culture and to antiquity charge the landscape with aesthetic value. In essence, Mamin-Sibiriak presents the Chusovaia as an object of fascination and contemplation.

Mamin-Sibiriak's second important contribution to the Chusovaia's image was to give the river a central place in the natural and social history of the Urals. The Urals are an ancient land, and the Chusovaia becomes a witness to that history: "Here on these exposed cliffs, one could see the water's destructive effects. Slowly, over the course of millennia, the river washed away the stone mountains, revealing huge rock walls, forged as if by the hands of giants rather than by blind elemental forces" (Mamin 5: 807).

It was Mamin-Sibiriak who made famous the local term for the cliffs, "warriors," or *boitsy*: "There are too many fields of battle on the Chusovaia to describe each one individually: the most dangerous *boitsy* have their own names. The rest are simply called battlegrounds..." (Mamin 5: 807). The people's war with the powerful river was reflected in a language unknown beyond the Chusovaia, but one that deserved wider recognition.

Mamin-Sibiriak underlined the social events that took place along the Chusovaia, weaving literature together with folklore to tell about the dangers of the river. For instance, he wrote about the Cossack ataman Yermak Timofeevich who traveled along the Chusovaia in the sixteenth century. And when writing about the punishing work of the river barge captains, Mamin-Sibiriak insisted that only thanks to these *splavshchiki* did Russia receive the Ural metal so essential to its development.

Mamin-Sibiriak emphasized the antiquity, the willfulness, and the power of the river, fully understanding that these repeated impressions would coalesce into an image of wildness (*dikost'*). In this way, the writer obliquely defined the character of the Chusovaia basin's inhabitants as courageous and strong, ready for constant and sustained struggle. At the same time, he challenged his coddled contemporaries who avoided places like the Chusovaia and knowingly deprived themselves of the opportunity for unexpected and intense experiences:

> Of course, the Chusovaia is a *wild* river, and this *wild beast* [dich'] *terrifies* Russian travelers, artists and scholars. They more often enjoy southern summers and seaside beauty, but on the Chusovaia you will see neither Scottish cottages, nor Swiss chalets, nor Italian villas, nor the poetic ruins of ancient castles and fortresses, nor will you see those lived-in and loved sportsmen's outposts to which the Scottish elite flock from all corners of the globe. Each seeks his own, of course, and has his own preferences. To each baron, his own fantasy.
> (Mamin 8: 364, emphasis added)

Gradually, through repetition from one essay to the next, Mamin-Sibiriak developed a picture of the Chusovaia as a powerful wild river which nevertheless formed an important part of world culture – that is, a river which deserved the interest and recognition of Russians. In his descriptions, Mamin-Sibiriak makes the Chusovaia into the main river of the Urals, a position subsequently supported by future writers and travelers. Thus, in Gleb Uspenskii's cycle, "Journeys to the Settlers" ("*Poezdki k pereselentsam*" 1889) the Chusovaia landscape is made to represent the greater Ural region: "*Beautiful...and emblematic are the Urals along the Chusovaia*: the broad river bends freely through a wide valley left between mountains that neither lean upon each other, nor crowd each other out..." (Uspenskii 34, emphasis added).

Chusovaia: tourist destination and site of class struggle

As the Chusovaia's economic importance for the region waned, it gained status as a tourist destination. But, of course, the transformation from a difficult and dangerous working river into a place of recreation does not happen spontaneously, but through active and conscious reinterpretation and the production of new meanings. In the case of the Chusovaia, written texts, and especially various guidebooks, played an integral role. Guidebooks are designed to make travelers feel the importance of the places they visit so that by following the guide, while moving through the space themselves, they transform the book's descriptions into personal travel experiences.

At the turn of the twentieth century, tourism became a broadly accepted use of leisure time in Russia (Koshman 5) and readers began to demand various types of travel writing, especially about the lesser known corners of the country (Guminskii 141). More and more city-dwellers began to travel in search of new experiences, creating a:

> need [for] authoritative instructions: where they should go, what they should see, and what they should look for in everything they saw. An enormous literature of travel was created to satisfy this demand and one of the sources of such literature was *belles lettres* – that is, descriptions in creative works. No guidebook would be complete without reference to such works. The feverish development of the travel industry, on the one hand, and the cult of local identity and the ambitions of local administrations, on the other, heightened the 'demand' for both contemporary and classical works of cartographic origin.
>
> (Abashev and Firsova 103)

As Sergei Kropotov and Natalia Cherniaieva note in their essay on the Chusovaia, the beginning of the twentieth century saw a qualitative shift in the spatial construction of the river: "from an economic object into a site of leisure and scenic recreation, from a practical space to a visual space, in other words, from a space constructed around 'useful values' to one based primarily on exchange values" (Cherniaieva and Kropotov 440). Recently a working river, the Chusovaia became a place of leisure, of recreation, a place that reinforced the traveler's historical knowledge, while also encouraging the consumption of "nature" for the sake of beauty, health, and personal enrichment.

From the beginning of the 1900s, excursions, including school trips, regularly traveled along the Chusovaia. The river gained an important educational function as "nature's open book" and as a text of local history.

The booklets and guides that began to appear in the Urals at the time borrowed readily from the writings of Mamin-Sibiriak and the travelers who followed him, and also from the local historical writings of the UOLE (Ural Society of Amateur Naturalists). Guidebook descriptions of the Urals at the turn of the twentieth century are built around the juxtaposition of River and Mountain. Defined by its geographic position embracing both the eastern and the western Urals, and flowing through both mountains and valleys, the Chusovaia was seen – following Mamin-Sibiriak – as representative of the greater Ural territory. The river's central position became especially important as the need arose to recast the whole geographic area as a single integral region.

Mamin-Sibiriak's strategy for aestheticizing the Chusovaia as an exotic place (strange, wild, and ancient) was adopted by guidebook authors, but was transformed into a collection of recognizable locales in order to better answer the demands of the genre. While maintaining the image of the river as a beauty, the guidebooks gradually "transformed" the dangerous Chusovaia into a safe and peaceful river.

In recounting the pleasures of traveling the West Ural Railroad, the editorial secretary of the newspaper *The Perm Journal* Viktor Vesnovskii improvised his own description based on images used by those who had written before him (the river is unique, powerful, a laborer and a witness to ancient history), even at times directly borrowing from Mamin-Sibiriak's texts:

> From Kyn to the Utka station, for almost a hundred versts [approximately 107 kilometers], the railroad follows the left bank of the Chusovaia. What a beautiful river! What a capricious river [*kapriznitsa*]!
>
> The train speeds along and scenes flash by, each more picturesque than the last.
>
> As is well known, before the opening of the Ural Railroad, the Chusovaia served as the main export route for Ural metal production. Fifty alpine mills sent their productions along these waters ..., with the total quantity of freight reaching 6–7 million poods [98,000–115,000 metric tons]; additionally, the river carried the goods of Siberian merchants: lard, oil, spirits, wheat, etc. ...
>
> Imagine the terrifying power that carved these corridors from the very heart of the mountains! Banks of huge exposed rock at each turn give the Chusovaia a wild but extraordinarily picturesque look. Gazing at these gigantic 50- to 70-*sazhen*-tall [approximately 100–150 meters] rock walls that stretch an entire verst along the river, one somehow senses one's own powerlessness in the face of a current so formidable as to have left these grand monuments to its eternal battle with the obstacles along its path.
>
> (Vesnovskii 4)

The river's "wildness" is preserved in the landscapes along its banks, but the river itself all but loses its bellicose nature, and is described instead as capricious ("*kapriznitsa*"). Its economic status is also explicitly transferred to the past, to the time "before the opening of the Ural railroad" (Vesnovskii).

The depiction of the Chusovaia as a beautiful river with a rich past, and as a potentially interesting tourist destination continued through the Soviet era, changing only to accommodate a new notion of what that "rich past" should mean. In line with Soviet priorities, class struggle occupied a central place in the river's history.

In A. Sheidlin's guidebook *Chusovaia*, published as part of the "Aqua Tourist" ("Turist-vodnik") series, the Chusovaia maintains its recreational function, offering attractions for tourists of various interests:

> Traveling along the Chusovaia by boat or by raft can be a wonderful mode of open-air recreation. ... The Chusovaia provides no small measure of entertainment for hunters and fishers. The river and its tributaries are rich in fish and various game. In the Chusovaia's clear cool depths swim pike, perch, and dace, while the rapids are home to grayling and the pools host dogfish. On the sandy riverbeds and along the rocky banks scuttle the claws of clumsy crabs. ... In the woods one might meet foxes, badgers, mountain goats, lynx, and, on rare occasions, bears and moose, and especially wild fowl: blackcock, woodcock, and wild duck.
> (Sheidlin)

At the same time, the Chusovaia is described as an arena of long-term class struggles between the poor *splavshchiki* and the rich mill owners, between the poor indigenous populations (*inorodtsy*) and the greedy Russian colonizers. "The history of the Chusovaia is extremely interesting and distinctive. Every settlement along its banks is closely tied to the memory of the bloody events that have happened here. Every turn of the river is a witness to the people's heroic war with autocracy"; "It was here that Russia's first capitalists began colonizing and appropriating Ural and Siberian lands"; "The Utkinskaia settlement, a colonial outpost, was founded here long ago. It is mentioned in chronicles as early as 1651. Before that, the land was populated with the yurts of ancient inhabitants – the Ostyaks and the Voguls. In defending their independence, the Ostyaks and the Tatars often attacked the colonial outpost, burned it, and took its inhabitants prisoner" (Sheidlin).

The class struggle, as Sheidlin constantly underlines, played out on the banks of the Chusovaia over many years, and although early folk songs about the river's tragic nature "disappeared along with the barge hands," "the popular memory still preserves the image of the old Chusovaia. The stories of the Chusovaia people along with the yellowed pages of history have much to tell the curious mind of the tourist" (Sheidlin). Conversations with *splavshchiki* and with their descendants, the guidebook's author imagines, should be an integral part of any river voyage.

All guidebooks correspond in some way to the ideology of the time and the society in which they were written, but the overt political intentions of Soviet literature make the connection especially clear. Sheidlin's guidebook was written during the early Soviet push for industrialization, when the USSR's manufacturing capacity stood at the center of attention. This helps explain an unexpected focus in the description of the Chusovaia. The author, after a quick nod to "the incomparably harsh beauty" of the banks of the Chusovaia and the wonderful natural riches of the river, turns his attention away from the landscape and toward what would not seem to be tourist attractions – the mills along the river: "The Chusovaia Mill is one of the giants of Ural metallurgy. It was founded in 1880. Its history is representative of the backwardness of 19th-century Russian feudalism, incapable of making any changes without foreign investment" (Sheidlin). The river, from this point of view, is attractive primarily as a source of natural resources, that is, as a potential site for new factories. "In certain hidden places, one can still find undiscovered deposits of gold, platinum, and precious stones, oil fields, copper, iron, coal... The Chusovaia basin is a true treasure trove still awaiting exploration. Undoubtedly, the enormous riches found here represent only a part of all the treasures hidden from human eyes" (Sheidlin).

This orientation toward future development, typical of the representation of the Soviet world of the 1930s–1950s was supported by a characteristic depiction of a war between man and river and the taming of the river (Rosenholm). The description of the river still underlines its power. "From the Kumysh to the warrior 'Bandit,' the Chusovaia flows along a narrow bed with a steep slope. The river falls 2.5 meters over a 7-kilometer stretch. There are many turns and bends. The major rapids drown out the sound of human voices. Everything is filled with the roar of waves, the noise of tumbling rocks, the air is filled with the ominous music of the raging elements" (Sheidlin). But the new Soviet people hear these "raging elements" as "music," which they set against the "music" of construction:

> No longer does anyone fear the looming *boitsy* of the Chusovaia. Long ago, the groans of wrecked barges and the cries of drowning men ceased to be heard here. ... Motors hum, jackhammers pound, and happy young voices can be heard. ... Near the *boitsy* limestone and alabaster are quarried for new apartment buildings, clubs, pioneer halls, etc.
>
> (Sheidlin)

Soviet guidebooks enhance prerevolutionary descriptions of the Chusovaia's visual and educational value by adding new historical interpretations and an orientation towards future development.

Interestingly, at almost the same time, in 1940, another key aspect of the Chusovaia's image was advanced by Pavel Bazhov in his fairytale "Yermak's Swans." The Chusovaia along with other Russian rivers became the setting for the tale of Yermak Timofeevich's conquest of Siberia. The Chusovaia's uniqueness as the point of connection between Europe and Siberia provided the grounds for Bazhov's neomythological interpretation of the mythical river: a river which not only tests the traveler, but also instills in him the desire to push on. The Chusovaia in the story is a full subject endowed with the special power of fate: according to the narrator, the river "leads you itself" (Bazhov 29) from the known into the unknown. By creating an alternative history of the Urals (Litovskaia 450–452). Bazhov creates a vision of the region which will play an active role in the representation of the Chusovaia through the turn of the twenty-first century.

After a hiatus for the war, tourism was once again advertised as an important aspect of well-rounded Soviet citizenship during Khrushchev's "thaw" at the end of the 1950s. At the same time, as a result of the latest wave of urbanization, there was a steep increase in the number of first-generation city-dwellers who longed, it was assumed, for their "roots." And so there arose an acute need for texts that would present the Chusovaia to the new generation.

From this time on, guidebooks about the river have been published regularly. Often these guides even provide sample travel itineraries which tourists can use to build their own. On the one hand, they provide "useful" information about the river's geography, its flora and fauna, and the code of conduct for visitors; on the other, they reproduce the "proper" image of the river. Creative texts usually make their way into such books in the form of quotations and references, amplifying the "authority" of the Chusovaia as a place worth visiting.

One of the first guidebooks of the postwar period – Evgenii Yastrebov's *Along the Chusovaia River: A Guide for Tourists* (1957) – starts with the words:

> This book is for those who love nature and who are ready to travel one of the most remarkable rivers of the Soviet Union – the beauty-Chusovaia. Along the whole length of the river, you will be met with picturesque islands, limestone caverns, enormous riverside cliffs or, as they are usually known, 'warriors' or *boitsy* which make the river particularly attractive.
>
> (Yastrebov 2)

The author describes the same Chusovaia beauty as have writers stretching back to Mamin-Sibiriak, but in contrast to his predecessors, Yastrebov all but completely ignores the river's rich history. However – consistent with the utopian ideas of the early 1960s – a second edition of the guidebook, published in 1963, includes a grandiose vision that imagines a canal connecting the Chusovaia and the Iset' rivers to "create a great water passage" that would link the European part of the USSR to Siberia and transform the landlocked and mountainous Yekaterinburg into a "port of six seas." Consequently, dreams the author, "without a doubt, new port towns and industrial centers will arise, and these broad, full rivers will attract an even greater flow of tourists than they currently do" (Yastrebov 26).

Just like Sheidlin before him, Yastrebov indefinitely sets aside the inevitable conflict between the economic growth of the region and leisure tourism. Furthermore, the guidebook does not consider the serious ecological issues of the Chusovaia, which was very polluted from many years of carrying freight. Attention would be drawn to these issues in the 1960s by Boris Riabinin in a series of publications for a Sverdlovsk newspaper.[1]

Guidebooks of the 1970s and 1980s put more emphasis on the river's functional aspects since the norms of Soviet literature required that any guidebook give due attention to the "base" with descriptions of economic life in the region. The river's heroic past nevertheless receded into the background, and a set image was established of a beautiful, peaceful river whose calm waters guarantee the safety and enjoyment of travelers. Even the explanation of the river's name is given in calming tones (Matveev 287).

These authors relegate to the distant past not only descriptions of the social struggles in the Chusovaia region and the river's economic importance, but also any definitions of the river that could be interpreted as martial. Thus the description of the Chusovaia as an energetic and working river is associated not with Mamin-Sibiriak, but with one of the founders of Yekaterinburg, Willen de Gennin, who saw the value of the Chusovaia in that it "passed over the Urals and cut through them, flowing into the Kama" (Arkhipova 145). The image of the river as a fighter (or a "sword") connects with the word for its cliffs: "warrior" (*boitsy*). But in accordance with Soviet usage, the author interprets this image as one of a protector – of the riches of the Chusovaia and of the Urals as a whole, of peace and calm. In the twentieth century, the main function of the *boitsy* is to educate travelers.

The Chusovaia, having completely lost its bellicose nature through guidebook descriptions, becomes an effective backdrop for alluring images of the charms of river tourism.

The Chusovaia: inventing the "message"

In the beginning of the 1990s, the dismantling of a unified Soviet territory, with its hyper-centralization, unified consciousness, and continued imperial distinction between center and periphery, led to yet another attempt to re-describe Russian geographies. That which was seen as homogenous began to be reconsidered.

In particular, Ural writers began an active search for representative symbols of their region. Local mythology was revised and into the foreground emerged images of the Urals as positioned between two parts of the globe, bordering diverse lands, and encompassing the colonial and industrial history of the region. "Uralness" began to be conceptualized as a sort of bridge between peoples, confessions, civilizations, and parts of the world.

Such a conception demands not only scholarly interpretations, but also popular texts accessible to a broader audience. The sense of regional identity, previously hidden under the mask of the "unified Soviet" space, inspired cultural activity and yielded several discursive incarnations. It also created a demand wonderfully fulfilled by the Chusovaia with its natural beauty and its sense of local meaning stamped by generations of writers. The representation of the Chusovaia that most resonated with readers inside Russia was that of the writer Aleksei Ivanov. As an experienced traveler himself, Ivanov knows his setting impeccably well. He poured his years of local outdoorsmanship into his first book on the Chusovaia, the traditional and factual guidebook *Down Through the River Narrows* (2004). He expanded on the same themes in his historical novel *The Gold of the Rebellion, or Down Through the River Narrows* (2005) whose popular success pushed Ivanov to write another guidebook, this time with more emphasis on conceptual and culturological analysis, called *Message: Chusovaia* (2007).

As literary scholars have correctly noted, it was Ivanov who "offered the widest-ranging and most fully realized cultural-symbolic construction of the region," based on "a harsh and fairly straightforward geographic determinism ...: he constantly highlights the definitive influence of topographical and geographical factors on the course of history, on the culture, on modes of production and ways of life in local societies" (Abashev and Abasheva 44).

For Ivanov, who considers it his scholarly, creative, and civic duty to "adopt" and "transfigure" the Urals (Ivanov, *Khrebet Rossii* 12), it is of principal importance that Ural history be rewritten from a contemporary perspective, one that is sensitive to current notions of ethnic and state discourse. He holds dear the idea of producing Russian historical reality as a polycentric social world of powerful cultural conflicts between Russians and non-Russians, Orthodox Christians and Old Believers, the natural and the cultural.

The central landmarks of Ivanov's Ural world are the Chusovaia river, the alpine-industrial civilization, rebellious populations, Old Believers, and the little-understood pagan belief systems (Iakshin and Itkin). His central problem is the peculiarities of Russian empire. The perspective of Ivanov's narrator is one of a principled Russian provincial.

In his texts, the Chusovaia becomes the thread that ties Europe to Asia. It is the river that tests one's spirit, a place that concentrates the great events of history, "the 'lifeblood' of the Ural alpine-industrial civilization" (Ivanov, *Message* 7). And, in accordance with the mythological-literary tradition, the topographically concrete and precisely described river is also endowed with a metaphysical dimension: to guide a vessel along the river is to guide one's soul through the narrows of religious and secular temptation.

Message: Chusovaia is written with this in mind. The first two parts describe the river from its sources to its mouth, the third tells of ancient history, as the river's banks were first populated 20,000 years ago, the fourth discusses the Chusovaia's transfer to Russian state control, the fifth and the sixth talk about the river's alpine-industrial past and about the "iron caravans," and in the seventh we find a description of the river's recent history.

Of course, the textual description of territory in any type of guidebook is motivated at least partly by practicality: that is, in order to create an image that would attract tourists. In the 2000s the practical importance of revealing local attractions became particularly pronounced. Literature, after all, is involved in the production of experiences – the most sought-after product of the new economy (Pine and Gilmore). Aleksei Ivanov's portrayal of the Chusovaia has undoubtedly had a positive impact on tourism in the region (Firsova).

The authors discussed here imaginatively invested in the symbolic adoption of a landscape – successfully transforming a small Ural river into an important local site. The capitalization of these imaginative productions over an extended period of time forms a sort of "bank of cultural information" ready to satisfy any demand for prepared images, or local mythologems of varying levels of originality, some identified with a single author, others anonymous, for simple reuse or for critical deconstruction.

From the very beginning, the image of the Chusovaia has included such characteristics as "labor-ready," "austere," "willful," "stubborn," "modestly beautiful," later augmented by its "glorious history," and the "alpine-industrial civilization," which connect the river to images of the broader Ural region. The imaginings of Mamin-Sibiriak, Bazhov, Ivanov, and many others form the interpretive tradition of the Chusovaia and with time became seen as the only possible, completely natural interpretations, as if they flowed "from the very heart" of each writer. In many prose and verse works the same repeated images come up again and again: the sportsman's river, the warrior cliffs, the juxtaposition of mountains and river, river and man, Ural iron mills, local patriotism.

"The River-beauty with the Ural sky / dashed herself against the corridor-cliffs. / And the source of all earthly beauties / The Water-delight, companion of the Ural mountains." "The glorious Ural Chusovaia / flows over and against all" (Mokronosov). As in the text which opened this chapter, here, in these unskillful but sincere lines, Iurii Mokronosov concentrates all the themes of independence, energy, and anthropomorphism of the river as an active agent.

This chapter has attempted to show the long-term development of themes and images initially produced by talented interpreters channeling broad understandings of the ideological demands of both society and the state. The established set of images transforms at every stage into a new system with an independent symbolic meaning as well as more or less evident economic motivations.

The guidebooks about the Chusovaia create a sort of "historical compromise." The Chusovaia forms a symbolic connection between the eastern and western Urals which, since the previous century, have often been administratively separated. By the same token, the river bolsters property values in the surrounding territory insofar its role in local history endows the region with national importance. It should also be mentioned that this historical literature advances an image of the river whose industrial past is far behind it, reinforcing the contemporary idea of a currently pristine territory in the "*old* industrial" Urals, attractive as a site of the *history* of industry, but ecologically conscientious today.

Note

1 The city of Yekaterinburg, founded in 1723, was named for Catherine (Ekaterina), the wife of Peter I ("the great"). On October 14, 1924 the city's name was changed to Sverdlovsk by the Yekaterinburg city soviet, in honor of the revolutionary Yakov Sverdlov. On September 4, 1991, after the fall of the Soviet Union, the city returned to its former name.

Bibliography

Abashev, Vladimir, and Marina Abasheva. "Gory i reki Alekseia Ivanova (zametki o poetike prostranstva v romane 'Zoloto bunta')." *Reka i gora: lokal'nye diskursy. Materialy mezhdunarodnoi nauchno-prakticheskoi konferentsii "Ural i Karpaty: Lokal'nyi diskurs gornykh mestnostei". Perm', 29–30 oktiabria, 2009.* Perm: Permskii gosudarstvennyi universitet, 2009, 41–57. Print.

Abashev, Vladimir, and Anastasia Firsova. "Tvorchestvo Alekseia Ivanova kak faktor razvitiia turizma v Permskom krae." *Vestnik Permskogo universiteta. Rossiiskaia i zarubezhnaia filologiia* 3.23 (2013): 182–190. Print.

Arkhipova, Nina. *Okrestnosti Sverdlovska.* Sverdlovsk: Sredne-Uralskoe knizhnoe izdatel'stvo, 1968. Print.

Bazhov, Pavel. *Malakhitovaia shkatulka. Skazy starogo Urala.* Sverdlovsk: OGIZ, Sverdlovskoe oblastnoe gosudarstvennoe izdatel'stvo, 1944. Print.

Blazhes, Valentin. *Satira i iumor v dorevoliutsionnom fol'klore rabochikh Urala.* Sverdlovsk: UUP, 1987. Print.

Cherniaieva, Natalia, and Serguei Kropotov. "Vniz po techeniiu, nazad k istokam: turisticheskie putevodoteli po reke Chusovaia i proizvodstvo prirodnogo landshafta." *Dergachevskie chteniia – 2008.* Ed. A.V. Podchinenov. Yekaterinburg: UUP, 2010. 437–449. Print.

Dergachev, Ivan. *Mamin-Sibiriak v russkom literaturnom protsesse 1870–1890 godov.* Novosibirsk: Izdatel'stvo SO RAN, 2005. Print.

Ely, Christopher. *This Meager Nature: Landscape and National Identity in Imperial Russia.* DeKalb: Northern Illinois University Press, 2002. Print.

Firsova, Anastasia. "Geograficheskoe prostranstvo v literaturnykh proizvedeniiakh kak resurs razvitiia turizma," Avtoreferat dissertatsii kandidata filologicheskih nauk. Permskii gosudarstvennyi universitet, Perm, 2013. Print.

Guminskii, Viktor. *Otkrytie mira ili puteshestvija i stranniki.* Moskva: Sovremennik, 1987. Print.

Hall, Tim. "(Re)Placing the City: Cultural Relocation and the City as Centre." *Imagining Cities: Scripts, Signs, Memory.* Ed. Sallie Westwood and John Williams. New York: Routledge, 1997, 204–222. Print.

Harris, James. *The Great Urals: Regionalism and the Evolution of the Soviet System.* Ithaca, NY: Cornell University Press, 1999. Print.
Harvey, David. *Justice, Nature and the Geography of Differences.* New York: Blackwell Publishing, 1996. Print.
Haussman, Guido. *Mütterchen Wolga. Ein Fluss als Erinnerungsort vom 16. bis ins frühe 20. Jahrhundert.* Frankfurt am Main: Campus Verlag, 2009. Print.
Iakshin, Ivan, and Vladimir Itkin. "Aleksei Ivanov. Zoloto bunta ili vniz po reke tesnin." Azbooka.ru: n. pag. November 2005. http://azbooka.ru/content/article/default.asp?book. Web.
Ivanov, Aleksei. "*Zoloto bunta, ili vniz po reke tesnin.*" St. Petersburg: Azbuka-klassika, 2005. Print.
Ivanov, Aleksei. *Message: Chusovaia.* St Petersburg: Azbuka-attikus, 2007. Print.
Ivanov, Aleksei. *Khrebet Rossii.* St Petersburg: Azbuka-attikus, 2010. Print.
Ivanov, Aleksei. *Gornozavodskaia tsivilizatsiia.* Ed. Elena Shubina. Moscow: AST, 2013. Print.
Kholmanskikh, Igor'. "Reka Chusovaia pomogla rodit'sia unikal'noi gornozavodskoi tsivilizatsii Urala." *Ural'skii federal'nyi okrug.* 10 June 2013. www.uralfo.ru/press_10_06_2013.html. Web.
Koshman, Lidiia. "Gorod v obshhestvenno–kul'turnoj zhizni." *Ocherki russkoj kul'tury XIX veka.* Moscow: Drofa, 1998. Print.
Kungurtseva, Nadezhda. "Etnokul'turnyi obraz reki Chusovoi v proizvedeniiakh D.N. Mamina-Sibiriaka." *Izvestija Ural'skogo universiteta. Seriia Gumanitarnye nauki.* 3.65 (2009): 137–143.
Kungurtseva, Nadezhda. "Ural'skii landshaft v maloi proze D.N. Mamina-Sibir'aka pervoi poloviny 1980-kh godov." *Vestnik Nizhegorodskogo universiteta imeni N.I. Lobachevskogo* 1.2 (2013): 190–193.
Litovskaia, Maria. "Zhanrovaia sistema tvorchestva Bazhova." *Evoliutsia zhanrov v literature Urala XVIII-XX vekov v kontekste literaturnyh protsessov.* Ed. V. Alekseev. Yekaterinburg: UrO RAN, 2010, 434–452.
Lovtsov, N. *Po Gorno-zavodskomu Uralu (Putevoditel').* Moscow and Leningrad: Fizkul'tura i turizm, 1931. Print.
Mamin-Sibiriak, Dmitrii. *Sobranie sochinenii v 8 tomakh.* Moscow: GIKHL, 1955. Print.
Mamin-Sibiriak, Dmitrii. *Polnoe sobranie sochinenii: v 20 tomakh.* Yekaterinburg: Bank kul'turnoi informatsii, 2002. Print.
Matveev, Aleksandr. *Geograficheskie nazvaniia Urala.* Sverdlovsk: Sredne-Uralskoe knizhnoe izdatel'stvo, 1980. Print.
Mokronosov, Iurii. "Sedoi Ural." *Literaturnoe kraevedenie: Uraloved.* 22 January 2013. http://uraloved.ru/literatura/stihi-pro-ural/stihi-mokronosova. Web.
Oparin, F.P. *Reka Chusovaia.* Sverdlovsk: Izdatel'stvo ural'skii rabochii, 1936. Print.
Pine, B. Joseph, and James H. Gilmore. *The Experience Economy: Work is Theatre & Every Business a Stage.* Cambridge, MA: Harvard Business Press, 1999. Print.
Postonogov, Evgenii, and Iurii Postonogov. *Po Chusovoi. Putevoditel'.* Sverdlovsk: Sredne-Uralskoe knizhnoe izdatel'stvo, 1980. Print.
Postonogov, Evgenii, and Iurii Postonogov. *Predaniia i legendy Urala.* Ed. Vera Krugliashova. Sverdlovsk: Sredne-Uralskoe knizhnoe izdatel'stvo, 1991. Print.

Primechaniia, sluzhashchie k poznaniiu mest estestvennoi istorii i domostroitel'stva v zapadnoi chasti Urala i po reke Kame. *Akademicheskie izvestiia* (June 1781): 728–759. Print.

Reshetnikov, Fedor. "Otryvki iz dnevnika." *Polnoe sobranie sochinenii.* Sverdlovsk: OGIZ, 1948, 261–329. Print.

Rosenholm, Arja. "Voda, vlast' i literatura v sovetskoi proze 30-kh godov." *Gumanitarnaia ekologiia i mir cheloveka: Materialy Vserossiiskoi nauchnoi konferentsii s mezhdunarodnym uchastiem "Gumanitarnaia ekologiia v sisteme kompleksnogo issledovaniia cheloveka". Kirov, 27–29 oktiabria 2011 g.* Ed. N.O. Osipova. Kirov: Konnektika, 2011, 135–144. Print.

Rubel', Raisa. *Po Chusovoi.* Moscow: GUGK, 1960. Print.

Sheidlin, A. *Chusovaia: puteshestvie na lodke.* Moscow: Izdanie tsentral'nogo soveta OPTJ. 1936. www.skitalets.ru/books/chusovaya_sheidlin/index.htm#01 [Accessed 23 August 2015]. Web.

Smith, Nell. *Uneven Development: Nature, Capital and the Production of Space.* Athens: University of Georgia Press, 2008. Print.

Sozina, E.K. "Severnye narrativy v literature puteshestvii nachala XX veka." *Narrativnye traditsii slavianskikh literatur: ot srednevekovia k novomu vremeni.* Novosibirsk: Omega, 2014, 206–216. Print.

Uspenskii, Gleb. *Sobranie sochinenii v 9 tomah.* Vol. 8. Moscow: GIKHL, 1957. Print.

Vesnovskii, Viktor. "Po zapadno-ural'skoi zheleznoi doroge." *Permskie gubernskie vedosmosti* 277 (1916). Print.

Vlasova, Elena. "Reka i gora v reprezentatsiiakh Urala XIX–nachala XX vv. (Po Materialam Putevoi Ocherkistiki)." *Reka i gora: lokal'nye diskursy. Materialy mezhdunarodnoi nauchno-prakticheskoi konferencii "Ural i Karpaty: lokal'nyj diskurs gornykh mestnostei."* Perm: Permskii gosudarstvennyi universitet, 2009, 59–69. Print.

Vorobiev V. *Chusovaia (putevoditel').* Moscow: Fizkul'tura i turizm, 1932. Print.

Yastrebov, Evgenii. *Po reke Chusovoi.* Sverdlovsk: Sverdlovskoe knizhnoe izdatel'stvo, 1963. Print.

7 A cup of tundra
Ethnography of water and thirst in the Bering Strait

Sveta Yamin-Pasternak, Peter Schweitzer, Igor Pasternak, Andrew Kliskey, and Lilian Alessa

Introduction

Looking down from aboard an aircraft, the hydrological landscape of the arctic tundra unfolds into an endless web of meandering creeks, with clusters of deep blue lakes dotting the luscious bedspread of mosses and grasses. In wintertime, bodies of fresh water are discernable by a smoother cover and hues that are slightly more saturated, offset by the blinding whiteness of the spectacular mountainous terrain. While aesthetically energizing, the landscape is arduous physically, especially for a walker who happens to be hauling load of water or ice. Yet, for many residents of contemporary Bering Strait villages, even those living in homes with tap water, hauling water or ice from a local source remains an everyday chore. Why? In Chukotka, the farthest northeast domain of Russia, this question will likely inspire affectionate comments about drinking tea. In the neighboring Alaska people may mention that water from certain sources makes better tasting coffee. On the Russian and American sides of Bering Strait, tea and coffee offer a way of comforting, celebrating, and welcoming. For many, these customs also serve to foster the relationships with local springs, ponds, creeks, rivers, and lakes. In the post-Soviet period, the paramount preference of either tea or coffee has also become a national identity marker for Chukotkans and Alaskans. The amounts of coffee and tea consumed by the United States and Soviet or Russian nationals, respectively, appear to be mutually bewildering for the residents of the two sides of the Bering Strait.

Narratives and practices surrounding tea and coffee figured prominently in the course of our research on the relationships between humans and water on Chukchi and Seward Peninsulas and on Saint Lawrence Island. Here, we examine the roles of these eminent beverages in the cultural construction of thirst, identity, and local hydrological landscapes. The ethnographic insight presented in this chapter speaks to the five themes – value, equity, governance, politics, and knowledge – that Orlove and Caton (404–406) identify as principal to the anthropological understanding of "waterworlds" (see also Hastrup and Rubow). Our findings indicate that the awareness and processes unfolding within each of the five domains are shaped by the lived contexts of consumption.

From the ice curtain to a steamy cup

The Chukotkan side of the Bering Strait is the indigenous homeland of Chukchi and Yupiget (*singular* Yupik, known also as Siberian Yupik). Yupiget also live on the Alaskan side of the Bering Strait, which they share with Inupiat (*singular* Inupiaq) – a more numerous indigenous population inhabiting the entire Arctic coast of Alaska. Both Yupiget and Inupiat of the Bering Strait are coastal maritime societies, whose subsistence livelihood and identity are tied to hunting marine mammals. Among the Chukchi, there are those who connect their cultural identity with marine mammal hunting and those who connect their heritage with reindeer herding. During the second half of the twentieth century, escalating Cold War politics between the Soviet Union and the United States transformed the bridging role of the Bering Strait into the "ice curtain." When in the late Soviet period the ice curtain began to "melt," after several decades of living exclusively within the national constraints of either United States or Soviet Union, the cross-Beringian relationships became infused with a renaissance spirit. The revived exchanges have furnished a vibrant stage for the emergence of region-wide festivals, conferences, and collaborative efforts in research and education. Taking turns in being hosts and guests, the long-separated relatives were triumphing over the collective enjoyment of their heritage foods and mourning the generational shift in the use of the indigenous languages (Kerttula; Schweitzer and Golovko). They were comparing the many facets of their daily lives, including the emergence of some strikingly distinct practices, like the consumption of tea on one side and coffee on the other.

The loved and ubiquitous beverage

A 13-year-old sister hands a "baby bottle" to her 16-month-old brother. Their mother enters the kitchen right as the toddler draws the nozzle toward his lips. For a moment she is struck with panic, scolding her teenage daughter for filling the bottle with tap water. "It is tea," the girl explains. Everyone breathes a sigh of relief. The toddler goes on to drink from the bottle (Yamin-Pasternak's edited field notes entry, 2009).

Taking place in the home of a contemporary Chukchi family, the above exchange speaks to our study theme in a number of ways. For many residents of Chukotka, the mixed blessing of being connected to a centralized plumbing system means that each opening of the tap releases a flow of rusty brown liquid, which people try to filter in a variety of ways. Those able to fetch water from other sources use tap water predominantly for cleaning

Figure 7.1. Municipal water delivery truck – *vodovozka* – operating in Sireniki in 2009. Photo by Sveta Yamin-Pasternak, 2009.

chores. In most settlements, public utilities services offer the option of having water delivered by a municipal truck – *vodovozka* – to homes with and without running water. During periods of warmer weather, residents may haul some bulky household items, such as blankets or area rugs, to wash in a nearby river or lake.

Year-round people visit their favored sources, which they consider to be especially good for tea and cooking, to draw fresh water or chisel some ice to be melted at home. Delivered water is typically stored in holding vessels made of refurbished 200-liter drums, formerly used to haul fuel. A side-effect of the early militarization and resource development in the Arctic, scores of such drums were being left to populate circumpolar regions near and far from human settlements (Fritz). The preferred galvanized drums are scarce, so the most common procedure of converting a fuel drum into a water barrel involves getting it aired out and painted. Weather and circumstances permitting, from Monday to Friday *vodovozka* is seen operating in different sections of a village.

On their scheduled delivery day, residents know to be on the lookout. Once the truck stops in front of their house or apartment building, the inhabitants make way for the long rubber hoses that reach their holding barrels through either the door or a window. In the regional hubs such as Provideniya and Chukotka's capital city Anadyr, people find themselves living too far from a good water source to facilitate their own supply. Areas categorized as "urban" are not serviced by *vodovozka*. Hub and city dwellers can either purchase bottled water – a fairly recent inventory item in Chukotka – or make do with whatever flows out of their faucets.

Although people do occasionally drink plain boiled water, cooled to room temperature, the principal beverage in today's Chukotka is tea. Tea is administered as a healthful tonic, cherished as a marker of celebration and hospitality, and commonly drunk to hydrate and quench thirst. To say "I am thirsty" typically implies "I am craving tea." People prefer steeping loose-leaf black tea, but settle for tea bags when the former is not available. Tea is consumed in between and following meals, during everyday and festive eating, out on the tundra, in reindeer herder camps, and at every type of workplace. The observation by Ho Chi-Tang *et al.* that "tea is the most widely consumed beverage in the world *after* water" (vii, emphasis added) does not hold up in Chukotka. Cooled and relatively diluted infusion of tea becomes a commonplace beverage for children at the earliest stages of life. In most families we have met, the temperature adjustments are made only for babies and very young toddlers. By preschool time, children in our host communities learn to ingest tea in the form they are likely to enjoy for life: steaming hot, infused within seconds after the water has come to a boil. Tea is on the menu for both breakfast and lunch at school cafeterias. A lush spread of sweets marks the ceremoniousness of *chaepitiye* – literally "tea-drinking" – a celebratory occasion put on at workplaces and schools.

Similar to Gail Fondahl's observation that fieldwork in village Siberia demands the ability to ingest "copious amounts of tea" (14), in today's Chukotka one can hardly find a social context that does not involve tea. In the tundra dwellings called *yaranga* (a Chukchi word used also by Russian and Yupik speakers), even in remote herding camps, the kettle hanging above the hearth is continuously refilled with water or snow. Vitebsky observes similar practices among the Eveny reindeer herders in the Sakha region, noting that throughout a prolonged segment of migrating to a new pasture, "granny had taken care to keep track of tea and sugar" (121) while "tending kettle hanging from three poles" (ibid.) was at the top of the to-do list for the herders arriving at a new camp.

For the coastal villagers, an outdoors excursion, whether it is to fish, to pick mushrooms and berries, or just to go on a pleasure hike is not complete without tea. Drinking tea on the tundra is, in and of itself, a fully warranted purpose – a much anticipated and celebrated way to spend time, endowed with spiritual and rejuvenating qualities.

Drinking tea on the tundra follows a rather uncompromising procedure that is specific and integral to the tundra experience. The smoke pillowing the sides of the kettle, filled with freshly drawn water, is believed to boost the flavor and aroma of the tea. In summertime, tundra tea is often

A cup of tundra 121

Figure 7.2. Third-grade students and teacher in a Chukotkan village, having a *chaepitie*. Photo by Natalya Kalyuzhina, 2006.

Figure 7.3. Tea on the tundra. Photo by Aleksandr Borovik, 2010.

Figure 7.4. Newer approaches to winter teatime. Photo by Natalya Kalyuzhina, 2012.

enhanced with wildflower petals, willow and cranberry leaves, and, when available, low-bush cranberries. The scent, the taste, the water quality, and the nutritive properties of the tundra tea are regarded as far superior to its indoor counterpart.

When heading to collect seaweeds or edible benthic specimens that wash up abundantly after storms, a coastal forager may haul tea from home in a thermos, as fresh water may not be available on the beach. In a handful of households that own a snowmobile, thermoses have also become part of snowmobile travel.

Neither thermoses nor snowmobiles were common household items at the time of writing, but the presence of both has grown notably over the last few years. For the tundra walks in the summer, the tea logistics continue to involve transporting bulky tin and aluminum kettles, no matter the distances (see Figure 7.6).

In a contemporary Chukotka household, whether it is in a coastal village or in the tundra camp, the only circumstances in which a welcomed visitor is not offered tea is when the receiving party is inadequately supplied with either tea products or water. Very distressing for the host, such instances tend to prompt a preemptive apology, offered within moments of a guest's arrival. Accustomed to the scarcely and irregularly stocked village stores, as well as to periodic difficulties in accessing adequate fresh water, people attempt to take proactive measures. On one occasion a neighbor, mindful of the fact that we had an electric stove, came to warn our host family about a likely power outage. "Better boil some water or you will be left without tea," she said.

Sometimes when out of tea products, people use leafs of *Vaccinium vitis-idaea* (known as lingonberry or low-bush cranberry) and other local plants to steep a "substitute" infusion. Curiously, the practice of infusing a hot "tea-like" concoction with parts of locally gathered plants came into being only after regular tea drinking became part of the local way of life. This is one of the ways in which diffusion of the tea drinking custom has expanded the range of engagement between local people and surrounding landscapes. Another domain of local knowledge influenced by the daily desire for tasty tea is manifested through the relationships between people and water sources. The pride in being able to drink and serve tea made with the water that is considered to be of especially good quality engenders the awareness of the local hydrological landscapes. Chukotkan tea has *terroir* – the indissoluble agency of transmitting sensuously the traits and processes of the place(s) where the product was made (Manning; Paxson), which also varies with seasons.

Tea time in the Bering Strait

Tea first came to the Bering Strait in the middle of eighteenth century, being one of the main commodities introduced by Russian and American traders. Prior to the spread of Euro-American influence in Alaska, which has replaced tea with coffee as the predominantly consumed hot beverage (*c.* 1950s), tea remained hugely popular on both sides of the Bering Strait. In contrast to the suspicious reception by the early consumers in Russia, where after its mid-seventeenth-century introduction tea was very slow to catch on (Toomre), the Bering Strait appears to have been a place of instant welcome. Upon the establishment of the Saint Michael trading post in 1833, on the coast of the Yukon-Kuskokwim Delta, tea was drunk in "enormous quantities" (Ray 179). In the early 1900s, Bogoras (200) observed Chukotka Natives drinking up to 40 large cups a day. At fairs, Russian traders treated their Chukchi customers to tea and hard rye bread several times a day. Since the 1850s, tea compressed into bricks also served as currency in the sales of firearms, priced in the range of 20 to 30 bricks per rifle. The American wares that Russians acquired from Chukchi in exchange for brick tea sold for prices significantly lower than their monetary value (Bogoras 68). In the second half of the nineteenth century tea had "become more important than anything else" and was used "in the remotest inland camps and along the Arctic and Pacific coasts" (ibid. 62). By the early 1900s tea consumption had become so conventional throughout Chukotka that the few people who did not own a kettle were mocked as tea-shunners. Bogoras's hospitality accounts from that period are remarkably telling:

> In other Maritime villages we were occasionally detained by a snowstorm for several days. All fuel has been consumed. We fed on raw walrus meat. Still some fire was necessary to melt snow to prepare tea... Then the house-master would take an axe and break one of his sledges,

or cut down one of the wooden house-supports at the risk of it tumbling down on our heads. When we remember how scarce wood is on the Arctic shore, and especially wood that is suitable for poles and house-supports, we can appreciate the real value of such a sacrifice.

(637)

Prior to the advent of tea, the only hot liquid ingested after meals was hot broth, provided that boiled meat or fish was the main fare. Eskimo languages throughout the Arctic region reflect a culturally drawn connection between broth and tea. In the languages of Canadian and Greenlandic Inuit, Central Yup'ik and Inupiaq of Alaska, Siberian Yupik, as well as in Aleut, the word for "hot beverage" is a "conflation of tea and soup" (Fortescue *et al.* 77). In Naukan Yupik (the language originally spoken in the now closed settlement of Naukan, near the easternmost point of the Chukchi Peninsula), the word *qayuq* stands for both "tea" and "meat broth." The *Comparative Eskimo Dictionary* also points out the related verb *qayur*, which stands for "drink hot liquid" (320).

Recalling a childhood memory, one of our hosts, a native of Naukan, talks about being awoken in the family *yaranga* to the sound of her grandmother softly calling for *qayuq*. Protruding from underneath the bedding on the fur-covered floor of a *yaranga*, without getting up, little Nadezhda would lift her face to the steaming saucer. The drink in the saucer was infused from a thin wedge, sliced off a compressed tea brick, just as the ones described by Bogoras. Nadezhda's grandmother placed the saucer on the log that sat on the outer side of the hanging hides, separating the sleeping quarters from the hearth area. Retaining the pose of a seal that is lifting its head to the sun while resting on a cozy ice flow – this is how Nadezhda described herself during such moments – in a series of prolonged audible slurps the little girl indulged in the moments of content that she will be recalling throughout her life.

Decades later, living in the Alaskan town of Nome, Nadezhda continues to observe scrupulously her treasured aesthetic of drinking tea. Making a point to follow every step of the prescribed procedure, she covers the bottom of her cup with the dark-brown base, made with loose-leaf black tea in a delicate steeping pot, and dilutes the tincture with boiling-hot water. Little by little, she proceeds to pour the tea out of the cup into the matching saucer, which she then picks up with both hands. Sending ripples across the shallow inlet, Nadezhda blows gently at the steaming liquid and takes a sip. Each time the saucer meets her lips, Nadezhda's face lights up, exuding an inimitable expression of tranquility and satisfaction. Once taken for granted, the procedure now has become an explicit articulation of her identity as a person from Russia. It is also a time-travel ticket to Naukan, the *yaranga*, and the voice of her grandmother announcing *qayuq* time. Nadezhda's friends and relatives in Nome, who overwhelmingly are coffee-drinkers, know that to her they should offer tea. When visiting, she politely drinks from whatever cup she is being given. However, at home, in spite of being teased for "drinking from a plate" by her American stepchildren, Nadezhda will not be caught with a coffee mug in hand, and she vows never to give up her precious saucer.

Nadezhda's experience represents a transitional phase in the time when most Yupik and Chukchi households regarded tea predominantly as an adult drink. Although it was given to children in small quantities, the youth of the 1930–1960s use the metaphor of "controlled substance" to describe their relationship with tea in that time. Having illicit tea parties, occasionally getting caught and being scolded by parents and grandparents, is a common plot. A Chukchi man who was born in 1931 said that it was not until his mid-twenties that he was allowed to enjoy tea regularly. Nadezhda's childhood is also unusual in that, having left the village to work in the district center, Nadezhda's parents managed to finagle a way for her to remain with her grandmother in Naukan. The majority of her peers had to reside in a boarding school. In boarding schools, tea was a regular part of the cafeteria meals and a much-anticipated evening treat. During the cold months resident students shared the chore of harvesting blocks of ice, which were to become water for the school cafeteria. One former resident recalled how during the evening hours in her dormitory, the caretakers would bestow upon the excitedly awaiting youth a kettle filled with boiling-hot tea. The enjoyment hour for her and roommates was also the waiting time for residents of the boy quarters of the dormitory, who were "in line" for their turn to host the kettle.

Finding "tasty tea" in contemporary water systems

I once took my daughter – she was five – with me on a work trip to Anadyr.

> A staff member shows us to our hotel room, we enter, and my daughter points to the table with a decanter and two glasses, cheering 'Momma, look, the decanter is filled with tea!' I felt so bad, I did not know what to say. Once the hotel worker was gone, I explained that it is not tea but tap water, and that they fill the decanter with it for decoration. The child had never seen piped water before.
> (Recounted by a Nunligran resident in 2009)

Thirty years after the incident, this Nunligran mother offers it as a telling anecdote. For her, it is the testimony to the child's recognition of tea as the core hospitality beverage and to the superior water quality in her home village. Having never seen rusty tap water and having been drinking tea since infancy, the six-year-old was prone to thinking "tea" upon discovering the decoratively placed decanter in the hotel room. The child's first visit to Chukoka's capital was also the first encounter with tap water. At that time, the water infrastructure in her home village consisted of the recycled fuel drums from which residents would scoop up water needed for the task at hand.

The Nunligran *vodovozka* gets filled at a freshwater lake situated just over two kilometers outside the village limits. Its local name, "Second Lake," has to do with the geospatial characteristic of its distance from the village. Third Lake is approximately five kilometers inland from Nunligran. The village itself sits on the shore of the lagoon known as "First Lake." The barrier spit between First Lake and the sea is characteristic for the prehistoric settlement geography in the region (Krupnik, *Arctic Adaptations*). Around the 1950s, the intensive implementation of the Soviet settlement consolidation policies imposed forced relocations throughout the region, lumping dozens of traditional coastal settlements into a handful of industrialized villages (Holzlehner). The surrounding land and water rapidly began to show signs of pollution resulting from coal plants and Soviet-built fox farms. This was the case with Nunligran's First Lake, which residents ceased using as a source of tea and cooking water in the 1960s.

Frequent combinations of perilous road conditions, breakage of the water delivery truck, and the need to draw water from the more distant sources make people vulnerable to lacking reliable access to fresh water. Nevertheless, the villagers we consulted felt fortunate to have access to water they thought to be far superior to that in cities. When regional managers ruled to discontinue the *vodovozka* service to the recently built housing units – with indoor plumbing – residents voiced dissonance at the level uncharacteristic for Chukotka villages, where assertion of agency in the face of state authorities is rare. Even more rare was the outcome: promptly and somewhat startlingly, the service was reinstated. What motivated the discord? "We fought so that our tea is tasty," said several residents, showing a sense of rectitude and pride. "I want to taste the tundra in my tea, not the pipe," explained one of the contesters, again invoking the corroded channels of tap water. The expression "so that the tea is tasty" shows to have historical depth. Several elders recited it verbatim in recounting the childhood chore of fetching water from a distant source that was favored by elders of their generation. Time and again, they would haul the kettle to the treasured spring or stream that assure "that the tea is tasty."

Water in cooking and cleansing

Prior to the dispersion of Euro-American culinary influences in western Alaska and of Slavic cookery in the Russian Far East, the indigenous cuisines of the Bering Strait required very little or no water. Aside from tea, the introduction of wheat flour was one of the major culinary catalysts for change. According to Bogoras, the annual quantity of wheat flour that whalers sold along the Chukotkan coast in the early 1900s averaged 2,500 sacks (44 pounds per sack) (62). Anchored in the earlier trade period, the consumption of flour products proliferated during Soviet times. The

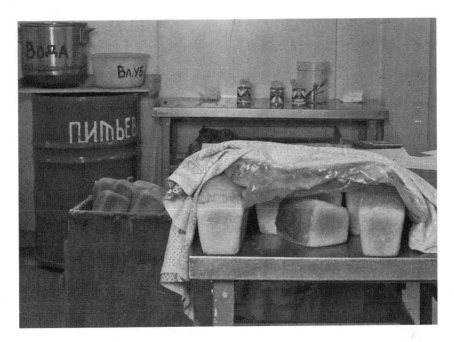

Figure 7.5. Municipal village bakery, with the marked vessels storing the drinking water and utility water. Photo by Igor Pasternak, 2008.

propagation of Russian values, in which bread is an enduring icon that epitomizes sustenance, was implicit to Sovietization. The proliferation of state-run baking facilities, still operating in every municipality in Chukotka, was in great part fueled by the perceived essentiality of bread in the Russian definition of food. When the dire economic crises of the late 1990s had nearly depleted the utilities infrastructure, village bakeries were among the few municipal entities that remained in operation.

The perceived qualities of local bread are also invoked as a barometer of water quality. Although municipal bakeries generally stick to a standard recipe and "brick" shape, the consumers detect discernable differences in the taste and texture of the loaves baked at specific locales. When visiting the nearby village of New Chaplino, a guest from Provideniya may make a bulk purchase of bread to distribute among the neighbors back home, while a New Chaplino resident may do the same at a rare opportunity to visit the closed village of Old Chaplino – now a military post. The distinctiveness of bread in certain locales is usually attributed not to the local baker, but to the quality of the bakery's water source. In addition to baking, the contemporary cookery in the Bering Strait features soups, kasha, pasta, and other dishes broadly representing Slavic and Euro-American cuisines. Unlike the indigenous cuisines that rely overwhelmingly on aging and fermentation (Yamin-Pasternak *et al.*), the preparation of these major imported staples require water.

Another essential of Russification in the building of Soviet settlements was the construction of municipal bathhouses, which in some villages preceded bakeries. Prior to those efforts, neither the personal hygiene practices nor the broader aesthetic of the indigenous worldview involved using water as a cleansing agent. People did not think that washing with water is healthy and many, especially the elders, were wary of the idea when it was first being introduced. A number of elders we consulted consider urine to be the most effective cleaning agent, particularly for washing greasy hands after working with animal products. Elders emphasize that in the old days they never had problems with skin, never experienced dryness or itchiness. They consider excessive washing of the body harmful to health, as it scrapes away the natural oils, thought to play a critical role for the immune system.

In the early 1930s, the incoming Soviet teachers began forming sanitary committees in Chukotkan schools. Committee members – usually the leading students – were responsible for the daily check-ups of their fellow student face, neck, hands, and ears. Those whose cleanliness was deemed unsatisfactory had to wash in the school tub prior to the start of classes (Menovshchikov). In 2012 the Provideniya newspaper *Polyarnik* printed a memoir account shared in a letter by a Soviet activist, who was recounting the experiences from 1957 – her first year in Chukotka. The author of the correspondence came to Provideniya to work as an accountant at a recently established vocational school.

Among the challenges she recalls was instilling the love for the bathhouse among the Yupik and Chukchi youth, sent from their home villages to study in Provideniya. Writes Semkina:

> Many of them never bathed and were afraid of water. They would come to the bathhouse, spend some time standing in the corner, then take their dirty undergarments [issued by the state for compulsory use among its new wards] and put clean undergarments on the dirty body... Soon we no longer had such problems: our students began to love the bathhouse.
>
> (2)

Writing about the late Soviet period, Kerttula describes the bi-weekly trip to the bathhouse as "one of the constants of life in Sireniki," which she says was "not just a place to clean the body but a social event, and, for some, a spiritual event as well" (70). This characterization rings true today and food and drink figure prominently into the bathing cycle, which consists of multiple rounds of taking in steam and sweating, washing off the sweat (using washtubs or showers, where available), and resting on the dressing benches while replenishing energy. People enjoy hearty snacks and tea between and after the steam sessions. Contemporary Chukotkans ascribe tea drinking

Figure 7.6. A spring catchment on a rocky slope near the old Yupik settlement of Imtuk, Chukotka, photographed in late August. Photo by Igor Pasternak, 2008.

in the bathhouse a healthful homeopathic function, whereas drinking cold water after exposure to heat is thought to be harmful.

Feeling and quenching thirst on each side of the Strait

The geography of ancient maritime hamlets in the Bering Strait does not always provide for easy access to fresh water. A typical source is a mountainside spring or a creek from which water or ice needs to be hauled over considerable distances and rough terrain. To a contemporary Western observer, who is unfamiliar with the human ecological adaptations in the Bering Strait and considers water essential to daily living, this arrangement is confounding: prior to the development of mechanized delivery infrastructure, how did Yupiget, Chukchi, and Inupiat of the Bering Strait procure water to meet their everyday needs? How, and how often, did they haul ice or water over strenuous distances? Why did they not live closer to a source?

An inquiry into the practices of cookery and living aesthetics of the elder and past generations of the Bering Strait societies helps explain why their social-ecological adaptations did not emphasize fresh water access as the

Figure 7.7. Resident of Gambell, Alaska, harvests from the village's preferred source of drinking water, photographed in February. Photo by Sveta Yamin-Pasternak, 2011.

priority. In the past, few sips of broth constituted the liquid consumed at mealtimes. While walking on the tundra, a reindeer herder would ingest a pinch of snow to moisten the mouth. However, this rather minimalistic usage should not be mistaken for lack of reverence. Year-round, people took care to preserve access to springs, constructing rock barriers around the catchments and maintaining manageable ice buildup around the water holes in wintertime.

The fact that water occupies a valued place in the worldviews of coastal dwellers and tundra nomads is manifested through its centrality in the ceremonial welcoming of harvested animals – a practice found throughout the Arctic (Lantis 1938; Spencer 1959; Nelson 1983; Birket-Smith 1976; Rasmussen and Calvert 1931).

In today's Chukotka, the physical act of quenching thirst continues to mean taking a few sips rather than ingesting through continuous gulping. In our discussions about beverages and thirst, numerous Chukotkans marveled at the cult of hydration they found to exist among visitors from Canada and the United States. Seeing the amounts of drinking water that visiting Canadians and Americans consume tends to leave lasting impressions. A vendor in Provideniya recalled a group of shoppers who in the course of one week bought out the store's entire supply of bottled water. The shoppers turned out to be members of a church group on a visit from the United States. The vendor was surprised to learn that this particular group was "not a battalion" but only a handful of people. In New Chaplino, the well

A cup of tundra 131

Figure 7.8. Welcoming a harvested seal with fresh water. Photo by Igor Pasternak, 2008.

that serves as the principal municipal water source suffers seasonally from seawater overflow. During such times, the operation of the water delivery truck comes to a halt and all the taps in the village turn salty. Remarkably, certain residents made the effort to deliver fresh ice, procured from a more distant source, to the dormitory that housed the visiting construction workers from Canada. Shortly into their stay, the workers became known for their noticeably non-Chukotkan way of being thirsty. Although the salty well dreadfully inconveniences the entire village, residents made sure to tend to the noted needs of the guests.

Tea, coffee, and national belonging within the shared Beringian heritage

A visitor in a contemporary home on Saint Lawrence Island and on Alaska's Seward Peninsula is likely to see a generous presence of tea paraphernalia – porcelain cups, saucers, steeping pots – that are recognizably "Russian," regardless of their actual manufacture place. Majorities of those collections consist of gifts, received over a series of visits to Chukotka or from the Chukotkan guests who have visited their shore. When a Yupik on Saint Lawrence Island recounts memoirs of a trans-Beringian family reunion, among the top impressions about the relatives from Chukotka is "they sure drink a lot of tea." Chukotkans, in turn, affectionately mimic their Alaskan hosts, recounting how throughout the day the latter chant "coffee… coffee… more coffee?"

In Alaskan villages the consumption of tea began to give way to coffee in the 1940s. Initiated through the influence of the stationed US soldiers (Hughes), over the second half of the twentieth century coffee drinking became a self-identifying signifier of the national belonging for the American Inupiat and Yupiget. The legacy of tea, its rootedness in the Russian heritage of Alaska (Unger), and its surrender to coffee are reflected in the oral histories, languages, and material cultures throughout the forty-ninth State. Contemporary speakers of Eskimo, Aleut, and Athabascan languages use variations of the Russian word for teakettle and teapot – *chainik*. In some cases these terms are also cognates for "coffeepot."

Coffee, today, is the principal hot drink and hospitality beverage in Alaska. Its consumption permeates the flow of everyday activities and interactions. Even the most minimally equipped kitchen will likely feature a "drip" coffeemaker. Evidence of its regular operation often spills beyond the living quarters: a home entryway may feature stacks of bulk-size containers that display a name of a major coffee brand (typically, these are intended for reuse as storage for dried meat). To quench thirst, a contemporary Alaskan resident of the Bering Strait is more likely to reach for water or another soft drink – thus the range of functions ascribed to coffee is not as universal as that which Chukotkans ascribe to tea. However, the social functions of coffee, as well as its *terroir* qualities, are similar to those of the Chukotkan tea. When a particular water source is valued by the community connoisseurs, using water that is not from that source may be taken as disrespectful, especially when making coffee for an elder (Marino *et al.*). The satisfying gustatory and olfactory experiences, facilitated through a cup of coffee or tea, are, in great part, derived from the qualities attributed to water harvested from a known place in the tundra.

In summer 2010, part of our work in the Bering Strait region involved assisting with a cultural exchange, which brought to Provideniya and New Chaplino students of ages between 16 and 18 from Saint Lawrence Island and Nome. Members of the Alaskan group stayed with local families, but participated in daily group activities with the Chukotkan youth. The activities included communal meals (certainly with tea), traditional Yupik dancing, athletic competitions, and hiking trips termed officially as "hike to drink tea on the tundra" (which involved the obligatory hauling of the kettle).

Boiling a large stockpot of water and filling the students' carrying bottles was the daily responsibility of the chaperoning staff. This task was usually done on the porch of our host's house. Among the questions we got from curious passers-by, who appeared at once puzzled and humored by the site, was "haven't you already filled all those bottles yesterday?"

A cup of tundra 133

Figure 7.9. Handcrafted potholder in a Koyukon Athabascan household in Galena, Alaska. Photo by Jake Pogrebinsky, 2014.

Concluding remarks

In a story told to anthropologist Igor Krupnik ("Gone With the Ice" 217–221), Yupik elder Ivan Ashkamakin recounts how as a young hunter he and 16 or so men were carried away by a windstorm and had to spend two weeks drifting on an ice floe. After days of struggle, with very little food and only clothing and their own bodies as the source of heat, the hunters were fortunate to have harvested a walrus. The elder of the brigade instructed how to cut through the walrus skin without puncturing the flesh. He then began to scoop up fresh snow and pour it onto the still-warm intestines, spared from the gush of blood through careful butchering. The snow was quickly melting, providing the first and only opportunity for the hunters to ingest fresh water until days later, when they were finally able to come ashore. "The snow was melting, and there was lots of water. We all drank aplenty because we hadn't drank much until then and were suffering from dehydration," describes Ashkamakin (Krupnik, "Gone With the Ice" 219). What does drinking "aplenty" mean for the narrator, who had found himself in the company of 16 dehydrated men slurping melting snow-water off the

Figure 7.10. Youth from Alaska and Chukotka, and the accompanying staff, heading out for teatime in the tundra near the village of New Chaplino, summer 2010. Photo by Sveta Yamin-Pasternak, 2010.

guts of a walrus? Those who had to melt snow in order to drink or cook can appreciate how meager the water yield is, relative to the volume of snow collected for the melting.

Studies that examine drinking through ethnography and ethnology reveal that the connections humans draw between hydration and health are indeed subject to great variability (see de Carnie and de Carnie). The comparative framework of the Bering Strait further authenticates thirst as a cultural experience that is subject to social change. The present-day beliefs about what constitutes the necessary and healthful consumption of water differ sharply between the two sides. Originating in a common ancestral set of human–water relationships, these ideas have taken on their present form through the distinct trajectories of colonial and globalizing influences, which helped produce the thirstier generations of Chukotkans and Alaskans. Tea and coffee have long been recognized as agents of emerging social and cultural contexts, such as the new gendered functions that were being fulfilled by coffeehouses and afternoon teatime in the seventeenth-century Europe (Smith). Our findings in the Bering Strait show that the consumption of coffee and tea helps foster not only contexts of interaction between humans and other humans, but also between humans and water, entangled in the surrounding landscapes, seasons, and social-environmental change.

Acknowledgments

We are grateful to our hosts in the Bering Strait region for their generous hospitality and enlightening conversations over many cups of coffee and tea. We also thank the National Science Foundation Arctic Social Sciences Program for the Award 0755966, which supported the work that enabled the preparation of this manuscript.

Bibliography

Birket-Smith, Kaj. *Anthropological Observations on the Central Eskimos*. New York: AMS Press, 1953. Print.
Bogoras, Waldemar. *The Chukchee*. New York: E.J. Brill Ltd, 1904–1909. Print.
Carnie, Igor de, and Valerie de Carnie, eds. *Drinking: Anthropological Approaches*. New York: Berghahn, 2001. Print.
Chi-Tang Ho, Jen-Kun Lin, and Fereidoon Shahidi. "Preface." *Tea and Tea Products: Chemistry and Health-Promoting Properties*. Ed. Chi-Tang Ho, Jen-Kun Lin, and Fereidoon Shahidi. Boca Raton, FL: CRC Press, 2008, vii. Print.
Fondahl, Gail. *Gaining Ground? Evenkis, Land and Reform in Southeastern Siberia*. Boston, MA: Allyn and Bacon, 1998. Print.
Fortescue, Michael D., A. Jacobson Steven, and D. Kaplan Lawrence. *Comparative Eskimo Dictionary with Aleut Cognates*. Fairbanks: Alaska Native Language Center, University of Alaska Fairbanks, 1994. Print.
Fritz, Stacey A. "Dew Line Passage: Tracing the Legacies of Arctic Militarization." Dissertation, University of Alaska Fairbanks, 2010. Print.
Hastrup, Kristen, and Cecile Rubow, eds. *Living with Environmental Change: Waterworlds*. New York: Routledge, 2014. Print.
Holzlehner, Tobias. "Re-Settlement – Life in the Ruins of the Past." Far Eastern Borderlands: Informal Networks and Space at the Margins of the Russian State 2013. https://sites.google.com/a/alaska.edu/far-eastern-borderlands/home/chukotka/abandoned-villages [Accessed 23 November 2014]. Web.
Hughes, Charles. *An Eskimo Village in the Modern World*. Ithaca, NY: Cornell University Press, 1960. Print.
Kerttula, Anna M. *Antler on the Sea: The Yup'ik and Chukchi of the Russian Far East*. Ithaca, NY: Cornell University Press, 2000. Print.
Krupnik, Igor. *Arctic Adaptations: Native Whalers and Reindeer Herders of Northern Eurasia*. Hanover, NH: University Press of New England [for] Dartmouth College, 1993. Print.
Krupnik, Igor. "Gone With the Ice." *Our Ice, Snow and Winds: Indigenous and Academic Knowledge of Ice-Scapes and Climate of Eastern Chukotka*. Ed. Bogoslovskaya, Lyudmila and Igor Krupnik. Washington, DC: Russian Heritage Institute, 2013, 217–221. Print.
Lantis, Margaret. "The Alaskan Whale Cult and Its Affinities." *American Journal of Anthropology* 40 (1938): 438–464. Print.

Manning, Paul. *Semiotics of Drink and Drinking*. London: Continuum International Publishing Group, 2010. Print.

Marino, Elizabeth, Dan White, Peter Schweitzer, Molly Chambers, and Josh Wisniewski. "Drinking Water in Northwestern Alaska: Using or Not Using Centralized Water Systems in Two Rural Communities." *Arctic* 62.1 (2009): 75–82. Print.

Menovshchikov, G.A. *Na Chukotskoi zemle [In the Land of Chukotka]*. Magadan: Magadanskoe Knizknoe Izdatel'stvo, 1977. Print.

Nelson, Edward W. *The Eskimo about Bering Strait*. Washington, DC: Smithsonian Institution Press, 1983 [1899]. Print.

Orlove, Ben, and Steven C. Caton. "Water Sustainability: Anthropological Approaches and Prospects." *Annual Review of Anthropology* 39 (2010): 401–415. Print.

Paxson, Heather. "Locating Value in Artisan Cheeses: Reverse Engineering *Terroir* for New-World Landscapes." *American Anthropologist* 112.3 (2010): 444–457. Print.

Rasmussen, Knud, and W.E. Calvert. *The Netsilik Eskimos: Social Life and Spiritual Culture*. Copenhagen: Gyldendal, 1931. Print.

Ray, Dorothy Jean. *The Eskimos of Bering Strait, 1650–1898*. Seattle: University of Washington Press, 1975. Print.

Schweitzer, Peter, and Evgeny Golovko. "Traveling between Continents: Native Contacts across the Bering Strait." *Russian-American Links: 300 Years of Cooperation*. Ed. Uri P. Trtyakov and Natalia A. Alexandrova. St. Petersburg: Akademicheskij proekt, 2004, 99–119. Print.

Semkina, Antonina S. "Once Half Century Ago." *Polyarnik* 17.8739 (2012): 2. Print.

Smith Woodruff, D. "From Coffeehouse to Parlour: The Consumption of Coffee, Tea, and Sugar in Northwestern Europe in the Seventeenth and Eighteenth Centuries." *Consuming Habits: Drugs in History and Anthropology*. Ed. Jordan Goodman, Paul E. Lovejoy, and Andrew Sherratt. New York: Routledge, 1995, 148–164. Print.

Spencer, Robert F. *The North Alaskan Eskimo: A Study in Ecology and Society*. Washington, DC: Government Printing Office, 1959. Print.

Toomre, Joyce. "Introduction." *Classic Russian Cooking: Elena Molokhovets' Gift to Young Housewives*. Ed. Joyce Toomre. Bloomington: Indiana University Press, 1992, 3–73. Print.

Unger, Suanne. *Qaqamiigux: Traditional Foods and Recipes from the Aleutian and Pribilof Islands: Nourishing Our Mind, Body and Spirit for Generations*. Anchorage, AK: Aleutian Pribilof Islands Association, 2014. Print.

Vitebsky, Piers. *The Reindeer People: Living with Animals and Spirits in Siberia*. Boston, MA: Houghton Miffin Company, 2005. Print.

Yamin-Pasternak, Sveta, Andrew Kliskey, Lilian Alessa, Igor Pasternak, and Peter Schweitzer. "The Rotten Renaissance in the Bering Strait: Loving, Loathing, and Washing the Smell of Foods with a (Re)Acquired Taste." *Current Anthropology* 55(2014): 619–646. Print.

Section III
Water rebuilding landscapes

8 Water on the Russian gentry estate[1]

E.G. Miliugina and M.V. Stroganov

As the title of this article suggests, it aims to explore the relationship between two independent entities: water and the human will. Our choice of this particular topic is largely informed by D.S. Likhachev's foundational works on the style of gardens and parks. We will apply these works' key ideas in examining the semantics of water features within the context of the gentry estate (Likhachev). Water on the estate, whether in a natural or artificial state, has yet to be studied as text, as an expression of the artistic consciousness of a particular country or era.

As an element of nature, water has always existed in and of itself and for itself and therefore is completely free of self-interest and ambition. Humanity has always been driven to modify the world to accommodate people in keeping with the historically evolving ideals and norms – both spiritual and material – of human society and civilization. This drive, in combination with humanity's lack of its own material resources, inevitably means that the human will is far from selfless in regard to nature. Nevertheless, while seeing nature's elements (earth, water, air) as the main material to be used in modifying the world, humanity has been compelled to recognize that this material, by definition, will never fully submit to its will and that in actuality, given the fact that the elements exist independently from humans, they will always influence human initiatives, shape and force changes to human plans, and complicate or even thwart the realization of human endeavors. Because of its dynamic nature, this is particularly true of the water element.

The confrontation between water as a natural element and the humans striving to civilize it is on vivid display within the space of the country estate. The prologue to this relationship is, of course, the long process by which ancient humans gained mastery over territories adjacent to sources of water, a process reflected in the mythology and folklore of archaic and traditional societies through stories in which a demiurge creates a new world or a cultural hero transforms an existing one (Miliugina, *Russkaia reka*). The creativity manifested in the design of country estates offers an opportunity to trace this process through a compressed period of intensive development and in a form representing human intelligence and planning. Furthermore, this process, culminating in recent history, is reflected not only in a neo-mythology and folklore contemporary to it, but in various genres of documentary and literary writing. Such sources provide a broader context for study.

The context within which the relationship between water and humans developed on the gentry estate offers two interrelated aspects for investigation: the pragmatic and the aesthetic. There are furthermore three essential components of this process: the actual circumstances under which people gained mastery over water; the human creative ego that sees itself and positions itself as a rival and tamer of the water element; and, finally, the artistic and aesthetic result that achieves the optimal (in terms of objective conditions) coordination between the human will and water.

Water on the gentry estate is a multifaceted phenomenon in that, in addition to fulfilling a pragmatic and aesthetic function, it plays a direct role in constructing the mythology that surrounds the estate. On the pragmatic level, the Russian gentry estate, like any place of habitation and agriculture, is inconceivable without sources of water: rivers, lakes, reservoirs, springs, and streams. However, while using water for practical purposes – to support and develop life and farming within the world of the estate – the creators of the Russian gentry estate were guided by ideas that went beyond the autonomy and self-sufficiency of their households in the economic sense (subsistence economy).

I.

The Russian gentry estate (like the European estate generally) was a self-sufficient world of its own. The creators of this world experienced and conceived it as a harmoniously organized system, a cosmos, in essence, created out of primordial chaos. The owners of estates saw themselves as the creators of their own universe (see Dmitrieva and Kuptsova; Evangulova). In fact, this universe was rather small; furthermore, even if the landowner's estate and its manor house[2] were quite large, this "universe" was enclosed within very real boundaries. This did little to reduce landowners' sense of themselves as creators since, even within the territory of fairly small estates, they contrived to create their own world.

All landowners began their work on the estate just as God began his: "In the beginning God created the heavens and the earth. And the earth was waste and void; and darkness was upon the face of the deep: and the Spirit of God moved upon the face of the waters" (Genesis 1: 1–2). A primordial syncretism of earth and water is embodied in the visual image of the swamp, and the estate comes into existence with the separation of these two elements. This is a process beautifully illustrated in a poem by Aleksandr Bakunin[3] called "Brook" (1799). This poem is highly pertinent to our analysis insofar as it describes the creation of the Nikol'skoe-Cherenchitsy estate owned by Nikolai L'vov,[4] who created many other estates and was a theoretician of estate design. Bakunin gives mythological form to L'vov's pragmatic experience. "Brook" begins with the following lines:

> The pathways through the mossy tundra
> How recently led but to doom?
> And o'er the streams and currents turbid
> There hung a cold and foggy gloom.
> The bowels of earth would like' devour
> Those bold enough to thither stray,
> And vicious beasts would make away with
> All beings mired in their way.
> (Bakunin 17)

Bakunin appended the comment that "The swamp in Cherenchitsy was previously impassable – it has been drained" (Bakunin 18). It is this comment that informs us that the poem refers to Nikol'skoe-Cherenchitsy, and we are familiar with the place where this swamp was located. We will return to the description of this estate. Bakunin's poem goes on to describe how, as a result of an act of creation, cosmos emerged where chaos once reigned:

> Where once no trace of life existed,
> Naught but the image of demise,
> There now the song of nightingales
> To joyous village dance gives rise.
> (Bakunin 18)

The separation of earth and water – this is the first stage, the first day of creation. This same natural philosophical motif is evident in Bakunin's neo-mythology:

> What is that sound of water flowing?
> A brook runs here? That cannot be,
> That's not a brook, that's Lel' the mighty,
> His image in the waters has poured,
> Life's genius that within them flow,
> Has to the valley life restored.
> (Bakunin 18)

According to these lines, "life's genius" comes specifically from the flowing waters. Water could come in all shapes and forms, but it was the small streams and brooks along whose banks the estates of the nobility were usually built that became a symbol of genuinely contented life. It is therefore not surprising that Bakunin titled a poem he devoted to describing his estate not with the name of the estate itself, but with the name of the small river on whose banks it was located – "Osuga": "Flow, oh brook, nature's adornment, / Show us the path to happiness..." (Bakunin 18). Bakunin goes on to list other types of flowing water: fountains broad rivers flowing to the sea, and waterfalls:

> You're able, as a roaring fountain,
> To cleave the air with lively stream,
> Or fall in glistening raindrops that,
> In sporting, make a rainbow gleam.
> You're able, as a lofty river,
> To bring to vast banks majesty,
> And choosing splendor over calm,
> Dispatch fast currents to the sea.
> But empty splendor you disdain,
> Toward it, you can be miserly,
> So as to best bring life to shores
> Where love frisks with you joyously.
> Not striving forward in fruitless rushing,
> You're not a thund'ring waterfall,
> The sight of which, most dread and frightening,
> Disturbs the gaze of passers all.
>   (Bakunin 18–19)

Bakunin's writing is fully in the spirit of Enlightenment sentimentalism, which placed personal qualities above social status. His reference to a waterfall at the end of the previous excerpt evidently alludes to Gavriil Derzhavin's ode "Waterfall" (1794), a contemplation of the renowned statesman and military leader Grigory Potemkin[5] on the occasion of his death. Bakunin's brook prefers the "calm" of the private individual over the "splendor" of the public figure; in fact it scorns "empty splendor." The poem ends with a description of the benefit the noble estate derives from the brook's water:

> Your babbling, like the voice of friendship,
> Allures to you from field and knoll;
> It lightens loads and eases hardship,
> Pours sap and strength into the soul.
> You don't exchange for granite walls
> Your verdant banks, where, as they grow,
> The living blooms that you bring forth
> With twice their beauty start to glow.
> Though whirlwinds may attempt to roil
> Your e'er pristine, and tranquil gaze,
> Descending on you, they can't spoil
> Your current, which they merely graze.

You summon herds, by heat exhausted,
As they in sultriness run loose,
You murmur, and the flow, disrupted,
You happily assign good use.
And when days take a turn for worse
Throughout cold winter, you still go,
Your currents, at their depths, coerce
The season's stiffened limbs to flow.
                    (Bakunin 19)

Given his thoughts about water as element, it is not at all surprising that in contemplating humanity's most elevated values Bakunin constantly compares them to flowing water. We see this imagery in his poem "To My Friend Nikolai Aleksandrovich" about his friendship with L'vov (1799):

Nearby the brook a doleful glade
Lay like a wasteland, void of fruit:
No buds or blossoms gave it shade,
And naught but rampant weeds took root –
Until the water's living current
Wellbeing in that glade induced;
The wasteland overgrew with grass,
And the first flower was produced.
It in bucolic freedom bloomed,
As such, I give it, from the earth;
Oh nature's friend, accept it please,
It was by nature given birth.
                    (Bakunin 16)

Clearly, Bakunin chooses his imagery very intentionally in discussing L'vov and his estate. The concept of flowing water repeatedly becomes an object of intensive reflection. In L'vov's conception of the Russian aristocratic estate, "flowing water" is seen as a form of energy that unites all spheres humanity's and the world's being. Bakunin therefore takes this concept as ready-made and makes liberal use of it in his poetry.

II.

We do not have at our disposal any written record of how L'vov chose the location for or determined the layout of his Nikol'skoe-Cherenchitsy estate. To some extent, he was forced to deal with what his parents had already done with the land. However, he did implement modernizations in accordance with his own ideas, and the guiding principle in his transformation of the estate was the use of water as "text" or symbolic system.

In addition to the land's topographical features and the fact that it sloped downward from the northwest to the southeast, the architect focused his attention on the location of groundwater. Using underground wooden aqueducts and a drainage system, he obtained water for artificial ponds designed for various purposes: agriculture, religion, fishing, and bathing. He also drained a swamp.[6] A cascade of ponds was built along the continuation of the axis running through the center of the main house, reflecting L'vov's belief that, for the estate as text, the human and water principles are of equal value and importance and are intrinsically unified and interdependent.

The organization of the estate economy was governed by practical expediency. At the high-elevation northwestern end of the estate, on land close to fields and at the estate's farthest point from sources of water, there were structures for storing and processing grain: a threshing barn and granary. In the middle zone, closer to the house and to water resources, fruit orchards were planted and a greenhouse and stables were set up. At the low-elevation southeastern end, close to meadows and cascading ponds ("flowing water"), was the livestock yard. This portion of the estate is depicted in a drawing by M.N. Vorobiev titled "View of the Village of Nikol'skoe" (1812). The dominant natural element of the estate's northern zone was thus earth, while in the southern zone, the architect used natural sources to compose a water text.

Water sources were also situated along the road, on an axis running through the estate's middle zone. To the west of the main house, a complex of structures relating to peasant economic activity was built. Southwest of the house, on the slope of Petrova Gora (Peter's Mountain), a forge stood at the edge of an old village. Here, L'vov created a miniature estate for his friend Petr Veliaminov,[7] with a two-story residence (kept warm with heat generated by the forge), along with various service buildings, including a stable and threshing barn. This complex came to be known as the "new village" and is depicted, along with neighboring wells, in a drawing by L'vov titled "View of P.L. Veliaminov's House on Petrova Gora on the Nikol'skoe-Cherenchitsy Estate" (1787). The Petrova Gora complex was not only functionally self-sufficient, it was exceptionally picturesque: structures built with a special earthstone blend were in harmony, in terms of materials and style, with the forge (made of limestone and slabs of boulder) and fit organically into the aesthetic whole of the English park.[8]

The estate's western zone was dominated, in both symbolic and practical terms, by the fire element, a counterpoise to the eastern zone, where the air element was dominant. East of the main house, on a hill artificially built up through the movement of earth that had been planted with birch and cedar trees and featured a complex water engineering system, L'vov placed a church with a burial vault (designed in 1784, built 1789–1806). The placement of the church raised it above all other neighboring structures, promoting the formation of a religious zone within the estate for the convenience of parishioners. This design was optimally suited to the church's preservation. It also incorporated water features, both of natural and artificial origin. The church was separated from the road by a deep and fast-flowing stream, and nearby, for the needs of the religious zone, a church pond was created that fulfilled both a practical and aesthetic function. Visitors approaching the estate from the east would have admired the double image of the church rotunda: one image seemed to hover in the air, while the other was reflected on the pond's surface, surrounded by centuries-old trees.

Nikol'skoe-Cherenchitsy's water text has largely been erased, but evidence of its leading role in the estate's aesthetic and pragmatic organization can be found in nineteenth-century iconographic material and the observations and measurements of twentieth-century investigators (Budylina *et al.* 69–70). These sources suggest that the estate's largest water reservoir was the lower system of ponds: two of this system's ponds were in the park, and the lowest one was located by the livestock yard. In designing them, L'vov did more than simply take the land's topographical features into account; he turned these features into genuine assets. For example, the long and narrow (approximately 300 x 20 meters) Balkhon Pond that meanders picturesquely in front of the house created the impression of a road of water leading to a pavilion (referred to as the "little temple") built in classical style that stood on the eastern edge of the park. The base of the pavilion's six-columned portico, which faced the water, was adorned with an arched opening allowing water to flow into an underground aqueduct used to channel water from the upper pond to the livestock yard. A small island and natural peninsula at the western end of Balkhon were adorned with a gazebo and rotunda pavilion. In his design of the second pond located on the house's main axis, L'vov constructed a small waterfall down which water cascaded over boulders, falling two meters. A picture of this water feature has been preserved in a sketch that L'vov made when he was designing it, titled "Cascade at Nikol'skoe-Cherenchitsy" (1789). The compositional center of this pond was a bathhouse whose archway faced south, its design incorporating large boulders. From this spot, a trench channeled water to the third pond. The successful realization of the system's artistic and ecological features required earthwork and stonemasonry (lining the bottom with flagstone, facing slopes with stone), as well as the creation of a number of hydraulic devices. In particular, the church pond was designed for easy cleaning: the upper end of an underground wooden conduit opened at the bottom of the pond, which was lined with white stone, while the lower end channeled water to the bottom of a diversion ditch.

The system of ponds worked in conjunction with sources of water and devices to propel it that were used for both aesthetic and practical purposes and were located throughout the estate. The estate's most powerful water jet was found at its entrance: a fountain fed, via aqueduct, by spring wells.

Since destroyed, it is depicted on a drawing by M.N. Vorob'ev, "Fountain in the Village of Nikol'skoe" (1812) and was later described by Aleksei Grech,[9] who visited the estate in the 1920s: "In front of the entrance into Nikol'skoe was a pool, an archway made of wild stone through which a stream of water passed into a semi-circular reservoir. This is one of the Italian obsessions of the owner and builder of Nikol'skoe, N.A. L'vov" (118). The fountain was a monumental stone structure: water poured from the mouth of a mask into a bowl sculpted out of the stone. Of exceptional importance in the world of the estate was the water engine that stood by the side of the road, captured in a woodcut by G.V. Gogenfel'den, "View of the Manor House and the Church in the Village of Nikol'skoe; In Front is a Machine with Bear in a Wheel" (1860s, based on a drawing by I.A. Ivanov made during L'vov's lifetime). Another source was at the foot of the hill on which the church and burial vault stood, in the wall supporting the ramp leading up to it. The source was fed by the church pond via aqueduct. In summing up the water features and fanciful inventions shown in nineteenth-century gouaches with views of Nikol'skoe-Cherenchitsy (no longer available to us), Grech notes: "There was a lake here with little islands and bridges, classical temples, gazebos, a waterfall, and even a cave filled with water, just like the Isle of Capri's Blue Grotto" (120).

We see further evidence of the degree of thought and planning that went into the design of the Nikol'skoe-Cherenchitsy complex in a 1799 letter L'vov wrote to Petr Lopukhin[10] concerning the latter's estate, Vvedenskoe, outside Moscow. While commenting on the natural beauty of the place, L'vov analyzes its topography and natural resources and demonstrates the irrationality of his client's original plan:

> [T]he promontory on which you intend to place the estate has marvelous views and there is beautiful forest on both sides, but the ridge is sandy and mean: not a drop of water, and whatever is planted on the promontory will grow slowly and feebly unless you undertake the necessary measures to avert inconvenience. The new fruit orchard located on the sandy mount also hasn't a drop of water, nor does the livestock yard; you will have to assign at least three pairs of oxen in the summer for watering and swill, and when the master is gone, instead of benefit, one of two necessary evils could occur: either the cows will be without swill or the oxen without hide.
>
> In terms of the current situation, the spot where you have asked me to begin building the stable yard, that is, to the right of the prospective road to the grove, the place is not entirely suitable because it is quite far from a watering place. It is quite impossible to have a good well on the mount, the 12-sazhen deep well holds very little water, which trickles in from the earth, but there is no true spring vein, nor can there be, because the horizon of the streams on either side, or even of the Moscow River itself, is very low, so if you are to seek good water, you will have to dig

to the very level of the Moscow River, and then, although there will be enough water in the well, it will be quite hard to draw it out. [...] Having examined the rivers on either side and their banks, it seems to me that there exists the capacity to invigorate the beautiful, but heretofore dead and waterless, situation of your estate, with living waters – there will be fountains in your orchard and livestock yard, a magnificent cascade near the house, and the stable yard will be built where you have indicated and have flowing water. In short, the wonderful situation of the place will be, truly, incomparable; everything will come to life and everything will be in motion.

(L'vov 350–351)

As we see, in this case as well, the decisive factor in planning the estate was the availability of water: this is the standpoint from which L'vov evaluated the placement of the fruit orchard and the stable and livestock yards, with an eye toward ensuring that plants and animals would not be left without water. Viewing it as irrational to expend the energy of people, animals, and machines on providing the estate with well water, L'vov set up "flowing waters" on the estate grounds – ponds formed by damming the Nakhabnia River – and enriched Vvedenskoe's nature with artificial water features. Where once forest had grown, he created a park and a glade, built fountains, and planted flowerbeds. This is what we see in a painting by I.I. Podchaskii, "The Vvedenskoe Estate: View from the Riverbank" (1812). The careful consideration of natural features, the systematic approach to an estate's organization, and the principle of rational management enabled the functioning of a significant number of components performing a variety of the tasks needed to keep the estate running (see also Miliugina, "Kontseptsiia" 140–146).

L'vov also applied the "flowing water" principle in planning other estates, especially estate complexes in the Tver' region. Here, we find further evidence of the main techniques the architect used in composing water texts.

The Mitino-Vasilevo estate complex that L'vov designed was, in its day, one of the most magnificent in Novyi Torg District.[11] Its impressive dimensions were remarked on not only by visitors to the estate, but by those traveling the highway between St. Petersburg and Moscow in those days (Glushkov 151). The complex's importance is tied to the landscaping innovations it incorporated. L'vov integrated two estates on opposite sides of the Tvertsa River into a single whole and the Tvertsa itself with existing structures of the Prutnia churchyard and Prutnia Lock (Kharlamova and Udal'tsova 14–18). The Prutnia Lock (which provided a way around a stretch of dangerous rapids), along with the military fort that protected it, were built in the early eighteenth century, when Peter I ordered construction of the Vyshnyi Volochek Waterway system. The L'vov estate was located downstream from the lock on both banks of the Tvertsa where the Vasilevo and Mitino streams fed into it (Nikitina 434–435). The Tvertsa River formed the axis of the estate complex. Along its right bank ran the road from Torzhok (part of the St. Petersburg–Moscow Highway). The Prutnia Church also stood on this side. On the left side, symmetrically radiating out from the church by L'vov's design, stretched the Vasilevo (Chertov) Bridge on one side and a cascade of ponds on the other.

The cascade of ponds created out of the Vasilevo Stream occupied the central position in the layout of the Vasilevo estate. It separated the estate complex's main area – residential and utility buildings, greenhouses and conservatories, fruit orchards, and a section of the park that featured numerous pavilions – from the park's main expanse. The upper pond, the largest, was created at the headwaters of the Vasilevo Stream and served practical purposes: the cultivation of fish and the keeping of waterfowl. The other three ponds were decorative. As they descended toward the Tvertsa, the surface area of each successive pond was reduced, as were, accordingly, the structures built over the water (dams that also served as bridges) flowing from pond to ponds. The Chertov Bridge featured a view of the dam that separated the upper decorative pond from the middle one.

The second pond's dam represents an interesting combination of a complex water engineering structure and a park pavilion:

> The dam extended 1.2 meters above the water level of the upper pond. The aqueduct pipes laid inside the body of the dam diverted overflow from the upper pond to the middle one, forming two picturesque flows down either side of the grotto abutting the dam from the east. The huge stones of the arch formed a deep niche grotto accessible by a spiral staircase mounted inside a special, vertical tunnel. The keystone of the grotto's arch and two adjacent stones created a sort of spout through which, using a special water gate, water could be released, and this water, cleaved by sharp stone edges, formed a translucent curtain for the grotto niche as it fell.
>
> (Nikitina 447)

The Mitino estate on the right bank was designed in accordance with the same principle. L'vov used weirs and dams to create a cascade of ponds out of the Mitino stream that was also joined with the Tvertsa and also divided the estate complex from the park.

To visually counterbalance the massive stone Chertov Bridge on the other side, L'vov erected a pyramidal vault with an arched entry of rough-hewn stone on the raised right bank. In his travel notes, S.N. Korsakov, who visited Mitino in May 1809, commented on this unity of human-made objects, visible from the Torzhok road:

> About seven versts beyond Torzhok on both banks of the Msta [Tvertsa] are the estates of the L'vovs. Right by the road one can see a rather large stone pyramid, looking like the glorious Egyptian ones, that is part of

Figure 8.1. The Chertov Bridge on the Vasilevo estate. Photo by Elena Miliugina.

the manor house and garden complex. From both sides of it there are entrances whose tall and broad archway is made of strange, rough-hewn blocks of gray stone. This is a wine cellar. On the other side of the river as well, one sees a manor house with gardens, with stone bridges over ravines, or with fanciful structures and kennels that were actually "little paradises" or *raeks*.[12]

(Budylina *et al.* 85)

The tiered structure of the Vasilevo cascade mirrored the tiered terraces on which the vault was placed: the lower tier was where ice was stored in the winter for later use, the middle one contained a cold-storage chamber for food, while the upper tier protruded out of the ground in the form of a pyramid, providing ventilation. Placing the vault on a sharp incline made it possible to have entrances at various levels, and while the main entrance led to the cold storage chamber from the upper landing, from the lower terrace, near the bank, ice was delivered from the stream – yet another sturdy bond connecting people's lives with the life of the river. Just as L'vov had conceived it, the Tvertsa and the streams that converged into it became a chain

Figure 8.2. Boulder bridge in the park of the Mitino estate. Photo by Elena Miliugina.

linking all aspects of the estate complex. This design represents yet another embodiment of the architect's cherished principle of "flowing waters."

Another estate for which L'vov composed an equally original water text was Znamenskoe-Raek.[13] The Logovezh River looped through the estate's land, giving it a distinctive topography. L'vov used the streams that fed the river to set up weirs that allowed him to create a system of ponds at the southern and northern ends of a park (Budylina *et al.* 82).

The ponds featured piers, bathhouses, and bridges, while the park was dotted with gazebos and pavilions. At the south end, the largest pond in the system had an island in the middle and an arched bridge made of rough stone. Roads branched out from the system of ponds at the north end to the manor house and to a large stone bridge across the Logovezh that had three

Figure 8.3. A system of ponds on the Znamenskoe-Raek estate. Photo by Elena Miliugina.

arches. The lower pond was given a sloping embankment paved with rough stone, and its southern side was adorned with sculptures of mermaids. These bodies of water served both utilitarian and decorative purposes, but Grech saw the chief function of Znamenskoe-Raek's water features as aesthetic:

> A wide glade along the main axis leads to the river. From here, the lime trees afford another view of the house, brightly lit by the sun: the space of the meadow is softened, and the architecture is perceived as something skillfully placed within a landscape painting. [...] Still other "flights of fancy" have been preserved within the English park – a grotto made of wild stone above the river and a monumental dam that diverts the river's flow, also built with rounded boulders.
>
> (Grech 126, 128)

L'vov's thoughts on the role of water on the urban estate were expressed in the album *The Garden of Prince Bezborodko in Moscow* (1797) and its opening essay, "How Prince Bezborodko's Moscow Garden Might Be Arranged" (Grimm 107–126; L'vov 316–325). This was L'vov's only essay on the art of landscaping gardens and parks that synthesizes the experience of the Western European experts William Kent, William Chambers, Alexander Pope, Thomas Whately, and C.C.L. Hirshfeld (Rossi 210–306). Prince Aleksandr Bezborodko,[14] whom Paul I granted "a vacant place on the Iauza near Nikola [the Church of Nikolai the Wonder Worker] in Vorobino [...] as an eternal and hereditary domain," had commissioned a plan to develop the estate (Glumov 144). Seeing himself as a champion of culture, Bezborodko, despite being mortally ill and lacking any hope of seeing the project brought to fruition, nevertheless ordered Giacomo Quarenghi and L'vov to design a magnificent estate with a vast park (1797): "I have decided to start on a new building that will at least show posterity that in our day and in our land there were people with a sense of taste" (*Arkhiv kniazia Vorontsova* 379). The freedom granted him by the client permitted L'vov to use his design of Bezborodko's garden in Moscow to express his conception of the art of Russian garden and park landscaping and his understanding of prospects for its development.

The essay comprises several thematically independent sections. According to a drawing titled "Plan for Prince Bezborodko's Garden in Moscow" (1797), the palace had two façades, one with the main entrance facing the street and an open courtyard and another facing a hill that sloped down to the river. Outside the latter, L'vov planned to install a park. "The entire hill in front of the house" L'vov divided "into three terraces" and adorned them "with a grotto, perrons, cascades, etc., blending them with the greenery of selected trees and setting this entire part of the hill in motion with flowing waters" (L'vov 316). In other words, the space would be rendered fluid not by virtue of the hill's slope in and of itself, but specifically by flowing waters. L'vov placed two large ponds with a slender neck of land between them at the center of the lower part of the park. The artist intended these ponds to be used to revive the magnificent games of antiquity: "He has turned a four-cornered pond into a semi-circular *naumachia*... The second pond, having an elongated figure, is turned into an aquatic lyceum for holding regattas of small gondolas" (L'vov 316). An amphitheater was built by the *naumachia* with a portico in the center and rostral columns along the edges that served as "pharoses" to illuminate the spectacles. In summertime, the amphitheater was used for illuminations and fireworks and the pond "for water games and for gondola outings" and, in the winter, "for ice skating." A hippodrome was placed around the "aquatic lyceum" for "chariot runs" (L'vov 318).

L'vov took the various times of day into account in his plans for the landscaped section of the park. An elevated spot to the right of the house was designed for morning walks, and a special garden was placed somewhat downhill for the afternoon. This area was rich in flowing waters; little lakes, streams, and small rapids enlivened the quiet with the sounds of running water. It also featured an aqueduct that channeled water to a Temple of Neptune. A rustic mill and cascade, in addition to their practical purposes, embellished the landscaped park in a manner consistent with the land's historic uses.

The plans for "Prince Bezborodko's Garden in Moscow" were not fated to be realized due to the death of the client, but L'vov did use many of the ideas from this project in his design of Aleksandr Razumovskii's Moscow estate on Gorokhovo Field.[15] The centerpiece of this magnificent complex was the palace, from which a vast, terraced park with ponds, grottos, gazebos, and statues stretched down to the Iauza River. For L'vov, the most critical component of the urban estates he designed were their gardens and parks, and the life's blood of these landscaped zones was water. His gardens and parks sloped down toward rivers, extended along rivers, and were fed by rivers and other bodies of waters, creating an ecological space enabling humans, animals, and plants to thrive within the world of the estate.

In the late eighteenth and early nineteenth century, the philosophical meaning attributed to water in the world of these estates also found expression in poetry. The image of "flowing waters" became a leitmotif of the particular genre of descriptive poetry devoted to the estate. The conventions of this genre reflect specific geographic realities: estates are located on the slope of a hill not far from a river, with the manor house sitting on an elevated spot near a spring. These descriptions appear, as a rule, to be realistic and topographically precise, to the point that they can even be used to reconstruct the layout of estates that have not survived. Such is the case, for example, of a description of Obukhovka, the ancestral estate of Vasilii Kapnist,[16] in a poem named for it:

> By mountain shielded from the north,
> Atop a fertile hill it [the house] stands
> And looks on glades and meadowlands;
> The Psel before it snake-like winds,
> As, burbling, toward the mill it rushes.
> (Kapnist 402)

Kapnist describes a real-world estate, but the manner in which he does this (intentionally or not – that does not concern us now) is based on the logic of myth. The poet's home is the functional center of a world, its pivot, a central point projecting outward to the four corners of the world: to the north stands a mountain, to the south, a glade and distant meadow, and in front of the house, from east to west, flows the Psel. This narrative of the gentry estate is reminiscent of the treatment of paradise in mythology – a universal center of the world.

In Aleksandr Bakunin's poem "Osuga" (1820–1830s), which was built around an aquatic mythology, we see an analogous approach to describing his ancestral estate, Priamukhino. As mentioned above, Bakunin uses the river on which the estate sat as the title of his poem, rather than the name of the estate itself, and addresses the river in a rapturous salutation that manifests a *naturphilosophical* cult of water and springs typical of Bakunin's poetry:

> Salute of love, to you Osuga,
> The gem of Priamukhino's fields,
> Unfailing friend who fed my children,
> Who nourished them upon her breast.
> (Bakunin 69)

For Bakunin, the land through which the Osuga flows is rich in traditions, legends, and fairy tales that also center on water:

> In bygone days, known far and wide,
> A source of waters, dead and living,
> Could bring back health to him who died,
> So potent was its wonder-working,
> When, flying to earth's farthest corner,
> On Firebird's feather for these trips,
> Lel' gave the dead men living water
> From a sweet soul-maiden's lips.
> (Bakunin 69)

Many of these originate in Slavic demonology: tales of a dismal swamp, the domain of devils who drag livestock and people away by the legs and where chthonic fires burn that are transformed into reptiles at the sign of the cross (such stories are part of the *bylichki* tradition, a genre of oral tale about encounters with demonic beings). There are also stories of a historical (or pseudohistorical) nature: about the Mogil'ovka monastery on the Tsna River founded on the site where the bodies of Lithuanian troops were piled (its name derives from the Russian word for grave) and two bubbling medicinal springs. Out of "the marital union of these two springs" (Bakunin 69) was born the Osuga – the part real, part fairy-tale river, sister to the mythic rivers of florescence, fertility, and abundance.

At the dawn of its formation, the culture of the Russian gentry consciously described the role of water in the dynamic and developing cultural and practical whole of the estate. Placing the water element's artistic and aesthetic functions on a par with its practical ones, Nikolai L'vov and Aleksandr Bakunin, two original theoreticians of the Russian gentry estate who put their theories into practice, while undoubtedly aware of the inevitable anthropocentrism of their landscape architecture, firmly believed in the effectiveness of the *naturphilosophical* approach. This approach was reflected not only in the design of estates, but in a neomythology of estate life that found artistic expression in estate poetry, painting, and theater. This neo-mythology and the works of art dedicated to the world of the Russian gentry estate that helped to spawn it demand closer investigation.

Notes

1 This publication is part of a scholarly project devoted to the waterways of the Upper Volga Basin in Russian culture ("Verkhnevolzhskie vodnye puti v russkoi kul'ture"), Project No. 14-14-69002, with grants from the Russian Foundation for the Humanities and the Government of Tver' Oblast.
2 Here, "manor house" is used to translate *pomest'e*. We fully appreciate the original differences between the terms *usad'ba* (translated here as "estate"), *pomest'e*, *votchina*, and *imenie* (see Miliugina and Stroganov, *Tekst prostranstva* 200–201, 339–347). For the purposes of this chapter, however, we use these terms interchangeably, as by the second half of the eighteenth century they were being used synonymously.
3 Aleksandr Mikhailovich Bakunin (October 17, 1768–December 6, 1854), was a natural philosopher, poet, social commentator, and the father of Mikhail Bakunin, one of the ideologues of the *narodnik* movement. The owner and architect of Priamukhino, his family's ancestral estate in the Novyi Torg District of Tver' Province (in the 1790s, now Kuvshinovo District in Tver' Oblast; the estate is 28 kilometers from the town of Kuvshinovo) that sat on the banks of the Osuga River. Guests spending time at his estate included Ivan Turgenev, Vissarion Belinsky, Nikolai Stankevich, and Timofei Granovsky, among other prominent cultural figures.
4 Nikolai Aleksandrovich L'vov (May 4, 1753–December 22, 1803) was one of the most fascinating and versatile figures of the Russian Enlightenment: Palladian architect, poet, translator, folklorist, playwright, graphic artist, and musician. He was the owner and architect of his ancestral estate, Nikol'skoe-Cherenchitsy in the Novyi Torg District of Tver' Province (in the 1780s through the early 1800s, now Torzhok District of Tver' Oblast, the estate is 18 kilometers west of the town of Torzhok), not far from the Talozhenka River. Guests spending time at his estate included Gavriil Derzhavin, Vasilii Kapnist, Ivan Khemnicer, Dmitrii Levitskii, Vladimir Borovikovskii, Mihail Vorobiev, among other prominent cultural figures.
5 A general and field marshal known by the honorific title "Most Serene Prince," Grigorii Aleksandrovich Potemkin-Tavricheskii (September 13, 1739–October 5, 1791) was a prominent figure during the reign of Catherine II who oversaw the incorporation of "Novorossiia" (a historical term used to denote the area north of the Black Sea – primarily, present-day Ukraine) into the Russian Empire and its initial development.
6 All water engineering at Nikol'skoe-Cherenchitsy has been destroyed. For a description, see Budylina *et al.* (53–55). This description is based on accounts from long-time residents and a manuscript stored in the Russian State Archive of Literature and Art: Koplan (RGALI, f. 244, ed. khr. 1).
7 Petr Lukich Vel'iaminov (died February 28, 1805) was a translator, writer, collector, and honorary member of the Imperial Academy of Arts, as well as an expert in and performer of Russian folk songs. A member of the L'vov-Derzhavin circle, he was close with Gavriil Derzhavin and Nikolai L'vov and was a long-time resident of the Nikol'skoe-Cherenchitsy estate.
8 The aggregate blend L'vov chose for his building material (4 percent 3–7 millimeter gravel; 58 percent sand; 20 percent fine soil; 18 percent clay) yielded a substance that was naturally moist and hardened to be as sturdy as reinforced concrete. It was spread into a sturdy sheathing in layers of 12–15 centimeters, tamped down, and covered with a 6-millimeter layer of lime mortar, onto which the next layer was added.

9 Aleksei Nikolaevich Grech (real name Zaleman; 1899–1938), a scholar of the Russian gentry estate of the nineteenth and early twentieth century. Author of the book *Venok usad'bam* (1932, first published in 1994), written from memory while Grech was imprisoned at the Solovki prison camp.
10 Prince Petr Vasil'evich Lopukhin (1753–April 6, 1827) was a prominent Russian government official and owner of an estate in what was then Moscow Province's Vvedenskoe-Zvenigorod District (now Moscow Oblast's Odintsovskii District, the estate is three kilometers southeast of Zvenigorod and a half kilometer from the Zvenigorod train station).
11 The Mitino and Vasilevo estate complex in Tver' Province's Novyi Torg District (in the 1790s; now Tver' Oblast's Torzhok District; the complex is five kilometers from the town of Torzhok) sits along the Tvertsa River; it was owned by Novyi Torg landowners Mariia Fedorovna (née Tyrtova; 1752–1822) and Dmitrii Ivanovich L'vov (1726–1782). See Miliugina, *Obgoniaiushchii vremia* (334–340), and Miliugina and Stroganov, *Genii vkusa* (60).
12 A *raek*, or "little paradise," was a device used for entertainment that features a panorama made up of moving pictures inside a box into which viewers looked through a magnifying glass, a common form of entertainment at fairs in Russia in the eighteenth and nineteenth centuries.
13 The Znamenskoe-Raek estate in Tver' Province's Novyi Torg District (in the 1790s; now Tver' Oblast's Tozhok District; the estate is 20 kilometers from the town of Torzhok) sits on the right bank of the Logovezh River, a left tributary of the Tvertsa. It was owned by Fedor Ivanovich Glebov-Streshnev (December 31, 1734–November 29, 1799), a general-in-chief and a senator. See Miliugina, *Obgoniaiushchii vremia* (334–340) and Miliugina and Stroganov, *Genii vkusa* (60).
14 A count who was later given the title "most serene prince," Aleksandr Andreevich Bezborodko (March 17, 1749–April 6, 1799) was a Russian statesman, the head of the postal service, and a chancellor of the Russian Empire. He owned an estate on Vorontsovo Field in Moscow on the banks of the Iauza River (designed 1797, Giacomo Quarenghi and Nikolai L'vov architects).
15 Count Aleksei Kirillovich Razumovskii (September 12, 1748–April 5, 1822) was a prominent government official, senator, and minister of education. The Gorokhovo Field estate was on the banks of the Iauza River. L'vov worked on the estate during 1800–1803. It was rebuilt later in the nineteenth century.
16 Vasilii Vasil'evich Kapnist (February 12, 1758–October 28, 1823) was a poet, playwright, and public figure and the owner of the Obukhovka estate in Poltava Province's Mirgorod District (now the village of Velikaia Obukhovka in Poltava Oblast's Mirgorod District in Ukraine) on the right bank of the Psel River.

Bibliography

Bakunin, A.M. *Sobranie stikhotvorenii*. Ed. M.V. Stroganov. Tver': Zolotaia bukva, 2001. Print.

Budylina, M.V., O.I. Braitseva, and A.M. Kharlamova. *Arkhitektor N.A. L'vov*. Moscow: Gosstroiizdat, 1961. Print.

Dmitrieva, E.E., and O.N. Kuptsova. *Zhizn' usadebnogo mifa: utrachennyi i obretennyi rai*. Moscow: OGI, 2003. Print.

Evangulova, O.S. *Khudozhestvennaia «Vselennaia» russkoi usad'by*. Moscow: Progress-Tradiciia, 2003. Print.

Glumov, A.N. *N.A. L'vov*. Moscow: Iskusstvo, 1980. Print.

Glushkov, I.F. "Ruchnoi dorozhnik" 1801, in *Tver' v zapiskakh puteshestvennikov XVI – XIX vekov*. Ed. E.G. Miliugina and M.V. Stroganov. Tver': Knizhnyi klub, 2012, 145–170. Print.

Grech, A.N. *Venok usad'bam*. Moscow: AST-Press, 2006. Print.

Grimm, G.G. "Proekt parka Bezborodko v Moskve: materialy k izucheniiu tvorchestva N. A. L'vova." *Soobshcheniia Instituta istorii iskusstv AN SSSR*, vol. 4–5. Moscow: Nauka, 1954, 107–135. Print.

Kapnist, V.V. "Obukhovka." *Russkaia poeziia XVIII veka*. Ed. G.P. Makogonenko. Moscow: Khudozhestvennaia literatura, 1972, 401–405. Print.

Kharlamova, A.M., and A.L. Udal'tsova. "Prutenskoi ansambl' na reke Tvertse." *Arkhitekturnoe nasledstvo*, vol. 35. Moscow: Stroiizdat, 1988, 14–18. Print.

Koplan, B.I. "Dni i gody zhizni i tvorchestva N. A. L'vova." RGALI, f. 244, ed. khr. 1. Manuscript.

Likhachev, D.S. *Poeziia sadov. K semantike sadovo-parkovykh stilei. Sad kak tekst*. Moscow: Soglasie, 1998. Print.

L'vov, N.A. *Izbrannye sochineniia*. Ed. K. Lappo-Danilevskii. Cologne, Weimar, Vienna, St. Petersburg: Pushkinskii Dom, RHGI, Akropol', 1994. Print.

Miliugina, E.G. "Kontseptsiia dvorianskoi usad'by v tvorchestve N.A. L'vova." *Rossiia i mir: vchera, segodnia, zavtra: mezhkul'turnaia kommunikatsiia v usloviiakh globalizatsii sovremennogo mira*. Moscow: MGI imeni E.R. Dashkovoi, 2009, 140–146. Print.

Miliugina, E.G. *Obgoniaiushchii vremia: Nikolai Aleksandrovich L'vov – poet, arkhitektor, iskusstvoved, istorik Moskvy*. Moscow: Russkii impul's, 2009. Print.

Miliugina, E.G. *Russkaia reka*. Moscow: Belyi gorod, 2012. Print.

Miliugina, E.G., and M.V. Stroganov. *Genii vkusa: N.A. L'vov. Itogi i problemy izucheniia*. Tver': Tverskoi gosudarstvennyi universitet, 2008. Print.

Miliugina, E.G., and M.V. Stroganov. *Tekst prostranstva: materialy k slovariu*. Tver': SFK-ofis, 2014. Print.

Nikitina, A.B. *Arkhitekturnoe nasledie N. A. L'vova*. St. Petersburg: Dmitrii Bulanin, 2006. Print.

Rossi F. *Palladio in Russia. Nikolaj L'vov architetto e intellettuale russo al tramonto dei Lumi*. Venice: Marsilio, 2010. Print.

Arkhiv kniazia Vorontsova. Ed. P.I. Bartenev, vol. 13. Moscow: A.I. Mamontov, 1879.

9 Celebrating the return of the flood

Polina Barskova

The city of Saint Petersburg is one of the most ambitious and, at the same time, most problematic designs of a single human mind: Peter the Great conceived of a city that would become his capital and the symbol of his re-conceptualized state, renewed and oriented towards the West. Spurred on by this ambition, Peter chose for the city a locale unfortunate both in its position in relation to the rest of the country and in its geo-climatic features. As if the brutal climate that allegedly inspired the most poignant pages of the great Russian literature to follow were not enough, the city was constantly inundated by the waters of the Gulf of Finland. The image and history of Saint Petersburg are inalienable from the waters that embrace it and run through it.

The history of the Saint Petersburg floods goes as far back as the history of the city itself: Pyotr Karatygin in his history of the city floods writes: "From the very first year when Petersburg was founded, the Neva poured onto the city that Peter was building as if challenging him to fight the likes of it" (6).

The first flood during the city's history had already occurred on August 20, 1703, and floods on various scales became a regular recurrence and an intrinsic part of the city's life cycle. The most destructive and most culturally significant of them happened on November 7, 1824, and caused hundreds of victims. The flood of 1824 engendered multiple descriptions by such literary notables as Polish poet Adam Mickiewicz and Russian playwright Aleksandr Griboedov, the most important of them being the poetic text by Alexander Pushkin, "The Bronze Horseman" of 1833, that forever coined the flood of 1824 as not only a natural – but, crucially, a political disaster.[1]

Pushkin's "Petersburg tale" (the new genre to which he assigned his poem) was banned from publication during the poet's tragically short life. His imperial censor, Tsar Nicholas I in person, refused to countenance it, and for an obvious reason: "The Bronze Horseman" presents the city of Petersburg as a whim inflicted on his subjects by the state sovereign, the site of a conflict between nature and politics while the flood becomes the trigger and expression of this conflict.

"The Bronze Horseman" describes the most severe flood to date in Saint Petersburg, on November 19, 1824. In this flood, caused by a storm, water reached 13.5 feet over the usual level. On that day, around 600 people were killed and 462 buildings were destroyed. Previous poems regarding Saint Petersburg tended to praise Peter the Great for its creation and glorify the city's architectural design and layout. Pushkin's poem is the first one to deviate from this tendency: it represents the city as a site of conflict between the imperialist, rational design and the elemental, almost mystical, force of nature.

As the story itself unfolds, Pushkin introduces the hero of the poem, Evgeny, a poor and hard working clerk, who loses his beloved, Parasha, in the muddy waters of the flood. Evgeny goes mad with grief and imagines his conflict with the creator of the perilous city, now existing in the form of the Bronze Horseman monument. The Bronze Horseman, a magnificent sculpture in the center of Petersburg, was created by the French sculptor Étienne Maurice Falconet in 1782: it shows Peter the I on the back of a fierce stallion looking at the Neva River embodying the power of the Russian Empire.

This work by Pushkin was the first masterpiece in what became a voluminous literature on the floods – and a genre-defining one; since his time, writing on the floods of Petersburg has evolved as a nature-cum-urban description with political undertones.

The present study gives an account of the literary reception and expression of one of the most overwrought and controversial natural disasters of the Soviet century – the Leningrad flood in the fall of 1924. Following the remark by political scientist Austin Sarat, "catastrophic events seem to have a revelatory quality" (Sarat and Lezaun 1), I offer my research question: what did the flood of 1924 reveal about the life of the city – both cultural and political?

The year 1924 became a macabre *annus mirabilis* for the city on the Neva banks though most of its "miraculous" transformations were of a disturbing sort. January of that year saw the death of Vladimir Lenin, chief organizer and ideologist of the Bolshevik political revolt that in the late fall of 1917 flooded the streets of the then capital with armed protesters.

Lenin's death occurred at a time when Bolshevik Russia was still in the process of overcoming anxieties surrounding Lenin's last big idea – the New Economic Policy (NEP) that saved a state struggling with the economic ruin left by Civil War (1919–1921). NEP, involving a synthesis of Communist ideology with the return of private property and free trade, was enabled by Lenin's authority; the fatal disappearance of the Party leader resulted in the overwhelming atmosphere of uncertainty that covered Russia in 1924. The flood of that year was "read" in this context as a sign of/from the future – but a very difficult one to decipher.

The rhetorical aftermath of Lenin's death became a defining context for two events that dramatically reshaped and sharpened Petersburg's relationship with its traditional self-identification: the change of the city's name to

Leningrad (by resolution of the Second Congress of Soviets, January 26, 1924), and the recurrence of an emblematic Petersburg disaster – the flood. These events laid bare the opposition of the two main vectors that perception of the Petersburg history took in the twentieth century: that of continuous, enduring tradition, and that of change and rupture. This dichotomy can be seen as a frame for all subsequent reactions: how, in other words, does the flood of 1924 correlate to its celebrated predecessor of 1824, and to what extent can its cultural reception be perceived as a symptom of post-revolutionary urban change? Connecting the renaming and the flood, "traditionalists" interpreted the latter as apocalyptic retribution for the city's break with historical continuity and meaning; paradoxically, in this reading, the city paid for its innovations with the most recurrent or "traditional" of all Petersburg punishments – the flood.

On September 23, 1924, a hurricane caused the waters of the Neva to rise four meters above the usual level, thus marking this one as the most severe Leningrad flood of the twentieth century. The flood began during the daytime and, with overwhelming speed, waters of the Gulf of Finland reached the city by night. More than half of the city's territory soon went under water: Petrogradsky, Vyborgsky, Vasileostrovsky, and Central city regions were cut off from the rest of the city for several days. Curiously, the flood was accompanied by *aurora borealis*, a rare phenomenon at this latitude – and this striking combination of the rare and spectacular natural phenomena only added to their perception as rather supernatural and even mystical, manifesting ominous signs. The flood took the lives of at least 14 people; 160 were wounded, and 6,000 urban structures were destroyed. One of the main blows in terms of the urban infrastructure was the flood's impact on the transportation system of the city – most of the streetcars and streetcar lines in the center were demolished. The flood also severely hurt parks and gardens of the city – hundreds of the old trees in the Summer Garden, created during Peter the I's reign, were uprooted and washed away. Several newspapers also reported that in the famous Leningrad Zoo, 88 animals drowned.[2]

The artist Valentin Kurdov, then a young and inquisitive newcomer to the city, vividly describes the flood in his memoirs:

> The flood did not start the way we had expected. The Neva had still not overflowed its banks when the water forced off the cast-iron lids of the water-line manholes and poured into the street. Amid the howling wind, from the basement of the Greek bakery came the heart-rending squeal of a piglet, which probably drowned.
>
> (21–22)

In the corpus of texts induced by this flood, Kurdov's reaction is rare for its eye for specific detail; in spite of the dramatic material impact, the flood of 1924 was viewed first and foremost not as a natural but rather historical, political, and cultural disaster, its pragmatic details and sober descriptions were often overshadowed by wild speculations. Articles in the press of the day with titles like "Deluge" ["Potop" – quotation marks in original – PB] or "Flood Literature" ["Literatura navodneniia"] made clear that this flood was part of a long textual tradition, and as such should be interpreted according to the rules of discursive analysis: what we're dealing with here is a discursive rather than just a natural disaster. The main task of this exploration is to demonstrate to what a profound extent natural phenomenon can be embedded culturally, what kind of intense connections can arise between a flood and the local culture's drive to interpret it, to make it a part of the discourse creating the historical momentum.

I. The new and the old: politics of the flood

Various authors (journalists, writers, scholars) offered their responses to the question of the meaning, and, moreover, the task of the flood. Pro- and anti-Bolshevik interpreters of the disaster had one point in common: the flood could not be more timely. Epitomizing the mythology of the centennial return of the Pushkinian "Golden Age" (the period of Russian literature of the second quarter of the nineteenth century considered its pinnacle due to the work of Pushkin and his literary circle), a powerful discourse in the first decades of the twentieth century, the flood of 1924 signified in this reading a connection to its catastrophic predecessor of 1824, which had served as the matrix for Pushkin's Petersburg text *The Bronze Horseman*.

This sensation of a centennial cycle come round was immediately picked up by the city *literati* of the day – hence Veniamin Kaverin's remark that "the Neva was celebrating the centennial of its struggle with Petersburg" (554) and Mikhail Zenkevich's that the year of the flood, "24, / Had once more come round as a hundred-year anniversary" (411–413).

It also resonated in the daily press. Based on pieces published in *Krasnaia gazeta* (*The Red Newspaper*), a reader could fully appreciate the construction of the historical "correspondence" of the two floods. *Krasnaia gazeta*, the most popular Leningrad publication of the 1920s, fully reflected the rich and self-contradictory ideological atmosphere of its time, publishing "politically correct" materials, in full accordance with the new Soviet discourse, side by side with more sensationalist texts aimed at satisfying more lowbrow readers. For that reason, *Krasnaia gazeta* serves as a very rich and curious source of utterances about the flood – belonging to different sides, registers, and genres.

Numerous articles rehearsed the topic of the centennial return of the disaster, describing various details of the flood of 1824 (e.g. the actions of the police, reactions of celebrated writer-observers like Pushkin, Griboedov, and Mickiewicz) and forming a sort of "call and response" between the two events: one journalist described a crowd anxiously observing the previous

Figure 9.1. Leningraders examine the memorial plaque of the 1824 flood during the flood of 1924. Archive of Film and Photo documents, TsGAFD, Petersburg, Russia.

high water mark (November 7, 1824), anticipating that the new flood would break its fierce predecessor's record ("Istoricheskaia doska" 1).

The November 7, 1924 issues of numerous periodicals saw the publication of pieces dedicated to "celebrating" the centennial of "Petersburg's most horrific flood" – thus amalgamating the two events in a common text. An article published in *Krasnaia gazeta*, "A Historical Plaque", attested to citizens' interest in the "dialogue" of the two floods:

> On the corner of Vasil'evskii Island's Pervaia liniia and Bol'shoi Prospect, a historical inscription has been carved into the wall of a building: the height of the water in the flood of 7 November 1824 was fourteen feet. The difference between the modern height, which reached thirteen feet on Vasil'evskii Island, is thus one foot. The height is marked on the building with a red line. A great number of curious onlookers crowd around the historical plaque.

Contemplating the flood from the Finnish shore, the émigré poet Vadim Gardner writes:

> I can imagine
> The proud Neva rebelling,
> As it did a hundred years ago in Alexander's time,
> Joining the islands to the sea;
> But, as of old, surrounded by water,
> All covered in spray,
> The bronze rider on his swift horse,
> Already green with time,
> Makes his oration to the wave:
> Rage, you beautiful tsaritsa,
> Neva overcome with wrath.
> Punish my crazy descendants!
> In your vengeance, you are justified!
> They have desecrated Peter's child,
> The wondrous city has been renamed Leningrad...
> 							(199)

Thus, in Gardner's vision, the centennial flood comes to chastise the city's renamers. This interpretation is a peculiar variation of a crucial, apocalyptic component of Petersburg literary mythology – that is, the notion that the city will eventually be made desolate as payment for its unholy ways and origins. The curious twist here, though, is that for Gardner, the flood comes to punish the city for the profanation of its design, whereas, according to earlier interpretations, it was this design itself, read as Peter's satanic heaven-daring, that would call forth punishment.

This interpretation of the flood as retribution for political developments was not only a cerebral, "remote" construction of an émigré outsider; it had adherents in the city as well. The flood was immediately and even enthusiastically read as the long-awaited eschatological deluge by ideologically passeistic citizens, a tendency promptly noted in the press:

> [A]ssistance was provided to a panicked crowd of hysterical women [klikush] gathered on a colonnade of St. Isaak's cathedral. These women were hysterically screaming that it was the end of the world, the great deluge, and some of them were jumping from the colonnade into the raging waves and dashing themselves on slabs of pavement and the cathedral's foundation. There were a lot of victims here, but Pioneers and Komsomol'tsy saved 150 women and children.
> 				("Spasenie na vodakh" 2)

An article by E. Laganskii shows how apocalyptic discourse of the 1924 flood operated. The title, "Deluge," is highly evocative – why "deluge" and not just flood? And why the quotation marks? Who is speaking here? It seems that the journalist serves as a ventriloquist for an opinion perhaps different from his own aspiring to express traditionalist sensibilities:

> The hurricane gathers its last ounce of strength to crash the whole weight of the massive body of the sea onto the doomed city.... Thousands of people caught unawares rush about aimlessly, in a panic, along the still-dry pavement.... The wailing of children, the cries of their mothers, the banging of hastily-closed shutters, and over this whole cacophony, the devilish, triumphant whistle of the wind.... Wherever you look, water and more water, as in the days of the great deluge. Only weakening gusts of wind and a light ripple on the vast expanse of the waters.
>
> (4)

Another characteristic feature of Laganskii's interpretation of the flood is that the disaster stands first and foremost as a spectacle, a performative artifact framed by the expectations of experienced readers of urban aesthetics – those "historically educated in flood practice": "Leningrad came out by the thousands to watch the raging of the obdurate river, the fast coursing of its foamy waves; to see the barges and scows break the fetters that had constrained them and, carefree, dance their dying dance" (Zenkevich 412). This dimension of the flood's perceived performativity is confirmed in the text "The Flood in Leningrad" by one of the "lesser" acmeists, Mikhail Zenkevich:

> In the theaters, the orchestra seats, the foyer, the dress circle,
> Dragging a cold shower of dress trains up the stairs,
> They seated themselves in chairs and even
> In theater boxes of red velvet and plush.
> They make a great racket: we paid full price;
> All the theaters are given over to a single show.
> With lightning as our spotlight, we shall let onto stage
> Ballerinas woven of foam.

The notion of the staged rehearsal or replay of a historical event that acquires the character of spectacle was nourished in early 1920s Petrograd by the popular series of festivals realized by such masters of stage design as Iu. Annenkov, S. Radlov, V. Khodasevich, and others. After the Bolshevik Revolution Petrograd saw a renaissance of a peculiar theatrical genre – a political festival when in the streets and squares of the city important historical events would be re-enacted – such as "Overthrow of the Autocracy," "Third International," "Popular movements in Russia," etc.[3] Interpreters of the 1924 flood depicted the event in this context, as a political act, staged on the historical stage with an ideological agenda that cried out to be identified with the utmost precision. The various observers among the flood's "audience" sensed the need to take ownership or authorship of this spectacle, hence Zenkevich's "we shall let onto the stage."

The last phrase of Laganskii's essay – "The island froze in fatal sorrow..." – has strong eschatological undertones, and the ellipsis seems to mark the inescapable submerging of Vasil'evskii Island. The day after Laganskii's piece appeared saw the publication in *Krasnaia gazeta* of an article by B. Andreev, "Flood Literature," which slyly but vigorously overwrote Laganskii's prophecy of doom. Granting that "the Petersburg flood has its own literature," Andreev goes on to undercut this "unfortunate" literary lineage; he outlines the "flood component" of the Petersburg text with references to N. Pomialovskii ("Rainy Night"), Ia. Polonskii ("There is a house on the Moika"), M. Dmitriev ("The Underwater City"), and V. Pecherin (Death's Triumph), concluding with the recent flood prophecies of Dmitrii Merezhkovskii, Zinaida Gippius, and Fedor Sologub, whom the author rather controversially connects to the watery element of Petersburg. (Andreev even hints at the suicide of Sologub's wife Anastasiia Chebotarevskaia in the waters of Petersburg, and ventures the guess that the same fate might await Merezhkovskii in Switzerland [! – PB].) Andreev appraises this literary flood tradition dismissively:

> Here there is everything the modern Russian emigration could say about a flood and could wish from it: the city of Lenin is a cursed city, an antichrist, the enemy of God; through this flood, heaven is punishing the godless Bolsheviks; and sooner or later the city will sink into the abyss. The poet-epigones of bourgeois literature persist even now in their faith in the omnipotence of the elements, which they go right on admiring.
>
> (5)

Andreev's contemptuous definition of the adherents of the apocalyptic tradition as "epigones" is furthered by his declaration that this lineage is degenerative, and should be supplanted by a new urban poetics:

> But the gloomy prophecies pass the new proletarian literature by, and the city is already not the same: it is a new city, come to take the place of the dying, neurasthenic old Petersburg; a city that will defend itself with levees against the flood, that will sing a new song of life, vigorous and joyous. This is why the flood will bring not a minute of confusion and fear, and why the theme of this literary day is: "Long live life!"
>
> (5)

These essays, published one after another in *Krasnaia gazeta*, reflect the primary rift in flood interpretations, the conflict between "traditionalist" readers contemplating an apocalyptic recurrence and "new" readers who see 1924 as finally marking a break (note Andreev's literal-metaphorical reference to the levee or floodwall with this century-long tradition). To put an end to this tradition, however, it was not enough merely to declare it obsolete: the creators of the new flood discourse proceeded to overwrite the old one, using the former prototype to express new ideas, topics, and rhetorical devices, and thus to attempt, through rhetorical replacement, to control ambient anxiety regarding the recurrent visitations of the past.

At the time, literary scholar and critic Viktor Shklovskii, as usual extremely sensitive to the ideological demands of his day, remarked: "In general, portraits are making their way through our streets. We await the arrival at some committee meeting of a local literary celebrity – the Bronze Horseman" (132). It is understandable that the Bronze Horseman, the cultural alter ego of the historical Peter the Great, should be cast as the central "protagonist" of the flood of 1924, which disaster rudely proceeded to disturb the monumentalized remains of the "real" tsar. *Krasnaia gazeta* highlights the catastrophic reunion of tsar and flood, referencing a particular modest historical site – Peter's cabin, where the charismatic ruler lived and which was memorialized as a unique reliquary of his life and work: "In Peter's cabin, too, there is chaos. Among the things of Peter I to be carried off by the waves were his slippers." This time, instead of being in control of the mighty elements, the tsar as personified by his slippers becomes the passive victim of their vengeance. Similarly, the above-mentioned poem by Zenkevich effects a shift of power, from the Bronze Horseman to Evgenii:

> Long ago deafened in the cast-iron din,
> Now fearless amid the banging and howling,
> The madman shouts gloatingly at the giant:
> "This is Lenin's city, not yours!"
> (112)

Arguably the first "little man" of Petersburg literary lineage, Evgenii finally gets his revenge on Peter's willful urbanism when the city is symbolically repossessed, given a new identity in its renaming.

We find another – and peculiar – strategy of the "new" flood writing's program of supplanting *The Bronze Horseman* in a poem by the proletarian poet Vasilii Kniazev. Though this piece is entitled "On the Verge of an Unprecedented Disaster," its rhythmic, strophic, and lexical choices show it to be, in fact, a text about an already-experienced and culturally mediated, rather than "unprecedented," disaster, a text that literally copies Pushkin's celebrated poem, producing a curious palimpsest:

> Our proletarian folk of iron,
> Full of iron tenacity,
> Formed druzhinas of rowers,
> And into the flooded lowlands
> Stubbornly sent skiff after skiff.
> ("Pered nevidannoi bedoiu" 2)

Overwriting Pushkin's text about the conflict between the state and individual, and/or about the civilizing will of humanity versus the elements,

Kniazev offers his reading of the flood as a political struggle between "old" and "new" interpretations of the disaster. On the very next day, this prolific poet-journalist produced his next "flood poem," "Children of October":

> Tradition was shouting about Judgment Day,
> Its perturbed soul submerged in darkness,
> But ardently, in heroic exertion,
> Worked the young of the proletariat.
> ("Deti Oktiabria" 2)

Incarnated by a fittingly obsolete vocabulary choice, "Tradition" is rendered in the line by the obsolete "star'" and then opposed to "youngsters of steel." This juxtaposition was extremely apt: in 1922, the Young Pioneers organization was founded, emblematizing, according to Catriona Kelly, the "tabula rasa" to be inscribed by the new Bolshevik state as its most ideologically pure embodiment. Who better suited than Young Pioneers to face down a natural phenomenon associated with the perilous return of The Past? For Kniazev, the youngsters of steel become the most prominent agents of opposition to the unruly elements of the bygone era. In 1925, a year after the flood, he composed a bizarre text, "A Frightening Dream," peculiar both in the overtness of its "borrowing" and the grotesque political application of the material borrowed. This poem narrates a nightmare ("My little son had a dream....") in which the animals from the Leningrad Zoo escape to wreak havoc among the city's population, especially the population of... monuments:

> The folks turn pale, the folks tremble,
> A tiger is running down Troitskaia Street...
> Ai-ai-ai! Oi-oi-oi! It's not a cardboard tiger – it's alive!
> Run home, people!
> On the Anichkov Bridge
> The horses stand frozen at their post,
> But, seeing the tiger, in a flash
> They jump to Oktiabr'skii Prospect!...
> Along the Moika gallop the horses.
> Running away from the chase,
> The silly tsar took fright
> And clambers up a lamppost....
> Here's the end of the story,
> Leaving the Astoria,
> Heading for the square,
> A Young Pioneer.
> The Pioneer does not despair:
> He takes out
> A pistol,
> Stuffs the cork into the muzzle,

>Hums,
>Having no fear!
>Pow, pow, ta-ra-ra –
>Down tumbles the tiger in mid-run!
>Bang, bang – right in the forehead!
>Stop, bronze horses! ...
>A fireman pulled the hapless tsar
>Down from the lamp post
>And neatly seated him back on his horse.
>   ("Strashnyi son" 65)

At first glance, Kniazev's nightmare poem seems primarily an act of shameless literary thievery, a copy of Kornei Chukovskii's famous "The Crocodile" (1901–1917), about the youngster Vania Vasil'chikov who fights off the eponymous crocodile in Petrograd. Kniazev knew perfectly well both this source text and its author; he and Chukovskii were colleagues at *Krasnaia gazeta* in the 1920s, with Kniazev, with his graphomania, alcoholism, and idiosyncratic political agendas figuring prominently in Chukovskii's journals of this period. It would be wrong, however, to dismiss "A Frightening Dream" only as a feeble copy of Chukovskii's masterpiece; it also stands as an important piece of historical evidence. From the standpoint of 1925, Kniazev's poem, unlike that of Chukovskii, narrates not imaginary, but quite real phenomena – the panic engendered by the flood, displaced zoo animals and monuments, and Young Pioneers on guard. In depicting monuments come to life, frightened by tigers and other animals themselves frightened in turn by the flood, Kniazev creates a double remake – both of "The Crocodile" and, again, of Pushkin's *The Bronze Horseman*.

Curiously, the flood itself is never mentioned in the poem; it seems suppressed, replaced and symbolized both by its psychological and pragmatic consequences – nightmares and urban chaos, respectively. From Pushkin's text, Kniazev lifts the imagery of historical monuments coming to life and interacting with the city's inhabitants. Kniazev's political message is not ambivalent: tsars, tsarinas, and their generals of bronze and marble are disciplined by representatives of the new Soviet state, a militiaman and a Pioneer who is uniquely immune to fear ("He hums, having no fear!"). The trauma of the flood-related chaos and its psychic aftermath of nightmares are civilized, dealt with by the new order.

Politicizing the disaster becomes a commonplace of flood discourse. Even the atmosphere of the city during the flood is experienced by observers as a *sui generis* repetition of recent revolutionary events: "Yesterday was the flood; it was like revolution: lines at kerosene and bread shops; streetcars overflowing with unpaid passengers; desperate, cheerful, as if drunk, mobs; and talk of different parts of the city" (Chukovskii 287). "The lines for bread and kerosene, the fussing of people having suddenly changed their accustomed notions – these called to mind the February Revolution" (Kaverin

554). Both Chukovskii and Kaverin here alertly render the restless atmosphere in a city undergoing catastrophic change, influencing urban routines, routes, and notions, with mnemonic reference to the political unrest of 1917–1918. But for many witnesses, equating the flood metaphorically with revolution was not enough; it was more urgent to ask: whose side was the flood of 1924 on? Was it a "red"/ "new" flood, or a "white"/"old" one? A "Komsomol" flood, or a "NEP, bourgeois" one? Once again, opinion was divided. The brochure *Leningrad's Fight against Flooding*, published by the Leningrad Gubispolkom in 1925, declares outright that "the flood is the legacy of tsarist power." Alongside such a verdict was the casting of the flood as an attempt at counterrevolution in the Zenkevich poem quoted above:

> Lines of white ones [*beliaki*, i.e. White Guards, and the white foam of the waves – PB]
> Move forward in assault
> Onto your Field of Mars, Revolution,
> Attacking the tribunes of tombs,
> Their black mobs keep pouring and pouring,
> Hailing the night of their own October.

And yet for Laganskii, the horrific "Deluge" is rather of Marxist convictions: "A new rainsqual socialized and depersonalized private property, turning it into primordial chaos." The flood, then, conveniently takes on the allegorical investment, and marks the political convictions, of its interpreter.

II. Desire and anxiety of the flood

The political ambivalence of the flood that was discussed above, so symptomatic of the epoch, is expressed with particular poignancy in that category of interpretations wherein the disaster is cast in erotic tones, as in the remarks of Kaverin and Kurdov on new opportunities exposed by the flooded city: "Women were taking off their shoes and boots and walking with their skirts hiked up" (Kaverin 554). "Two pretty young ladies were put into my boat; they seemed frightened to death. The wind whipped up pictures of denuded artist's models" (Kurdov 222). Anxiety regarding the recurrence of politically suspect yet unnervingly exciting phenomena endows the discourse with erotic undertones, which can extend to darker implications of sexual violence. The importunate natural phenomenon takes on the hideous connotation of a sexual crime; as Eric Naiman puts it: "Repetition, particularly in its sexual, physiological, and reproductive hypostasis, was a repugnant and politically urgent symbol of Soviet man's recent lapse from communism into pseudocapitalism" (161). The flood, bursting upon the city as if a vengeance of the past, gave new expression to anxieties regarding historical repetition, at once abhorred and desired.

Figure 9.2. Preservation of the monuments in the Summer Garden after the flood of 1924. Archive of Film and Photo documents, TsGAFD, Petersburg, Russia.

Zenkevich, and the proletarian poet N. Semenov, depict the flood in terms of rape:

> You raideress-waves, that's enough raping!
> (Zenkevich 413)

> The enraged Neva does not scare me,
> But shall my red-bodied country fear it??
> (Semyonov)[4]

Alongside this obvious allegory of nature/chaos raping (new) civilization/order, we find far more ambivalent constructions and evocations of flood erotica in the texts of Tat'iana Vechorka and Evgenii Zamiatin. Vechorka's cycle of poems *The Flood* (1925) offers a peculiarly multifaceted, even fragmented perspective, governed, among other significant factors, by the author's fluctuation at the time between symbolist and futurist poetics:

1. The Summer Garden trembles in blast.
   Buildings have collapsed. The windows are blots.
   For all those not in love with Leningrad, it's cold and unpleasant.
2. Just as a husband who has drunk himself to the point of hoppy hiccupping,
   Red-hot in his jealous abomination, sees to it that the doors swear off opening,
   And creeps to drag his wife out of bed,
   So has the wind, running riot in its groggy fury …
   Picked up the Neva half-asleep from her shore, and spun her and squeezed her
   And enabled her to trust him…. The battered wife
   Is not silent; she must seek out the one who wronged her,
   And, her moist body, convulsing,
   Creeps to come down in a heap upon the city.

Vechorka's poem begins and ends with musings on how the flood is viewed by those who are "in love" with Leningrad, that is, who understand its traditions: executed in traditional rhythmic and strophic distributions, these fragments confirm the regularity ("rhythmically inhaling the atmosphere") of the inhabitant's attitude toward the city's emblematic disaster, which is apparently "unpleasant" only if one is not "in love" with this city, does not understand the excesses of this difficult business that recurrently brings ruination ("the remains of junk") and fragmentation ("Buildings have collapsed. The windows are blots"). To demonstrate how these aspects of urban disaster function textually, Vechorka executes the second part of her cycle according to futurist poetics, with irregular line lengths and a brutally experimental rhyme scheme. This part represents, through a convoluted metaphor, a dysfunctional ménage à trois of wind, river, and city, with desire seemingly indistinguishable from violence. As in many anthropomorphic representations of flood erotica, the gender allocation is somewhat puzzling and unstable: both male (wind, in Russian grammatically masculine) and female (river, wave – in Russian grammatically feminine) allegorized agents commit acts of sexual aggression, victimizing either the "feminine" country or "masculine" city. The motivation of this sexual aggression is also remarkably ambiguous: in Vechorka's telling, the river is punishing the city because the river has been sexually assaulted by the wind, and all this dangerous excess is, moreover, framed by the poet's consolatory rhetoric of a true (if masochistic) love that knows no "measure," especially when nurtured by the atmosphere of the "heavily-fused" Neva.

A similarly uneasy dynamics of disturbed attractions and mixed metaphorical correspondences characterizes Evgenii Zamiatin's novella *The Flood* ([*Navodnenie*] 1930),[5] which, according to Shklovskii's somewhat condescending remark, is nothing but one long "comparison unfolded"

("We easily figure out this device, which, after it is guessed, is uninteresting" [147]). Indeed, the main arc of the novella's plot is the metaphorical study of the correlation between transgressive (and fatal) sexual desire and the flood of 1924; but what remains interesting even after one "figures out" the device is Zamiatin's whimsical interweaving of the imagery of urban disaster with an erotic plot. During the flood of 1924, the heroine of the story realizes that her relationship with her husband is threatened. "As if connected with the Neva by underground veins, her blood was rising. Sof'ia did not sleep.... Trofim would leave her, would drip out entirely" (11). Eventually Sof'ia decides to take vengeance on her younger rival ("without thinking, seized by a wave, she picked the ax up from the floor" [38]), but the crime of passion leads to delirium ("a blue foam swelled on her forehead like the Neva" [46]; "Sof'ia stopped sleeping at night, as outside the window, the heavy, bright water kept heaving" [56]), and Sof'ia's cathartic recovery of consciousness erupts in a crisis depicted as the return of the flood with which this circularly constructed novella had opened: "Somewhere very close, a cannon boomed; the wind rabidly pounded against the window. 'A flood?' – asked Sof'ia, her eyes wide open.... The cannon boomed, the wind droned in her ears, and the water rose ever higher – in a moment it would gush in, carry off everything.... [S]he poured out entirely" (65).

Zamiatin insistently anthropomorphizes the flood, matching it to every twist and turn of his main character's passions – her desire, jealousy, fear, and quest for liberation – thus multiplying the possible dialogic connections between the urban disaster and its subject/observer. The flood stands as an overwhelmingly rich signifier of multiple emotional possibilities, recalling the central inquiry of this study: what does the flood of 1924 mean, or rather, what, as a device of urban politics and aesthetics, does it enable the expression of: the desire for tradition to be continued or, to the contrary, the necessity to control and deform tradition, dam it up with various rhetorical "levees" or "floodwalls"?

Curiously, the flood of 1924 remained on the witnesses' minds even decades after this event. And even then, it was interpreted and remembered as a symptom: the flood continued to signify anxiety and uncertainty. We find one of the most peculiar methods of interpreting the 1924 flood in Mikhail Zoshchenko's 1943 attempt at self-psychoanalysis, *Before Sunrise* [*Pered voskhodom solntsa*], in which therapeutic gesture the writer connects his lifelong depression to his fear of water, especially the uncontrollable water of the Petersburg flood:

September 23rd.

The window of my room looks out on the corner of the Moika and Nevskii.

I approach the window. An amazing picture: the river has swollen and turned black. Another half-meter, and the water will overflow the banks....

I walk down Nevskii. I am worried and agitated. I come to the Fontanka.... I hop on a streetcar and go to the Petrograd side. This is where my family lives – my wife and tiny son....

Now I am hurrying to see them. They live on the first floor on Pushkarskaia Street. They may have to move to the second floor....

I make chalk marks on the steps to see the [water's] rising.... I go outside. A horrific spectacle. There is a barge with lumber on the avenue. Logs. Boats. There is a small craft with a mast lying on its side.

Everywhere is havoc, chaos, and destruction.

(113)

Here Zoschenko's self-reading distinctly betrays at least one diagnosis, that of the author's desire to see himself as a new "poor Evgenii" (in this text he also compares his state to that of Gogol' and Nekrasov), driven by the guilt of having abandoned his family to the flood, overwhelmed by the cataclysmic, uncontrollable scale of its spectacle. Yet in conjunction with the writer's desire to connect himself with the authoritative literary tradition via partaking in the disaster, we see here another peculiar gesture – to interpret the flood as the symptom of the author's psychopathological state. Zoschenko perceives and depicts the flood here as both symptom and metaphor of his inability to be close, intimate with his family, but also, crucially, the flood stayed in the writer's imagination as a mark, both historical and personal, natural and cultural of a significant and ominous change.

The 1924 recurrence of the flood was perceived by discourse-shapers as an urgent opportunity to reevaluate their relationship with the urban text, with mythology and, indeed, with the city itself, at the time undergoing enforced political change, yet remaining faithful to its difficult self. The richly varying reactions to the flood, from rapture to horror to ambivalence, metonymically mark the spectrum of existing views on the meaning and viability of the Petersburg cultural tradition at this decisive historical moment of 1924. As Mark D. Anderson notes, "natural disasters must be mediated through culture" (3): it is at this intersection of the natural disruption of societal mechanisms and cultural appropriation of this disruption that one can observe the emergence of rich and complex discursive reactions. The 1924 flood of Leningrad was made into a textual phenomenon with striking energy, or rather energies, since agendas and opinions about the flood were many and they often contradicted each other. This complex matrix of interpretations and appropriations of natural disaster by culture lies at the core of my inquiry, which aims to reveal the curious mechanisms of mutual dependence between the city and its flood, in order to make meaning and history.

Notes

1 For a brilliant analysis of the genesis and contextual repercussions of Pushkin's *Bronze Horseman*, see Ospovat and Timenchik.

2 For background information on the flood of 1924, I found useful Pomeranets; Sherikh.
3 See von Geldern.
4 Cited in Pomeranets.
5 See Zamiatin.

Bibliography

Anderson, Mark D. *Disaster Writing: The Cultural Politics of Catastrophe in Latin America*. Charlottesville: University of Virginia Press, 2011.
Andreev, B. "Literatura navodneniia." *Krasnaia gazeta*, 27 September 1924.
Chukovskii, Kornei. *Dnevnik: 1901–1929*. Moscow: Sovremennyi pisatel, 1997.
Gardner, Vadim. "Navodnenie 1924 g." *Pod dalekimi zvezdami*. Paris, 1929, 98–101.
Geldern, James Von. *Bolshevik Festivals, 1917–1920*. Berkeley: University of California Press, 1993.
"Istoricheskaia doska." *Krasnaia gazeta*, 24 September 1924.
Karatygin, Pyotr. *Letopis' peterburgskikh navodnenii*. Quoted in Pomeranets, *Tri veka peterburgskikh navodnenii*, 187.
Kaverin, Veniamin. "Skandalist, ili vechera na Vasil'evskom ostrove." *Sobranie sochinenii*. Moscow: Khudozhestvennaia literatura, 1963–66.
Kelly, Catriona. *Children's World: Growing Up in Russia, 1890–1991*. New Haven, CT: Yale University Press, 2007.
Kniazev, Vasilii. "Pered nevidannoi bedoiu." *Krasnaia gazeta*. 25 September 1924, 2.
Kniazev, Vasilii. "Deti Oktiabria." *Krasnaia gazeta*, 26 September 1924.
Kniazev, Vasilii. "Strashnyi son." *Russkaia poeziia detiam v dvukh tomakh*. St. Petersburg: Novaia biblioteka poeta, 1997.
Kurdov, Valentin. *Pamiatnye dni i gody*. St. Petersburg: Arsis, 1994.
Laganskii, E. "Potop." *Krasnaia gazeta*, 26 September 1924.
Naiman, Eric. *Sex in Public: The Incarnation of Early Soviet Ideology*. Princeton, NJ: Princeton University Press, 1997.
Ospovat, Aleksandr, and Roman Timenchik. *Pechal'nu povest' sokhranit'*. Moscow: Kniga, 1985.
Pomeranets, K.S. *Tri veka peterburgskikh navodnenii*. St. Petersburg: Iskusstvo SPb, 2005.
Sarat, Austin, and Javier Lezaun. *Catastrophe: Law, Politics, and the Humanitarian Impulse*. Amherst: University of Massachusetts Press, 2009.
Sherikh, Dmitrii. *Iz Petrograda v Leningrad (1924)*. Moscow: TSentrpoligraf: MiM-Del'ta, 2004.
Shklovskii, Viktor. *Gamburgskii schet: stat'i, vospominaniia, esse, 1914–1933*. Moscow: Sov. pisatel', 1990.
"Spasenie na vodakh." *Krasnaia gazeta*, 24 September 1924.
Timenchik, Roman, and Vladimir Khazan. *Peterburg v poezii russkoi emigratsii*. St. Petersburg: Akademicheskii proekt, 2009.
Zamiatin, Evgenii. *Navodnenie*. Leningrad: Izd-vo pisatelei, 1930.
Zenkevich, Mikhail. "Navodnenie v Leningrade." *Sankt-Peterburg, Petrograd, Leningrad v russkoi poezii*. Ed. Mikhail Sinel'nikov. St. Petersburg: Limbus Press, 1999.
Zoschenko, Mikhail. *Pered voskhodom solntsa*. St. Petersburg: Azbuka, 2012.

10 Water and power
The Moscow Canal and the "Port of Five Seas"[1]

Cynthia Ruder

In his book *Landscape and Memory*, Simon Schama discusses "rivers ... as lines of power" (260–261). Such natural advantages lend authority and influence to the government that can harness the inherent power of these resources and thus display its ability to control nature. This kind of dominance emerges even more clearly from canal-building, itself an exercise in power and a method of control. Political systems build canals to demonstrate their capacity to achieve various goals, including most importantly the wielding and display of power broadly defined. To manage a large-scale construction project, the state must mobilize its fiscal resources, reveal its capacity for intelligent engineering and planning, and supply considerable physical labor, usually coupled with expensive heavy equipment. Earth must be moved, water channeled, physical barriers removed, and people displaced. The state that manages such a project wins an ideological victory by demonstrating its capacity to overcome any obstacle thanks largely to its ideology.[2] The physical structures – the locks, dams, dikes, reservoirs, pumping stations, and control towers – that adorn waterways exude power through the fact of their existence.

This context frames the construction of the Moscow Canal, along with its "sister" canals Belomor and Volga–Don, and illustrates how this waterway celebrated, personified, and implied Soviet power most notably through a trope that emblematized the significance of the Moscow Canal not only to Moscow and the USSR, but to the world: Moscow – "Port of Five Seas." Contemporary and recent treatments of this metaphor offer valuable insights into this trope. Especially evocative are the materials produced by and for the Gulag that integrated the trope of Moscow as "Port of Five Seas" into a broader discussion grounded in pronouncements that operated outside the parameters of popular culture (Binder 319–320). In a system that prided itself on its ability to harness nature to serve man, the canals provided a rich ideological opportunity as well as a practical solution to transportation issues. These projects were intended to show that the political system responsible for them was strong, ideologically sound, and capable of taming nature. When such structures successfully performed the tasks for which they were designed, their physical existence would provide physical proof of the validity of the ideology and the wisdom of the state. The metaphor of landlocked Moscow as a port reaching five seas was irresistible to a system intent on proving its legitimacy as a world power and viable alternative to the capitalist system.

The notion of landlocked Moscow gaining access to major bodies of water was not a new one. Even before the time of Peter the Great, Russian rulers had sought to connect Moscow to the Volga River and beyond to exploit the rich natural resources of the Russian interior, to link the city with the wider world through the Caspian Sea, and to provide a reliable channel to move goods, services, and military hardware/people to and from Moscow via the upper and lower reaches of the Volga. This project was as metaphorical as it was physical for just as the Moscow–Volga Canal brought the Volga's waters to the Kremlin steps, so, too, did it allow the world to sail to Moscow.

The Belomor, Moscow, and Volga–Don canals' histories were rooted in their shared pedigree as NKVD-supervised construction sites in the Gulag economy, the system that by its very nature demanded large infusions of human capital in order to complete its projects.[3] At the behest of the Soviet of People's Commissars of the USSR, the NKVD established camps to undertake canal construction: the Belomorsko-Baltiiskii ITL (1931–1941), Dmitlag (1932–1938), and Volgdonstroi ITL (1948–1952) (Kokurin and Morukov 523).[4] In addition, the canal projects were included in corresponding Five-Year Plans, thereby locating them within the larger context of the Soviet economy. Each canal garnered official approbation for the engineering feats achieved with minimal mechanization (especially the Belomor and the Moscow canals), maximum exploitation of local natural resources, and tightly regulated monetary support.

The Belomor, Moscow, and Volga–Don canals were constructed to connect important waterways with each other and with major urban centers. The projects were both economic and strategic, intended to insure more efficient transport of goods and raw materials from their points of origin to potential markets and to allow the Soviet military to move men and machines in virtually any direction, including to the open seas, in the case of naval blockades in the north or south. Just as important were the ideological designs of the projects: successful construction of the canals underscored the ability of Stalinism to achieve goals that the Tsarist regime was incapable of realizing as a consequence of its misguided ideology. Moreover, the Belomor and Moscow Canal projects were archetypal events in the development of the Gulag, a parallel and intertwined economic and social universe with Soviet society at large, charged initially with "reforging" state enemies, yet ultimately responsible for undertaking projects that demanded large labor supplies with little thought for the repercussions. The figurative transformation of landlocked Moscow into the "Port of Five Seas" was as important as its literal connection through this canal system. The canals secured

Moscow's position as the metaphorical center of the Soviet Union and as a *world* capital, to which every body of water ultimately flowed.[5]

In an article from a volume devoted to Stalinist landscapes, Boris Groys argues that totalitarian art results from the battle fought between those who support the totalitarian state and everyone else. The prize at stake in this battle – the ability to "ascribe one's meaning" to the system of signs present in the culture – is waged on two fronts. One front marches toward the reclamation of "the means necessary for aesthetic production." The other front, Groys notes, strives to conquer not only time, but space as well.

> The creation of any image, the erection of any building, the composition of any literary text could never be a neutral aesthetic act: it represent[s] either victory or defeat in the battle for symbolic occupation of space. Works of totalitarian art do not describe the world – they occupy the world. The aim of totalitarian art is to fill the largest possible territory with specific signs that are identifiable as 'our' signs, in contrast to 'their' signs, or the signs of the enemy power.
>
> (98)

Groys' framework permits not only art, but also totalitarian construction projects to stand as significant attempts to control Soviet space and exercise Soviet power. All spatial production – artistic, cultural, political, and ideological – not only comprises the "landscape" of Stalinism, of which water was an integral part, but also functions as an aesthetic and artistic enterprise.

The Belomor Canal was one of the first projects that sought to physically reshape the Soviet Union's landscape as part of the effort to achieve economic and ideological superiority, establish social control, and epitomize Soviet power. Yet Belomor, safely tucked away in the northwest corner of European Russia, failed to deliver that which subsequent projects managed to achieve. As Stalin himself noted, the Belomor Canal was "narrow and shallow" and thus incapable of fulfilling its proposed strategic function: to provide a safe channel for Soviet naval vessels, especially submarines, to sail via the Belomor Canal to the north to avoid potential naval blockades in the Baltic Sea. The products shipped via the canal, typically timber and furs, were found in greater numbers elsewhere in the USSR, as well as the roughly six-month shipping season, further diminished Belomor as a viable conduit.

Like its predecessor Belomor, the Moscow Canal project took thousands of lives, flooded villages out of existence, and forcibly resettled peasants to construct a reliable transportation route and series of hydroelectric stations. Conventional wisdom argued that such a canal between the Volga River and Moscow would bring the Russian interior closer to its capital. Engineers (many of whom had worked on Belomor) designed a project that was built as economically as possible through the use of slave labor and natural materials – rock, timber, peat, and dirt – found along the construction route.

Concrete and mechanized construction equipment were used sparingly. Natural waterways, such as the Dubna, Sestra, and Khimki Rivers, were incorporated to further economize.

The Moscow Canal officially opened on July 15, 1937. Dmitlag, the NKVD camp that constructed the canal, was headquartered in the ancient Russian city of Dmitrov, the halfway point between Moscow, the canal's terminal point, and Dubna, the canal's starting point at its confluence with the Volga River. At its peak, the inmate population of Dmitlag was almost 196,000 (April 1, 1935) (Dmitlag was officially organized on September 14, 1932 and dissolved on January 31, 1938). Official statistics cite inmate deaths in Dmitlag 1933–1938 to be 22,842 persons, although it is widely thought that the death toll was much higher.

Over the course of four years, eight months (fall 1932 to summer 1937) canal workers produced a waterway that is 128 km long with a minimum width of 85.5 meters at the water's surface and 46 meters on the bottom of the channel, with a minimum depth of 5.5 meters. The waterway is replete with 240 man-made structures on the canal route that include 11 single and double-chamber locks, 14 dams, five pumping stations, eight hydro-electric stations, two tunnels – one in Dubna under Lock #1, and the other where Moscow's Volokolamsk Highway under the canal at Lock #8 – as well as railway and highway bridges. Six reservoirs were constructed along the canal route; most significantly the Volga River was rerouted thanks to the creation of the Ivan'kovo hydro-electric station, dam, and attendant reservoir informally known as the Moscow Sea, whose surface area is 327 km^2 (126 sq. miles).

The Moscow Canal reduced the travel distance between Moscow and Nizhny Novgorod to the east by 68 miles and between Moscow and St. Petersburg to the north by over 600 miles. According to official Soviet rhetoric of the time, "At the initiative of the great Stalin, the city of Moscow, which was formerly far removed from 'big water,' has thus been transformed into a port of three seas: the White Sea, the Baltic, and the Caspian Sea" (Komarovsky 24). (Notably here Moscow is cast as the port of *three* seas, a metaphor that would soon disappear from official and unofficial discourse.) More importantly the Moscow Canal provided and continues to supply 60 percent of the potable water and significant amounts of electricity that keep Moscow's thirst slaked and its lights illuminated.[6]

The Moscow Canal also constructed identifiable, influential, unmistakably *Soviet* space. As Henri Lefebvre argues, space refers not only to a physical area, but to the psyche and imagination as well (358). To create a truly Soviet space, it was necessary to dominate spatial parameters in both the imagination of Soviet citizens and on the ground in city and countryside. Most important was the idea that Soviet power could control water – that element vital to life and difficult to confine or dominate. As Schama notes, water was the element that directly linked Marxist-Stalinist ideology to the origins of life itself:

> ...the ideology professed by modern hydraulic despotisms – Marxist dialectical materialism – has been linear, not circular, pushing history relentlessly downstream. So if the self-regulating arterial course of the sacred river, akin to the bloodstream of men, has constituted one permanent image of the flow of life, the *line* of waters, from beginning to end, birth to death, source to issue, has been at least important.
>
> (261)

The Moscow Canal, in its appropriation of this elemental power, thus became the life blood of Moscow in particular and the USSR in general.

In an article from the January 6, 1935 issue of *Pravda*, Lazar Kogan (NKVD officer and head of construction of the Moscow–Volga Canal project) asserted that

> Under the leadership of the Party this attractive canal is growing. It grows not by the day, but by the hour. In 1937 Moscow will become the *Port of Three Seas* [emphasis added]: The Caspian, Baltic, and the White Seas. And in a few years, then the Volga–Don Canal will be built, Moscow will become the "Port of Five Seas": The Caspian, Black, Azov, Baltic, and White Seas.
>
> (No page)

No sooner had Kogan first pronounced the phrase "Moscow Port of Five Seas" on the pages of *Pravda*, then the metaphor became one of the most oft-repeated and potent tropes uttered in the context of the construction of the Moscow–Volga Canal. Moscow magically became the "Port of Five Seas," as though uttering those words aloud made them so (Gorham; Tolczyk).

That Moscow so effortlessly assumed the mantle of the "Port of Five Seas" when other Soviet cities, including Leningrad, Gorky, Stalingrad, Kazan', and Saratov, had better claim on it lays bare the ideological nature of the term. Any city situated on the banks of these connected waterways could have easily made this same claim (RedShon). The epithet itself is a misnomer of sorts since Moscow does not stand on the banks of any sea. Like most of the cities noted above, Moscow is a *river* port, landlocked and only reachable via a system of waterways that includes canals, lakes, and rivers, but no bodies of water that rival the size of any sea. Yet Moscow emerged as the "Port of Five Seas" precisely because it was Moscow: the ideological, cultural, political, and economic center of the Soviet universe. Hence in preparation for the 1937 May Day celebration, P. German composed a song entitled "Moscow will be the 'Port of Five Seas,'" in an NKVD booklet produced at Dmitlag. The song's refrain proclaims:

> That, about which the people have sung,
> That which echoed in [their words]
> Has become today's reality.

It is ready, our Canal! Soon our Moscow
Will be the "Port of Five Seas"!

(1)

The combination of verb tenses here is especially revealing. While the refrain starts with the past tense, a transition occurs with the phrase "Has become today's reality" that simultaneously denotes a past action, yet moves to the present. In turn, the use of the present tense in "It is ready" brings the action fully to the present, while German uses the future tense "will be" to denote Moscow's impending, although not-yet-realized, status as a "Port of Five Seas."

Similar examples of the exploitation of this trope appear in the work of Dmitlag inmates who contributed to "The Library of Reforging" booklet series published by the NKVD and distributed predominantly within the confines of the Dmitlag camp. Series publication commenced in late 1934 and continued through 1936, the period of the most intense labor on the Canal. Archival holdings contain 18 of the purported 50+ published issues. The circulation of each issue (three booklets were released per month at a cost of 15 kopecks each) ranged from 10,000 for the first two to 1,000 for later issues. Forthcoming issues were advertised in the camp literary journal *Na shturm trassy* [*Storming the Work Site*], typically on the inside back cover. As one advertisement for the series noted, "The stories and verses of canalarmyist [Ruder, *Making History* 34] authors are published in the 'Library', as well as methodological and popular-scientific sketches" (*Na shturm trassy*). The "Port of Five Seas" trope resonated both within and outside the Gulag, thereby securing its rhetorical importance for the entire Soviet empire. Gulag inmates (unlike those outside the Gulag) could access both internal and external pronouncements of Moscow as the "Port of Five Seas" through wall-newspapers and at sector cultural centers on the Canal work site, as well as through the "Library of Reforging."

Foremost among the Gulag treatments of the "Port of Five Seas" trope stands Veniamin Riumin's work through his 1935 booklet *PPM. Stories*. The initials "PPM" of the title signify "Port of Five Seas," a sobriquet that also serves as the name for the first cycle of six stories in the work. The sixth story, entitled "The Port of Moscow" narrates the arrival of a ship that has traversed the Moscow–Volga Canal and triumphantly arrives at Moscow, referred to not by its proper name, but as the: "PPM. 'Port of Five Seas.'" (16). Another Dmitlag contributor to "The Library of Reforging" series, Sergei Riabonon, refers in his 1936 poem "Tomorrow" to "Here, at the 'Port of Five Seas'" (55). Both Riumin and Riabonon were writing in 1935 and 1936 respectively, one to two years prior to the completion of the Moscow Canal, which suggests that Moscow as the "Port of Five Seas" was aggressively promoted on the canal work site and in the Gulag press.

Moscow as the "Port of Five Seas" also illustrates various deceptive rhetorical practices that prevailed in the construction of the Stalinist/Soviet state. The notion of the "Port of Five Seas" was not actually realized by the Moscow–Volga Canal. Rather, the completion of the canal meant that Moscow was granted access to only three seas – the Baltic, Caspian, and White Seas – just as they gained access to Moscow. Not until the completion of the Volga–Don Canal in 1952 would Moscow fill – in real time and space – the imagined rhetorical space created with the trope "Port of Five Seas" with access to the Sea of Azov and the Black Sea.

References to the "Moscow-Port of Five Seas" metaphor were not limited to the 1930s, and appear in subsequent official publications about the Moscow Canal. A large-scale brochure, replete with a map of the Moscow Canal and lavishly illustrated with color photographs appeared in 1987 to mark the canal's 50th anniversary. The first page notes,

> "Moscow-Port of Five Seas." This epithet appeared after the creation of the Moscow canal, thanks to which the European part of the USSR turned into a single deep-water river system. Snow-white passenger ships depart from Moscow to Gorky, Leningrad, and Astrakhan and to many other cities in our Motherland. Freight ships… promote international non-stop freight hauling along these river and sea routes to ports in Europe, North Africa, and the Near East.
> (*Kanal imeni Moskvy* inside cover)

The author of these lines, like his predecessors, mistakenly proclaims that Moscow became the "Port of Five Seas" upon the completion of the Moscow Canal.

A still more recent application of this metaphor appeared in materials celebrating the Moscow Canal's 70th anniversary in 2007 (Ruder, *70th Anniversary*). In honor of this occasion, the Moscow Canal Authority (FGUP-KiM) produced a softbound 22-page booklet with articles about the history and exploitation of the Moscow Canal. One particular article, "Moscow: Port of Five Seas" guilelessly discusses Moscow's place as a major port. With language clearly lifted from the eponymous 1987 article, the text begins, "This epithet appeared after the creation of the Moscow Canal, thanks to which the European part of the USSR turned into a single deep-water river system" (Eremenko 8). After an abbreviated history of the canal's evolution from Peter the Great's dream to Stalin's reality, the article notes that "To this day the Canal responds to all contemporary technological demands and is a deep-water transport artery that guarantees the linkage of the capital with Russia's main river, the Volga, and provides an outlet for the capital to five seas: The Baltic, Azov, Black, White, and Caspian Seas" (Eremenko 8). The resilience and longevity of the original Stalinist idea and the canal itself resonate in this recent description. The metaphor links the two eras historically, while ignoring the ethical and moral dilemmas the

Moscow Canal continues to pose – the human cost exacted by the project on its Gulag builders.

Upon the completion of the Moscow–Volga Canal the *reality* of whether or not Moscow became the "Port of Five Seas" was not as important as the imagined space this metaphor created. Because feats of engineering within the Soviet context were conceived as manifestations of totalitarian art and culture, the Moscow Canal physically demonstrated Socialist Realism in practice. That is, the Moscow Canal, and consequently Moscow itself, simultaneously existed while in the process of becoming, a chief tenet of the aesthetic method of Socialist Realism. Socialist Realism held, among other ideas, that Soviet art in its many forms had to capture the "bright future" of the Soviet state both as it should be and as it was being realized through actual practice. This metaphor triumphed over time and space by promising that even though Moscow physically, in 1937, was not a "Port of Five Seas", it should be thought of as one; its future was being realized as its reality was unfolding. This was the dictum of imagining life as it *ought to be* and living in this imagined future.

This is not unexpected given the tendency of totalitarian regimes to occupy their spaces as fully as possible so that no physical feature, no geographic location remains untouched by their power. Even sites that were not yet realized became part and parcel of the Soviet enterprise as ideologues, engineers, and construction crews rushed to claim spaces that had not yet been created on the map. A map from Pavel Lopatin's 1938 book *The Volga Goes to Moscow* (a title that underscores the motion of the Volga *toward* Moscow) convincingly illustrates this point.

The map is labeled "Moscow: 'Port of Five Seas.'" (196 recto). As the map illustrates, the title does not fully align with reality. The legend at the bottom of the page notes that the map features both *completed* and *proposed* canal routes. The only completed canals in this proposed system of "five ports" are the Belomor and Moscow–Volga Canals. The Volga–Don Canal, and lesser waterways, are merely projected, but not completed.

As one of the more prolific chroniclers of the Moscow Canal, Lopatin addressed the notion of Moscow as a port city in all of his works, but with variations. Whereas in his children's book *Moscow-Volga* Lopatin initially notes that "Moscow must be the central port for Soviet seas" (9), he also declares that "So according to the idea of the great Stalin, arid Moscow, hundreds and thousands of kilometers from 'big water', will turn into the port of *three* [emphasis added] seas – the White, Baltic, and Caspian" (71). Later in the same work, however, Lopatin discusses the future plans for the Volga–Don Canal and explicitly concludes that "And in the center of this new route, at the crossroads of these waterways stands Moscow, the port of five seas" (74). In both *The Volga Goes to Moscow* as discussed above, as well as in his 1937 work *Canal Moscow-Volga*, Lopatin wavers between identifying Moscow as a port of three or five seas. In *Canal Moscow-Volga*, Lopatin initially notes that a placard at the Northern River Port should identify Moscow as "… The port of three seas – the

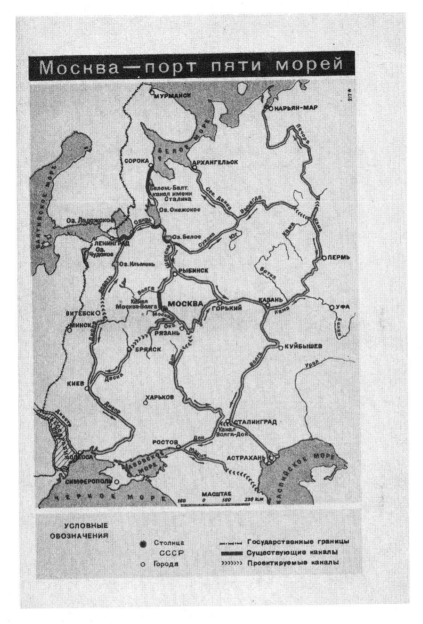

Figure 10.1. "Port of Five Seas" map.

White, Baltic, and Caspian" (8). Later in the same work Lopatin includes a map entitled "Moscow Port of Five Seas" that predates the one included in *The Volga Goes to Moscow*, but that includes the same notations for existing and proposed canal routes. Lopatin's vacillating description of Moscow as the port of either three or five seas makes the confusion palpable. The system hoped to substantiate the notion that the imagined reality of Moscow as a port of five seas was equal to – if not stronger than – the actual reality of Moscow as a port of three seas when the Moscow Canal was completed.

The metaphor of the "Port of Five Seas" captured the notion of motion and energy, images prevalent throughout the intense construction of the first three Five-Year Plans. A canal is a conduit that connects geographical locations that otherwise would not be linked. Like a river, a canal sustains two-directional transport. As such it not only links geographical map points, but it also carries cargo and passengers from one place to another. The cargo and passengers can be both real and symbolic. In the case of the Moscow Canal during the 1930s, the tactile cargo comprised building materials, foodstuffs, and tourists that traversed to and from Moscow from points south and north. This could be a pleasure trip from Moscow to Kalinin (now Tver') to the north as Lopatin describes in *Canal Moscow-Volga* or grain from the lower Volga, fruit from Central Asia, or building materials from Siberia. More significant was the symbolic cargo, comprising Soviet Stalinist ideology and the image of Moscow as the beacon of Soviet power for the world as personified in the passengers themselves, as well as in the names of the steamships that plied the canal's waters – the *In Memory of Kirov*, the *Dynamic*, and the *Sergo Orzhonikidze* among others. Barges laden with melons or timber and happy tourists enjoying shipboard entertainment and the sights along the canal, such as sculptures and natural landscapes, failed both then and now to sense the heavy emotional cargo that the canal carries with every voyage: the memory of those who suffered and died building it.

A different kind of cargo sailed along the Moscow Canal in 2007 during the commemoration of the 70th anniversary of the Great Purges. A barge laden with a cross embarked from Solovki, sailed through the White Sea, along the Belomor Canal, reached the Volga River, and sailed down the Moscow Canal to Butovo in southern Moscow. There it was erected in honor of the martyrs who perished during the Great Purges at the Butovsky Poligon, one of the NKVD's bloodiest killing fields ("Pokaianie" 8). It is fitting that this barge sailed to its destination given that waterways, by their very nature as constantly flowing conduits, embody the notion of the ceaseless current of time and space. As this barge plied the waters it cut through time and space to link past events with contemporary reality, while churning up memories in the process. Generally this episode illustrates the metaphor of the "river of life," which in this case, symbolized the "river/s of death." In particular, the event organizers were keenly aware of the history of the Moscow Canal's construction and the martyrs it produced, so that the cross as cargo served as a potent, meaningful counterweight to the typical 1930s cargo.

Vladimir Paperny's discussion of the importance of water to totalitarian culture is significant here as well. As Paperny notes:

> There is a possible connection between the development of the culture and the special attitude toward water that appeared in the early 1930s. Of all the architectural endeavors of Culture Two, the canals were always given top priority. The White Sea-Baltic canal was the first to be built (1931–1933). It was followed by the Volga–Moscow canal in 1932–1937 and the Volga–Don canal in 1949–52. The idea of water – understood by Culture Two almost as it is by truly 'hydraulic' societies, which view water as the basis of existence – was gradually superimposed onto the idea of the city, which in turn was understood archaically, that is as the center of the world. As a result of that superimposition, the project for the Volga–Moscow canal and the General Plan for the Reconstruction of Moscow mutually penetrated and enriched each other.
>
> (Paperny, *Men, Women* 149)

Moscow's primacy as the "Port of Five Seas" was literally and figuratively inscribed into the landscape, just as the elaborate Northern River Port and the monumental statues of Lenin and Stalin at the canal's confluence with the Volga further inscribed symbols of Soviet power into the landscape (Bulanov 132).[7] These "inscriptions" created a new Soviet geography that physically and visually manifested Soviet ideology. Indeed, one commentator noted that not only was Moscow the "Port of Five Seas," the Moscow Canal itself was the "main connector for five seas" (*Volga, Kama* 15).

In characterizing Moscow as the "Port of Five Seas" Soviet rhetorical practice created the image that Moscow actually extended to the very borders of the USSR. Moscow metaphorically subsumed the entire Soviet land mass so that even though its shores touched no seas or oceans, landlocked Moscow's reach extended to the very edges of the country. Its power reached from shore to shore. Moscow became the metaphor for the nexus of Soviet power, just as the "Port of Five Seas" became the metaphor for Moscow's political and ideological reach. As a result there would be no "neutral" space that was susceptible to forces other than Soviet power; any space created would be unmistakably politicized, controlled, ideologically laden Soviet space. The lingering question, however, is whether Russia has reclaimed and russified these Soviet spaces, the answer to which remains a topic for future consideration (Taplin).[8]

Notes

1 This article is part of a larger project that examines the construction of the Moscow Canal as a signature event in the construction of Soviet space. The author sincerely thanks volume editors Jane Costlow and Arja Rosenholm for their cogent and insightful comments, suggestions, and editorial corrections. The author alone

assumes full responsibility for any errors in content or in the translation of primary sources from Russian into English.
2 The construction of the Panama and Suez Canals bears witness to this process. US water projects in the 1930s, such as the construction of the Hoover Dam, followed a similar pattern. See McCullough; Greene; Karabell; and Hiltzik.
3 In this discussion variations from the official names of the canals are used. Belomor or Belomor-Baltiiksii kanal originally bore the name of its initiator Stalin, a sobriquet later removed. The Moscow–Volga Canal underwent a name change in honor of Moscow's 800th anniversary in 1947 after which it was called the Moscow Canal or Kanal imeni Moskvy. The more popular title Volga–Don Canal is used more frequently than its official title – *Volga-Donskoi sudokhodnyi kanal imeni Lenina* – the Lenin Volga–Don Shipping Canal. For the most detailed account of the NKVD's (Narodnyi komissariat vnutrennikh del [The People's Commissariat of Internal Affairs] that later became the KGB in the Soviet era and the FSB since the fall of the USSR) efforts to build these three canals, see Kokurin and Morukov, as well as Khlevniuk.
4 These figures are taken from *Stalinskie stroiki Gulaga 1930–1953*, 523. The figures I cite are for the period during which canal construction at each site reached its most fevered pitch, which means that the total number of prisoners that passed through each of these camps is much larger. I have resisted using a total figure for the Belomor and Moscow–Volga projects so as to err on the side of caution simply because it is not clear from the data how many prisoners remained on each site throughout the construction process and, therefore, might be counted two or more times in the statistics. On the other hand, Kokurin and Morukov note that a total of 236,778 zeks participated in the entire Volga–Don project (*Stalinskie stroiki* 121). For similar statistics, see Khlevniuk (358–363). Note that Khlevniuk provides no figures for the Volgodonstroi.
5 For all their similarities, differences exist among the three canal projects, notably as a consequence of the eras that produced them. Whereas the Belomor and Moscow Canal projects were permeated with the rhetoric of rapid industrialization, nation-building, and reforging (*perekovka*), the Volga–Don is less so due largely to its construction after World War II in a time that paid significantly less attention to industrialization at any cost and more to the burgeoning Cold War. The most significant difference among the canals is the level of exploitation each waterway presently enjoys. The Belomor Canal never reached projected usage levels from its inception. Because of the harsh climate in which it is situated and thanks to its shallowness, the Belomor never transported the heavy military equipment and large shipments of raw materials that were supposed to traverse the waterway. A 1979 statistic notes that typical yearly traffic on Belomor averaged 6 million tons for a shipping season of roughly six months. In the same period the Volga–Don handled 12 million tons of cargo, while the Moscow–Volga handled 17.2 million tons. In addition, the opening of the Kazakh oil fields to foreign firms, as well as the full exploitation of the Baku oil fields, has made the Volga–Don Canal a significant waterway vital for the transport of crude oil and petroleum products. During the 2002 shipping season the Volga–Don handled 2,500 ships carrying a total of 3.7 million tons of cargo. Throughout its now over 60-year history it has handled over 400,000 ships with a total of 350 million tons of cargo. Of course, the Volga–Don's geography supports its broader exploitation given the milder climate in which it operates. Even the Moscow Canal suffers from a reduced shipping season because its waters freeze in winter.
6 Engineers and supervisory personnel who presently work on the Moscow Canal echo this sentiment, although they admit that the amount and variety of cargo traffic has diminished over the years. Nonetheless, the importance of the canal as

the main source of potable water and electric power for metropolitan Moscow has not subsided. Personal interviews, summer 2004, winter 2007, summer 2009.
7 The monument to Lenin still stands, while the monument to Stalin was removed in the early 1960s during de-Stalinization. It lies at the bottom of the Moscow Canal channel at the approach to Lock 1. The dimensions of the two statues are: Lenin Monument: height: 37 meters [121 ft.]; weight: 450 tons; Stalin monument: height: 37 meters [121 ft.]; weight: 540 tons. Both monuments were constructed by Dmitlag laborers and designed by renowned sculptor S.D. Merkurov.
8 For a recent treatment of Moscow "Port of Five Seas," see Taplin.

Bibliography

Barkovsky, V.S. *Tainy Moskva-Volgastroia*. Moscow: n.p., 2007. Print.
Binder, Eva. "Moskau-Hafen von funf Meeren: Die stalinische 'Wasserkultur' und ihre symbolischen Bedeutungen." *Wasser und Raum: Beiträge zu einer Kulturtheorie des Wassers*. Ed. Doris Eibl. Göttingen: V & R Unipress, 2008, 319–340. Print.
Bulanov, M.I. *Kanal Moskva-Volga: Khronika Volzhskogo raiona gidrosooruzhenii.* Dubna: n.p., 2007. Print.
Eremenko, Elena. "Moskva-Port piati morei." *Kanal imeni Moskvy 70 let*. Moscow: OOO "Fond prazdnik" i zh-la "Korporativnaia kul'tura," 2007. Print.
Fedorov, N. *Byla li tachka u ministra?* Dmitrov: SPAS, 1997. Print.
German, Pavel. "Moskva budet port piati morei!" *Stikhi i pesni o Kanale Moskva-Volga k 1 maia 1937 goda*. Dmitrov: Tsentral'nii klub stroitel'stva Kanala Moskva-Volga i Dmitlaga NKVD SSSR, 1937. Print.
Gorham, Michael S. *Speaking in Tongues: Language Culture & the Politics of Voice in Revolutionary Russia*. DeKalb: Northern Illinois University Press, 2003. Print.
Greene, Julie. *The Canal Builders: Making America's Empire at the Panama Canal*. New York: Penguin Press, 2009. Print.
Groys, Boris. "The Art of Totality." *The Landscape of Stalinism: The Art & Ideology of Soviet Space*. Ed. Evgeny Dobrenko and Eric Naiman. Seattle: University of Washington Press, 2003, 96–122. Print.
Hiltzik, Michael. *Colossus*. New York: Simon & Schuster, 2011. Print.
Kanal im. Moskvy. www.fgup-kim.ru. Web.
Kanal imeni Moskvy. Moscow: Rechflot, 1987. Print.
Karabell, Zachary. *Parting the Desert: The Creation of the Suez Canal*. New York: Vintage, 2009. Print.
Khlevniuk, Oleg. *The History of the Gulag*: New Haven, CT: Yale University Press, 2004, 111–119, 338–339. Print.
Kogan, Lazar. "Kanal Moskva-Volga." *Pravda*, 6 January 1935, no pag. Print.
Kokurin, A.I., and Yu. N. Morukov, *Stalinskie stroiki Gulaga 1930–1953*. Russia. The 20th Century: Documents Ser. Moscow: Izdatel'stvo Materik, 2005, 9–166. Print.
Komarovsky, A. *The Moscow-Volga Canal*. Moscow: Foreign Languages Publishing House, 1939. Print.
Lefebvre, Henri. *The Production of Space*. Trans. Donald Nicholson-Smith. Oxford: Blackwell Publishers, 2000. Print.
Lopatin, P. *Kanal Moskva-Volga*. Moscow: Partizdat TsK VKP(b), 1937. Print.
Lopatin, P.I. *Moskva-Volga*. Moscow-Leningrad: Izdatel'stvo detskoi literatury, 1939. Print.

Lopatin, P(avel). *Volga idet v Moskvu.* Moscow: Moskovskii rabochii, 1938. Print.
Maslov, V.I. *Kanal imeni Moskvy: Stroika veka, Sud'by liudei.* Mytishchi: Administratsiia Mytishchinskogo munitsipal'nogo raiona, 2012. Print.
McCullough, David. *The Path Between The Seas: The Creation of the Panama Canal 1870–1914.* New York: Simon & Schuster, 1978. Print.
Na shturm trassy. No. 1(6), 15 January 1935. Inside back cover.
NKVD SSSR. Biuro tekhnicheskogo otcheta o stroitel'stve Kanala Moskva-Volga. *Kanal Moskva-Volga, 1932–1937.* Moscow-Leningrad: Gos. Izd. Stroitel'noi literatury, 1940. Print.
Paperny, Vladimir. "Men, Women, and the Living Space." *Russian Housing in the Modern Age: Design & Social History.* Ed. William Craft Brumfield and Blair A. Ruble. Cambridge: Woodrow Wilson Center Press and Cambridge University Press, 1993, 149–170. Print.
Paperny, Vladimir. *Kul'tura dva.* Moscow: Novoe literaturnoe obozrenie, 1996, 18–19. Print.
Paperny, Vladimir. *Architecture in the Age of Stalin: Culture Two.* Trans. John Hill and Roann Barris in collaboration with the author. Cambridge: Cambridge University Press, 2002. Print.
"Pokaianie." *Dmitrovskii vestnik* No. 8 (21) August 2007: no page given. Print.
RedShon. http://redshon.livejournal.com/1066867.html. Web.
Riabonon', Sergei. *Novaia Volga. Sbornik stikhov lagerno-stroitelei Kanala Moskva-Volga.* Biblioteka Perekovka, Vyp. 31. Dmitrov: Izd. Kul'turnogo-vospitatel'nogo otdela Dmitlaga NKVD SSSR, 1936. Print.
Riumin, Veniamin. *PPM. Rasskazy.* Biblioteka Perekovka, Vyp. 6. Dmitrov: Izd. Kul'turnogo-vospitatel'nogo otdela Dmitlaga NKVD SSSR, 1935. Print.
Ruder, Cynthia A. *Making History for Stalin: The Story of the Belomor Canal.* Gainesville: University Press of Florida, 1998. Print.
Ruder, Cynthia A. "The 70th Anniversary of the Moscow Canal." NCEEER Working Papers, www.ucis.pitt.edu/nceeer/2009_822-13g_Ruder.pdf. Web.
Schama, Simon. *Landscape and Memory.* New York: Vintage Books, 1995. Print.
Taplin, Phoebe. *The Moscow News*, 15 June 2015. http://themoscownews.com/columnists/20090914/55387704.html. Web.
Tolczyk, Dariusz. *See No Evil: Literary Cover-Ups & Discoveries of the Soviet Camp Experience.* New Haven, CT: Yale University Press, 1999. Print.
Volga, Kama, Oka, Don. Putevoditel'. Moscow: Izd. Rechnoi transport, 1955. Print.

Section IV
Aesthetics and poetics of water

11 A woman in nature/A WOMAN IS NATURE

The eternal feminine as a conceptual blend of human and liquescent ontologies in Russian Symbolist poetics

Anastasia Kostetskaya

Introduction

The Russian Symbolist movement, predominant at the end of the nineteenth and beginning of the twentieth century, praised metaphor as a central device in its stylistics, strongly impacted by a Baudelairean vision of the world as full of innumerable *correspondances* across nature's colors, sounds and smells. Symbolist artists, just like their Western European counterparts, drew attention to "music and nuance, paradox and oxymoron, dream and symbol" (Pyman 11). They perceived material reality through the senses and considered it to be full of tangible representations of phantasms that pointed to higher realities. In its attempt to escape the apocalyptic *fin de siècle* moods, Symbolism engendered a world in which "an Arcadian landscape of pristine myth and fable" seamlessly blended with "a utopian synthesis of art, religion and organic life" (Bowlt 67). The symbolist universe, where ghosts and people could seep through each other's realms, "inextricably linked material *realia* to its superior double of ideal *realiora*[1] via a fluid transmutation" (Kostetskaya 413).

Making woman their vehicle of transcendence, Symbolist artists employed a metaphor which points to liquescent connectivity across the notions of the feminine, the natural and the otherworldly: female apparitions appear in their poetics as ever-shifting fluid visions which transfuse mundane reality by their mystic presence. While "water is a deep, organic symbol of a woman" (Bachelard 82), female apparitions epitomize "the synthetic image of water, woman and death" (86). In their pursuit of new modes of expression Symbolist artists challenged the previously acceptable view of *mimesis* as imitation of nature and matter. They sought to convey nature's inner organizational, essentially spiritual, patterns through the use of metaphor. Communicating transcendental experiences via familiar images of the natural world, Symbolists made them part of a higher spiritual reality. The *metaphor of world liquescence* becomes instrumental in mapping symbolist transcendence as a fluid transmutation; this metaphor encompasses fluid changeability and permeability of all natural elements, including people and human emotion.

I use the trope of a liquescent female phantom to illuminate one of the Symbolist central themes of eternal femininity. The trope of the eternal feminine ("vechnaia zhenstvennost'") as a psychological archetype and philosophical principle idealizes woman as embracing Beauty, Truth, Good, and Love. It becomes epitomized by the final words of Goethe's *Faust*, Part Two: *Das ewig weibliche zieht uns hinan* ("The eternal feminine draws us upward"), which pronounces the spiritual potential of woman to be an agent of love in life's eternal renewal and a conduit for the human transcendence to the divine. The specific understanding of the feminine on Russian soil, which evolved in the course of the nineteenth and at the turn of the twentieth century, was informed by German religious and philosophical ideas. Along with Goethe's *Das Ewig Weibliche* ("the eternal feminine") it included a related concept of *Weltseele* ("the World Soul" or "anima mundi"), which originated from primeval pantheistic attitudes to nature proposed by Friedrich Wilhelm Joseph Schelling.

The eternal feminine of the Russian *fin de siècle* emerges as a fantasy that embodies the anxiety of the transition into the unknown associated with the turn of the century. It reflects rapidly shifting attitudes towards the very idea of femininity during the nineteenth century. Femininity and female spirituality were *not* recognized as a spiritual attribute of a woman (Zhukovskii 137) and not distinguished from that of a man (Kantor 157–159). The trope of woman as a muse re-appears with the advent of a new European consciousness through Romantic and Realist literature (Kantor 163–164). Vladimir Solov'ev's turn-of-the-century reanalysis of the concepts of the eternal feminine and the World Soul had as its aim the reconciliation of religious and secular aspects of Russian life, as well as Russian tradition and Western influence, through the prism of Plato's Sophia.

The Russian Symbolist trope of a liquescent female apparition, I contend, is an attempt on the part of male Symbolist artists to "grasp the fleeting shadows," to use a line from Bal'mont's programmatic poem opening the cycle *In Boundlessness* (30). A female apparition becomes a symbol expressing a transcendental experience in the love of an earthly woman. It achieves the balance between the "high" and the "low" spheres of love (Kling 442) by way of blending the tangible and the esoteric. It becomes a metaphor for the on-going search for the ever-elusive and unattainable feminine, its very definition still in flux at the turn of the century in Russia.

In this chapter I analyze the trope of the liquescent female apparition across verbal and visual media of the Russian *fin de siècle* in two distinct artistic modes of poetry and art: specifically, Konstantin Bal'mont's poem "Apparitions" (from the cycle *In Boundlessness*) and a painting by Viktor Borisov-Musatov (henceforth Musatov) likewise titled *Apparitions*. An encounter with a female apparition principal to these works also features in early Russian film as a distinctly Symbolist trope, although cinematography was excluded from Symbolist arts by contemporaries (Bird 68). Evgenii Bauer's *After Death*, a screen adaptation of Ivan Turgenev's story "After Death (Klara Milich)," while not included in this chapter, draws on the earlier story by Turgenev, "Apparitions," which may have inspired both Bal'mont and Musatov.

My choice of Symbolist artists for this analysis of liquescence is motivated by deep resonance between the patterns we find in their aesthetics, fluid interactions between the verbal, the visual, and other sensory modes in their works, and their emphasis on the liquescent synthesis of various art forms for the purposes of Symbolist transcendence. The poem and the painting I discuss share a male emotional memory of the unattainable feminine across the threshold between life and death, and conceive of the soul as a feminine entity. The two works bring together fluidity of the life cycle and woman as the locus of emotion in its mystery, while evoking the processes of dreaming and retention of emotional memory as inherently liquescent. Hence, blending between the *feminine* and the *fluid* entails references to memory of the prototypical ancestral home, water as a feminine element, and womanhood as a liquescent universe. The all-pervasive female presence in the poem and the painting becomes symbolically marked: Bal'mont and Musatov explore the feminine as both symbol and natural element conducive to spiritual transcendence, which, I contend, blends in various ways with the primary element of water.

Approaches: cognitive framework

In my discussion of the apparitional eternal feminine I rely on a conceptualization, which presents people, human emotions and spiritual transcendence in terms of *liquescence*. This metaphorical mapping reflects a vision of the human domain as becoming or apt to become liquid and is pervasive throughout world cultures (Isham; Norwick; Toporov). We conceptualize our emotions in terms of the primary element of water when we speak about emotional *waves*, *outpouring* our emotions, *immersing* or *dissolving* in them or in each other. The metaphor of liquescence also proves instrumental in speaking about the dissolution of boundaries and removal of dualities, such as God-world, self-others, mind-body, good-bad, male-female, light-darkness, unity-plurality, in which the second member is always viewed as inferior in its opposition to the first (Voss Roberts xvii–xix). Liquescent presence is thus tangible in our everyday life even without water physically present in the picture. With Symbolism's proclivity for metaphor and synesthesia and its close attention to emotion, the metaphor of *liquescence* becomes paramount in discourses of spiritual transcendence via mystical experiences involving *blending* of physical sensations.

My interpretation of the Symbolist liquescent apparition draws on a historic cognitive framework, which makes it possible to "retain the emphasis on the specific socio-cultural environment" of Russian *fin de siècle* while "recruiting and selectively adapting paradigms from cognitive science" (Spolsky 84). I employ conceptual metaphor and conceptual blending theories for my analysis of both verbal and non-verbal metaphor, examining the trope of liquescent symbolist apparition as "an ongoing interplay between human cognitive architecture" (Zunshine 61) and the *fin de siècle* atmosphere of mysticism and spiritualism flourishing amidst its apocalyptic moods.[2] This approach enables me to view the metaphor of liquescence as an agent of shaping the cultural context of Russian *fin de siècle*, not just an aspect of it. The cognitive focus on the shared embodied experiences with fluids demonstrates that metaphor of *world liquescence* allows us, as readers and viewers, to recognize and understand symbolist innovations. An analysis of how the liquescent metaphor functions in the poem by K. Bal'mont and the painting by V. Musatov brings us closer to how these Symbolist artists *intuited* transcendence, closer perhaps than if they had theorized their use of the metaphor. According to Slingerland, "such theoretical accounts will almost inevitably invoke a metaphor in a revealing way" (13), which, for instance, Bal'mont's own thoughts about the nature of poetic creativity demonstrate, as quoted below.

The metaphor of world liquescence emerges from humans' capacity to establish mental connections between themselves and the physical world of ever-changing nature, and can be presented as HUMAN IS LIQUID, with an extension HUMAN EMOTION IS LIQUID.[3] It exemplifies the central argument of conceptual metaphor theory that "reason is shaped by the body" (Lakoff and Johnson, *Metaphors* 5). In other words, it demonstrates that our "reason" grasps and articulates intangible emotions largely in terms of concrete physical sensations we experience in or with water.[4] On the premise that "metaphor is not a figure of speech, but a mode of thought" (Lakoff and Johnson, *Metaphors* 7), my chapter shows how the metaphor of liquescence reveals itself across verbal and visual art modes. I analyze the liquescent eternal feminine of Russian Symbolism as a metaphoric *blend*[5] composed of diverse elements or "mental" spaces – the feminine, the liquescent, the mundane, and the otherworldly, each of which represents a particular scenario. An amalgam of these elements results in a new mental construct where culturally specific inferences emerge, as will be demonstrated.

I show how the two artists rely on the metaphor in question to achieve liquescent effects by way of commingling sensations. Synesthesia, or blending of individual art modes and evoking the effects of one mode (e.g. poetry, with its rhyme and meter) by means of another (e.g. painting operating with line, shape, and color) – suggests that Symbolist metaphors simultaneously blend elements represented in different sensory modes, like, for example, vision, hearing, and movement. By doing so, they "activate multisensory imagery – aural, visual and non-visual (olfactory, concerning smell and sometimes taste; haptic, concerning grasp and touch; motor/kinesthetic, concerning movement and sometimes proprioception (perception of one's own body position); gustatory, concerning taste) *fundamentally*" (Starr 275–276 [emphasis added]).

Bal'mont's and Musatov's shared Symbolist poetics of the eternal feminine

Bal'mont's poetry and Musatov's painterly art provide an experience of the eternal feminine by immersing a female ghostly figure in an ever-shifting liquescent landscape. Their poetics evokes boundless lyrical memoryscapes or *landscapes of the soul*, "where ethereal symbolic beauty emerges through the elements of the earthly landscape" (Mints and Bogomolov 372). The feminine of the two artists draws on pantheistic sources remounting to Romanticism, which see Nature[6] as a spiritualized feminine whole (Rusakova; Grashchenkova; Pyman). The essence of their shared poetics is condensed in Bal'mont's observation on Afanasii Fet's[7] poetry, where tropes of blending the life of the human soul with the life of Nature predominate. This blending results in the creation of "the realm of the unuttered, the kingdom of translucent shadows, of something that can be perceived but can not be expressed" (Bal'mont 264).[8]

The eternal feminine for the two artists is, in Bal'mont's words, mysterious Nature in constant flux, which "eternally *blends* and recreates various incarnations of Beauty"; it is "an apparitional bride, the spiritualized Nature" which "transcendentally weds the poet's enamored soul" (264). According to the poet, the male artist cognizant of Nature's unity either "*blends* with the Universe, losing himself in it *like a stream loses itself in the Ocean*" or "flares up brightly within constraints of his 'I' before he disappears forever in *the boundless sea of World Beauty*" (262, emphasis mine). The poet and the artist encode liquescence of Nature as a female apparitional being in the languages of their artistic medium. Thanks to Symbolist synesthesia of the senses, the language of the poem, with its rhyme and meter, evokes painterly elements. Thus the poem and the painting also reveal their flux iconically as they "leak" various types of imagery, visual and non-visual, across their liquescent boundaries, consequently blending our perceptions.

Comparing Bal'mont's poetry with Musatov's canvases and watercolors, Avril Pyman sees the two artists' works as united by Turgenevean themes and moods related to the feminine. Bal'mont has a longish poem about Turgenevan country estates, and Pyman may well have had the painting *Apparitions* in mind. This painting uses delicate pastel shades without any primary colors to convey the wavering transparency of the "phantoms" in the picture. The poet, likewise, uses "nuances only" in "To Turgenev's Memory": the pond is "half-overgrown," the rustle of leaves is "just" audible, the "enamel moon" shines "faintly" and its beam "scarcely" trembles (Bal'mont, *Polnoe* 22). Just as the artist indicates ghostly figures by a few impressionistic brush strokes, making no attempt to offer realistic portraits, so, in the poem, Bal'mont suggests the presence of elusive beings by "someone's" melancholy whispering, by "someone's regret for something" and, dimly glimpsed at a distance, an aerial flutter of imaginary women: "Elena, Masha... etc" (Pyman 57). The genesis of a ghostly woman in Turgenev can be traced to his 1864 story, whose title is the same as Musatov's painting, "Apparitions." It tells of the encounters of an earthly man and a ghostly "alien" woman across the threshold of a dream. A pale and semi-transparent woman called Ellis flies the hero to various places on moonlit nights, holding him in her embrace. It is notable that all these swift flights are accompanied by detailed descriptions of the atmosphere – misty, damp, and overall liquescent.

Pyman's observation that Symbolist poetry "with its extreme subjectivity, its concentration on the reverberations of the moment and its skeptical attitude to linear sequence and causality, [is] ill-adapted to narrative" can be well applied to Symbolist painting. Both Symbolist poem and painting tend to "consist entirely of a theme and its variations and modifications. It is held together not by plot or chronology, but by an underlying emotional structure more nearly comparable to architecture or music" (62). Just like Bal'mont's poems, Musatov's paintings "cannot be turned into a verbal narrative," Rusakova claims (180). Both Bal'mont's poem and Musatov's canvas must be experienced in their entirety: they convey a *stream* or a *wave* of emotion that *floods* the emotional terrain of the reader and the viewer and come into intense fluid interaction with her emotional condition. The all-pervasive female presence in Bal'mont's poetry and Musatov's canvasses[9] is symbolically marked as the artists explore the feminine both as a symbol, and a natural element associated with water.

Konstantin Bal'mont: "Apparitions"

"Apparitions" belongs to Bal'mont's poetic cycle *In Boundlessness* (1895), which exemplifies the Symbolist aspiration to reveal the boundlessness and profundity of the spiritual world via the boundedness of the physical world. Like many poems in the cycle, embracing symbolic water vistas from ocean to moor, "Apparitions" presents an emotional memoryscape as a liquescent space. The poem unfolds as a reverie for an idyllic childhood, in which the lyrical hero reflects on sensations he experienced while splashing in river waves amidst the nocturnal landscape. As his memory merges with fantasy, his bodily sensations commingle with emotions. He renders his transcendence via the images of nymphs riding the waves and interacting with an elf, the whole scene illuminated only by the pale light of the Moon. The sounds and sights of nature as well as the rhythm of splashing water, the poem communicates, form a fluid channel for the reader into the land of fantasy.

The first stanza of the poem iconically represents the world in flux, where sounds, color, and tactile sensations of splashing in water intermingle, as perceived by an innocent child. The stanza contains only nominative constructions and appears to be seemingly devoid of action. The scene however rapidly becomes filled with intense activity, as the poet introduces nouns containing ceaseless repetitive action – *rustle* of leaves, *whisper* of grasses, *splash* of a river wave, *murmur* of the wind ("*shelest* list'ev, *shepot* trav, *pereplesk* rechnoi volny, *ropot* vetra"). The repetitive sounds eventually flow into continuous resonant monotony where the already blended sound, *rumble* of groves ("*gul*[10] dubrav"), starts blending with image – steady pale brilliance of the Moon ("rovnyi blednyi *blesk* Luny"). The verbal nouns preserve and reinforce the lexical aspect of the verbs: all of them refer to atelic events which do not have intrinsic endpoints and can continue indefinitely;[11] all the aural events – rustle, whisper, splash, and murmur – can be graphically presented in the form of a regular sound *wave* which only has slight variations in pitch. This transition from the real to the "true higher reality" via the reference to the moonlight prepares the reader to perceive imagery as if seen through the veil of a childhood dream – nymphs dancing in the river's waves. The sound/image wave evoked takes the reader back to childhood as if on a wave of memory. The vision of nymphs riding up and down on a river wave suggests metaphoric transfer to the fluid and wave-like nature of emotion and emotional memory, which *sweeps over* or overwhelms the lyrical hero of the poem and carries him away to his reverie. The picture painted in the first stanza therefore produces an impression of eternity, of recurrence of myth. The moon's roundedness, incorporated into this picture, evokes the idea of full circle or a Symbolist trope of the eternal return to the origins.

The image of the river waves quietly splashing against each other comes only third in the succession of fluid images but its appearance is foreshadowed by the liquescent sounds of quiet rustling and whispering, which iconically mimic the sounds produced by water. The cognitive conceptualization of *world liquescence* is translated into meter and the choice of auditory imagery created by the liquids "r" and "l" prominent throughout the poem.[12] Bal'mont manipulates the length of trochaic lines through the different number of fulfilled and unfulfilled feet to alternate magnitude levels of the river waves evoked via multisensory imagery. The blending of auditory and visual imagery of the *splash* ("pereplesk") triggers the motor sensation of rocking and further perception of one's own body being rocked on the waves. This liquescent imagery infuses one with a sensation of boundlessness both in terms of time and space, hence replaying the title image of the cycle the poem belongs to.

Just as the liquescent elements blend with the theme of childhood, the garland of nymphs embrace and intertwine with each other riding on the waves. The motif of the feminine as a natural element thus becomes entwined with the theme of eternity and recurrence, the blending of which constitutes happy memory. In the two middle double-quatrains the Symbolists' key vision of motion along the vertical axis, connects the riverbed with the water surface via upward motion – from the depths of memory to its surface, from oblivion to remembering: *As if in my childhood,/ Over the river depths,/ Nymphs in a pale garland/ Embraced, intertwined*. This visual vector persists through the haze of the unfamiliar further up to the *unknown far-away*. As UP presupposes GOOD (Lakoff and Johnson, *Metaphors* 17), the reader initially attaches positive meaning to this unexplored boundless space. In "Apparitions," the *unknown far-away* and the water surface are also connected via the downward movement of a *wonderful elf* who descends to join the nymphs *on a straight moonbeam, as if on a golden thread*. Along with forgetting the harsh reality and escaping into a childhood reverie, this downward movement also symbolizes the return to the beginning of the natural cycle. Since DOWN is also conventionally conceptualized as BAD (Lakoff and Johnson, *Metaphors* 17) – the downward movement of a mystic creature leaves a vague under-taste of danger and a sense of vulnerability inalienable from childhood.[13]

Here Bal'mont also evokes the theme of emotional memory via the spatial metaphor of REMEMBERING IS AN UPWARD MOVEMENT (IN WATER)/ FORGETTING IS A DOWNWARD MOVEMENT (IN WATER).[14] Clashing mental frames – contradictory emotions caused by the juxtaposition of GOOD and BAD via upward and downward motion, remembering and forgetting – contribute to an organizing frame for the blend of the feminine and the fluid that includes parts of each of those organizing frames. Water, as the mother element, balances negative and positive implications and creates a safe environment of happy childhood, to which the poet would like to return. The conclusion Bal'mont comes to in the finale of the poem resolves the tension between elements of the blend in an emergent structure of its own. The poet situates the absolutely autonomous and thus uncanny universe of the feminine, with its Mystery of Creation, above and beyond both Good and Evil: *Above the earthly truth,/ More seductive than evil,/ In the quiet of night is this life,/ This ghostly mist*.

Viktor Borisov-Musatov: *Apparitions*

The images of nymphs with their wavelike trajectories from Bal'mont's happy childhood memory could be directly mapped onto the women in *Apparitions* by Musatov, which belongs to a series of the artist's "procession paintings." Women's movement through the landscape in these paintings metaphorically stands for the journey of the psyche through emotional terrain.[15] The fluid outline of the whole procession evokes the particular shape and contour of waves, which in Musatov's Symbolist art stand for the waves of emotion. By reproducing the procession pattern the artist draws on the metaphoric conceptualizations of LIFE AS A JOURNEY and TIME AS A FLOW OF LIQUID that are part of human cognitive architecture and, hence, the world of art. These two universal schemata when blended with images

Figure 11.1. Viktor Elpidiforovich Borisov-Musatov. *Apparitions* (1903). Oil on canvas. The State Tretyakov Gallery, Moscow.

of females suggest the liquescent unity of (wo)man and nature. They allow us to see the symbolic landscape as the *ocean of human emotionality* across which emotional waves rise and wane. In Musatov's painting, Bal'mont's nymphs transform into transparent wavering phantoms, stretching their hands after sister apparitional women whose lugubrious fluid movement through the doleful autumnal country estate also conveys emotion, in this case a profound nostalgia. The liquescence of the rainy day in the painting is a natural corollary of the motif of apparitions, be they emanations of the past or of another world.

The painting depicts the palace on the estate Zubrilovka in Saratov region, which the artist last visited in late autumn of 1902. Musatov's sister recalls that the painting was inspired by the pale colors of dying autumnal nature and the grey melancholy weather of the season:

> Late Autumn in Zubrilovka carried my brother away with its pale shades of the colors of dying nature... Around the house where he painted our portraits on sunny summer days, the colors were already elegiac, greyish, everything harmonizing with the dark autumnal sky, overcast

with clouds. The house seemed to have frozen together with the vegetation surrounding it. All this infused my brother with the mood for the painting *Apparitions*... As far as I remember, he said that, together with the end of the abandoned estate, 'everything started to disappear into the past,' just like the moving phantom-like female figures in the foreground.

("Zubrilovka")

Immersed in the cultural environment of Symbolism and influenced by the Symbolist poetics of synesthesia (Bal'mont's among others), Musatov consciously builds his artistic system on blending across various sensory modes to underscore the fluidity of the human emotional domain. In his letter to fellow-artist and art critic Alexandre Benois he speaks about it in terms of Symbolist *Correspondances*:

The endless melody, which Wagner found in music, is also present in painting. This melody is in the lugubrious, northern landscapes of Grieg, in the songs of the medieval troubadours, and in the Romanticism of our native, Russian Turgenevs... In frescoes this leitmotif should correspond to line. Endless, monotonic, impassive, without angles. It could only be expressed on big expanses like walls.

(Bowlt 207)

Musatov transcends mimetic constraints by blending the visual images of maidens with rises and falls of the fluid poetic meter and elegiac musical tempo elicited by his heroines' gestures and trajectories of their movements. The color scheme of the painting captures the haptic sensations of autumnal humidity that chills to the bone. The inference a viewer draws from this blend of embodied sensations is unrestricted emotionality, which *pours* out from the painting and *floods* the emotional landscape of the viewer. The images of visible but intangible fluid apparitions engender frustration, due to the impossibility of breaking through the immaterial, yet insurmountable, divide between those departing and the dead. This occasions the Symbolist longing for the unattainable.

"Refined sadness" over the disappearance of a culturally superior and subtler past is the dominant mood in Musatov's works. His predilection for "Turgenevean" young women[16] set against the background of dilapidated dreamy estates testifies to his regret for a refined culture that will not remain anywhere but in his art. Although rendered via familiar cues – typical Russian vegetation and architecture – the landscape through which Musatov's apparitions process appears de-familiarized and detached, as the artist casts a nostalgic look at his own native land through the lens of the incorporeal and the unattainable. Historical distance in his painting metaphorically stands for the unbridgeable space between the earthly and the ideal.

Phantoms reportedly appear at twilight, when objects start to lose their clear-cut outlines, merging with the environment due to changing light. The color scheme and the general gloaming mood of Musatov's painting is that of a late autumnal day threatening rain. The subdued colors flow into each other in the pervasive grey of imminent rain. The painting creates a sense of psychological tension, which becomes associated with the liminal state between autumn and winter, pre-storm tension and rain, the ambivalent vagueness of which suggests flux as an existential constant connecting the two poles of life and death. On the emotional plane, it is the state between resignation and tears and the uncannily poignant experience of premature nostalgia, supposedly influenced by bitter experiences in the past.

This elemental and emotional instability finds its correspondence in the architecture: the lopsided shape of the building in the background is reminiscent of a semitransparent vision and not of a solid structure. The elongated columns of its façade and its windows have started to lose their shape, as if melting. The whole structure, somewhat like Edgar Allan Poe's "House of Usher," produces an impression of a liquid changing its state to that of gaseous vapors, as if the whole edifice is going to either evaporate or dissolve into the fluid landscape once the last ghostly inhabitant is gone.

Movement in the painting occurs along a serpentine-like path, which mimics the outlines of blurry paths, muddy from rain. The female cortège moving from the center of the composition and vanishing off canvas – we see only the woman closing the procession and the voluminous skirts of the one in front of her – is seen as if through a veil of rain or tears. The procession starts on the building's stairs, which are flanked by female-shaped white-greyish statues lining up on both sides of the staircase. They look like phantoms extending their arms in silent appeal to the woman in the center of the canvas, who walks sadly toward but past the viewer, without noticing us. This inverted perspective where "getting closer" stands for "departure," as well as the inability of the phantoms to see us, suggests the Symbolist transfer to a reality bound to be more true than the earthly one. The observer of Musatov's painting becomes intimately involved in the experience of mournful leaving, as the emotion *pours out* at us from the canvas and *floods* our emotional terrain with empathetic melancholy. The similarity of the Symbolist landscape to the space we occupy as viewers, points not only to the continuity across the realms of life and death, of people and apparitions, but also of them being part and parcel of each other.[17]

The apparitional women against the background of ghostly statues invite associations with Bal'mont's "pale garland of nymphs" riding river waves (*Polnoe* 39). While the ambience of Bal'mont's poem is reverie, and his reader dissolves in the translucence of a primordial world, Musatov's mood is elegiac: he is attempting to grasp the "fleeting shadows" of the past, but their diaphanous bodies seem to pass through his fingers like water; hence, their movement seemingly toward but ultimately past the viewer.

A female apparition who fuses natural elements, imagination, mood, and weather yields, however, different inferences in the blended spaces of Musatov's painterly *Apparitions* and Bal'mont's poetic ones. Viewpoint appears to be the decisive factor here: Bal'mont recounts his childhood sensations of being inalienable from nature in his interactions with river nymphs; he includes himself into this blend, and his sensations are reproduced all over again. In Musatov's painting the viewpoint is that of a person aware of life's transience: he feels he is already close to the end of his earthly existence – hence he is more detached and observant, although maintaining the sensation of oneness with nature as it flows toward the end of the life cycle. He is aware of the inevitability and imminence of his "floating away" together with the apparitions to their realm and becoming one of them. While Bal'mont in his poem maintains the sensation of oneness, Musatov's painting is an attempt to suspend in time the moment of leaving. Musatov's fluid feminine is thus simultaneously both route and vehicle to the destination of a higher spiritual reality.

I believe the study of the liquescent eternal feminine in cognitive terms enriches the discussion of Symbolist epistemology. My article traces how the selected artists' cognitive systems, with the metaphorical conceptualization of *world liquescence* ingrained in them, relate to the world outside of their embodied experiences and to Symbolist artistic ideology. It also delineates how the cognitive process of conceptual blending allows us as the artists' reading/viewing audience to recognize and understand their innovations in the way they create poetic extensions of the existing metaphorical conceptualization of *world liquescence* across verbal and visual (static and dynamic) media.

As my chapter recasts the discussion of Symbolist synesthesia in cognitive terms of conceptual blending and multimodality, it provides a new understanding of the famous eternal feminine trope, expanding on literary and art-historical interpretations. As discussed, the two Symbolist artists capture the "fleeting shadows" of the unattainable feminine via the liquescent imagery of female apparitions, which by their fluidity underscore the liquescence of the human – including the male artist's – emotional domain. Bal'mont and Borisov-Musatov metaphorically grasp the eternal feminine by employing the conceptual metaphor of the *world liquescence* which understands the human domain in terms of water: Bal'mont *dissolves* in a reverie shaped by the images of the river nymphs; Musatov *floats away on the wave* of mourning for the past, which takes a female shape.

Notes

1 Viacheslav Ivanov's motto *a realibus ad realiora* – "from the merely real to the highest reality" – offered in 1908 is a cornerstone of Symbolist aesthetics, especially for "the second generation" of Symbolists. It postulates the desirability of moving from visual (concrete) reality and "through" it to the true reality of the innermost and supra-material spheres (Ivanov 94).

2 Vladimir Solov'ev and Konstantin Bal'mont were among many who "were touched in their day by Theosophy and Spiritualism" (Solov'ev and Kornblatt 31).
3 Conceptual metaphor theorists use small caps as a convention for indicating the presence of conceptual metaphor.
4 Cognitive linguist Eve Sweetser also argues that the development of metaphorical meaning "proceeds from concrete to abstract" (29). She writes, for instance, that the statement "physical brightness is conductive to cheerfulness" offers an example of how this transition from concrete to abstract points to the "inseparability of physical sensation from emotional reaction, or of emotional state from concomitant physical change..." (28–30).
5 The idea of metaphorical ubiquity was further developed within the framework of conceptual blending theory by Fauconnier and Turner, which accounts for "creativity, metaphoric or otherwise" (Forceville and Urios-Aparisi 20) and allows to account for more complex mental constructs than the ones of A IS B type that conceptual metaphor theory operates with.
6 I follow Bal'mont in capitalizing the word "Nature" (see the quotation below).
7 In his article "Elementary Words about Symbolist Poetry," Bal'mont considers Afanasii Fet, along with Fedor Tiutchev, to be the first Russian Symbolist poets. "Subtle penetration into the life of Nature and religious merger with it" is also characteristic of such Romantic authors as Johann Wolfgang von Goethe and Percy Bysshe Shelley, according to Bal'mont ("Elementarnye Slova" 257).
8 Translations are mine.
9 The increasingly lyrical aspect of Musatov's oeuvre is connected to the disappearance of male figures from his paintings after 1900.
10 According to Ozhegov Dictionary, *gul* is "unclear, *blended* noise."
11 Lexical aspect refers to the inherent temporal properties of an event (e.g. rumble of the groves). Based on these properties, events can be temporally classified into categories, such as states, achievements, activities, and accomplishments. A principal distinction in lexical aspect is that of telicity. Telic events progress towards a specific goal or endpoint and are considered completed once the endpoint is reached, whereas atelic events do not have intrinsic endpoints and can continue indefinitely (Becker *et al.* 212).
12 The term "liquid" in phonetics denotes a consonant sound in which the tongue produces a partial closure in the mouth, resulting in a resonant, vowel-like consonant, which in certain phonetic environment can form a syllable of its own. The etymology of the phonetic label remounts to the Greek word *hygros*, "moist," which reportedly refers to the "slippery" effect these consonants produce on poetic meter when they occur as the second member of a consonant cluster.
13 According to Lakoff and Johnson, "most of our fundamental concepts are organized in terms of one or more spatialization metaphors and are rooted in physical and cultural experience." "There is an internal systematicity to each spatialization metaphor," such as GOOD IS UP/BAD IS DOWN. For example, conceptualization DIVINE REALITY IS UP/MUNDANE REALITY IS DOWN, revealed in Bal'mont's "Apparitions," "defines a coherent system rather than a number of isolated and random cases." UNKNOWN IS UP/KNOWN IS DOWN appears incoherent with GOOD IS UP/BAD IS DOWN because it is based on a different kind of experience. It has a similar experiential basis with UNDERSTANDING IS GRASPING, as "it is easier to grasp something and look at it carefully if it is on the ground in a fixed location than if it is floating through the air" (*Philosophy in the Flesh* 17–20).
14 This trope also appears in the poem "The Steppe Grass" ('Kovyl'") from the same poetic cycle, where the *sunken past emerges above the burial mounds* (35).
15 The most prominent of these paintings includes *The Emerald Necklace, 1903–1904* ("Izumrudnoe ozherel'e"), *Requiem, 1905* ("Rekviem"), *Autumnal Evening, 1904–1905* ("Osennii vecher"), etc.

16 As mentioned above, Musatov and Bal'mont shared a love for Turgenev's poetical evocations of the Russian countryside. The artist dressed his models in eighteenth-century costumes and placed them into the atmosphere of Russian "nests of the gentry."
17 A similar idea appears in a Joseph Brodsky poem "Hills": Death is not a nightmarish skeleton/ with a long scythe covered with dew./ Death is that bush,/ we are all standing in (Brodsky 28).

Bibliography

Bachelard, Gaston. *Water and Dreams: An Essay on the Imagination of Matter.* Dallas, TX: Pegasus Foundation, 1983. Print.

Bal'mont, Konstantin D. "Elementarnye Slova o Simvolicheskoi Poezii." *Kritika russkogo simvolizma.* Ed. N.A. Bogomolov. Moskva: Olimp, 2002, 246–267. Print.

Bal'mont, Konstantin D. *Polnoe Sobranie Poezii i Prozy v Odnom Tome.* Moskva: Izd-vo "Al'fa-Kniga", 2011. Print.

Barthes, Roland. *Camera Lucida: Reflections on Photography.* New York: Hill and Wang, 1981. Print.

Becker, R.B., T.R. Ferretti, and C.J. Madden-Lombardi. "Grammatical Aspect, Lexical Aspect, and Event Duration Constrain the Availability of Events in Narratives." *Cognition* 129.2 (2013): 212–220. Print.

Bird, Robert. "Russkii simvolizm i razvitie kinoestetiki: nasledie Viach. Ivanova i A. Bakshi i Adr. Piotrovskogo." *Novoe literaturnoe obozrenie* 5 (2006): 67–98. 10 June 2013. Web.

Bowlt, John E. *Moscow & St. Petersburg 1900–1920: Art, Life & Culture of the Russian Silver Age.* New York: Vendome Press, 2008. Print.

Brodsky, Joseph. *Kholmy: Stikhotvoreniia.* Sankt-Peterburg: Izd. Dom "Azbuka klassika", 2007. Print.

Budnikova, Larisa I. *Tvorchestvo K.D. Bal'monta v kontekste russkoi sinkreticheskoi kul'tury kontsa XIX – nachala XX veka: monografiia.* Cheliabinsk: Cheliabinskii gosudarstvennyi pedagogicheskii universitet, 2006. Print.

Budnikova, Larisa I. "Kliuchevye motivy knigi stikhov Bal'monta "V Bezbrezhnosti" (problemy genezisa i interpretatsii)." *Konstantin Bal'mont: sait issledovatelei zhizni i tvorchestva* (balmontoved.ru). 2 December 2012. Web.

Chéroux, Clément. *The Perfect Medium: Photography and the Occult.* New Haven, CT: Yale University Press, 2005. Print.

Coulson, Seana, and Esther Pascual. "For the Sake of Argument: Mourning the Unborn and Reviving the Dead through Conceptual Blending." *Annual Review of Cognitive Linguistics* 4.1 (2006): 153–181. Print.

Croft, William, and D.A. Cruse. *Cognitive Linguistics.* Cambridge: Cambridge University Press, 2004. Print.

Ellis, Lev L. *Russkie Simvolisty: Konstantin Bal'mont, Valerii Briusov, Andrei Belyi.* Tomsk: Vodolei, 1996. Print.

Fauconnier, Giles, and Mark Turner. "Principles of Conceptual Integration." *Discourse and Cognition.* Ed. Jean-Pierre Koenig. Stanford, CA: Center for the Study of Language and Information (GSLI), 1998, 269–283. Print.

Forceville, Charles, and J. Eduardo Urios-Aparisi. "Non-verbal and Multimodal Metaphor in a Cognitivist Framework: Agendas for Research." *Multimodal Metaphor: Applications of Cognitive Linguistics.* Berlin: Mouton De Gruyter, 2009, 19–42. Print.

Grashchenkova, I. "Serebrianyi vek. V poiskakh litsa." *Iskusstvo kino*, 2007. 2 May 2011. Web.
Isham, Howard F. *Image of the Sea: Oceanic Consciousness in the Romantic Century.* New York: Peter Lang, 2004. Print.
Ivanov, V. "Dve stikhii v sovremennom simvolizme." *Rodnoe i vselenskoe.* Ed. V.I. Ivanov and V.M. Tolmachev. Moskva: Izd-vo "Respublika," 1994. Print.
Kantor, Vladimir. ""Vechno zhenstvennoe" i russkaia kul'tura." *Oktiabr'* 11 (2003): 155–176. Print.
Kling, Oleg. "Mifologema "Ewige Weiblichkeit" (Vechnaia zhenstvennost') v gendernom diskurse russkikh simvolistov i postsimvolistov." *Pol. Gender. Kul'tura: Nemetskie i russkie issledovaniia.* Ed. E. Shore, K. Khaider, and G. Zvereva. Moskva: RGGU, 2009, 438–452. Print.
Kochik, Ol'ga I.A. *Zhivopisnaia sistema V.E. Borisova-Musatova.* Moskva: Iskusstvo, 1980. Print.
Kostetskaya, Anastasia. "Symbolism in Flux: the Conceptual Metaphor of World Liquescence across Media, Genre and Realities." *Slavic and Eastern European Journal* 59.3 (2015). Print.
Lakoff, George, and Mark Johnson. *Metaphors We Live By.* Chicago, IL: University of Chicago Press, 2003. Print.
Lakoff, George, and Mark Johnson. *Philosophy in the Flesh: The Embodied Mind and Its Challenge to Western Thought.* New York: Basic Books, 1999. Print.
Mannherz, Julia. *Modern Occultism in Late Imperial Russia.* Dekalb: Northern Illinois University Press, 2012. Print.
Metz, Eric. "Konstantin Bal'mont's Oxford Lectures on Russian "Fin de Siècle" Poetry: Publication, Introduction and Comments." *The Slavonic and East European Review* 87.1 (2009): 78–99. Print.
Mints, Z.G., and N.A. Bogomolov. *Poetika russkogo simvolizma.* Sankt-Peterburg: Iskusstvo-SPB, 2004.
Norwick, Stephen A. *The History of Metaphors of Nature: Science and Literature from Homer to Al Gore.* Lewiston, NY: Edwin Mellen Press, 2006. Print.
Ozhegov, S I. *Slovar' Russkogo iazyka.* Moskva: Gos. izd-vo innostrannykh i natsional'nykh slovarei, 1960. Print.
Pyman, Avril. *A History of Russian Symbolism.* Cambridge: Cambridge University Press, 1994. Print.
Rusakova, Alla A. *Viktor El'pidiforovich Borisov-Musatov, 1870–1905.* Leningrad: Iskusstvo, 1966. Print.
Rusakova, A.A. *Simvolizm v russkoi zhivopisi.* Moskva: Iskusstvo, 1995. Print.
Shilov, Konstantin. *Borisov-Musatov.* Moskva: "Molodaia gvardiia," 2000. Print.
Slingerland, Edward. "Conceptual Metaphor Theory as Methodology for Comparative Religion." *Journal of the American Academy of Religion* 72.1 (2004): 1–31. Print.
Solov'ev, Vladimir Sergeevich, and Judith Deutsch Kornblatt. *Divine Sophia: The Wisdom Writings of Vladimir Soloviov.* Ithaca, NY: Cornell University Press, 2009. Print.
Spolsky, Ellen. "Making "Quite Anew": Brain Modularity and Creativity." *Introduction to Cognitive Cultural Studies.* Ed. Lisa Zunshine. Baltimore, MD: Johns Hopkins University Press, 2010, 84–103. Print
Starr, Gabrielle G. "Multisensory Imagery." *Introduction to Cognitive Cultural Studies.* Ed. Lisa Zunshine. Baltimore, MD: Johns Hopkins University Press, 2010, 275–292. Print.

Sweetser, Eve. *From Etymology to Pragmatics: Metaphorical and Cultural Aspects of Semantic Structure*. Cambridge: Cambridge University Press, 1990. Print.

Toporov, Vladimir Nikolaevich. *Mif, ritual, simvol, obraz: issledovaniia v oblasti mifopoeticheskogo: izbrannoe*. Moskva: Izdatelskaia gruppa "Progress." 1995. Print.

Voss, Roberts M. *Dualities: A Theology of Difference*. Louisville, KY: Westminster John Knox Press, 2010. Print.

Zhukovskii, Vasilii A. *Polnoe sobranie sochinenii i pisem: v dvadtsati tomakh*. Moskva: "Iazyki russkoi kul'tury,"1999. Print.

"Zubrilovka." *Proselki: putevoditel' dlia avtoputeshestvennikov*. 12 November 2012. www.proselki.ru. Web.

Zunshine, Lisa. *Introduction to Cognitive Cultural Studies*. Baltimore, MD: Johns Hopkins University Press, 2010. Print.

12 Parched

Water and its absence in the films of Larisa Shepit'ko

Jane Costlow

In considering the films of Larisa Shepit'ko (1938–1979) from the standpoint of water, it is tempting to begin not at the beginning, but at the end of her all too brief career. The film Shepit'ko had begun filming at the time of her death was to memorialize and lament the life of a Siberian village about to be drowned in the rising waters behind a hydroelectric dam. Based on *Farewell to Matyora*, a 1976 novel by Valentin Rasputin, and ultimately completed by her husband Elem Klimov, the film suggests the violation of both human and more than human communities in the massive engineering of hydrological systems. But the film also celebrates water, both as visual delight and matrix of life: from the opening shots rising from the sparkling translucence of the Angara River, to the moist, hummocky "mother earth" of the heroine Darya's animistic prayer, to the final cosmic mist that surrounds the engineers attempting to force Darya at last from the island. The film (like Rasputin's novel) precedes by decades the vigorous protests that have arisen against dam-building worldwide, from India to China and the US. What Paul Josephson has called "brute force technology" – massive dam projects – has agitated publics since at least the 1960s, with the building in Egypt of the Soviet-funded Aswan Dam (completed in 1970). Shepit'ko's final film however was to show not the massive face of the dam itself, but the beautiful flowing water it would impound, and the centuries- and millennia-old forms of life that its building would bring to an end.

Farewell to Matyora was not Shepit'ko's first foray into the cinematic exploration of water either as hypnotic visual medium or environmental resource. As I will argue in these pages, the realities of drought, along with the costs and consequences of hydrological engineering, enter into Shepit'ko's work from her very first films, and the aesthetic and psychological resonances of water clearly fascinated the film-maker throughout her career. To some extent this attention may be attributed to the importance of hydrology and engineering in the history of Soviet economics and agriculture; in making films about the Virgin Lands Campaign, or drought, or the building of dams, Shepit'ko was simply representing key parts of the economic and political reality of the society in which she lived and worked. But she enters this world with her own particular mixture of intensity, lyricism, and psychological focus, producing films which give us an extraordinarily *tactile* sense of place and conflict. To say that the films engage with environmental or sociopolitical issues, while true, leans too heavily on the cognitive and rhetorical potential of film-making, precisely that "logocentrism" which numerous Thaw film-makers sought to challenge with their innovative and exploratory cinematography (Kaganovsky 485). *Heat* (1963) and *Motherland of Electricity* (1967) – the two films this chapter will focus on – throw us into worlds of excruciating heat and the absence of water, in a kind of radical gesture of abandonment to the elements. Official slogans and promises of a bright future give no comfort in these worlds. The only relief comes from a still, small spring, or seemingly miraculous rain on parched earth.

Shepit'ko began her film-making career as one of a group of talented directors who came of age during the Thaw, the period of relative cultural liberalism conventionally bracketed by the dates of Stalin's death (1953) and Khrushchev's departure from the Kremlin (1964). Films from this period were long overshadowed by the rich and fraught cinematic legacy of other Soviet and post-Soviet eras, from the early avant-garde to Stalinist film-making and the cinema of perestroika. More recently, however, film scholars have begun to explore the aesthetics and cinematic practice of this generation, moving beyond political interpretations grounded in Cold War paradigms. As Alexander Prokhorov has argued, changes in cultural and political life in the post-Stalin era enabled the production of "innovative works that revived the avant-garde spirit of the 1920's and revolutionized the visual and narrative aspects of film art" (7). Making films that were set up "against or counter to the cinema of Stalinism," film-makers of this generation – including Andrei Tarkovsky, Andrei Konchalovsky, and Kira Muratova as well as the slightly older Marlen Khutsiev and Mikhail Kalotozov – experimented with film-making techniques endebted both to the Soviet avant-garde and to the New Wave of European cinema. Exemplary of this innovative spirit, and perhaps best known to non-Russian viewers is Kalotozov's *The Cranes are Flying*, with its "sophisticated techniques for creating visual uncertainty" and camera work that intentionally quotes the great Soviet photographer Alexander Rodchenko (Stiegler). Much of this innovative film work aimed to challenge the "master narratives" of Soviet modernization, two fundamental aspirations that Prokhorov characterizes in the following way: "that of raising the new Soviet race to Marxist consciousness and that of the war on nature with its subsequent transformation into post-historical paradise on Earth" (26–27). The Russian film scholar Evgenii Margolit argues that nature itself *returns to film* in this period, allied to a "spontaneity" which he sees at the heart of cinema as art, a spontaneity which had been rigorously expunged from all aspects of life in the Stalin era (29).

In a recent essay on Shepit'ko and her contemporary Kira Muratova, Lilya Kaganovsky has suggested that both women were centrally concerned with the "question of seeing differently," developing a kind of "counter cinema," that involves challenging cinematic convention (483). While Shepit'ko's fame has justly rested on her 1966 *Wings* and the 1976 *The Ascent* (for which she won a Golden Bear), both *Heat* (her graduation film) and *Motherland of Electricity* are talented and provocative "revisionings" of Soviet narratives of human mastery. Water and its absence are at the center of both films, with central plots revolving around agriculture, irrigation, and technology. Both films however represent water as more than merely utilitarian, as something essential to life that fundamentally escapes human control. The challenges of both films are oblique, embedded in their visual language and in what Shepit'ko called their "internal rhythm" – not just the structuring of the film at the level of plot and character confrontation, but in the shaping of particular frames and the "movement of actors or objects within a frame" (Beaver 132). Shelved along with one other experimental film made as part of a triptych to celebrate the 50th anniversary of the revolution, *Motherland of Electricity* was seen by contemporary cultural arbiters as too much at odds with prevailing narratives of Soviet history. But even the earlier, gentler *Heat* challenges Soviet ambitions to *force* (through sweat and tractors) cultivation in a world where, as two different characters in the film put it, "there is no water." Where official Soviet narratives insisted on heroic triumphs, these films leave us with uncertainty and doubt. To borrow terms used by the American historian William Cronon, these are closer to *declensionist* than progressive narratives (11).

Heat was Shepit'ko's first full-length film, serving as her diploma work for a degree from the prestigious VGIK (All-Union State Institute of Cinematography), where she had begun her study in 1955 under the tutelage of Aleksandr Dovzhenko. The film is based on a story by the Kyrgyz author Chingiz Aitmatov, "The Camel's Eye," published in 1961. When the preliminary version of the screenplay was not approved, Shepit'ko and her crew wound up working on it as they went along, partly in response to the landscape itself.[1] The film was shot in the spring of 1962 with actors and much of the production crew from Kyrgyz film studios.[2] Regional film studios, as Alexander Prokhorov has noted, played key roles in "fragmenting totalitarian mythology" during the Thaw period; it was "no coincidence" that Shepit'ko and others made their first films in studios where the dominance of studios in Moscow and Leningrad could be challenged (21). The shooting location – near the village of Anrakhai in present-day Kazakhstan – is located north of "Frunze" (present-day Bishkek), a locale referred to in the film's opening scene. The film was shot in punishing conditions of extreme heat and aridity, with temperatures reaching 40 degrees celsius: "the plot meant you had to film in completely barren, water-less steppe" (Aitmatov 28).[3] Shepit'ko herself suffered physically but (as was to be characteristic throughout her career) insisted on continuing filming despite exhaustion and a bout of hepatitis. Visually, the film captures the excruciating climatic conditions of arid steppe: the absence of moisture in both soil and air, manifest both as clouds of dust and dehydrated human bodies. The English title *Heat* in fact seems too mild for the Russian *Znoi* and the film's visuals: *Parched* or *Burning* might be more like it.

The plot of the film is quite simple. A young Komsomol enthusiast (Kemel') comes to an isolated encampment in the steppe, where a small tractor brigade is plowing up steppe land in anticipation of planting the following year. These are ground-level participants in one of the grand ventures of Nikita Khrushchev's rocky term as General Secretary of the Communist Party, known as the "Virgin Lands Campaign." Kemel' dreams of driving a tractor, but is instead assigned to be the water delivery boy. He shares the day-to-day life of the brigade, clashing repeatedly with Abakir, an older man who is romantically involved with Kalipa, a young woman who (unlike Kemel') submits to his verbal and physical abuse. Kemel' gets so fed up that at one point he walks off into the steppe, intending to leave, but by day's end he has returned to camp. The film's climax comes when Kemel' sits in Abakir's seat on one of the brigade's two rusty tractors, a usurpation which triggers a violent outburst in Abakir. Abakir's response is to strike Kalipa, a displacement that suggests the ways in which women bear the brunt of men's disputes. The film ends with a long shot of Abakir striding off into the steppe, as the brigade members (who we see from behind) watch him leave.

The "Camel's Eye" of Aitmatov's story is a small spring and pool, a rare and essential feature of the steppe landscape that we are introduced to in the story's first lines, as the young hero Kemel' draws water from it. The spring has several functions in both story and film: it is the crucial source of water for what one critic has called the "antediluvian" tractors that the crew is using to plow land (Ezerskaia). Incredibly enough, the tractors only run if a horse-drawn cart makes its rounds bringing water from the spring out into the surrounding steppe. Aside from this utilitarian (and ironic) function, the spring plays additional roles: in Aitmatov's story it is associated with the genesis of poetry, and becomes a locus of poetic reverie for Kemel', who we learn is an aspiring poet; it's also the place he meets a young herding girl who brings her animals to the spring to drink. To this mix of lyricism, love, and relief from thirst Aitmatov's story adds the name itself, *Camel's Eye:* it's a name Kemel' thinks up, linking the spring to a creature who – unlike tractors – can subsist in this landscape for long periods of time without needing to rehydrate.

By the time Shepit'ko's film was made the Virgin Lands Campaign had been underway for over seven years; as with the aggressive conversion of arid grazing land to grain cultivation that led to the American Dust Bowl, the Virgin Lands Campaign was predicated on the availability of water in landscapes ecologically marked by water's scarcity or absence. It was a huge gamble. In the wake of Khrushchev's announcement of the campaign in 1953, hundreds of thousands of young communist enthusiasts like Kemel' journeyed to steppe regions to participate, and millions of hectares of virgin lands were plowed up. The state aggressively propagandized the campaign, with films and posters projecting images of strapping young men and women in abundant and fertile landscapes, images that show resolute and capable Soviets whose labor links mechanization and an abundant organic world. Harvest results, however, were profoundly disappointing, and by the second year of the campaign it became doubtful whether initial high yields could be sustained (McCauley 90–91). The soils and climate of Russia's steppe regions had been the object of both practical concern and scientific study since the mid-nineteenth century; by the early twentieth century research had elucidated what David Moon has called the "central paradox of the steppe soils: the very fertility that gave such bumper harvests in good years, when the rains came, was largely a consequence of the low rainfall that, in years of drought, led to harvest failures and famine" (86). What environmental historians have called "one of Khrushchev's most environmentally-devastating and costly programs" assumed that such knowledge could be ignored, or that water supply could be engineered to suit human needs (Josephson *et al.* 145). Discounting both local ecology and historical experience with the difficulties of agriculture in these regions, the campaign led to "poor harvests, accompanied by soil erosion and dust storms. Vast areas were ruined. The outcome resembled the 'Dust Bowl' on the southern plains of the USA in the 1930's" (Moon 293).[4]

Within this context, Shepit'ko's film about a work brigade involved in the transformation of native steppe to arable land takes on particular resonance. Numerous commentators, and Shepit'ko herself, have tended to talk about the film primarily in terms of the conflict between its two central characters, representatives of contrasting Stalinist and Thaw generations: the young enthusiast Kemel' (with whom Shepit'ko apparently identified) and the older Abakir – a domineering man with a shadowy past (and awards for record-breaking plowing). But at least as important to the film is its setting – which Shepit'ko in her written companion to the film (submitted as part of her diploma work) referred to as "one of the film's main characters" (Shepit'ko 162). Again and again the broad, flat steppe landscape fills Shepit'ko's frame, often with a solitary figure silhouetted, virtually invisible, against it, or with the seemingly constant wind whipping at awnings and stealing men's words from their mouths. Again and again we see great clouds of dust lift into the air. And then we are brought to a very different place – a spring and pool of water, shadowed by a small cleft in the landscape and suddenly lush vegetation. The music shifts as we move from one place to the other: Roman Ledenev, who composed music for the film, recounts working to reinforce the "juxtaposition of spring and desert [*istochnik i pustynia*]" (Shilova). The spring is associated with reverie, play, and light – with a space of meditation as Kemel' stands looking at light glimmering on water – but also with flirtation and the potential for romance, when the unnamed herd girl shows up and teases Kemel' by tossing pebbles at his bucket. The world of the steppe on the other hand is associated with aridity, sweat-inducing, less-than-voluntary labor (from which at least one member of the crew longs to escape; when Kemel arrives another worker begs to leave, but the driver won't take him), and violence: this is most apparent in the figure of Abakir when he is abusive of Kalipa, but it is also implied more broadly in the film's machines, vehicles of a different kind of violence.[5]

The film begins, interestingly enough, with Kemel' sound asleep, a posture that emphasizes his childlike face and features, but also suggests the "dreams" that motivate his journey. We see him in the back seat of a car at night, on his way to Anrakhai, where the brigade is working. The driver and another passenger chat quietly about the sleeping boy and about how the work is going. Within a minute and a half the men are talking about the weather: "How is it in Anrakhai? Hot?" "Spit on a rock and it sizzles." "What about water?" There's a pause, and the driver's voice slips into a lower register and takes on a completely different tone. "There is no water [*net vody*]." When the men shift from talking about Kemel' to talking about heat and water they shift from an almost maternal, bemused tone to one that is suddenly sober. It's as though they're admitting that the young idealist's dreams will soon confront sizzling and intractable reality. Water and its absence come up again in a later conversation, this one between Abakir and the brigade chief, as they argue under a wind-blown awning about production goals and the pace of plowing. In this exchange it's Abakir who states the obvious – "So where's the water?" – while the chief insists they have to follow orders. As far as Abakir's concerned, he's being asked to "plow dust."[6]

Both conversations put into words what the film makes visually evident in a range of ways. They verbalize a kind of creeping doubt about the whole enterprise that is reinforced by the film's visual strategies – although it might be more accurate to put the visual first, and say that the characters' episodic language merely confirms what the film shows us. It's worth considering in some detail just how the film asks us to see, since it's here that Shepit'ko is most obviously taking issue both with Stalinist figuration and Khrushchev era rhetoric. Her use of exaggerated and angular shots, intercutting of dissonant points of view and frames that echo both masterful and schlock work of Soviet propaganda – all of this suggests a young and creatively ambitious director figuring out how to get her viewers to *see things differently*.

Machines in the film, and how they are represented, are key to this process of revisioning. As I've noted above, the tractors – all two of them – are antediluvian, rusting and difficult to start, wholly dependent on regular deliveries of water from a horse-drawn cart. Hardly modern technology. There's a moment immediately after Kemel's arrival when we're reminded that somewhere out there in the larger world technology and machines have evolved, and interestingly enough the insight depends on water. The brigade is sitting under an awning, out of the sun, having breakfast. Kemel' sits holding his *piala* – a central Asian tea cup – and becomes mesmerized by the play of light on the liquid (just as he'll later be mesmerized by the play of light on water at the spring). "It's a solar battery," he says. The group looks at him quizzically. "On the *sputnik* they turn toward the sun, and make electricity. Just like this *piala*." The reference might be taken to establish Kemel' as "brainy" (in Aitmatov's story he's aggressively – even combatively – teased by Abakir and called "scholar" [*uchenyi*]), but it also refers to the parallel but infinitely distant world of cosmonauts and the Soviet space program, with a visual allusion that links tradition (the teacup), sun, and water.

Just prior to this exchange we've heard Kemel' speculate about an "Abakir" he's heard of (who might or might not be the one in this brigade) who was a famous tractor driver, a *traktorist*. Tractors occupy a significant place in the visual rhetoric – and political/environmental history – of Soviet aspirations to modernity, and Shepit'ko's film seems quite cognizant of that. From early Soviet film-makers to Stalin-era musicals to the recruiting posters for the Virgin Lands Campaign, tractors occupy an almost sacred place in the Soviet cult of the machine. One of the most famous moments in the visual history of Soviet tractors comes, in fact, in Shepit'ko's beloved teacher Dovzhenko's most famous film, *Earth* (1930). That film includes a justly celebrated sequence of a tractor's arrival in a Ukrainian village. With much anticipation and a long build-up of intercut shots of villagers and cows, the tractor arrives. Dovzhenko's tractor raises a fair amount of dust, but is accompanied by an almost cosmic excitement, surrounded by men in their Sunday best, signifying perhaps the human dignity and promise of leisure brought by the machine. Dovzhenko does remind us, however humorously, that the machine needs water: the triumphal procession pauses while one of the dandies unbuttons his fly and "waters" it with human fluid.

This solitary, human-scale tractor multiplies in later Soviet films into echelons of plowing machines, following a visual strategy apparently initiated by Sergei Eisenstein in *The General Line* (1929). As Gilbert Perez notes, that film ends with a "vast ballet of tractors": what is initially one tractor hauling a long line of horse wagons without the horses gives way to a squadron of tractors, plowing an ever-widening circle of rich dark earth (71). The 1939 musical *Tractor Drivers* (*Traktoristy*) combines romantic comedy with a heroic vision of record-setting tractor drivers (of which Abakir is an aging example) and their place in what we might call the military-agricultural complex. Released at a moment of high anticipation of impending war, *Tractor Drivers* in its final minutes makes an explicit analogy between tractors and tanks. Both tanks and tractors are represented as heroic defenders of the Soviet Union, territory metonymically implied by the lush, dark landscapes of the film (shot in Ukraine). This is not dust, it is *chernozem*, the country's most fertile and moisture-laden soil. Finally, another of Shepit'ko's teachers, Mikheil Chiaureli, in his 1949 *The Oath*, superimposed burgeoning tractors in a dream-like trance as Stalin imagines the Soviet future. Tractors predictably proliferate in posters for the Virgin Lands Campaign, repeating this idealized, fertile constellation of tractor–earth–humans. The tractors are all new; the earth is dark, moist, and productive of bumper crops; and the strapping young men are paired with equally strapping young women, suggestive of (moist?) Mother Russia and the fertile bodies that the campaign promises to feed.[7] All of this, of course, depends on water.

In Shepit'ko's *Heat*, however, *there is no water*, and her tractors suggest both inhuman scale and outmoded (or inappropriate) technology. Her shots of tractors – and later of earth-moving dump trucks – explicitly quote a tradition of heroic rendering of the machine, but here what was heroic has become rusty, demonic, and destructive. The relatively benign world of Dovzhenko's tractor is left behind (there's a nicely composed sequence early in *Heat* that shows the horse cart with the water barrel descending diagonally and disappearing screen right, immediately followed by the inverse shot, with a much larger tractor rising from where the cart had disappeared). We enter instead an ominous, more Eisensteinian universe. Kemel' arrives with his bucket and barrel of water to keep Abakir's tractor from overheating. He jumps down from the cart and prepares to pour the water in, at which point Abakir tells him he must first drain the old stuff. Kemel' crawls under the massive tractor while Abakir towers above him, laughing (another example of the confrontational "teasing" the older man engages in). The scene is shot in such a way that we see Kemel' on the ground beneath the tractor, with Abakir's almost demonic face glimpsed through gaps in the metal. The impression is of technology that overwhelms the human and demands literal submission, but also of a machine that isn't working at all well. Unlike Dovzhenko's tractor, this is a rusty, water-guzzling behemoth controlled by a bully.

More menacing still are the machines that appear in one of the film's later sequences, when Kemel', fed up with the teasing and with having to drive a donkey cart, stalks out of camp. Headed we're not sure where, he encounters a massive line of enormous dump trucks – machines which seem considerably less rusty than the antiquated tractors. Kemel' hitches a ride, and after a brief exchange with the driver (he finds out that they're "digging" – building a reservoir to hold "underground rivers"), the sequence mutates from meditation (Kemel' staring into space from the cab door window) into manic rally. What begins with a geometrically composed view from above (highly reminiscent of Stalin-era films that show planes, boats, and marchers in tight formation)[8] shifts into a series of lurching close-ups accompanied by foreboding percussion and the sounds of racing motors. We see speeding trucks and dust from ground-level, interspersed with massive human faces, all rapidly cut and at disorienting angles. Kemel' himself is drawn out of his reverie into this stampede (we see him waving other drivers on), but the most disconcerting face, to which the camera repeatedly returns, is a grizzled driver with a cigarette in his blackened teeth. It's a face that hesitates between leering grin and menacing grimace; the music leans heavily toward the latter. When the trucks hit the highway Kemel' decides to get out, and walks back to camp.

What are we to make of this sequence? In the theoretical portion of her diploma Shepit'ko reports having to defend the scene against a Kyrgyz "culture worker" who took offense at the depiction of irresponsible drivers. Shepit'ko claims instead that the scene was intended to capture the "living pulse" and the "new song that sounded beneath the scorching sun of an ancient region...." (162). If this is indeed a new song it is a deeply disturbing one. The exaggerated faces, distorting angles, pace of editing – all give a sense of adrenaline, aggression, and violence. The Kyrgyz cultural worker may have been on to something: the scene gives the impression of men and machines *out of control*, and the potential for enormous destruction. The scene might be viewed as anomalous (it doesn't exist in Aitmatov's text), but for the thematic link to *water* (the reservoir the trucks are building for those supposed underground rivers), and a lingering sense of menace and destruction, a set of images that gives a sense of what will happen to the "ancient region."

And what is this "ancient region" aside from the steppe itself? In Aitmatov's story the region's antiquity is embodied in a *kamennaia baba*, or handwrought stone effigy in the shape of a woman, which stands near the tractor brigade's camp. Stone figures like this are found throughout the steppe regions of Central Asia, Mongolia, and southeastern Europe; archeologists surmise that they are connected to cults of the ancestors, giving physical embodiment to the spirits of place. In Aitmatov's story the *baba* is a mute and unsettling observer. The *baba* doesn't exist in *Heat*; instead we might see a link to "ancient culture" in the young herd girl – part of a lifeway and ecological tradition that characterized the steppe for millennia. The film makes a strong link between her, her animals (sheep, goats, and horses), and the wild steppe – but a steppe that is seen as a site of traditional herding culture, rather than as "virgin" slate for Soviet remaking (Murphy 43–44). In a scene that bears comparison with the manic truck race, Kemel' sees the girl on horseback, is clearly mesmerized, and unharnesses the pony he's been using to haul water. We're shown an extended sequence of both Kemel' and the girl on horseback, intercut with shots of the herd of wild horses alternately standing still and racing through open steppe. As with the later truck scene, there's a race (accompanied by less foreboding percussion) that raises lots of dust; diagonally shot faces, and rapid cutting back and forth between the human and the non-human. The scene ends with the horses disappearing over a hillside, and an abrupt shift from frenetic movement to almost uncanny stillness (a stratagem that Shepit'ko would use to brilliant effect in *The Ascent*). As when he gets out of the truck, Kemel' is left alone, but here his meditative solitude is interrupted but high-pitched laughter; it turns out the herd girl is right beside him, and she's laughing (whether *at* Kemel' or simply from sheer joy, is unclear).

These two "race scenes" suggest that the film tracks a conflict not just between Abakir and Kemel', but within Kemel' himself, a division suggested but not exhausted by the contrast of mechanization and the animal world, or hard labor versus joyful movement – the latter vividly apparent in the body language of scenes when Kemel' and the girl interact. Just before Kemel' sees the herd girl and her horses, he is startled by a flock of birds, wheeling and diving in flight over his head. Both horses and birds are prime examples of what Margolit calls spontaneity; the birds' tumult was no doubt caught on film by chance. All of this – birds and horses, girl and spring, play and free movement – are instances of what the film's machines seem likely to compromise if not destroy.

The Motherland of Electricity, which Shepit'ko made in 1967, strikes the viewer of *Heat* as an almost surrealist revisitation of the landscape of *Heat*. This time we're in the steppes of Astrakhan, and it is 1921, a year of famine and civil war. Shepit'ko's film is again based on a work of literature, a bizarre and visionary story by Andrei Platonov in which a hydraulic engineer is sent to a distant village to construct an irrigation system. The short (36-minute) film was intended as one of a group of films that would celebrate the 50th anniversary of the revolution with screen versions of some of the best writing of the 1920s. The project, conceived at the recently inaugurated Experimental Film Studio, was to include short films based on stories by Platonov, Isaak Babel', Yurii Olesha, and Konstantin Paustovskii (Fomin 34). Rooted in the fast-fading creative possibilities of the Thaw, the project foundered from the outset; both *Angel* (story by Olesha, filmed by Andrei Smirnov) and Shepit'ko's film were shelved completely, to be screened only 20 years later under Gorbachev.

Even more than *Heat* this film focuses not just on desiccated land but on parched bodies, bodies without water and without the food that drought has destroyed. When the young engineer walks into this dried-out, dusty landscape he comes like a Bolshevik Christ, in a frame composed to echo Alexander Ivanov's famous nineteenth-century painting, "The Appearance of Christ Before the People." In Ivanov's painting Christ comes to John, who is baptizing believers in the River Jordan. In Shepit'ko's frame there is no water, just a procession of believers who have paused briefly to rest from the punishing heat; they are carrying icons and church banners and offering desperate prayers for rain. Here and throughout the film Shepit'ko links earth and the human body: her engineer is so still as he sleeps on the ground that a large, dark beetle crawls over his cheek; the procession of the cross is enveloped in dust, an ancient woman bares her head to show a hairless skull that looks like the ravaged ground. Bodies lie on earth, including at least one that is motionless, perhaps dead.

These bodies' gaunt emaciation is visually produced at least in part by a special lens suggested by the cameraman, D. Korzhikhin, which "deformed the image, slightly narrowing it along the horizontal" (Fomin 39). Shepit'ko's intention was to find a visual counterpart for Platonov's remarkable and uncanny verbal style, but the device also focuses our attention on these haunting faces. As with her later *Ascent*, the camera lingers on faces so that they become almost iconic, a parallel that the Procession of the Cross scene makes explicit, as the camera moves slowly from icons to mortal faces.[9]

The religious allusions of the film are thematically (and visually) connected to the engineer's promise to deliver water, and the evocation once more of the Soviet Union's cult of the machine.[10] The water that peasants have in the past prayed for, the new state promises to deliver with technology. "Nature," as the young engineer explains to the ancient hairless woman, "fears only reason and work." In Platonov's story the state (in the person of the young engineer) delivers: by story's end a jury-rigged British motorcycle is generating power for an irrigation pump, and the engineer walks away from the village, understanding that "one of my tasks in life had been completed" (Platonov 279). Remarkably, radically, Shepit'ko gives us a different ending. At the end of Platonov's story the still that produces grain-alcohol fuel for the operation blows up, but the pump/motorcycle itself continues to work. In Shepit'ko's film it's the motorcycle-pump machine *itself* that blows up. The machine fails; the village peasants stand watching it burn; and suddenly – miraculously? – it begins to rain.

One really can't overstate the extent to which this cinematic logic undermines the Soviet promise of technology, as implied by the engineer's words to the old woman – however well-intentoined they may be – that technology will replace God. The voice over at film's end (the prose is Shepit'ko's, not Platonov's) declares that it is *hope alone that makes us human*. Given the failure of technology and the arrival of what the peasants had been praying for, just what the object of *hope* should be is at best ambiguous. In fact, the film's ending seems more like an *apotheosis* – the villagers have arrived in their nightclothes to watch the motorcycle burn; their bodies are lit with a kind of uncanny light, and with the reflection of sparkling water, as the camera moves slowly from one gaunt face to another. They are bathed not just in light but in water that seems almost baptismal.

It is hardly surprising that Shepit'ko's film was shelved, given its revision of the progressive narrative (however humorously embedded) in Platonov's story. Censors and bureaucrats charged with ideological oversight took issue with the film's representation of villagers as "the living dead" and a finale that suggested that it is "God that supplies water, not the Bolsheviks."[11] But it seems at least possible that the film's visualization of rain and its absence might have led to other inferences, having to do with histories of drought, histories of famine, and the failures of technology in the Soviet Union. One wonders, in fact, if Shepit'ko herself, with strong Ukrainian roots, didn't have the bodies of Ukrainian famine victims in mind when she shot the film. Seen in this light, the finale is a kind of apotheosis of the martyred, alluding to the millions of peasants dead from starvation for their resistance to Stalin's forced collectivization, rendering them not as corpses but as filmic icons of transfiguration. The distance between this final image and the cheery-tractor-drivers-in-moist-and-fertile-land of Soviet propaganda couldn't be greater; it is in fact cosmic.

The role of water – and its absence – in these two films certainly doesn't exhaust the ways in which Larisa Shepit'ko was to film water, or reference cultural mythologies of water, in her work as a director. A vaudeville extravaganza that Shepit'ko produced for New Year's TV in 1970 romps through Russian folk tales – including the *rusalka* or mermaid figure of Slavic folk tradition – suggesting Shepit'ko's thoroughgoing and unsurprising familiarity with folk traditions.[12] Folk tradition and belief associated with water are part of what structures *Farewell to Matyora*; the film as ultimately released begins with the island of Matyora rising from watery depths, like the hidden city of Kitezh (a kind of Russian Atlantis, a righteous city protected beneath the waters of Lake Svetloyar by divine intervention) (Costlow, *Heart-Pine*). Even *Wings*, a film explicitly devoted not to water but air (the film dramatizes the alienation of a female fighter pilot in post-World War II Soviet life), includes an intriguing and seemingly anomalous sequence in which a diver begins, but doesn't complete, his dive. The diver's hesitation – a sequence repeated twice in the film – is both an external event and a filmic icon for the heroine's own inchoate desires, her longing but also her hesitation to *jump in*. In this sense the diving-board scene functions in *Wings* in ways not unlike the spring scenes in *Heat*, when Kemel' is lost in reverie and indecision. Later in *Wings* when a sudden shower washes both the heroine and the cherries she's bought – and clears the streets of people so that she's suddenly alone – it feels as miraculous as the final rain in *Motherland of Electricity*.

The visual vocabulary and ethical urgency of *Heat* and *Motherland of Electricity* derive from revisions of Soviet propaganda and avant-garde forefathers, but also from encounters with actual landscapes. These films practice (in extremely challenging political contexts) what one wants to call *environmental cinema*, film-making that represents with visual and tactile power the connection between human lives and particular landscapes. Particularly in *Motherland of Electricity* a lament that moves toward despair at human suffering and the vulnerability of hope is palpable.

Environmental cinema, as I understand it, emerges not as a pre-defined genre of visual production, but as a praxis situated in multiple and changing contexts of place, politics, and visual possibility.[13] These particular environmentally inflected films emerge from encounters with desiccated and destroyed places; they take stock of and challenge rhetorics of heroic transformation; they ask us to pay attention to the impact of climate and technology on human and earthly bodies. Made within a context of uncertain and then vanishing liberalization, they had to contend with what could and could not be said, or shown. Perhaps environmental cinema, in this case, is deeply allied to moments of reverie and indecision, to the *hesitation* I've suggested is embedded in the diver's pause. As an alternative to the violent heroics of remaking at the center of these films, such hesitation seems both ethically and environmentally imperative.

Notes

1 "It was when we'd driven through half the Republic that we understood what the screenplay was lacking, and how it needed to be reshaped" (Shepit'ko 154).
2 Tolomush Okeev, whose 1966 film *The Sky of Our Youth* is a stunning drama of generational divides within traditional herding families, worked on the sound crew for the film.
3 The temperature comes from Okeev's reminiscences (112); for him the filming came down to three things – "the Sargo sands, heat and the artesian well" (114).
4 Moon's study is primarily concerned with pre-revolutionary attempts at agriculture in Russian steppe land, but his conclusion suggests continuity between nineteenth-century settlers' tendency to see the region in terms of the wetter regions from which they had come and the twentieth (and twenty-first) centuries.
5 It's worth noting that there's a visual parallel between violence against Kalipa and violence against the earth – exactly the sort of argument that ecofeminists have made.
6 The film gives Abakir a truth-telling function here. He may be abusive and obnoxious, but he clearly knows what he's doing when it comes to plowing, and he also realizes the futility of their undertaking.
7 For a contemporary critique of these posters, see Ioffe.
8 Including *Aerograd* by Dovzhenko, or *The General Line* by Eisenstein, which includes a "tractor ballet" (Perez 71).
9 See also Costlow, "Icons."
10 "In an age lacking faith, in the age of a weakening not only of the old religious faith but also the humanistic faith of the nineteenth century, the sole remaining strong belief for a civilized person is the belief in technology, its power an dun-limited development." Nikolay Berdyaev, quoted in Hellebust (1).
11 This reading of the ending apparently occurred to the censors. Fomin quotes V. Ognev to the effect that "they banned [the film] because in the rain that nature gives at the end they saw an allusion to the fact that it's God who waters the earth, and not the Bolsheviks" (53).
12 As a student at VGIK Shepit'ko also produced a course film entitled "Living Water," which I have not yet been able to see. The title is, presumably, an allusion to the notion in Russian folk (and religious) tradition of water's miraculous powers to revive the dead and nearly dead.
13 See Ivakhiv for an overview of contemporary directions in green film criticism.

Bibliography

Aitmatov, Chingiz. "Verbliuzhii glaz." Translated from the Kirgiz by the author and A. Dmitrieva. *Pervyi uchitel'. Povesti.* Kiev: Veselka, 1976. Lib.ru. 28 May 2003. Web. 12 August 2015.

Aitmatov, Chingiz. "Larisa – debiutantka." *Larisa: Kniga o Larise Shepit'ko.* Ed. Elem Kilmov. Moscow: Iskusstvo, 1987, 28.

Beaver, Frank. *Dictionary of Film Terms: The Aesthetic Companion to Film Art.* New York: Peter Lang, 2006. Print.

Costlow, Jane. *Heart-Pine Russia. Walking and Writing the Nineteenth-Century Forest.* Ithaca, NY: Cornell University Press, 2013. Print.

Costlow, Jane. "Icons, Landscape and the Boundaries of Good and Evil: Larisa Shepit'ko's *The Ascent*." *Border Visions: Borderlands in Film and Literature.* Ed.

Jakub Kazecki, Karen Ritzenhoff, and Cynthia Miller. Lanham, MD: Scarecrow Press, 2013. Print.

Cronon, William. "A Place for Stories: Nature, History, and Narrative." *The Journal of American History* 78.4 (1992): 1347–1376. Print.

Ezerskaia, Bella. "Postmortem: Elem Klimov i Larisa Shepit'ko." *Chaika Seagull Magazine*. 15 August 2006. [Accessed 12 August 2015]. Web.

Fomin, Valerii. "Nachalo nevedomogo veka." *Polka: dokumenty, svidetel'stva, kommentarii*, vypusk 3: 32–54. Print.

Hellebust, Rolf. *Flesh to Metal: Soviet Literature and the Alchemy of Revolution*. Ithaca, NY: Cornell University Press, 2003. Print.

Ioffe, M. "Agitatsionnye plakaty na sel'skokhoziaistvennye temy." *Iskusstvo* 4 (1955).

Ivakhiv, Adrian. "Green Film Criticism and Its Futures." *Interdisciplinary Studies in Literature and Environment* 15.2 (2008): 1–28. Print.

Josephson, Paul. *Industrialized Nature: Brute Force Technology and the Transformation of the Natural World*. Washington, DC: Island Press, 2002. Print.

Josephson, Paul, et al. *An Environmental History of Russia*. Cambridge: Cambridge University Press, 2013. Print.

Kaganovsky, Lilya. "Ways of Seeing: On Kira Muratova's *Brief Encounters* and Larisa Shepit'ko's *Wings*." *The Russian Review* 71.3 (2012): 482–499. Print.

Klimov, Elem, ed. *Larisa: Kniga o Larise Shepit'ko*. Moscow: Iskusstvo, 1987. Print.

Kuznetsov, V.V. "Periodicheskaia pechat' o nachal'nom periode osvoeniia tselinykh I zalezhnykh zemel' Zapadnoi Sibiri." *Izvestiia altaiskogo gosudarstvennogo universiteta* 4.4 (2009): 138–140. Print.

Margolit, Evgenii. "Landscape with Hero." *Springtime for Soviet Cinema: Re/Viewing the 1960's*. Ed. Alexander Prokhorov. Pittsburgh, PA: Russian Film Symposium, 2001. Print.

McCauley, Martin. *Khrushchev and the Development of Soviet Agriculture. The Virgin Land Programme, 1953–1964*. New York: Holmes & Meier Publishers, 1976. Print.

Moon, David. *The Plough that Broke the Steppes: Agriculture and Environment on Russia's Grasslands, 1700–1914*. New York: Oxford, 2013. Print.

Murphy, Rhoads. "An Ecological History of Central Asian Nomadism." *Ecology and Empire: Nomads in the Culture and Evolution of the Old World*. Ed. Gary Seaman. Los Angeles, CA: Ethnographics Press/USC, 1989, 41–58. Print.

Okeev, Tolomush. "Kak molody my byli…" *Larisa: Kniga o Larise Shepit'ko*. Ed. Elem Kilmov. Moscow: Iskusstvo, 1987, 112–114.

Perez, Gilbert. "All in the Foreground: A Study of Dovzhenko's "Earth." *Hudson Review* 28.1 (1975): 68–86. Print.

Platonov, Andrei. *Soul and Other Stories*. Trans. Robert Chandler et al. New York: New York Review Books, 2008. Print.

Prokhorov, Alexander. "The Unknown New Wave: Soviet Cinema of the Sixties." *Springtime for Soviet Cinema: Re/Viewing the 1960's*. Pittsburgh, PA: Russian Film Symposium, 2001. Print.

Shepit'ko, Larisa. "Znoi. (Teoreticheskaia chast' diplomnoi raboty L. Shepit'ko)." *Larisa: Kniga o Larise Shepit'ko*. Ed. Elem Kilmov. Moscow: Iskusstvo, 1987, 153–165.

Shilova, I. *Fil'm i ego myzika*. Moscow: Sovetskii kompozitor, 1973. Wikipedia.ru. [Accessed 12 August 2015]. Web.

Stiegler, Bernd. "When a Photograph of Trees is Almost Like a Crime: Rodchenko, Vertov, Kalatozov." *Etudes photographiques* 23 (May 2009). Web.

Filmography

Dovzhenko, Oleksandr, dir. *Aerograd*. Mosfil'm, 1935.
Dovzhenko, Oleksandr, dir. *Zemlia [Earth]*. Kiev Film Studio, 1930.
Eisenstein, Sergei, dir. *The General Line*. Sovkino, 1929
Pyr'ev, Ivan. *Traktoristy*. Mosfil'm, 1939.
Shepit'ko, Larisa, dir. *Rodina elektrichestva [Motherland of Electricity]*. Mosfil'm (Experimental Creative Studio), 1968.
Shepit'ko, Larisa, dir. *Znoi [Heat]*. Kirgizfil'm, 1963.

13 "Water flows and teaches"
Marietta Shaginian's novel *Hydrocentral*

Arja Rosenholm

Water flows and teaches: one must not split me; I'm fused, united. Be united too, then I'll supply you all with water in equal measure. And then, further on, about the water: how people decided to use its power, to force it to serve up to them its flow. There is nothing better for such purposes than small Armenian rivers, because they are powerful rivers that flow down from the high mountains...[1]

The words above, detailing how "water flows and teaches" us, are those of Anush Malkhasian, an elderly female schoolteacher and mediator figure. They echo the main idea of the massive novel *Hydrocentral*, written by the Soviet-Armenian writer Marietta Shaginian (1888–1982). *Hydrocentral* is regarded as one of the "forgotten classics" (Nicholas 34) of Socialist Realism, one of the movement's "flagships" (Terras 484), and a "pioneer work" describing socialist construction (Kuznetsov 194). The novel was published in 1930–1931, first serially in the journal *Novyi mir*, and then as a separate volume in 1931.

In the novel, Malkhasian wants to teach her pupils – the future working class of the still young Armenian Soviet Socialist Republic – that water is inherent to all life; it is a powerful force that cannot be divided, since it is fluid and continuously in movement. Furthermore, it belongs to all: water is a common good, a vital element gushing through, touching, animating, and connecting both the human and non-human environment. The story ends with the teacher and her pupils visiting the construction site; they hear the main hydro-engineer state that the "electrification is the most important basis for our country," "warmth – steam – electric and hydroelectric energy – is bred for our machines; it is the foundation for us all" (345). They are also told that the hydrocentral power plant will eliminate the imbalance between the north and south of the country, since water will be delivered in balance and equally to all.

The passionate desire of the teacher to understand both the enigma of electricity and how water works in the hydroelectric power plant crystallizes the main idea of the novel. Both the teacher and the author wish to contribute to their country's transformation from a backward and isolated province into a dynamic member of the modern Union of Soviet Socialist Republics. They dream of its legitimate place as part of the united network of the Soviet Union's electric and hydropower plants, with the "Armenian electric network organically linked" (347) to the whole.

Shaginian's diaries and journalistic work indicate that the novel was based on her own observations while visiting similar construction sites in Soviet Armenia during the latter half of the 1920s (Shaginian, *Kak ia rabotala* 29; Nicholas 79). The story is situated on a construction site on the River Mizinka,[2] where a bridge and a water power plant is being built at the beginning of the second Five-Year Plan (1928–1932). The novel is known in the Soviet literary canon as one of the most seminal Soviet "production novels" (*proizvodstvennii roman*), even as "a model 'production novel'" (Clark and Dobrenko 116). Its thematic focus is on construction, and it "relies on the metaphor of building to make its case" (Nicholas 19). However, it is far from being a cheerleading story of success that only celebrates socialist construction work and the "heroic" (Kovalev 6).[3] Surely, it may have served as a "catalyst in developing the consciousness of 'Soviet man'" (Terras 484), as did also other production novels written in the transformative period of the late 1920s and early 1930s. However, in spite of its construction topic and the strong commitment to the socialist utopia and Soviet economic modernization, Shaginian's novel does not conform to the expectations of the Socialist Realist production novel as a genre marked "from above" with a highly ritualized "master plot," as has been suggested (Clark, *The Soviet Novel* 4–5). Several scholars (e.g. Guski; Shepherd 39–59) have already pointed out that the production novel was rather a complex genre mirroring the dynamic transformations of the period. Mary Nicholas (20) argues in her work on the production genre that the "early production novels provide an important key to the tortuous process of constructing Soviet culture, a process that was both more personal and more organic than has been appreciated." According to her, Shaginian's *Hydrocentral* is interesting since it refuses to "offer any pat answers which did not coincide with Shaginian's personal experience in researching and writing the novel" (ibid. 80).

The plot of *Hydrocentral* is complex. By the abundance of the episodic acts, sketches, and the many voices of the characters, the novel resists closeness and a clearly defined story-line while intertwining the author's contemplations on aesthetics with the collective interest in imagining a modern society. At the center of the building process is the bridge to be built for the hydropower plant; this bridge is seen as a symbol of the new life. The characters are configured in two groups; those of the future, and those of the past. Committed to the future are the teacher Malkhasian; the young female communist Mardzhana; the engineer-student Fokin, who is fascinated by cement as the newly found building material; the chairman Agabek; and the mediator protagonist, the philosopher-archivist, Arno Arevian. The past is reserved for the sceptics representing the old "cadre" embodied by the pre-revolutionary specialists, the non-party engineers and the managers of the construction, like Levon Davydovich and Sahar Petrovich, whose stiffened bureaucratism merges with their indifference toward any new forms of labour. The novel, being enthusiastic about the future, is critical of the various negative and contradictory phenomena of poor planning and badly organized labour, and these sins are depicted in a rather realistic manner. Thus, the construction plot shows its "readiness to negotiate" (ibid.) competing worldviews – between the pathos and high ambitions of modern hydro-engineering, on the one hand, and the detachment of both the working men and the management, their ideological resistance, and even sabotage, on the other. The novel reveals what happens when a construction site lacks disciplined labor ethics and the plant is hindered by an imbalance between abstract theories and an adequate knowledge of the local material conditions: the badly built bridge does not hold back the wild floodwater, and the plant descends into chaos, as represented by the collapse of the bridge, the very symbol of united ideas and people. The hydropower plant is not completed, though it is still "in the process of becoming," as promised at the end of the story by the hydro-engineer.

Shaginian writes that her aim with this novel was to "reflect in the arts how socialist construction arises through struggle and resistance" (Goriachkina 7). We can easily assume that the struggle in and with the production novel includes also her own artistic self-reconstruction. This meant overcoming her ambivalences and doubts, and processing her past as a member of the early Symbolist intelligentsia[4] before becoming a prolific Soviet writer and Lenin Prize winner (1972) who was drawn to the "realist novel," as she later wrote (Goriachkina 8; Nicholas 20). Aquatic imagery plays a significant role in this struggle toward a new literary identity, and it is thus important to keep an eye on the two lines intertwining in the novel: the discourse on Soviet modernization, on the one hand, and Shaginian's personal artistic desire to apply aquatic metaphors for her own aesthetic self-reflection, on the other. It is obvious in the drafted modern Soviet landscape that Armenian history and culture are mapped in images of water – in the landscapes of the snow-capped mountains in the wet north; in the dry waterless south, with its rivers and *aryks* (the small aqueducts providing water to the inhabitants); and in the newly planned water channels and dam projects. The recurrent metaphors of water are constitutive in social and individual agency construction.

It is for this water imagery that the "classic" *Hydrocentral* deserves to be revisited. A re-reading, focusing on ambivalent water, shows the text as a paradoxical celebration of Soviet modernity *and* a critique. Correspondingly, it is also a blend of the struggling streams of Symbolism and newly discovered Socialist Realism. The novel shows life in a ceaseless state of flux which blurs the past and present, and makes the inner self and the physical world dissolve. Water flows through various agencies; it overwhelms through its logic of circulation. The aquatic metaphors not only challenge the gaps between the past and present, but also between the natural and cultural in the human and non-human worlds.

Water dissolves boundaries and dual hierarchies through its elementary fluidity, generating dynamics of interchange between human and non-human qualities.

Accordingly, my analysis follows the ideas of scholars emphasizing the new materialist shift of dual structures, such as between nature and culture and mind and body. This reading helps us to understand "our entanglements with the lively materiality" of water (Chen *et al.* 5) and its presence in every aspect of our lives. As Chen *et al.* (ibid.) point out, it is important to pay attention to the "[...] continuity of watery materiality (for example, its capacity to gestate life, transform, or destroy) with discursive practices and ways of knowing." Böhme (16) also points out that since we cannot separate ourselves from the natural circulation of water, we cannot cut ourselves off from practices linked to water technologies either. This means that with respect to Shaginian's novel, the constructors of the hydropower plant are both actors and at the same time the targets of the very damming actions that are simultaneously directed at the aqueous environment and the streams of imaginary desire. Accordingly, by focusing on the meanings of water, I can shed light on both the historical and aesthetic potential of the novel. I also hope to contribute to the study of Soviet mythology, since despite the obvious role water plays in the novel, hardly any attention has been paid to it in analysis. Water can be considered to have mythology its own, like the already familiar "myth of metallization," which Hellebust has determined as one of the obligatory characteristics of the socialist "positive hero," with socialist society being characterized by comparisons with iron and steel, both in physical and psychological transformations. In my analysis, I claim that water – as one of the main spatial elements and tropes in the Soviet-Russian modernization discourses of the 1930s – strongly influenced cultural self-understanding as part of the imagined new world.

The power plant of desire production

The story plays with analogies, and Malkhasian's story of the power of water is integrated within the main story as a *mise en abyme*. Like the schoolteacher, the author also wishes to teach and to find the right words to resolve the enigma of water. Similar to the teacher and the schoolchildren, who "fantasize of the hydropower plant as a wishful and an alluring image of desire, just as Paris or London is to some provincial inhabitants" (337), the author regards the hydro-electrical plant as a topos of desire. Shaginian's power plant generates and absorbs the dreams and utopian concepts that intersect the private and public-collective spheres of life. The power plant thus confirms the cultural-historical conclusions made regarding the Soviet mega-dams – that they not only required an immense amount of physical manpower, but also became power centers, absorbing millions of peoples' imaginations and fantasies (Gestwa 117–132; see also Epstein).

Analogous to the fantasy-absorbing function of the power plant, Shaginian's text abounds with images that emphasize productive "energy" as "the most precious" (10, 16) for "our new Soviet system" (212); it encompasses both physical and imaginary flows, currents, movements, and fluidities, both within human bodies and without (e.g. 10, 43, 59, 66), and it makes life stream in a great flow. Not only do physical rivers and aqueducts flow in the story, but so do humans, things, and thoughts. People "stream" (246), "swim" and "splash like fish" (47, 58); crowds of workers "stream" back and forth (62, 106, 107, 335); the club hall at one point is filled to bursting by a "thick ocean of people" (107); the hall "whooshed like ocean surf" with workers (107); the club room turned into an "ocean of heads" (107); it was like a "human sea" (106); the barracks "swim" (83); ideas and thoughts "stream" (103, 105); speech "floods over" (88); and words "flow" (9, 43) "like a river" (14, 43, 63).

The aquatic metaphors provide the construction site with energy-producing fluidities that are implicit forces of the production of human desire: not only does the River Mizinka flow in the novel, human desire also expresses itself in a streaming mode. The artist Arshak Gnuni verbalizes his futurist ambitions and the newly discovered possibilities: "All my inner gateways are raised, the energy flows like a stream. It seems that I have enough energy to perform all possible work in the Soviet Union. The immense passion to work..." (15–16). Human desire flows and produces a socially embodied reality in a process of coupling, binding, and splitting. The novel becomes a site, and the author's desire, with the logic of a machine, produces ever new couplings and meanings according to the fluid mobility of the human psyche (Deleuze and Guattari, *Anti-Oedipus* 1–50). Streams of desire couple with other streams and split from them again, which makes this "hydraulic model" (Deleuze and Guattari, *A Thousand Plateaus* 361) remind us of a "desiring-machine" (Colebrook, *Gilles Deleuze* 140–144). Flux in this hydraulic model is thought of as reality itself and opposes "the stable, the eternal, the identical, the constant" (Deleuze and Guattari, *A Thousand Plateaus* 361). Agency, being thus spatially marked through the flows of desire, is in a permanent process of coupling between "territorialization" and its concomitant "de-territorialization" (West-Pavlov 178, 183):

> The basic process of life is dynamic and eternal, but the local territorialities formed by desiring couplings are only ever contingent and temporary, subject to entropy and renewal in another form elsewhere. Territorialization and its concomitant *de*-territorialization are the two hallmarks of life, as contingent couplings dissolve so as to make space for new connections.
>
> (Ibid. 183)

To the same extent, the various forces, streams, and fluidities in Shaginian's world of human and non-human agencies are perpetually interacting with each other, and they contribute to an endless processuality of "becoming"

(Deleuze and Guattari, *A Thousand Plateaus* 361). The novel shows how in this multifunctional circuit of streams and constant state of flowing desire, the boundaries between human and non-human matter become destabilized. This is expressed, for example, in recurrent hybrid human–non-human creatures: new busy Soviet people become the "happy migratory birds of the railroads" (62), and the power plant looks like a "big whale" (203). Respectively, social coding is also compromised: the River Mizinka shows its resistant, independent, and material flow, mirroring the ever-flowing desire also to couple with unexpected objects, ideologically improper names, and disturbing memories. The interaction of various – discursive, geo-physical, corporeal, technological, and social – forces and agencies calls for an understanding of Shaginian's view of hydro-modernization as a rich, complex, and ambivalent process where the material and discursive and the natural and cultural are not separated but belong to one and the same multifunctional universe that interconnects imagery and social desire. The flow of desire is constantly seeking a new "alluring" object (337) to couple with (i.e. territorialization), then to be dissolved in an ongoing process of "de-territorializing," thus making space for new connections (West-Pavlov 179). Occasionally, the modernization process celebrates the rising of inner and outer "gates," as Arshak demonstrates, but then the consolidation of free waters into an "aggressive onslaught of concrete" (207) point to how people's passion and prejudices were supposed to be disciplined and seized upon by society, and their dreams "codified" (Deleuze and Guattari, *Anti-Oedipus* 33; West-Pavlov 178) according to social and political power.

Shaginian follows the stream of her time with *Hydrocentral*, which is certainly a politically correct name for the desire being re-coded and channelled according to the modernization processes reflected in the Soviet literature of the 1930s in general. However, the dynamics of the flow challenge the hallmarks of modernization – that is, the teleological, forward march of evolution – leaving the power plant unfinished. Accordingly, when we bring water forward, we see Shaginian working out an original, rather paradoxical concept that aims at the integral wholeness of the human and the non-human realm, but it is also simultaneously in a permanent state of disintegration into its individual parts. Wholeness draws from the lesson water teaches us; from the schoolteacher Malkhasian we know that water is a balancing, interrelating, and uniting force, and a source for generating true creativity – both for socialist labor ethics and artistic activity. It is the elemental mediator of the view of life as an organic assimilation and an interrelation of the material and non-material and the human and non-human spheres. Balance is pursued: in order to build a bridge as the very topos of unity, the "symbol(s) of connection" (199) between nations, classes, and aesthetic styles, one needs to find a balanced interrelation between the aquatic substance – "this vital force" (106) of human desire – and a cultural-material form that is "plastic" enough to hold up the matter.

The palimpsestic text of the "sea of life"

The metaphorical semantics, consisting of numerous images of seas and oceans – the "ocean of work" (103) and the "ocean of people" (107) – point to a hydro-cosmos that contains the symbolic analogy of the "sea of life." Water as the bearer of all life indicates a creation story; it is both life-giving and a stormy, chaotic realm. The amorphous sea of life attracts metaphors that imply the moment of metamorphosis: humans become fish, and the construction workers become fishermen laying and drawing their "fishing nets" (227), connoting – due to their use in mythological tradition – change and transformation. This encapsulates the novel's theme: everything streams and swims in the sea of life where stories and identities mix in an organic multi-layered reality, with "apparent" (171) knowledge on the surface and the mysterious below, in the invisible depths.

Analogically, it is the mission of the author-storyteller to spread her story nets across the broad and deep waters in order to catch the flow of life "onboard" the "steamer" (150, 210, 65, 230), as the power plant is imagined. This steamer is close to a "shipwrecking" (225) due both to the inadequate decisions made by the indifferent crew on the construction site and to the implicit logic of the de-coupling desire that is haunted by memories; what is regarded as forgotten has not disappeared but only lies in the depths of the "well of time" (17, 199). The author-storyteller must be ready to dive into the depths, become an "archivist," like the protagonist Arno Arevian, the author's alter ego. The role of the Soviet writer, as is indicated, is to be a complex actor recreating the world out of flowing pieces, like Arno Arevian does by telling a new story by reordering the chaotic archive of past events on the construction site. Arno Arevian thinks, that one "should [...] be able to excite those who are sitting in the crowd, to raise the inner powers which the depth advances. And after that, to inflame oneself with ideas delegated by the depths. And after that... after... it's not clear yet" (107–108). Both the uneducated lower class and the streams of unconscious desire are connoted as unpredictable, still uncontrollable in the "depths," untouched by the modernization process. Despite not yet exactly knowing how to proceed with what has been achieved, the storyteller has to dredge up what lies in the depths, to "regulate" the diffuse energy (103) and streams of unconscious in order to enable the "birth of the Soviet citizen" (123) – as Arno Arevian recognizes. The analogy of the unconscious and water is brought about by the "inherent structural commonality" between them, which Young and DeCosta (69) have pointed out as the "'undifferentiated matrix' into which all things are submerged and from which all things arise."

What may seem "apparent" (171) – as emphasized several times in relation to the bridge "being [only] apparently solid" (ibid.) – is not the whole story: different stories are coupled to each other in the fluid process of storytelling. The text pays attention to what flows deep down, under the visible level of the construction project – the unattainable water, desire and memories – as the driving force of creativity. Accordingly, the narrative has a palimpsest dual structure. It consists of both a collective history and the author's individual reflection on her own mission to become a Soviet author; this process is constantly interrupted by "cursed memories," indicating the vulnerability of feelings. In the words of the young female Bolshevik: "Memory is something damnable, damnable. [...] There are many things in the world that would be better not to remember" (83–84). While collective history is conceived of as the "sea of labourers' voices," the individual voice resonates with Shaginian's own history as a writer in transformation. Thus, the story of hydro-engineering also re-routes and re-channels the disturbing memories and doubts of the author, who asks questions regarding the patronizing attitude of society to its people: "Didacticism, enlightenment and watching your every step, taking care of you – is that good?" (105). The author thinks like Arno Arevian, and both have the same aim – to correlate with the utopian socialist future. The palimpsest storylines are coupled to each other in the "double-layered" narrative structure; the cultural artefact – be it the narrative or the map of Armenia – corresponds with the multi-layered structure of the material world of nature – of living water, and the "living layers" of soil (201) that geology should "account as a whole" (201), according to the new dialectic world view. As individual history merges past and present, so collective history is depicted as a "double-layered" map of a network of water channels, comprising different historical periods: "A big pink-green map of Armenia with a black network of channels was hanging on the wall. [...] The map represented a kind of a unique ancient culture." (203) This idea is repeated: "There was a double track of new channels created by the revolution, and two-colored lines of the planned channels appeared as newborn grandchildren who get ready to say their word in the future" (204).

Challenging modernization

Along with the refashioning of both the self and the surrounding environment, one story-line of the palimpsest narrative obviously deals with nature and ecology. The novel acts as a point of reference for the intense modernization projects of the 1930s through hydro-engineering and the construction of the Soviet "cartography of power" (Clark, "Socialist Realism" 8; Dobrenko 117–134). The "great transformation of Nature" (Weiner 169ff) as the landscaping of the central power perspective expressed the idea that conscious history could be planned and made. The hydro projects – like the White Sea–Baltic Sea Canal (Ruder), and the later mega-projects of DniproGES and the Moscow Canal (Hausmann; Gestwa *Die Stalinschen*) – became constructions of superlatives to convince the world of the superiority of Soviet hydro-engineering. The enforced modernization of the 1930s was marked by dam-building, amelioration projects, and flooding caused by established dams and hydroelectric power stations to produce energy for the country's ambitious industrialization program (Richter 72). Hydropower plants, canals, reservoirs, and mega-dams became an essential feature of Soviet rivers[5] and the Soviet-Russian landscape more generally. The plans to divert rivers in particular became "one example of a long and painstaking development of the[se] utopian projects" (Vorobyev 177).

As already noted, the hydropower plants are not only the products of modern industry; they are also a special spatial trope in negotiation with nature and culture and the conscious mind and spontaneous affect – the two hallmarks of Socialist Realist identity constitution. Many contemporary authors – such as Paustovsky, Pil'niak, and Platonov – and film-makers – such as Dovzhenko and Sol'ntseva – took part in the imagery construction of the country by depicting dam- and canal-building (Westerman; Shtil'mark). Shaginian also followed the "pathos of water culture," as Paperny calls the warming up of the Soviet atmosphere with special relation to the water culture of the 1930s (Paperny 172–173; Binder), which was in contrast to the "fire culture" of the 1920s. In his article "Struggle with Nature" (1931), Maxim Gorky called writers to the "struggle of collectively organized reason against elemental forces of nature and against everything 'elemental' [...] in the formation of man [...]" (Gorky, in Weiner 170).[6] However, these "elementary forces" (146) are highly valued by Shaginian and not to be considered separate from human culture. Although the framework is inspired by didacticism and the socialist pathos of the technology that would "resolve all" in the words of Stalin (Paperny 158), the taming of water in the novel is in no way an unapologetic celebration of human mastery over the environment and hydrological systems, in contrast to many other contemporary novels.[7]

Instead of regarding modern water as a pure commodity of industrial use-value that should be predictably modelled and calculated through measurements, credits, and numbers, Shaginian defies the reduction of water to an abstract concept divorced from social and ecological relations. Her water is a powerful agentic force – the very "heroine" (150, 461) of the novel embodied by the River Mizinka. The river is an autonomous agent and an ecological subject of its own; it speaks in its own part (46, 102, 163). Shaginian provides the river with an anthropomorphic identity, ascribing to it human physical traits and emotions, but also non-human animal attributes:

> The river runs breathing convulsively as a skinny little girl with straight green hair. [...] Her small foot slipped and checked the road here and there. Her hair clung to the stones and left green glitter between sandbanks. If it was impossible to run, the river grinned its silvery teeth and penetrated into the land – who could stop her?
>
> (157)

The Mizinka has its own logic and ethical identity, and, as a living body, it is vulnerable when "injured" by inadequate human interventions to its flow-body: critical irony is directed at the blind faith in the superior technology of water measurement by the hydro-technician, Areulski, who ignores the river as a living body of water: "The Mizinka runs past Areulski and whisks away its wounded and beaten in its gentle liquid body" (165).

The narrator's critical irony emphasizes the organic understanding of nature and humanity's part in it. Everything is interrelated: rivers to each other and to the seas, famine to the oppression of peasants by landowners, drought to the lack of energy and irrigation systems, ecology to political economy, and spiritual creativity to the flowing matter of desire. In Shaginian's conceptualization, all parts should work together; this correlates with the Soviet ideal of the disciplined harmony of hydrological system-thinking where river-taming becomes part of socio-economic logic. However, Shaginian questions the anthropocentric instrumentalization of nature in the consequent quest for an organic reading of the world. The "dialectic" (204) complexity of that world becomes obvious in the shared working of the human and non-human alike in the hydro-realm and the circulation of water as a life-giving energy through human and non-human bodies, between and across borders. Distinctions between human and nonhuman worlds, as the hallmark of the modernist project, dissolve by perpetual interchange; the narrator points out that there exists an analogy between organic and machine parts, as well (195). An obvious analogy is created between the human characters and their shared animalistic qualities and attributes: humans resemble birds, bees, rats, parrots, bugs, hedgehogs, mice, wolves, and gamecocks, among others. Who teaches whom and which came first – nature or culture – becomes elusive. As hydroculture is shared by human and animal alike, so hydro-building skills are similarly mediated from one generation to the next among both the human builders and the "beavers" (204). The teacher contemplates how, in Armenian history, "water had been meticulously researched [...] and there was a unique construction culture connected with water, while people didn't understand its importance and simply passed on the delicate skills of using water like the construction skills of a beaver" (204). Odd metamorphic agents are born, such as the cliffs on the riverbank being washed by the river and taking on an "elephant's skin" (163), the car that "passed by with a cockcrow as elastically and soundless as a lacquered rat" (82), or the "steamsoul" (76) of the locomotive being endowed with a human soul. The world becomes a heterogeneous mixture consisting of human–machine–animal hybrids, the river looks like a "tiger" (162), humans may seem like "broken motors" (226) who look at you with fear in their "cat eyes" (226).

This kind of constructed discontinuity between the human and the non-human seems to follow the conjunctive logic of the multifunctional "becoming," where alliances are changed and cohesions revert in the interplay of forces (Colebrook, "The Space of Man" 192). The process comes close to those transgressions pointed out by the "material turn", or what Donna Haraway (149–181) has identified as a concept of "nature/culture." The multi-layered dynamics of Shaginian's world of analogies and transgressions creates metamorphic creatures. The transgressions show qualities that contemporary material ecocritical studies have formalized as the concept of "transcorporeality" (Alaimo, "Trans-corporeal Feminisms" 238; *Bodily Natures*). Alaimo's construct indicates that there is a number of "material interchanges across human bodies, animal bodies, and a broader non-human world" (Alaimo, "States of Suspension" 476). Material corporeality draws on the idea that there are reciprocal interchanges and diverse interconnections across diverse natural entities. This indicates that the human is part of a material and constantly changing world and that the human-self is interconnected in an inevitable way to other networks – be they political, cultural, economic, or material. While being integrated into diverse environments in this fundamental way, humanity is also made vulnerable by unpredictable and often unwanted effects caused by other humans, non-humans, ecological systems, chemicals, and other agencies (Alaimo, *Bodily Natures* 2, 18, 20).

Drawing its dynamics from ever-circulating water, Shaginian's concept resists becoming consolidated, much like water resists becoming fixated as an abstraction; the many interchanges resist the modern logic of "false distinctions" (Latour 85) between nature and culture, and the human and non-human. The quest for balance and the wholeness of matter and form unsettles binaries of culture/nature, male/female, mind/body, reason/matter and human/non-human. The collapse of the bridge in the novel represents the absence of balance and wholeness: the whole construction project will fail if a balanced interconnection is not achieved with flows of substances, the agencies of the environment, and adequate human cultural and technological knowledge. Furthermore, balance will be evasive if local, peripheral environments are not respected but are instead subjected to the needs of a distant center (Moscow), with the "form" not corresponding to the "content," and theory not corresponding to practice.

In the utopian construction process of socialism, every subject and every part should become integrated into the collective. In the continuous process of concatenating natural forces and human qualities, humans and the power plant become one in their analogous working: "Obviously, the hydrocentral is like a human: so far, it works alone, its achievements are low, its thought is limited, but when it is linked to another, it will flow into a collective, and it will be of more use to others, and others will be of use to it too. And besides that…" (347).

As the ellipsis indicates, since everything is in a continuous state of transformation, the future can only be unknown and open. Rather than a revolutionary development, the future is imagined by Shaginian more like an involution of a complex process generated by the interchanges of organic bodies and machines, of matter and spirit. Shaginian's hybrid creatures – the cliffs with "elephant skin," the small, "smart," and "grumbling" concrete mixer with teeth in its jaw (161), the "talkative" river tiger "holding its tongue" (269), and the many comparisons of human and animals – come about in metamorphic symbioses and articulated combinations. Thus, Shaginian's metamorphic creatures also accompany the various other human-fish swimming in the Soviet science fiction literature of the 1920s (Rosenholm 41–54), a genre which uses water as a gestational space for a new world.

Aqueous dissolution and metonymic discourse

Besides the storyline of modernization and its attitude to the natural environment and especially water, the novel considers aesthetics and Shaginian's own re-creation. Reality, conceptualized as diverse systems' and agencies' flow of interchange, has an obvious impact on the novel's aesthetics and how creativity is understood as one of the layers within the palimpsest sea of life. The creative representation of social reality is not separated from the idea of matter, which is endowed – in the terms of material ecocriticism – with agentic capacity and meanings (Iovino 56). Water is a changing realm of effects: both human and non-human agencies are continuously interrelated with each other. Shaginian's water acts in a twofold manner: it unites the Soviet Armenian landscape through the common electric network, and as a fluid element it also challenges and dissolves opposites and dual hierarchies. Simultaneously, the dissolving dynamic possesses a chaotic and dispersing power. This resonates with Latour's (34) conclusions that the modern constitution gives rise to the paradox in which modernity allows a proliferation of hybridities but necessarily denies their existence. In Shaginian's world, this means that the fluid element of water unites by dissolving boundaries, but it also has a disintegrating effect.

While reviewing *Hydrocentral* in *Krasnaja nov'* in 1933, the Russian literary critic Boris Aikhenvald (195) mentions the "method of watery sentences," by which he means that the "uninterrupted flow" (ibid.) of the narration is constantly looking at all possible directions of life. What ensues in this "organic flow" (ibid.) of narration is the large number of subtexts and plotlines coursing from the text: reflections on pedagogy, the arts and aesthetics, love and sexual behaviour, people's justice, quotidian life (*byt*), technical training, and ecology and modernization. There is a linkage between authenticity, representation and fluid reality, as already pointed out, that explains the rhetorical thoroughness of the storyteller. Things and words cross over formal boundaries from chapter to chapter, small and large flow into one, and "a detail grows into another detail" (ibid.). There is a constant interplay between the whole and the part as *pars pro toto*, whereby the whole is constantly in danger since it is fragmented and disintegrated by the obvious abundance of details that almost live an autonomous life. The novel mentions innumerable technical tools and utensils used in the construction work, it repeats rather mundane objects of quotidian life, and it stops several times at the "modern" short hairstyle of the female workers. Furthermore, it pays careful attention to the dishes in the canteen and the eating habits of the peasants. We come to know details that are both irrelevant but also "telling," like the Belgian tableware in the house of Levon Davydovich (87), the linen napkins (87), and the "oil-clothed" folder (90) of the female people's judge. Furthermore, the barracks furniture and the office walls tell the stories of the inhabitants' lives, since "things spoke even before people opened their mouths" (303).

Human bodies are a particular target of disintegration, and they become the very embodiments of hybridization. They are fragmented into "nostrils," "pike-profiles," "fish stomach[es]," "gouty bones," "stork-legs," and "eyebrows," etc. The hidden love story of Arno Arevian and the young Bolshevik Mardzhana takes place between his "broken glasses" (59, 80) and her "attractive eyebrows" (59). The protagonist, Arno Arevian, is a hybrid, both in social and gender terms, and as the alter ego of the author: the figure implicates the author's self-reflection. Arno Arevian's "centaurian" (80) habitus in particular is a patchwork pieced together from various parts emphasizing his Otherness (80). His constantly repeated "broken glasses," his stork-legs, and his arbitrarily composed attire, composed of female equestrian dress (Amazonka) and American-style shoes, is constantly brought up when he appears. The outer patchwork corresponds to the flowing identity of his hybrid character, which defies any fixed meaning, both in social and gender categories.

What the project stands for is signified by the close attention paid to details and parts of the whole, the interchange of the subject and object positions, so that the plot action is subjected to the characterizing details, the anthropomorphic reflection of the non-human world, and the replacement and substitution of the actions and thoughts of the protagonists through frequent references to parts of the body, architecture, tools, and hydro-technical and political systems. MizinGES is a metonym, a synecdoche for the modern socialist society, and even for the whole cosmic sphere in the stream of life. The novel displays many elements listed by Roman Jakobson (41–48) in his article on metonymy in language. Two aspects are of special interest. First, the metonymic discourse in the novel operates according to the principle of contiguity, which prefers closeness and combination, and locates events and objects side by side in space and time without being connected by causality. As already pointed out, the boundaries of binary logic are in flux and blurred; the novel is created from episodes which point to an immediate connection to the material realm. The details, the fragmented parts and pieces, are placed side by side in the novel like a paratactic syntax (Donovan 87) that "reflects the associative, random connections of consciousness in immediate response to the environment" (ibid. 88). Second, the paratactic syntax and the fragmentation of the whole that is obvious in Shaginian's metonymic narration comes close to what Olga Matich has called the "rhetorical fragmentation" that she identifies as "the aesthetic device of decadent poetics." This device, she writes, was deployed by the Russian decadent utopians who "saturated their work with the dissolution of society's and nature's whole" (Matich 18).

This connection is of interest as a "living layer" in Shaginian's own palimpsest literary history, which obviously contains her Symbolist past. According to Matich, "these early modernists infused the severed part with a fetishizing, mystical aura, while indulging their nostalgia for the whole" (ibid.). Shaginian's past continues to live on in this later "realist" work. What the metonymic discourse may also tell us is that the author does not only think *about* water, but *with* water (Chen et al. 3–5; also Linton 38): the formal and rhetorical choices of the metonymic discourse with its paratactic syntax and non-dualistic approach to life imitate a fluid text-movement in collaboration with the corporeality of water. The text-movement consists of circulating details (e.g. of technical tools and processes), and lists (e.g. the agendas of meetings) that interrupt the linear story-line, and the plot prefers open-endedness to closeness, as demonstrated by the ending of the novel: the river is still free at the end of the story. The process of becoming with the logic of fluids dissolves solid identities and produces the open-endedness and the horizontal expansion of the plot with an abundance of details from the close environment. The novel moves on a kind of a boundary between literature and the non-literary, incorporating extra-literary genres, such as archive material, letters, technical inventories, party congress resolutions, political speeches, reflections on aesthetic programs, and so on.

The metonymic text-movement shows the author as if trying to conceive of (the sea of) life as a ceaseless state of flux, which, however, being as "impetuous" (165) as the River Mizinka, is too powerful to be harnessed. In constant reference to something that is not there in its totality but only in its singular parts, the metonymic discourse appears to be more than a simple rhetorical trope. The metonym can also be a trope of desire (Lacan 447–461)[8] coursing in correspondence to the constant de/territorializing flow. The text tries to catch the absent utopian dream in the details present, constantly changing the objects of desire, from large to small and vice versa, from the quotation of Stalin's speech at the 25th Party Congress to the hairstyle of the female workers or a detailed lecture on a hydro-technical procedure. The text goes on, endlessly referring to what is not there in its entirety. Desire wishes to flow, and it flows in the rhythms of de-couplings between becoming and un-becoming. The cyclical rhythm in the sea of life also resonates in the mingling of the past and present. Since water has in its materiality the capacity to recycle and communicate memory (Bachelard 52, 134), it is no wonder that however controlled and deeply submerged memory is, the symbolist stream still rises to the surface in the text-flow.

Shaginian tries to reroute her modernist past along the regulations of Socialist Realism. The novel itself becomes a hybrid genre; it shows how unleashed, "deterritorialized" utopian openings made in the name of "Communism [as] Soviet power plus the electrification of the whole country," in the words of Lenin, experience a re-codification. Openings and liberties are taken back by society "to see that no flow exists that is not properly damned up, channelled, regulated" (Deleuze and Guattari, *Anti-Oedipus*

33). The construction engineer's speech at the end of the heterogeneous construction process confirms that relative liberties are rescinded as the design of the new power paradigm. When the narrator states that "the first aggressive onslaught of concrete had already started to float under the raised bridge" (207), we can read the image as an anticipation of the future "re-territorialization,", that is, the cementing of utopian and free-flowing dreams. It is as if the novel foresees how Soviet society will reroute the flows, harness both physical and the human fantasy production into regulated channels of the future mega-dams, and drain the vivid aquatic streams with "gusts of concrete" (211).

"Concrete-water factor"

The novel's long and detailed debates on the role of concrete not only refer to the contemporary debates on construction negotiated between traditional stone and concrete as the element of modern construction technology (207); as the narrator states, the "debate [on concrete] lies much deeper than only on the surface of the words" (208). Again, we have the act of diving into the deeper levels of water imagery, where memory unfolds. This becomes clear in chapter 13, which begins with the narrator's rather long reflection on age:

> Turning forty is a milestone for everyone. [...] In one's forties one suddenly begins to feel one's forgotten past in its strange, growing, tenacious resilience, in the petrification of all, gone and forgotten, rashly made and said words and deeds. It's the time of "waiting-on-cement"/ схватыванье for any person, a terrible time of human life, as it happens for concrete, and now it's too late. [...] The time, the "concrete-water factor", holds the whole past, every small detail, in the process of solidification – and now the whole past is here.
>
> (278)

The reflection can also be assigned to the author, who was in her forties at the time of writing the novel. The depiction expresses sensual awareness of time past and a sense of sorrow. Communication of one's feelings and memories in the recurrent image of water resonates with what Gaston Bachelard has called the "material imagination." Fundamental ideas are communicated and felt in the material sense, which explains why past experiences and dreams are often, he suggests, imagined in figures of deep water. The streams, or rather, their regulation by the channels, dams, and power plants, utilize the meanings of water as a symbol for the undifferentiated source of the unconscious and memories. Different narrative streams mix in Shaginian's "sea" of potential (Strang 67; Böhme 24–25) – one intertwines human culture and ecology, and another deals with aesthetics and creativity.

The author seems to have reached an existentially experienced juncture that is a culmination of what she calls the "concrete-water factor." Shaginian borrows from construction terminology to characterize her own life, including its creative processes and crises. The concrete-water factor indicates the stage of life when one's flowing vitality of youth, flexibility, and plasticity is over and the process of "setting" and hardening takes place. Both good and bad memories hold one's identity together; they are now inseparable from one's present identity. The reflections imply that due to the setting material of memory, the narrator lacks the capacity to be as pliable as she had once been earlier in the sea of life. The difference is obvious in the comparison made to the lives of the young Bolshevik girls working for the idea of future socialism in the peripheral Armenian villages: the narrator makes note of their youth, and states that they had not yet experienced the "moment of setting." Quite in accordance with the idea of a swimmer taking up the challenge of violent water as a schema for courage (Bachelard 168), the narrator sees the girls putting themselves in a position – like that of a swimmer – where the surroundings are unpredictable and difficult to determine. Nevertheless, the girls have the courage to do so. Swimming is a metaphor for living one's life, and life is full of tasks and surprises that the girls cannot yet anticipate – they must rely on their courage to get them through:

> [the] method [of working] demanded from them, as water demands from a swimmer, that they would be able to immediately rise to the surface in the unknown environment, gain status, get the right to speak out, and that this all would be based on two or three essential principles, the same two or three basic movements needed by a swimmer.
> (279)

The attention paid to the "methodic swimming" is important, since it is analogically applied by Shaginian both to the ethics of work and to aesthetics. Full dedication to the socialist construction work and artistic creativity needs a "methodic" approach – those "two or three basic movements needed by a swimmer" – to accumulate energies that can be released and discharged at the "right moment" to deliver hydropower, art, or children. The "gestational" process (Chandler and Neimanis 62–63) of construction and creativity is saturated with water and its "enigma of energy"; humans and machines are both charged by streams of "electric loading" (e.g. 187, 189, 308, 310) to become "diesel stations" (309) generating valuable new life. With this imagery, Shaginian shares the Bolshevik discourse on the magic of electricity, which is seen "as heavenly fire" and as a "mystical life force" (Hellebust 19; Stites 49). However, the novel also shows how energies and streams flowing both outside and inside human bodies and minds include and route libidinal and sexual energies, making humans dangerously unpredictable; they are endowed with affective resonance and are thus in need of methodic restructuring. This is made obvious by images of how the crowd of people "streams into [the hall] like an elementary force" (106), how "the first rows [of people] broke toward the stage like the sea foam onto a beach" (106) in a way that the whole hall "whooshes like splashing surf" (106). The "thick sea of people" (107) is ambivalently powerful in its "elementary" incalculability; inner streams may begin to "boil" and burst out like "lava" (146). The crowd must be regulated in its urges, quite like the water power being dammed and transformed into positive energy. Two opposite "methods" of energy dissipation are presented; the one is embodied by Klavdia Ivanovna, the wife of the head of the construction bureau, of whom the ascetic hero Arno Arevian thinks this "woman before him is devilishly loaded with electricity" (137). Klavdia "discharges" this electricity spontaneously in erotic caresses (139). She is described as being animal-like, which she is compared to in appearance (52). It is also mentioned several times that her apartment is reminiscent of an animal's "hole" (136, 169).

As already pointed out, for example by Nicholas (83), Shaginian struggled with her Symbolist past in trying to catch the new "magnetic and electric force" as an author, and thus to mediate her commitment to the socialist order. It is thus not surprising that the author-narrator shares the same struggles with the agitating alter ego, Arno Arevian. They both share the same vague past, the same passion for storytelling, and the need for self-regulation. Arevian's habitus is marked by his "methodical" cleaning activities and washing images (9–10, 50), which correspond to the purification of one's mind of re-emerging memories that distract from the future orientation. Like Shaginian, Arno Arevian is also committed to disciplined work and to the working class, whose words "blend in a peaceful flow with his own thoughts" (103). The narrator and her alter ego become identical in their thoughts of re-territorializing, damming, and self-regulation:

> There is an ocean of work to be done – great, new, free, highly inspiring work at any, even insignificant, workplace. Educate, form a man – in yourself and in others – patiently teach the backward ones; study, measure, dig and build up the land; conquer, direct and keep the rebellious river in check.
>
> (103)

While Klavdia is endowed with erotically assigned "electric loading" (137), which she extravagantly and generously squanders without giving birth to new life – as her abortions testify (55) – Arno Arevian is her opposite: his strategy is ascetic, that is, "methodic" self-regulation. In the way Arno Arevian works "there was a method as actual as in all his behaviour" (130). He may want to dance, but only in his "thoughts" (130), while keeping the affective resonance of his inner "music" (130) and erotic desire under control. His erotic desire is reduced to metonymic eye contact, which becomes the fetishized medium of his emotions.

The method of self-regulation is imagined in the hydro-technological analogy of dam-building, which is extended to desire production and creativity processes in general; the higher the dam, the more effective is the water energy accumulated behind it (342), and the more controlled the imagery and desire production. The chief engineer states that the very goal of the construction project is to build a dam as high as possible to "hold up the greatest pressure ever" (342) to be released "in maximum" and at the "right moment" (270). The flow of desire becomes rerouted, "reterritorialized," even halted occasionally, to accumulate pressure in order to be released, not in Klavdia's false, squandering way, but only at the right moment:

> In every work – at the machine or the steam boiler, in piano playing, being a rider who leaps through the hoop, taking care of a patient with typhoid fever – there is a moment when you can't waste even a second, and need to rearrange your full intelligence and sustained attention on this culmination point not to lose focus.
>
> (270)

The release of the loaded energy at the "right moment" means giving birth to a new wo/man, a new society, and a new kind of art. Arno Arevian manages to store away his bodily energies – into eye contact – and thus overcome the temptations embodied by Klavdia. The painter Arshak, "breathing" and "panting," also "delivers" his libidinal energies into a piece of art in a "wave of creativity," like a woman giving birth (56).

The mechanism of dam-building represents a libidinal self-regulation that points to the utopian desire of the modernizers to extend social transformation to the corporeal realm. Matich (7) calls this oxymoronic sexual practice "erotic celibacy," which was "considered a prerequisite for abolishing death and immortalizing the body." Not only does it "erase nature's reproductive dictum and celebrate unconsummated erotic desire, it also reflects the radical idea that sexual renunciation is the agent of change" (ibid.). Matich makes sense of this paradoxical economy of desire by considering it as a two-stage process:

> In the first stage, loaded in history, the practitioners of erotic celibacy would store their libidinal energy in their mortal bodies; in the second stage, marking the transition to time after history, the accumulated erotic energy would be expended collectively – in a grand orgasm, so to speak, whose release of energy would immortalize the body.
>
> (Ibid.)

Shaginian, who shared the culture of the modernists in her past, ascribes to the ideas of the paradoxical "erotic celibacy" in the new Bolshevist utopia. The fetishized love-affair of Arno Arevian and Mardzhana embodies the paradox of sexually liberating asceticism; the sublimated and postponed culmination of the moment of sexual consummation is subjected to the utopia of socialism as the collective union that will take place in the future. Thus, the dam-building is provided with different functions; it can be read as the politically correct symbol of the new production literature responding to the challenge of the electrification of the country, and as a defence mechanism (Theweleit 271) against the final fragmentation concerning the psychic, aesthetic, and material realms that are obvious in the novel. Each realm is affected by the dam-building, which is disguised as an idealized human energy production that erupts into transformative creativity for the grand idea of the socialist future.

As I have suggested in this analysis, water in *Hydrocentral* is not a passive resource subjected to the enforced modernization that took place in the Soviet Union in the 1930s. It is rather a powerful force generating an interplay of energies and an active medium of artistic and aesthetic self-reflection; thus, it is a strong participant in the modernization discourse. Water dissolves dualities and distinctions between the real and imaginary and the human and non-human. Instead of closed, fixed, or even politically univocal meanings, Shaginian's *Hydrocentral* favors process and constant transformation, that is, the heterogeneity of becoming that produces hybrid forms both in the aesthetic and socio-political spheres of life. As the hybridity designates the fluid multi-layeredness of the aesthetic approaches – that is, modernism and emerging Socialist Realism – and the interconnectedness of the human mind with its surrounding environment, respectively, the hybrid agitator-philosopher Arno Arevian also corresponds to the artistic and political activities of the actual author Marietta Shaginian, who did not fit in any clear-cut category, either as an author or as a political being. The novel highlights how strongly human self-representation is intertwined with water. People are interconnected with the natural circulation of water, and are simultaneously both subjects and objects in respect to water. As a material substance, water is not only essential to life; it holds polyvalent spiritual and philosophical meanings as a cognitive means for knowing the world. Accordingly, we can also conclude that the open ending with the undammed waters and the unfinished power plant, still in "becoming," resonates with Shaginian's philosophical involvement in the Hegelianian dialectic "Werden." The ever streaming waters entail dialectics of transformation that may also explain the blurring of metaphors and metonymies within the same story, or in other words, the idealistic dialectic of "becoming" confronts the accomplishment of the socialist utopia. Shaginian's water has the ability to generate new communities of workers, engineers, party members, and artists; it creates the identities and stories of the new Soviet citizen and the Soviet author who are required to gain control over water. However, as we see in the Mizinka's self-determined acts, in its elementary force water is as uncontrollable as the flow of desire.

Notes

1 Quotations are from the 1982 edition of *Hydrocentral* (page 46). The author edited the original over the years. Nicholas (295) points out that the "first rough

draft of *Hydrocentral* [is] apparently no longer extant." Further quotations from the book are marked with the page number only. All translations are my own.
2 The actual river of the construction site was the Dzoraget. See the notes on the history of the novel in Shaginian (*Sobranie* 802–805).
3 The novel was received sympathetically by Soviet critics, although it was also criticized for its overwhelming "lecturing idea," the incorrect description of communists and the lack of a "united party collective." For example, Kuznetsov (194) and Kolpakova (25) criticize the fact that Arevian, a non-party figure, is more convincing than the party members. The critic also accuses the author for "staying, both in life and in creative work, behind the door of the party bureau and without a clear knowledge of what happens inside."
4 Shaginian, who began her career as a poet, was strongly influenced by Symbolism, and especially by the work of Zinaida Gippius, one of the key figures of modernist and Symbolist aesthetics.
5 The interest in Russian rivers increased, especially in the Volga, which was an anthropomorphic actor in paintings, posters, and especially film during the 1930s. See, for example the 1938 film *Volga-Volga* (e.g. Binder 319–340, especially 324 and 329), and such documentary films as Dziga Vertov's *Odinnatsatyi* (1928), Esfir Shub's *Komsomol – shef elektrifikatsii* (1932), and *Belomorsko-Baltiskii Vodnyi Put'*, which was the cinematographic equivalent of the literary volumes of Gorky, Averbach, and Firin.
6 Gorky himself was one of the first to claim the status of "water construction author" while initiating and editing (together with Leopold Averbach and Sergei Firin) the collective anthology with 36 writers on the White Sea–Baltic Sea Canal (1934), which was celebrated as an "act of heroism and re-education work" (Gestwa, *Die Stalinschen* 271 and 62), not as the first large construction project of inhuman forced labour and the Gulag economics.
7 See, for example, Konstantin Paustovsky's novels *Kara-Bugas* (1932) and *Kolkhida* (1934), or Mikhail Ilin's *Men and Mountains: Man's Victory over Nature* (1935). Also, contemporary critics saw the main idea of the novel in "the combat for concrete" and in showing how "blind elementary nature is heroically overcome" (*Krasnyi mir*, 1931, No. 9, 164).
8 Eva Hausbacher (71–78) has found metonymic discourse in the work of another Russian female modernist author, Elena Guro.

Bibliography

Aikhenvald, Boris. "Metod Gidrotsentrali." *Krasnaja Nov'* 2 (1933): 195–208.
Alaimo, Stacy. "Trans-corporeal Feminisms and the Ethical Space of Nature." *Material Feminisms*. Ed. Stacy Alaimo and Susan Hekman. Bloomington: Indiana University Press, 2008, 237–264.
Alaimo, Stacy. *Bodily Natures: Science, Environment, and the Material Self*. Bloomington: Indiana University Press, 2010.
Alaimo, Stacy. "States of Suspension: Trans-corporeality at Sea." *Interdisciplinary Studies in Literature and Environment* 19.3 (2012): 476–493.
Bachelard, Gaston. *Water and Dreams: An Essay on the Imagination of Matter* (1942). Trans. Edith R. Farrel. Dallas, TX: Pegasus Foundation, 1983.
Binder, Eva. "Moskau – Hafen von Fünf Meeren: Die stalinistische "Wasserkultur" und ihre symbolischen Bedeutungen." *Wasser und Raum*. Ed. Doris G. Eibl, Lorelies Ortner, Ingo Schneider, and Christoph Ulf. Göttingen: V&R unipress, 2008, 319–340.

Böhme, Hartmut. "Umriss einer Kulturgeschichte des Wassers. Eine Einleitung." *Kulturgeschichte des Wassers*. Ed. Hartmut Böhme. Frankfurt am Main: Suhrkamp Verlag, 1988, 7–44.

Chandler, Michelle, and Astrida Neimanis. "Water and Gestationality: What Flows beneath Ethics". *Thinking with Water*. Ed. Cecilia Chen, Janine MacLeod, and Astrida Neimanis. Montreal and Kingston: McGill-Queens University Press, 2013, 61–83.

Chen, Cecilia, Janine MacLeod, and Astrida Neimanis. "Introduction." *Thinking with Water*. Ed. Cecilia Chen, Janine MacLeod, and Astrida Neimanis. Montreal and Kingston: McGill-Queens University Press, 2013, 3–22.

Clark, Katerina. *The Soviet Novel. History as Ritual*, 3rd ed. Bloomington: Indiana University Press, 2000.

Clark, Katerina. "Socialist Realism and the Sacralizing of Space." *The Landscape of Stalinism. The Art and Ideology of Soviet Space*. Ed. Evgeny Dobrenko and Eric Naiman. Washington, DC: The University of Washington Press, 2003, 3–18.

Clark, Katerina, and Evgeny Dobrenko. *Soviet Culture and Power: A History in Documents, 1917–1953*. Ed. Katerina Clark, Evgeny Dobrenko, Andrei Artizov, Oleg Naumov, and Marian Schwartz. New Haven, CT: Yale University Press, 2007.

Colebrook, Claire. *Gilles Deleuze*. New York: Routledge, 2002.

Colebrook, Claire. "The Space of Man': On the Specificity of Affect in Deleuze and Guattari." *Deleuze and Space*. Ed. Ian Buchanan and Gregg Lambert. Toronto: University of Toronto Press, 2005, 189–206.

Deleuze, Gilles, and Félix Guattari. *A Thousand Plateaus: Capitalism and Schizophrenia*. Trans. Brian Massumi. Minneapolis: University of Minneapolis Press, 2003.

Deleuze, Gilles, and Félix Guattari. *Anti-Oedipus: Capitalism and Schizophrenia*. Trans. Robert Hurley et al. Minneapolis: University of Minneapolis Press, 2005.

Dobrenko, Evgenii. "Iskusstvo sotsial'noi navigatsii. Ocherki kul'turnoi topografii stalinskoi epokhi." *Wiener Slawistischer Almanach* 45 (2000): 117–134.

Donovan, Josephine. "Style and Power." *Feminism, Bakhtin, and the Dialogic*. Ed. Dale M. Bauer and Susan Jaret McKinstry. New York: State University of New York Press, 1991, 85–94.

Epstein, Mikhail. *After the Future: The Paradoxes of Postmodernism and Contemporary Russian Culture*. Amherst: The University of Massachusetts Press, www.emory.edu/INTELNET/af.rus.postmodernism.html.

Gestwa, Klaus. "Sowjetische Zukunfts- und Erinnerungslandschaften: Die 'Stalinschen Grossbauten des Kommunismus' und die Schaffung eines neuen Zeit- und Raumbewusstseins." *Ordnungen der Landschaft. Natur und Raum technisch und symbolisch entwerfen*. Ed. Stefan Kaufmann. Würzburg: Ergon Verlag, 2002. 117–132.

Gestwa, Klaus. *Die Stalinschen Grossbauten des Kommunismus*. München: R. Oldenbourg Verlag, 2010.

Goriachkina, M.S. "Daiushchii zhizn'" Marietta Shaginian. *Gidrotsentral'*. Moskva: "Sovetskaia Rossiia", 1988, 5–18.

Gorky, M. "O bor'be s prirodoi." http://gorkiy.lit-info.ru/gorkiy/articles/article-173.htm.

Guski, Andreas. *Literatur und Arbeit. Produktionsskizze und Produktionsroman im Russland des 1. Fünfjahrplans (1928–1932)*. Wiesbaden: Harrassowitz Verlag, 1995.

Haraway, Donna. *Simians, Cyborgs and Women: The Reinvention of Nature*. New York: Routledge, 1991.
Hausbacher, Eva. *"... denn die Geschöpfe lieben Aufmerksame." Weiblichkeit in der Schrift Elena Guros (1877–1913)*. Frankfurt am Main: Peter Lang, 1996.
Hausmann, Guido. *Mütterchen Wolga. Ein Fluss als Erinnerungsort vom 16. bis ins frühe 20. Jahrhundert*. Frankfurt and New York: Campus Verlag, 2009.
Hellebust, Rolf. *Flesh to Metal. Soviet Literature and the Alchemy of Revolution*. Ithaca, NY and London: Cornell University Press, 2003.
Iovino, Serenella. "Material Ecocriticism: Matter, Text, and Posthuman Ethics." *Literature, Ecology, Ethics*. Ed. Timo Müller and Michael Sauter. Heidelberg: Winter Verlag, 2012, 51–68.
Jakobson, Roman. "The Metaphoric and Metonymic Poles." *Metaphor and Metonymy in Comparison and Contrast*. Ed. Rene Dirven and Ralf Pörings. Berlin and New York: Mouton de Gruyter, 2003 [1956], 41–48.
Kolpakova, E.G. *Romany s sotsialisticheskom stroitelstve perioda pervoi piatiletki. Doklady i soobshcheniia filologicheskogo instituta*. Vy.2. Leningrad: Izd. Leningradskogo god-go ordena Lenina uni-ta, 1950, 17–47.
Kovalev, Valentin. *Khudozhnik-myslitel', svidetel' glavnykh sobytii veka. Marietta Shaginian, Sobranie sochinenij*. T. 1. Chelovek i vremia: M. Khudozhestevennaia literatura, 1986, 5–8.
Kuznetsov, M.M. *Sovetskii roman*. Ocherki: M. Izdatelstvo Akedemii Nauk SSSR, 1963.
Lacan, Jacques. "The Instance of the Letter in the Unconscious or Reason since Freud." *Literary Theory: An Anthology*, 2nd ed. Ed. Julie Rivkin and Michael Ryan. Malden, MA: Blackwell, 2004 [1957], 447–461.
Latour, Bruno. *We Have Never Been Modern*. Trans. Catherine Porter. Cambridge, MA: Harvard University Press, 1993.
Linton, Jamie. *What is Water? The History of a Modern Abstraction*. Vancouver and Toronto: UBS Press, 2010.
Matich, Olga. *Erotic Utopia: The Decadent Imagination in Russia's Fin-de-siècle*. Madison: University of Wisconsin Press, 2005.
Nicholas, Mary. *Writers at Work: Russian Production Novels and the Construction of Soviet Culture*. Lewisburg, PA: Bucknell University Press/Rosemont Publishing, 2010.
Paperny, Vladimir. *Kul'tura dva*. Moskva: Novoe Literaturnoe Obozrenie, 2006.
Richter, Bernd Stevens. "Nature Mastered by Man: Ideology and Water in the Soviet Union." *Environment and History* 3 (1997): 69–96.
Rosenholm, Arja. "'Chelovek-amfibiia', ili Novii chelovek kak kiborg." *Kul't-tovary-XXI: Reviziia tsennostei (masskul'tura i ee potrebiteli)*. Ed. Irina Savkina and Mariia Cherniak. Ekaterinburg, Sankt-Peterburg and Tampere: Izdatel'skii Dom "Azhur", 2012, 41–54.
Ruder, Cynthia. *Making History for Stalin: The Story of the Belomor Canal*. Gainesville: University Press of Florida, 1998.
Shaginian, Marietta. *Kak ia rabotala nad 'Gidrotsentral'iu'*. Moskva: Profizdat, 1933.
Shaginian, Marietta. *Gidrotsentral'*. Moskva: Dnepropetrovsk, "Promin'", 1982.
Shaginian, Marietta. *Sobranie sochinenii v deviati tomah*. T. 3. Moskva: Khudozhestvennaia literatura. 1987.
Shepherd, David. "Canon Fodder? Problems in the Reading of a Soviet Production Novel." *Discontinuous Discourses in Modern Russian Literature*. Ed. Catriona

Kelly, Michael Makin, and David Shepherd. New York: St. Martin's Press, 1989, 39–59.

Shtil'mark, F.R. "Evoliutsiia predstavlenii ob okhrane prirody v sovetskoi literature." *Gumanitarnyi ekologicheskii zhurnal* 1.2 (1999): 25–37.

Stites, Richard. *Revolutionary Dreams. Utopian Visions and Experimental Life in the Russian Revolution*. Oxford and New York: Oxford University Press, 1989.

Strang, Veronica. *The Meaning of Water*. Oxford: Berg, 2004.

Terras, Victor. *The Twentieth Century: The Era of Socialist Realism 1925–53*. The Cambridge History of Russian Literature. Ed. Charles A. Moser. Cambridge: Cambridge University Press, 1989, 458–519.

Theweleit, Klaus. *Männerphantasien. I. Frauen, Fluten, Körper*, Geschichte 1. Reinbeck bei Hamburg: Rowohlt, 1982.

Vorobyev, Dmitry. "Ruling Rivers: Discussion on the River Diversion Project in the Soviet Union." *Understanding Russian Nature: Representations, Values and Concepts*. Ed. Arja Rosenholm and Sari Autio-Sarasmo. Aleksanteri Papers 4, Helsinki, 2005, 177–208.

Weiner, Douglas R. *Models of Nature*. Pittsburgh, PA: University of Pittsburgh Press, 2000 [orig. 1988].

West-Pavlov, Russell. *Space in Theory. Kristeva, Foucault, Deleuze*. Amsterdam: Rodopi, 2009.

Westerman, Frank. *Ingenieure der Seele*. Berlin: Ch. Links Verlag, 2003 [orig. in Dutch 2002].

Young, W., and DeCosta, L. "Water Imagery in Dreams and Fantasy." *Dynamic Psychotherapy* 5.1 (Spring/Summer 1987): 67–76.

14 Spatriotism

Water recycling in literary polemics (late eighteenth- to early nineteenth-century Russia)[1]

Gitta Hammarberg

Peter the Great is widely celebrated as the first to develop and visit spas in Russia, but numerous legends give Russian curative waters (and thus Russia itself) much earlier provenance, linking them to native tribes, horses, and cattle that indulged in water cures well before Russians developed spas per se.[2] But pre-Petrine legends also lend Russian spas prestige by linking them to the West, for example, Alexander of Macedonia or Roman *thermae*. Peter himself saw the development of Russian spas as a distinctly Westernizing enterprise. After visiting European spas, he issued a decree to "locate in our State … spring waters, which can be used for illnesses, in applications, waters of the kind that are used in our part of the world like those in Pyrmont, Spa, and other waters" (Kugushev, Appendix). European engineers, spa landscapers, and medical experts were invited to develop and run Russian spas. Like spas in other countries on the edges of Europe, Russian spas were thus developed on Western models and by Western expertise to showcase Russia as a European power. Nevertheless, Russian discourse about spas, be it technical or literary, often became the site of patriotic expressions of superiority to the West or a vehicle for questioning behaviors deemed Western, such as a lavish lifestyle, conspicuous consumption, or dandyism.[3] Dandyism, or the art of self-creation and self-display, entered spa accounts especially prominently after Richard ("Beau") Nash was made Master of Ceremonies at Bath and later at Tunbridge Wells, and made them the most fashionable European resorts. Beau Brummell, who set the tone for all subsequent dandies, would accompany his royal mentor, the regent and subsequently king, George IV to Brighton, another fashionable English seaside resort. Many British playwrights set their comedies at spas and poked fun at "fashionable" dandy behavior and conspicuous consumption, notably Richard Brinsley Sheridan's "The Rivals." Similar satires on fops had appeared in Russian satires at least since Antiokh Kantemir and later saw a renaissance in Russian spa comedies and polemical works set at other bodies of water. Dandyism became particularly prominent as a means of parodying the adherents of Nikolai Karamzin, many of who used a dandified jargon and showed all the hallmarks of dandyish behavior. Since dandyism was always perceived as something foreign (to the English it was something French, to the French it was English, to the Russians it was distinctly non-Russian) it could be nicely combined with the theme of patriotism or its lack. The pros and cons of patriotism and/or a Western lifestyle at Russian spas were in turn used to question literary skills. I will investigate how spas, dandyism, patriotism, Westernization intersected in literary polemics in late eighteenth- to early nineteenth-century Russia and what sorts of literary devices using water were perfected in the process. I will look at two Sentimentalist spa texts from 1803 set at Lipetsk spa, which show the basic themes for later spa literature, at a major polemical manifesto and a "dialogue of the dead" set at the rivers Styx and Lethe, which set the polemical tone for the later texts, and finally I will focus on the specific literary devices perfected in spa dramas and the ensuing verse retorts.

Among the first official Russian spas are Olonets in northern Russia opened in 1714 and Lipetsk, south of Moscow, opened in 1717. Peter visited both and presumably set out to "cure [his] body with the waters and [his] subjects – by example" (Maikov, *Rasskazy* 35). In both cases he foresaw a slow cure. Most texts about Russian spas are scientific, focusing on the curative properties of water and the various designs used to promote water cures. Lipetsk is possibly the first Russian spa celebrated in literature – notably in two arch-Sentimental accounts, one by a Mr Bekhteev, who left an unsigned epistolary account of his visit in 1803 and the other by Nikolai Kugushev, a minor Sentimentalist writer.[4] The Caucasus soon became the major center of spa culture in imperial Russia and was praised for the *variety* of its waters, superior in its concentration to any single region in Europe. Many early spa accounts, steeped in Petrine patriotism, compare Russian waters favorably to their European prototypes, while at the same time evincing spa envy and expressing the need to develop Russian spas to their full (European) potential (Hammarberg, "Spas *in spe*").

Ever since Alexander the Great interrupted his military campaigns for mineral cures in Abbas-Tuma (not far from the celebrated Borzhomi waters in today's Georgia) Russian spa accounts have celebrated both imperial conquest and domestic healing (Sviatlovskii 9). Lipetsk was famed both for its iron foundry where weapons were produced for wars and its healing springs that would cure wounded soldiers. Bekhteev's account (41–42) contains several passionate verse encomia to Peter the imperial warrior and Peter the domestic healer, alternating praise for the simple old Russian ways with laments about European frivolity and extravagance. In one such poetic outburst, he intones:

You [Peter] discovered iron ore
You named the place Lipetsk;
You ordered iron cannons to be cast,
To subdue daring neighbors,
To ward off enemy evil;
And You found springs there.

Springs, flowing from mountains,
Give us the extract of life,
Cure peoples' illnesses,
And give them health instead.
They return strength through water
And revive the fibers of life...[5]

Both Kugushev and Bekhteev implement the essential features of early Russian spa accounts: Russia's status as a major European power, competitive with or superior to the West in imperial lineage, natural resources, and scientific and humanitarian initiatives. They contrast war to healing, upper-class frivolity to simple living, leisure to productive activity, art to nature, and social graces to naturalistic descriptions of ailments. These contrasts were also typical of Western European spa discourse.[6] Benedict, discussing English spas, notes that even as spas advertise a retreat into nature, they also vie for customers "with a dazzling array of luxuries," and thus mirror the conspicuous consumption in the city people are getting away from. Life in Russian spas, as in European ones, could be quite ostentatious. A Doctor Kimmel (39) describes General J***'s spa trip in 1812: "This nobleman also went to the Caucasus waters with a large company: the number of persons, masters as well as servants, was almost a hundred, the number of carriages of all kinds was 26, and the number of fully equipped horses about 130." An account by Kh. Sh. (259) mentions one Titular Councilor who came in two *koliaski* and three *britchki* (specific Russian carriages) with 24 horses harnessed and four extra ones. With him came his wife, children, doctor, dwarf, teacher, governess, nurses and nannies, maids, laundresses, and other servants – all of them healthy except the man of the house.[7] Russian spas, like their European counterparts, also provided the setting for a variety of literary texts.[8] Kugushev and Bekhteev produced what could be called travel journals with aspects of today's tourist guidebook with several verse inserts. They both affirmed Sentimentalism, the innovatory literary current, spearheaded by Karamzin, and part of their aim was to familiarize Russian readers with Lipetsk. In themselves not polemical, their accounts prepared the ground for what is generally referred to as the "Lipetsk flood" of Russian spa literature, which was a vital aspect of the major literary polemic that colored all aspects of culture in late eighteenth- to early nineteenth-century Russia.

In 1803, A.S. Shishkov's treatise "Discourse on the Old and New Style of the Russian Language" ("Rassuzhdenie o starom i novom sloge Rossiiskogo iazyka") set the tone for the opposition, criticizing the Karamzinist pandering to foreign models and their Frenchified literary language.[9] As pointed out by Ol'ga Vainshtein (493), the treatise makes frequent connections between language and dress, linking questions of political freedom and fashion. Shishkov made the case for a literature in a special written language modeled on an abstractly conceived and uncontaminated ancient Slaviano-Russian (*slaveno-rossiiskii*) language and traditional texts, such as church books. His adherents were since 1811 concentrated in a literary grouping he presided over, Colloqui of the Lovers of the Russian Word (*Beseda liubitelei russkogo slova*). The followers of Karamzin (epigones of Sentimentalism) espoused a new literature based on the spoken conversational language of educated society (especially its women) and on taste rather than genre, with the aim of modeling the new Russian literature on its modern West European (mainly French) counterparts.[10] As the polemics grew increasingly heated, the younger Karamzinists in 1815 founded a parodic anti-Colloqui grouping, the Arzamas. Both camps saw language and literature as an important part of nation-building and strove for reform, but emphasized different means: the Karamzinists looked to create a Russian culture, evolutionary in content and based on commonalities with the West, while the Shishkovites aimed to reform what they saw as a contaminated culture by appeal to a *sui generis* pure Russian language and behavior. It is telling that many of the Karamzinist polemicists (e.g. S.S. Uvarov, D.V. Dashkov, P.A. Viazemskii) later became important government officials involved in various reforms. One stream of the polemic used references to bodies of water and culminated in the Lipetsk flood of polemical texts, mentioned above.

Soon after Shishkov's incendiary treatise some of the younger Karamzinists, especially P.I. Shalikov and P.I. Makarov, mounted an eloquent and intelligent counterattack, while also flaunting their admiration for Napoleon and their fondness for French culture, their feminization, their dandyism, and their Karamzinolatry. Makarov in particular broke all the rules of his era's "gentle" criticism and aimed to shock and provoke his readers in numerous critical pieces in his journal, as well as epigrams and other satirical jabs at his opponents. The earlier spa pieces by Bekhteev and Kugushev defined the specific site (Lipetsk) for the polemical flood of subsequent texts. A number of these other texts featured other waters (the rivers and swamps in Hades) as the battleground. One such piece was S.S. Bobrov's "dialogue of the dead" entitled "An Event in the Kingdom of Shadows, or the Fate of the Russian Language" ("Proisshestvie v tsarstve tenei, ili Sud'bina rossiiskogo iazyka") written in 1804 and long unpublished. Makarov and Bobrov set the tone of sharp mutual accusation.[11] In Bobrov's text Makarov, alias Gallo-Rus, is "half-Russian, half-Gall" and has crossed the Styx, drunk from the river Lethe, and forgotten his past while continuing to display his Frenchified speech and foppish behavior. He meets numerous shadows, incuding Boyan (a Shishkovite figure of wisdom and proper old-time values). Boyan upon first seeing Gallo-Rus wonders "Who in the world is this? – Not a fellow-countryman? – No; – He has little in common with my contemporaries; one must assume that he speaks a different language." His clothing and behavior also seem alien to Boyan. Gallo-Rus counters that nowadays everything has changed in Russia: "Instead of your awkward clothing, your *zhupans*, people now wear tailcoats according to the latest fashion as you see me doing; –our hairdo is a glorious *à la Tite*, – people shave their beards, – the customs of old geezers are out ... nowadays all's younger, all's *fresher*; all's cheerful; – feelings are more refined; – the Russian language is *purified*; the pen of our Authors is so much more *sentimental* than before, livelier, more playful; that's the kind of *reformation* there is in everything" (Uspenskii and Lotman 469).[12] Bobrov uses Lomonosov to give a grim sentence to Gallo-Rus (and other Karamzinists) for their exaggeratedly sentimental elegies, love songs, and various other "bagatelles" (*bezdelki*) in prose and verse, represented with a heavy layer of quotations from both second-rate writers and the leading figures of Sentimentalism. Lomonosov, as a foundational reformer of the Russian literary language and versification, is particularly appropriate here. He now condemns, among other things, a song with incestuous implications from Karamzin's "Bornholm Island" ("Ostrov Borngol'm" in Karamzin 2: 661–73) for its immoral contents: "The error lies not so much in the language but in the very sentiments" (Uspenskii and Lotman 486). The Karamzinists were equally severely judged for their main criterion (taste) and for their "new" language and literature, which results in "false glitter, a wild mixture of things, pomposity ... fake sensitivity, amorousness, tearfulness, scariness – even to the point of fainting spells" (Uspenskii and Lotman 471). They speak in a dandified style, where every other word is French, a calque, a translation, or otherwise pointedly non-Russian. The Karamzinist ailment is diagnosed: a dandified jargon, feminine weakness, and moral decrepitude.[13] They are punished by death and oblivion. The metaphors of Hades and its rivers enter the polemical water discourse, anticipating the spa accounts and recalling some aspects of Kugushev's and Bekhteev's texts.

Francomania had long been the target of Russian satirists, and was a reality for many a Karamzinist epigone. The timing of Shishkovite attacks became particularly propitious with the onset of the Napoleonic campaigns in 1805, when many Russians became less enamored of French culture and the anti-Karamzinist polemic became a site where literature, esthetics, morality, and politics fused. Uspenskii and Lotman (351–360) show the effect of the Napoleonic campaigns on the polemic. The Shishkovites went so far as to blame the traitorous unpatriotic Karamzinists for Napoleon's invasion, and even for the French occupation of Moscow.[14]

An energetic pro-Karamzinist campaign, responding to accusations by Bobrov, P.I. Golenishchev-Kutuzov and others was mounted by Karamzin's defenders, P.A. Viazemskii, K.N. Batiushkov, A.E. Izmailov, and many others, some of them replicating Bobrov's Styx setting. A swamp suspiciously like Bobrov's muddy Styx is the setting for the pseudonymous Karamzinist "Opinions and Notes of an Hermit" ("Mneniia i zamechaniia pustynnika," summarized in Proskurin, *Literaturnye skandaly* 132). Here a dream scene reverses the Bobrovian Styx scene. We see (the Russian) people stuck in a black swamp of pre-Enlightenment ignorance, unwilling to change, until one of them (Karamzin) extricates himself and tries to pull out the rest to dry in the sun. One of the saved writers (Sergei Glinka, here a Shishkovite sympathizer) threw himself back into the Styx. His real-life prototype took the masked identification personally and in response published "A Model of Fashionable Wit" ("Obrazets modnogo ostroumiia").[15] He saw the Stygian picture as a slur on Old Russia and cast aspersions on the patriotism of the Karamzinists. The Shishkovites increasingly accused the Karamzinists of loose morals, abandoning "true Russian" values, and a lack of patriotism when they found themselves powerless to mount a viable *literary* alternative to the Karamzinist "new" style.[16]

The Karamzinists payed back in the same coin in pieces such as K.N. Batiushkov's "A Knight of our Era" ("Rytsar' nashego veka," in Batiushkov 150), where the self-styled Shishkovite patriot, while lamenting the loss of Old Russia, guzzles champagne and fine French sauces, and plays card games.[17] The satirical Styx hilarity is perhaps most fully expressed in Batiushkov's 1809 response to Bobrov's attacks, "A Vision on the Banks of Lethe" ("Videnie na beregakh Lety," in Batiushkov 96–103), which broadens the parodic scope to depict canonical eighteenth-century Russian writers (Lomonosov, Sumarokov, Kheraskov, Kniazhnin) basking in Elysian glories, while contemporaries face lethal drownings and oblivion. Among the latter are not only Shishkovites (including a cruel satire on the three women members of Colloqui), but also Karamzinist epigones, such as Shalikov – presumably for excessive epigonic Karamzinism.[18]

These swamp and river texts represent the kinds of issues that were raised in the polemic, and dangerous waters served to mutually drown and silence enemy poets. We also see healing Castalian springs, the Parnassus, and the Elysian fields, where virtuous poets are rewarded, mirroring the duality of water symbolism in the earlier Lipetsk accounts by Bekhteev and Kugushev. Lipetsk itself had gained in popularity as a curative resort over the decade since they wrote about it.

In 1815 the time was ripe for A.A. Shakhovskoi's spa play "A Lesson for Coquettes, or the Lipetsk Waters" ("Urok koketkam ili Lipetskie vody," in Shakhovskoi 119–263), which unleashed the Lipetsk flood of polemical texts.[19]

The comedy makes fun of the younger Karamzinist polemicists – and, indirectly of Karamzin himself.[20] Shakhovskoi targets their style, the literary genres they favor, their Francomania in dress and behavior, and their lack of patriotism – the already familiar topoi. Lipetsk Russianness is contrasted to foreign lands. For instance, the effete Karamzinist fop Ol'gin is trying to court the female libertine Leleva with a lover's aria from a Paisiello opera (244).

The positive (Shishkovite) characters, Prince Kholmskii, his sister Olen'ka, and his friend Colonel Pronskii are idealized as "true Russian" landowners and their happy servants. They are brave warriors, though lacking in slick social graces (130) and they parade their hardships in war, their part in the Russian victory at Leipzig, and the triumphant Russian march into Paris in 1814, as well as their proud rebuilding of Moscow (132). Even the shy and modest Princess Olen'ka is a true patriot, or so the defeated coquette Leleva refers to her (247).

Pronskii, though in love with Olen'ka, is now overcome by infatuation for the corrupt spa queen, Leleva. His rivals are the bad Karamzinists: the 75-year-old spendthrift Baron Wolmar, the retired Hussar Ugarov, and the Sentimentalist poet, Fialkin, "Mr Violet." Wolmar (a V.L. Pushkin satire), who once participated in a siege at a Prussian fortress, has now turned to silly gallantry, including fireworks to surprise Leleva.[21] Fire now serves to entertain the ladies rather than forge weapons for European wars, as had been the case in the earlier Lipetsk texts. Ugarov (a satire both on S.S. Uvarov and V.L. Pushkin, two of the most active Karamzinists) retired from the Hussars as soon as the Napoleonic war started and now, dressed in half-military garb, enjoys his hounds, horses, and Gypsies – sporting the typical European jockey dandy pose.[22] Now his Hussar gear is turned against women: with "the weapon of his military spurs" he endangers Leleva's dress (158). He is accused of cowardice: "when the entire nobility went against the enemy [Napoleon] and was covered in glory, you, as I recall, dashed off and battled the local bunnies with utmost bravery" (178). The feminized Sentimentalist poet Fialkin (a lampoon on Zhukovskii) tenderly strums his guitar rather than engage in swordsmanship.[23] Count Ol'gin, known for his nasty tongue, is an example of a French education that misfired: he has learned to babble, interspersing his chit-chat with French words and despises his native land. He knows all "the salacious couplets and free-thinking nonsense by French authors" (134–135). His professed love for the "philosophical century" is as shallow as his interpretation of Enlightenment freedoms. His hairdo is more important than deep discussion, as we see him in his *ekipazh* heading for Pronskii's *ermitazh* where his man will apply his *papil'ioty* and fix his *tualet* (206–207).[24] All this makes him amiable in society, but ignorant of Russian culture. The playwright predicts that such "aping a frivolous nation," such "Parisianizing will not be fashionable for long" (219).[25]

On the Shishkovite side we have patriotic masculine bravery and a lack in social skills, while the Karamzinists are dandified, non-patriotic, Frenchified social butterflies. As in traditional spa texts, the wounded soldier (Pronskii) needs spa treatment both for love-sickness and stress. Ol'gin has been prescribed a spa cure for "frayed nerves, migraine and vertige." Both war wounds and linguistic ailments come from Paris. Another unpatriotic warfare that holds sway in Lipetsk (as in European spas) is foreign card games, such as boston and whist (171–171, 182).

The Russian Lipetsk waters are a cure for foreign infections and the patriotic Prince is glad to see the post-Napoleonic changes in attitudes towards the Russian language and culture, especially among Russian women (135). Olen'ka, the positive heroine, speaks Russian naturally and nothing could be more pleasant to Pronskii than her tender and sweet Russian (136). Countess Leleva, however, has infected the air at Lipetsk and polluted the waters (127) she is both an "infection" and a "pox"

(259), though even she now follows the current anti-Napoleonic fashion of speaking Russian only, with forfeits for those who accidentally use French, anticipating Julie Karagin in *War and Peace*.[26] Her problem is her upbringing by a Parisian *madame* (234), and soon enough she lapses into French. On her toiletry table she keeps a copy of Pierre Charles Levesque's *Histoire de la Russie*, mainly to impress the good Pronskii by being cleverer than other women who read only novels (197–199). A typical Sentimentalist combination of toiletry, sewing, and reading is here ridiculed, and Leleva's reading is certainly a direct slap at Karamzin, who at the time was official court historiographer, writing the monumental *History of the Russian State*.

Lipetsk, like European spas is presented by Shakhovskoi as a marriage market and the widowed Leleva is seeking eligible men, not unlike Moll Flanders in Bath. Her seductive tactics are the usual: flattery, gossip, slander, and intrigue.[27] She is ultimately not receptive to Wolmar's fireworks, Ugarov's wit, or Fialkin's poetry. Fialkin's view of poetry captures the essential features of Karamzinist poetics. A poet, Fialkin declaims, needs an ardent heart, constant tears, ample emotions, delicate taste, and he lives only through his "darling" (*milaia* – a high-frequency Sentimentalist word) (163). Here Shakhovskoi captures the gist of epigonic Sentimentalist poetics and, placed on the lips of the syrupy poet, they are effectively ridiculed together with Fialkin's fondness for the ballad with its corpses and dark forests (Zhukovskii's forte), complimentary madrigals to women, witty wordplay, trifles, and light verse couplets (166–167).

The other suitors, too, are ridiculed for Karamzinist behavior, for example Wolmar's flowery phrases, excessive flattery, and adoring compliments in the eighteenth-century fashion, Fialkin's penchant to "sing one and the same tune to all women" (167), indicating the generic nature of the "individualized" Sentimentalist verse apostrophies, and his insistense on reading his own verse (a habit that Sentimentalist salon poets like Shalikov or V.L. Pushkin were notorious for).[28] While the rivals ridicule one another, Shakhovskoi aims to kill all Karamzinists by ridicule, or as O'lgin puts it, make them "ridikiul'nymi" (205). Everything from women to spa cures to the Battle of Leipzig is lampooned with an anti-Karamzinist slant. Not unexpectedly, in the final scene only the positive characters remain, and Shakhovskoi's patriotic message rings out loudly against foreign dandyism and coquetry in behavior as in language:

> All swagger is the fruit of foreign science.
> Coquetry was unknown in the olden holy Russia,
> The very word cannot be translated into Russian.
> (261–262)

The ridicule was not lost on either side. Right after the performance, Shakhovskoi's play was celebrated by the Shishkovites, and the author was crowned with a laurel wreath by the Petersburg governor's wife (*Arzamas* 1: 529). Meanwhile Shakhovskoi's victims walked home after the play and Zhukovskii, according to A.N. Turgenev's letter to Ia. Bulgakov, improvised a witty punning reaction: "Oh wondrous miracles on high: / He made up waters, wholly dry!" (*Arzamas* 1: 239–40, 59). The very next day Dashkov parodied both the play and the Shishkovite crowning in a hymn, "The Crowning of Shutovskoi/Jester" ("Venchanie Shutovskogo" in *Arzamas* 1: 246–248) – the punning 'Shutovskoi' became the recurring moniker for Shakhovskoi. Shakhovskoi, "The evil persecutor of Karamzin, / Threat to ballads" is given the line: "I write [of] the waters with water." His hymn ends with nasty hints at plagiarism and loose morals (*Arzamas* 1: 240–242).[29] The oxymoronic dry waters and dry watery writing were to characterize Shakhovskoi in Karamzinist counterattacks for a long time to come, as for instance in the seventh of Viazemskii's cycle of epigrams "Shutovskoi's/Jester's poetic wreath bestowed on him once and forever for many feats": "In 'Fur Coats' [one of Shakhovskoi's plays] you're the cold Shutovskoi, / In 'Waters' you're the dry Shutovskoi" (*Arzamas* 1: 247). Here two of Shakhovskoi's anti-Karamzinist texts enter one of Viazemskii's typical witty double oxymorons. Similar oxymoronic double entendres became a staple in Karamzinist attacks. The first epigram in the same cycle describes Shakhovskoi's satires and comedies (and by implication all Shishkovite texts) as containing the fun of a dictionary, the ingeniousness of a calendar, and the salt and sarcasm of an alphabet book (246). The second epigram concludes that Shakovskoi's comedies make his friends weep, while his tragedies make them laugh (246). Number nine, "Healing Waters" ("Tselitel'nye vody" 247) puns on Lipetsk the place and Lipetsk the play: if you suffer from insomnia or passion that doctors or medicine cannot cure, Lipetsk waters and "Lipetsk Waters" will put you to sleep (*Arzamas* 1: 248–249). Long unpublished, some of the wittiest lines in these texts were subsequently incorporated in published works by both friends and enemies. Zhukovskii's quip about "dry waters," for instance, was used by M.N. Zagoskin in his anti-Karamzinist "Comedy Against Comedies, or A Lesson for Fops" ("Komediia protiv komedii, ili urok volokitam," excerpted in *Arzamas* 1: 252–256) performed in 1815. The second act satirizes the Karamzinists and specifically Shakhovskoi's Lipetsk play and the epigrams it provoked. One example will show how the wittiest lines got second and third wind in the polemics:

> The Count: "Nothing can be greater – a totally French turn of phrase. In the first line there is something about nature and in the second about dry waters."
>
> The Princess: "About dry waters! This is actually great! Too bad only that I don't understand it."
>
> The Count: "This is an allusion to the name of the play. Dry waters! Don't you feel Princess how witty this is! What a caustic double

entendre! Dry waters! How nasty! Honestly, in these two words there is much more intellect that in this entire comedy."

(*Arzamas* 1: 255)

I have tried to show that the Lipetsk spa serves as setting both for a parody, a parody of parody, and an ensuing chain of mutually parodic spa rhetoric. Parody is one of the more efficient products of a culture recycling its metaphors and puns, and parody of parody perpetuates this cycle of cultural invigoration. The fondness for quotation is part of this recycling – the quotes of old material retain both its old meaning and take on new value each time they are re-quoted and thus accumulate ever new layers of cultural capital.

This cycle of mutual ridicule promoted Russian parodic skills and especially the creative use of witty lines and double entendres. Vatsuro (20) perceptively describes the spirit of the polemic and emphasizes its "literariness," its "citationality" (*tsitatnost'*). It was a polemic that increasingly amused the participants themselves, as an insider's game, and depended on the their familiarity with the twists and turns of the battles and the specific lines uttered. Indeed Shakhovskoi's spa drama precipitated the very formation of the Karamzinist insider Arzamas society, dedicated solely to poking fun at the Colloqui and wittily implementing and abusing all key concepts in the debates, carrying on their anti-Shishkovite polemic in the spirit of galimatias, cacophony, anti-taste, in all sorts of parodic and satirical genres. This gave Shakhovskoi's spa drama impressive longevity and, I believe, proves that Shakhovskoi was a more worthy opponent than Shishkov himself and a better comedy writer than he has been given credit for.

I shall conclude with a few samples of the backwash that followed the Lipetsk flood. Lipetsk spa patriotism continued to figure both as discourse within discourse and discourse about discourse for almost half a century.

Viazemskii's "Letter from Lipetsk Waters" ("Pis'mo s lipetskikh vod," *Arzamas* 1: 248–252) was published in *The Russian Museum* (*Rossiiskii Muzeum*) in 1815 with a note: "Here we refer not to our Lipetsk waters, but to the German Leipzig waters," and a reminder: "we recall that Leipzig in ancient times was called Lipetsk and was built, according to legend, by Slavs." In Shakhovskoi's play two of the positive Shishkovite characters had mentioned their (heroic) participation in the Battle of Leipzig, and Viazemskii, no doubt also counts on his readers' recognition of true patriotism: one of his fellow-Karamzinists, Batiushkov, in real life served as Adjutant to General N.N. Raevskii, one of the heroes of the Napoleonic campaigns (Maikov, *Batiushkov* 183). Lipetsk waters are like any waters, the epistolary spa patron writes, "and if the main virtue of water, as is generally accepted, is the total absence of taste, then Lipetsk waters can compete with all the waters in the world." Here he comes up with a quintuple entendre on Lipetsk spa waters, the play "Lipetsk Waters," taste as the main criterion for good art and for good spa water, and the Russian patriotic proclivity to surpass European waters. The Lipetsk patient proceeds to describe and parody, in typical spa discourse, his boring fellow patients, all of them drawn from Shakhovskoi's play, studding his description with quotes from anti-Shakhovskoi pieces and epigrams by his friends. Shakhovskoi, author of "Lipetsk Waters" and critic of Karamzinism is himself now the patient most seriously ill in the virtual spa he himself created. He is now taking the Lipetsk waters to cure the bilious water fever that Zoilus acquainted the Greeks with and that has now spread to Petersburg and infected this poor victim and dried up his brain and hair. Shakhovskoi, the prime recipient of criticism, judging by pictures, as a young man had a bad comb-over and was quite bald as he got older; his ugliness was endlessly buffooned, as Julie Cassiday ("Of Dandies") has shown. His body is now poisoned, his moral sense and writing skills have washed away, and his works have become watery. Lipetsk waters cannot cure even the present writer himself: they don't grant him oblivion (as the Hades waters had done to many a writer before) and though he was prepared to put up with spa boredom, he cannot forget the bad verses and lukewarm comedies and now gives up on Lipetsk waters.[30]

D.N. Bludov's speech (*Arzamas* 1: 337–339) at an Arzamas gathering in 1816, apostrophizes V.L. Pushkin, one of Shakhovskoi's victims, and an eager contributor to the flood. Pushkin, en route from Petersburg, is alerted to the "dangers" of the town of Arzamas and prescribed a stop at Lipetsk waters to purify him from Colloqui contagion. Just a sprinkle of Lipetsk vapor can change everything, he is told: ballads become sins and objects of ridicule, fools become smart, honest people become monsters, and so on – all of which of course describes Shakhovskoi's comedy. The speaker here twists many familiar quotes from flood texts and varies the recipe for parody of parodies, by stripping the villains (Fialkin, Ugarov, Wolmar, Leleva) of their masks and then making them monstrously bad – the syrupy poet now becomes a criminal, etc. Appropriating Shakhovskoi's label and exaggerating it a hundredfold was designed to de-fang the enemy and turn the parody back on itself. Both theatricality and demasking fit the discourse of spa drama.[31]

These instances of parody on parody show the amazing skills at infusing new power into old water expressions and the kinds of innovation that Karamzinian "gallimatias" yielded. The polemics continued with further variations on parodic devices and on Lipetsk waters. Viazemskii, for instance, makes water and an empty wine cellar just punishment for drinkers of the Shakhovskoi ilk in a poem, "The Cellar" ("Pogreb" in Viazemskii 102–103), where "waters make only water." In the 1818 "The Pothole" ("Uxab" in Viazemskii 112–113) the road to happiness is full of potholes and a traveler trying to get to Lipetsk via Thalia (as did Shakhovskoi with his comedy), sinks into a pothole after the first act. Even as late as the 1850s Lipetsk spa still haunted Viazemskii when he himself visited European spas in the footsteps of Peter the Great. His poem "Baden-Baden" describes how his pre-season spa paradise is ruined once all the Parisian and London Duchesses, Viscountesses, Ladies, Lords, and Cavaliers arrive. He describes how they set their nets for their prelapsarian loves (or literally pre-flood, *dopotopnye*, the same word root as was used for the Lipetsk polemical flood) and how "my" Baden turns into a madhouse. A.F. Voeikov's "The Madhouse" ("Dom sumasshedshikh" in *Arzamas* 2: 167–173), was the title of one of the polemical Karamzinist poems. Perhaps the sexagenarian poet is nostalgically looking back at his youth's virtual spa season. While in Karlsbad around the same time he wrote an inscription to Peter, whose 1711–1712 visit had inspired him to develop Lipetsk. Viazemskii's poem was eternalized on a marble boulder in the area named for Peter, the Petrine Heights, near this spa, and in 1877 a bust of Peter was erected above his inscription. Viazemskii's inscription connects spas once again with legends about Peter and Russian patriotism with hints of imperialism and a symbolic Russification of a European spa:

> Great Peter, your every trace
> Is a holy monument for a Russian heart
> And here, amidst proud cliffs, your unforgettable image
> Rises in rays of love, and glory, and victory.
> Ancient legends about you are holy to us,
> Russian life is still illumined by you,
> And to your Memory, Great Peter,
> Your Great Russia remains faithful.
>
> (Viazemskii 312)

Notes

1 A version of this article was presented at a spa conference organized by Bath Spa University of Humanities and Culture Industries Centre of History and Culture, in Corsham, England, October 21–22, 2011. I am grateful for colleagues' comments.
2 For historical surveys and legends of Caucasian spas, see Sviatlovskii (1–93), Neliubin (1: 4 and 2: 3), and Bogoslovskii (7–8). For a summary, see Hammarberg, "Spas *in spe.*"
3 Peter's visits to European spas (Baden in 1698, Karlsbad in 1711 and 1712, Pyrmont in 1716, Spa in 1717, as well as Aachen) are mentioned in virtually all early Russian spa accounts. Petrine travelers, such as V.I. Kurakin, who visited Karlsbad and Teplitz in 1705, give us the first enthusiastic accounts (222–227). On Peter and indigenous Russian spas, as well as foreigners' reactions to them, see Křížek (213–216). Mansén shows how spas in Sweden, Finland, Estonia, and Denmark fit within the West European context. Swedish patriotic attitudes are not unlike those in Russia.
4 Juxtaposition of data in *Puteshestvie k Lipetskim mineral'nym vodam* makes Bekhteev the likely author (11, 59, 162). I have not been able to further identify him. Thanks to Sara Dickinson for sharing this text. Kugushev (1777–1825) published in journals such as *Ippokrena, Vestnik Evropy, Novosti russkoi literatury,* and *Zhurnal dlia milykh.* See *Slovar' russkikh pisatelei XVIII veka.* Peter's *ukaz* and his "Ob"iavlenie o Martsial'nykh vodakh" are appended to Kugushev's account.

5 All translations here and elsewhere are mine. I aim to convey content rather than poetic form.
6 Weingrod Sandor (xv) characterizes the spa as "a site where characters who identify with dialectically opposed interests meet, conflict, and eventually resolve their conflict." Spa drama inverts ordinary hierarchies of gender and power and portrays binary contrasts, such as aristocratic/fortuneless people, landed/moneyed, country/city, virtuous/vicious romantic/anti-romantic characters and serves as a liminal space mediating between such binaries (ix–xviii). Spas were typically credited with the ability to "drive all ill out / And cure what e're you please" and some spa texts contain amazingly naturalistic descriptions of the dismal hygienic conditions and list illnesses that presumably could be cured. See Hammarberg, "Spas *in spe*" (354) for examples of non-euphemistic descriptions of illnesses.
7 Commodification accompanies pastoral and historical aspects in Kugushev's and Bekhteev's accounts, and Kugushev gives examples of how Petrine sites were made into tourist attractions. See Benedict (206–208, 216).
8 See Benedict for a variety of spa discourses in English spas, including question-answer poems, spa toasts, panegyrics to wells, and various kinds of resort compendia. See Hill (92–93) on Fanny Burney's and Horace Walpole's descriptions of Lady Miller's Parnassian fairs, poetry readings, and competitions in Bath.
9 See Uspenskii and Lotman (331–466, esp. 370–374), on the distinctions between the *slaveno-rossiiskii*, *slavenskii*, and *russkii* languages.
10 This is an oversimplification in that there was much variation and generational divides on both sides. For simplicity's sake I will refer to them as Shishkovites and Karamzinists. Tynianov is the classic on this topic. The most concise corrective to Tynianov is Vatsuro. See also Uspenskii and Lotman for a detailed discussion of the participants and the interrelationship between socio-political and linguistic questions that underpinned the polemics.
11 Bobrov's text, though not immediately published, circulated in both camps. See Uspenskii and Lotman for a detailed analysis of the polemic and the first published version of Bobrov's text with extensive commentary. P.I. Makarov and S.S. Bobrov serve as masks for the respective groups (360). In Bekhteev's account similar imagery of the nether world, the river Styx is mentioned, and the local mount Ostrov is described as a new Parnassus with healing Castilian springs and attendant ode production.
12 Here and elsewhere, Bobrov mercilessly parodies the Karamzinist new style and dandyish feminized behavior and Karamzin himself, as in the reference to a hairdo *á la Tite* that Karamzin sported after his European journey. He peppers Gallo-Rus's speech with Gallicisms, French syntax, italics for emphasis, as well as all the ellipses, dashes and exclamations of the Karamzinist style.
13 Effete dandies are ubiquitous in spa dramas. Weingrod Sandor finds them in for instance Thomas D'Urfey's 1701 play "The Bath, or the Western Lass" (52–53), Thomas Baker's 1703 play "Tunbridge Walks, or the Yeoman of Kent" (70–76), Gabriel Odingsell's 1724 "The Bath Unmasked," which connects foppishness to Frenchness and which features a female libertine (113–122), and Richard Brinsley Sheridan's 1775 comedy "The Rivals," where two wannabe dandies and a super-sentimental figure are satirized (136–138, 147–153).
14 Maikov, *Batiushkov* (199–200). The idea of Karamzinism as an "infection," harming young minds, was used by Karamzin's old enemy, P.I. Golenishchev-Kutuzov in his 1810 denunciation. He now laments the fact that young people worship Karamzin and memorize his works, and he feels that "we must think of the Universitites and somehow exterminate this infection" (quoted in Proskurin, *Literaturnye skandaly* 113).

258   *Gitta Hammarberg*

15 "Opinions" is signed by Vasilii Efimov (a pseudonym for A.E. Izmailov), and published in 1810 in the journal *Tsvetnik*. The setting and specific topoi lead me to see it partly as a belated repartee to the Bobrov piece. Proskurin, *Literaturnye skandaly* (116–142) unravels the complexities of the larger context.

16 See Proskurin, *Literaturnye skandaly* (81–116). The moral accusations by Golenishchev-Kutuzov against Karamzin as an apostate Mason had started as early as 1790 when he returned from abroad.

17 It appeared in the same issue of *Tsvetnik* as Efimov-Izmailov's piece and was subsequently re-titled "The True Patriot" ("Istinnyi patriot"). See Proskurin, *Literaturnye skandaly* (104). The epigram recalls the title of Karamzin's only novel *A Knight of Our Time* (*Rytsar' nashego vremeni*, in Karamzin 2: 755–782), where an innocent Russian boy is seduced by a sophisticated older woman, a text that might have added to the moral ire of his opposition.

18 The Shalikov circle of Karamzinist epigones drowned here include B. Blank and M.N. Makarov. The three women, A. Bunina, M.E. Izvekova, and E. Titova, particularly the talented poet Bunina, were repeatedly drowned elsewhere as well for example in a pithy 1809 madrigal by Batiushkov, repeating one of the legends about Sappho and her lover Phaon, while also alluding to I.I. Dmitriev's rumored rejection of Bunina: "You are Sappho, I'm Phaon / I don't dispute it / But to my sorrow / You don't know the path to the sea." See Proskurin, *Literaturnye skandaly* (158–159). Much later, in 1815, in a speech at one of the first meetings of Arzamas, S.S. Uvarov nastily connects her (real) planned trip to England for breast cancer treatment and is unstinting with sexual innuendo as to the provenance of her children-poems, this time involving Shishkov, her Beseda mentor. Proskurin (*Literaturnye skandaly* 164–187) argues that the subtext for Uvarov's speech is Karamzin's "Poor Liza" and the heroine's drowning in a pond. Water here, too, serves as punishment for moral transgression.

19 For an analysis of the play, see Cassiday, "Of Dandies," and "Spa as Theater." The latter compares Shakhovskoi's play to Lermontov's "Princess Mary" in *Hero of Our Time* set in Caucasian spas.

20 Targeting Karamzin by proxy was a widespread tactic. See e.g. Proskurin, *Skandaly* and Hammarberg, "Karamzinolatry." The specific targets here are V.A. Zhukovskii, S.S. Uvarov, and V.L. Pushkin. Karamzin himself did not actively participate in the polemic.

21 A Rousseauan character by name, a Karamzinist for trying to please the ladies, and, like V.L. Pushkin, much older than his rivals and suffering from gout, he is the originator and recipient of epigrams and is warned that love and gout are equally dangerous for him. The word "dangerous" is a subtle allusion to his "A Dangerous Neighbor" ("Opasnyi sosed" in Pushkin 155–161), where he placed Shakhovskoi's earlier satirical play "The New Sterne" ("Novyi Stern" in Shakhovskoi 735–752) in a bordello, read by the prostitutes.

22 V.L. Pushkin had indeed fled to Nizhnii Novgorod when Napoleon threatened Moscow, as had Karamzin, but so had numerous other Muscovites. Dandyism was most directly connected to spas by Beau Nash, "the uncrowned king of Bath," as Hill (16) refers to him, from 1705 till 1761. George IV installed riding stables adjacent to his famous Royal Pavillion in Brighton. See Moers (60–65) on the "jockey" dandy.

23 The Karamzinist in their idyllic fervor would include flowers in their minor verse, incorporate flower codes in their texts, and adorn their journals with fancy flowery names and engravings.

24 The portrait of Ol'gin evokes the real life Shalikov who was known as a dandy with a nasty tongue. P.I. Makarov, V.L. Pushkin, and many other Karamzinists also stood out for their dandyism, as did in his youth Karamzin himself. On Makarov's dandyism, see Uspenskii and Lotman (352). On V.L. Pushkin's

dandyism, see I.I. Dmitriev's mock travelogue, "N.N.'s Journey to Paris and London, written three days before the journey" ("Puteshestvie N. N. v Parizh i London, pisannoe za tri dni do puteshestvia," in Dmitriev 348–351).

25 The ape and the parrot were long-standing satirical labels for dandies and imitators of the French used in e.g. Ia.B. Kniazhnin's comedies, P.A. L'vov's poems, and Catherine the Great's satire. It was used by Karamzin himself. See Uspenskii and Lotman (463–464, 498). The same images fit European spa discourse; for example, the frontispiece for *The Bath, Bristol, Tunbridge and Epsom Miscellany*, satirizes vanity using the images of a beau, a monkey, a parrot, and a mirror (Benedict 207).

26 The name Leleva could be pure coincidence, but Kugushev (45) mentions a spa patient with a similar last name, a Mrs Eleva, who in 1799 was persuaded by General L'vov to go to Lipetsk, where she was miraculously healed.

27 Hill (90–106) singles out the hypocrites, the "tonish" characters, and the courtship among Bath characters. "Behind the gilded surfaces and the illusions of decorum, elegance, and morality, Bath harbored [...] greed, adultery, drunkenness, and profligacy" (24). Weingrod Sandor (95, 132, 174) analyzes several plays where the spa is a marriage market full of intrigue and scandal. Titles like Sheridan's "A School for Scandal" or "The Slanderers" are indicative.

28 On Shalikov's antics, see Hammarberg, "Karamzin After Karamzin." On V.L. Pushkin's behavior, see Vigel' (vol. 1, part 1: 131–133). Proskurin, "Chto skryvalos'" discusses the uses of fashion in the Karamzinist-Shishkovite polemic.

29 Shakhovskoi and his common-law wife were mercilessly lampooned on several occasions. See Cassiday, "Of Dandies."

30 Boredom is part of the generally accepted spa cure, its regulated leisure, its daily schedules (Mackaman 1–3).

31 This is laid bare succinctly by Pander in Odingsell's 1725 play "The Bath Unmasked": "People always come to the Bath with the same happy Disposition for Idleness and Pleasure. [...] The Wise and Witty are content to play the Fool, and Fools pass for Wits: Politicians turn Gamesters, and Gamesters to the Politique among 'em: Intrigues of the Council-board are turned into Intrigues of the Chamber: Lord and Pickpockets consort very amicably together" (quoted in Weingrod Sandor 105).

Bibliography

"Arzamas" Sbornik v dvukh knigakh. Ed. V.E. Vatsuro and A.L. Ospovat, 2 vols. Moscow: Khudozhestvennaia literatura, 1994.

Batiushkov, K.N. *Sochineniia*. Ed. N.V. Fridman. Moscow: Gosudarstvennoe izdatel'stvo Khudozhestvennaia literaturea, 1955.

[Bekhteev]. *Puteshestvie k Lipetskim mineral'nym vodam v 1803 godu*. Moscow: Tipografiia Krazheva i Meia, 1804.

Benedict, Barbara M. "Consumptive Communities: Commodifying Nature in Spa Society." *The Eighteenth Century* 36.3 (1995): 203–219.

Bogoslovskii, V.S. *Piatigorskie i snimi smezhnye mineral'nye vody. Sbornik istoricheskikh, statisticheskikh, ekonomicheskikh ivrachebnykh svedenii, otnosiashchikhsia k mineral'nym vodam*. Moscow: Tip. A Suvorina, 1883.

Cassiday, Julie A. "Of Dandies, Flirts, and Cockatoos: Shakhovskoi's Antitheatrical *Lesson to Coquettes*." *The Russian Review* 65 (2006): 393–416.

Cassiday, Julie A. "Spa as Theater in Nineteenth-Century Russia." Paper presented at the spa conference organized by Bath Spa University of Humanities and

Culture Industries Centre of History and Culture, in Corsham, England, October 21–22, 2011.
Dmitriev, I.I. *Polnoe sobranie stikhotvorenii*. Ed. V.N. Orlov *et al*. Leningrad: Izdatel'stvo Sovetskii pisatel', 1967.
Hammarberg, Gitta. "Karamzin After Karamzin: The Case of Prince Shalikov." *A Window on Russia*. Ed. Maria di Salvo and Lindsey Hughes. Rome: La Fenice Edizioni, 1996, 275–283.
Hammarberg, Gitta. "Spas *in spe*: Castalian Springs, Muses, and Muzhiks in Lipetsk." *Eighteenth-Century Russia: Society, Culture, Economy*. Ed. Roger Bartlett and Gabriela Lehmann-Carli. Berlin: LIT Verlag, 2007, 341–355.
Hammarberg, Gitta. "Karamzinolatry and Epigonism." *Russian Literature* 75: 1–4 (2014): 189–217.
Hill, Mary Kate. "The City of Bath in Eighteenth-Century English Novels." PhD dissertation, University of Southern Louisiana, 1984.
Karamzin, N.M. *Izbrannye sochineniia*. Ed. P. Berkov and G. Makogonenko, 2 vols. Moscow and Leningrad: Izdatel'stvo Khudozhestvennaia literatura, 1964.
Kh. Sh. "Pis'ma k F. Bulgarinu, ili Poezdka na Kavkaz." *Severnyi arkhiv* 33.6 (1828): 259.
Kimmel, Le Docteur, *Lettres écrites dans un voyage de Moscou au Caucase pour servir de guide aux persones qui se rendent au Eaux de ce pays*. Moscow: l'Imprimerie de N. S. Vsevolojsky, 1812.
Křížek, Vladimir. *Kulturgeschichte des Heilbades*. Stuttgart: Verlag W. Kohlhammer, 1990.
Kugushev, Nikolai Mikhailovich. *Kurs moi v Lipetske v 1804 godu*. Moscow, 1804.
Kurakin, V.I. "Dnevnik i putevye zametki (1705–1708)." *Rossiia i zapad: gorizonty vzaimopoznaniia. Literaturnye istochniki pervoi chetverti XVIII veka*. Ed. E.N. Lepekhin and N.D. Bludilina. Moscow: Nasledie, 2000, 215–310.
Mackaman, Douglas Peter. "Doctoring on Vacation: Medicine and Culture at the Spas of Nineteenth-Century France." PhD dissertation, University of California at Berkeley, 1993.
Maikov, L.N. *Rasskazy Nartova o Petre Velikom*. Petersburg: Tipografiia Imperatorskoi akademii nauk, 1891.
Maikov, L.N. *Batiushkov, ego zhizn' i sochineniia*. Moscow: Agraf, 2001.
Mansén, Elizabeth. *Ett paradis på jorden. Om den svenska kurortskulturen 1680–1880*. Stockholm: Atlantis, 2001.
Moers, Ellen. *The Dandy: Brummell to Beerbohm*. New York: The Viking Press, 1960.
Neliubin, A. *Polnoe istoricheskoe, medico-topograficheskoe, fiziko-khimicheskoe i vrachebnoe opisanie Kavkazskikh mineral'nykh vod*, 2 vols. Petersburg: v tip. Meditsinskogo departamenta vnutr. del, 1825.
Proskurin, Oleg. "Chto skryvalos' pod pantalonami (Korreliatsiia 'moda – iazyk' v 'Evgenii Onegine' i ee kul'turnyi kontekst." *Poeziia Pushkina ili podvizhnyi palimpsest*. Moscow: Novoe literaturnoe obozrenie, 1999, 301–343.
Proskurin, Oleg. *Literaturnye skandaly pushkinskoi epokhi*. Moscow: OGI, 2000.
Pushkin, V.L. *Stikhi, Proza, Pis'ma*. Moscow: Sovetskaia Rossiia, 1989, 156–161.
Shakhovskoi, A.A. *Komedii i stikhotvoreniia*. Leningrad: Sovetskii pisatel', 1961.
Shishkov, A.S. "*Rassuzhdenie o starom i novom sloge Rossiiskogo iazyka*." Petersburg, 1803.

Slovar' russkikh pisatelei XVIII veka. Ed. G.N. Moiseeva *et al.* Petersburg: Nauka, 1999.
Sviatlovskii, V.V. *Kavkazskie mineral'nye vody: vo vrachebnom, istoricheskom i drugikh otnosheniiakh, s prilozheniem Ocherka kak nado pit'mineral'nuiu vodu i kupat'sia v nei*. Ekaterinoslav: Izd. M.S. Kopylova, 1898.
Tosi, Alessandra. *Waiting for Pushkin: Russian Fiction in the Reign of Alexander I (1801–1825)*. Amsterdam and New York: Rodopi, 2006.
Tynianov, Iurii N. *Arkhaisty i novatory*. Leningrad, 1929, rpt. Munich: Wilhelm Fink Verlag, 1967.
Uspenskii, B.A., and Iurii Lotman. "Spory o iazyke v nachale XIX v. kak fakt russkoi kul'tury ('Proisshestvie v tsarstve tenei, ili sud'bina rossiiskogo iazyka' – neizvestnoe sochinenie Semena Bobrova)." In B.A. Uspenskii, *Izbrannye trudy*, vol 2: *Iazyk i kul'tura*. Moscow: Gnosis, 1994, 331–466.
Vainshtein, Ol'ga. *Dendi. Moda. Literatura. Stil' zhizni*. Moscow: Novoe literaturnoe obozrenie, 2005.
Vatsuro, V. "V preddverii pushkinskoi epokhi." Introduction to *"Arzamas" Sbornik v dvukh knigakh*. Ed. V.E. Vatsuro and A.L. Ospovat, 2 vols. Moscow: Khudozhestvennaia literatura, 1994, vol. 1, 5–27.
Viazemskii, P.A. *Stikhotvoreniia. Ed.* Iu.A. Andreev. Leningrad: Sovetskii pisatel', 1986.
Vigel', F.F. *Zapiski*, vol. 1. Moscow: Artel' pisatelei Krug, 1928.
Weingrod Sandor, Louise Elisa. "Spa Drama from Shadwell to Sheridan." PhD dissertation, Brandeis University, 1988.

Index

After Death, by Evgenii Bauer 193
"After Death (Klara Milich)" by Ivan Turgenev 193
Aitmatov, Chingiz 209–10, 213, 215
Alaimo, Stacy 232
Alaska 117, 118, 123, 124, 126, 131–2
Angara, river 5, 38, 39, 42, 207
Apparitions 192, 195, 196, 198–202
"Apparitions" 9, 192, 193, 196–8
aquatic imagery 69, 143, 197, 202, 224, 236
Arctic, the 117, 118, 119, 124, 130
Arzamas 248, 254, 255
Ascent, The 209, 215
Astrakhan 181, 216
Avvakum, Archpriest 32–3, 37
Azov Sea 179, 181

Bachelard, Gaston 235, 236, 237
Baikal, Lake 35–47, 94
Bakunin, Aleksandr 140–3, 153–4
ballad 252, 255
Bal'mont, Konstantin 195–8, 199, 200, 201, 202
Baltic Sea 177, 178, 179, 181, 182, 184
bania *see* bathing
barge haulers (*burlaki*) 92
bathing 8, 20, 23, 42, 47, 128–9, 144, 145, 150, 217 *see also* washing
Batiushkov, K.N. 249, 250, 254
Battle of Stalingrad 86, 90–2, 179
Bauer, Evgenii 193
Bazhov, Pavel 113
Belomor Canal 175, 176–7, 182, 184
Benois, Alexandre 200
Bering Strait 117–8, 123, 127, 129, 132, 134
Black Sea 177
Bludov, D.N. 255

Bobrov, S.S. 248, 249, 250
Borisov-Musatov, Viktor 198–9, 202
bread 19, 21, 123, 127
Bronze Horseman, The 158–9, 161, 166, 168
Brummell, Beau 245
Bruno, Andy 2
Buddhism 33, 38, 45
Bukha-noion-babai 35
Bulagat tribe 35, 36
Buriat 33, 35–9, 40–7
Böhme, Hartmut 225, 236

Cape Burkhan 38, 39, 43
Caspian Sea 176, 177, 178, 179, 181, 182
Catherine II (the Great) 92
Caucasus, the 222, 223, 224, 246, 247
chapels 53–6, 57–8
Chen, Cecilia 225, 235
Chernetsov, Grigory and Nikanor 84
Chiaureli, Mikheil 213
childhood 88, 120, 124–5, 197, 198, 202
Chukchi people 117–18, 123, 125, 128, 129
Chukotka 130–3, 134
Chusovaia, river 98–113
coffee 117–18, 123, 124, 131–2
Colloqui of the Lovers of the Russian Word (*Beseda liubitelei russkogo slova*) 248, 250, 254, 255
colonization 44, 67, 84, 92, 108
conceptual blending 194, 202
conceptual metaphor 194, 202
conspicuous consumption 245, 247, 248, 252
construction projects: bathhouses 128 *see also* bathing; dams 5, 10,

222–3, 224, 226, 228, 232–3, 236–9; Moscow Canal 9, 175–85; Vyshnyi Volochek Waterway system 147
cooking 126–9, 134
creation myths 20, 35, 46, 47, 141, 198, 228
Cronon, William 2, 3, 209
cult: ancestor cults 215; of the Volga 85–6; of water 15, 20, 21, 52, 55, 61, 84, 154; Soviet cult of the machine 213, 217
cultural semantics 15–29

dams: dam building 5–6, 10, 147, 148, 207, 224, 229, 230, 238–240; hydroelectric dams 207, 225 *see also* hydroelectricity; mega-dams 5, 6, 207, 225, 229, 230, 236
dandyism 245, 246
Dashkov, D.V. 248, 253
Deleuze, Gilles 226, 227, 235
dialects 15–29, 71
dissolution 193, 233–4
Dmitlag labor camp 176, 178–80
Dmitrov 178
double entendre 253, 254
Dovzhenko, Aleksandr 209, 213, 214
drought 10, 66, 207, 211, 216, 217, 231
Dubna, river 178

earthquakes 33, 37, 47
Eisenstein, Sergei 213, 214
Ekhirit tribe 35, 36
Eliade, Mircea 34, 35, 36
embodiment: of death 89–90; of divinity 58; of experience 192, 194, 200, 202; of femininity 28, 83, 215; of freedom 92; of hybridization 239; of the power of nature 19, 66, 140; of Russianness 85, 89
emotional memory 193, 196, 197, 198
Enlightenment, the 67, 142, 229, 251
environment 5, 8, 41, 47, 102, 194, 207, 211, 213, 218, 222, 225, 230, 232, 233
environmental cinema 218
epigram 248, 253, 255
estates: Nikol'skoe-Cherenchitsy 140, 141, 143, 145, 146; Znamensk-Raek 150–1; Mitino-Vasilevo 147–8; Priamukhino 153–4
eternal feminine, the (vechnaia zhenstvennost') 192, 193, 194, 195, 202

Evenks 33, 37, 41, 43, 44
Evtushenko, Evgeny 89, 93
Experimental Film Studio 216

Farewell to Matyora: Rasputin's book 70, 207; Shepit'ko's film 207, 218
fashion 245, 247, 248, 251, 252
Faust 192
female spirituality 192
femininity 19, 36, 46, 81, 84, 92, 93, 171, 192, 193, 195–8, 202
feminization 93, 248
fertility 15, 35, 36, 38, 88, 93, 154, 211
Fet, Afanasii 195
fishing 8, 33, 37, 40, 42, 47, 76, 144
five-year plans 85, 176, 184, 223
floods: dangers of 20, 66, 229; and folk beliefs 25; of Lipetsk 10, 247, 248, 254; of Saint Petersburg 8–9, 158–73; spring 1, 20, 25, 57
flow 25
fluidity 193, 200, 202, 225–6
folk culture 16–17, 18, 19, 23, 26–8, 72, 75, 218
food 118, 127–8
FORGETTING IS A DOWNWARD MOVEMENT (IN WATER) 198
Francomania 249, 250
frivolity 246, 247, 251

galimatias 254
Gardner, Vadim 162–3
gender 7, 81–2, 86, 88–9, 91, 171
German, Pavel 179–80
Gestwa, Klaus 225, 229
Gold of the Rebellion, or Down Through the River Narrows, The 112
ghosts 9, 74, 191, 202
Great Patriotic War *see* World War II
Great Purges 184
Griboedov, Aleksandr 158, 161
Groys, Boris 177
Guattari, Félix 226, 227, 235
guidebooks 99, 106–12, 113, 247
gulags 175, 176, 180, 182
Gulf of Finland 158, 160

Hausmann, Guido 3
Heat 10, 208, 209, 210, 214, 215, 216, 218
historic cognitive framework 194
holy springs 51–3, 55, 60, 61, 62
Holy Synod, the 52, 55, 56
holy water 20, 55, 59

holy wells 53, 54–8, 59–61
homelands 102, 118
hospitality 120, 123, 125, 132
"House of Usher" 201
HUMAN IS LIQUID/HUMAN EMOTION IS LIQUID 194
hunting 22–3, 33, 37, 40–2
Hydrocentral 9, 222, 223, 227, 233, 240
hydroelectricity 178, 207, 222–3, 224, 225, 229
hygiene *see* bathing

iconography 145, 195, 197, 216, 217
icons 52, 53–5, 56, 57–63, 216
identity: gender 91 *see also* gender; local 8, 161, 99, 106, 112, 117–18; national 81, 83, 93, 99, 117–18
idioms 15–29
In Boundlessness 192, 196
Ivanov, Alexander 216
Ivanov, Alexei 112, 113
Izmailov, A.E. 249

Josephson, Paul 6, 207, 211

Kalotozov, Mikhail 208
Kama, river 17, 19, 21–2, 24–5, 70, 111
Karamzin, N.M. 249–53
Karamzinist poetics 247–56
Kazakhstan 209
Khada, Sagaan 42
Khagdaev, Valentin 38, 43, 45
Khimki, river 178
Khlebnikov, Velimir 70, 89
Khori tribes 35
Khrushchev, Nikita 110, 208, 210, 211, 212
Kitezh 218
Klimov, Elem 207
Kliuchevskii, Vasily 2
Kniazev, Vasilii 166–8
Kogan, Lazar 179
Kugushev, N.M. 245, 246, 247, 248, 249, 250
Kyrgyz film studios 209

landscape: aesthetics 102, 104–5; co-spatial 73–4; human connection to 41, 66, 67, 123, 211; man-made 152–4; Soviet 5–8, 177, 185, 213, 224, 230, 233; spirituality 74–7; and Symbolism 191, 195–6, 198–201; and water 3, 65–7, 72, 73, 104–7, 117, 123, 195, 200, 201, 209–210

Lefebvre, Henri 178
Lenin, Vladimir 85, 159–60, 235
Leningrad, 159–60, 163, 164, 167, 169, 171, 179, 209 *see also* Saint Petersburg
Leningrad Zoo 160, 167
leisure 106, 111, 247
LIFE AS A JOURNEY 198
light verse 252
Lipetsk 246, 247, 250, 251, 252, 253
literary devices 246
literary polemics 245–54
liquescence 192, 193, 194, 195
local knowledge 123
Lopatin, Pavel 182, 184
L'vov, Nikolai 140, 141, 143, 144–54

Makarov, P.I. 248
Mamin-Sibiriak, Dmitrii 113
masculinity 86, 91, 171, 251
materiality 99, 139, 225, 227, 231–4, 236
Matich, Olga 234, 235, 239
memoryscape 195, 196
mental space 194
mental worlds 65, 68
mercy 40, 88–89, 93
Message: Chusovaia 112
meta-geography 72
metaphor 8, 9, 69, 73, 82–4, 89, 92, 169, 172–85, 191–202, 223–8, 237
Mickiewicz, Adam 158, 161
modernization 5–7, 10, 208, 223–5, 227–8, 229–233, 240
Moscow 2, 176–85, 232, 250
Moscow Canal 9, 175, 176–85, 229 *see also* construction projects
Moscow, river 5, 146, 147
"Mother Russia" 81–93, 214; in political mobilization, legitimization and delegitimization of power 82, 83, 86, 89, 90; and stereotypes of Russianness 15, 16, 81
"Mother Volga": ambivalence of 88–9; "Let us defend Mother Volga!" poster 91; maternal traits of 81–92; monument 86; Russians as children of 89; substitute for "Mother Russia" 81, 89, 93; symbol of suffering of Russian people 85, 90, 91–2; as a tool of inclusion/exclusion 83, 84, 90
motherland 83, 85, 86, 89, 91, 181 *see also* "Mother Russia"

Motherland of Electricity 10, 208, 209, 216, 218
movement: in art 194–5, 198–201, 209, 215–16; of water 19, 25, 26, 65, 66, 67, 71, 103, 222, 226, 235 *see also* landscape and Symbolism
multisensory imagery 194, 197
mythology: Ket 72; local 111, 113, 139; of the river 22, 65, 66, 71, 72, 154; Russian national 3, 70, 83, 89, 161; of Saint Petersburg 161, 173; Soviet 225; of water 15–19, 22, 23, 28, 153, 218 *see also* creation myths

Na Shturm trassy 180
Napoleon 248, 249, 251
Nash, Richard (Beau) 245
nationalism 7, 81, 82, 85, 93
natural disasters 8–9, 33, 37, 159, 160, 161, 166–9, 173 *see also* earthquakes, *see also* floods
natural holy places 51–3, 56, 57, 60, 61, 62
Neimanis, Astrida 237
Nekrasov, Nikolay 84, 92, 173
neomythology of estate life 154
Nerpa seal 35, 36, 37, 38, 40, 41
Neva, river 5, 77, 158, 159, 160, 161, 163, 171, 172
New Wave cinema 208
Nicholas, Mary 222, 223, 234, 238, 240
Northern River Port of the Moscow Canal 182, 185

ocherk 98–9
Old Russia 250
Ol'khon island 35, 36, 37, 38, 40, 42, 45
Olonets 246
Orthodox Christianity 7, 15, 37, 38, 56, 112

Paperny, Vladimir 185, 230
parody 254, 255
Pasternak, Boris 70, 71, 72
patriotism 8, 10, 113, 245, 250–4, 256
Peter I (the Great) 147, 158, 159, 160, 166, 176, 181, 245, 246, 255, 256
petroglyphs of Sagan-Zaba 43
Platonov, Andrei 216, 217, 230
Poe, Edgar Allan 201
poetics: Futurist 170, 171; Sentimentalist 252; Symbolist 170, 191, 195–6, 200; urban 165

"Port of Five Seas" 5, 9, 175–6, 179, 181–5 *see also* Moscow
"Port of Three Seas" 178, 179, 181, 182, 184 *see also* Moscow
production novel 9, 223–4
propaganda 6, 7, 9, 82, 86, 90, 91, 210, 212, 217, 218
Pugachev, Yemelyan 92
Pushkin, Alexander 69, 84, 88, 158–9, 161, 166, 168
Pushkin, V.L. 251, 252, 255
Putin, Vladimir 83, 87

quotation 110, 249, 254

Rasputin, Valentin 46, 70, 207
Razin, Stepan 92
religion 15, 33–5, 38, 47, 56, 144 *see also religions by name*
REMEMBERING IS AN UPWARD MOVEMENT (IN WATER) 198
representation of water 7, 8, 15, 68, 99
Reshetnikov, Fedor 102
Riabonon, Sergei 180
ridicule 252, 254, 255
ritual 4, 6, 15, 16–17, 20–3, 24–8, 33, 34–5, 38, 40–5, 47, 66
Riumin, Veniamin 180
rivers 1–7, 22, 24, 26, 37, 40–2, 65–72, 81–4, 93, 99, 103, 109–11, 153–4, 224, 230
rivers as national symbols 83, 84, 85, 89
Rodchenko, Alexander 208
Rozanov, Vasily 85, 88
rusalka 20, 218,
Russian Civil War 67, 159, 213
Russian gentry estate 139–40, 154
Russian national identity 5, 7–8, 81, 83, 85, 87, 90, 93, 117, 124

sacred water 4, 7, 18, 32–9, 42, 43, 46–7, 84, 179
Saint Petersburg 147, 158–60, 163, 165, 166
satire 245, 248, 249
Schama, Simon 175, 178
sea: "of life" 228, 233, 235, 237; "Moscow" 178; "Sacred" *see* Baikal
sentimentalism 10, 84, 142, 246–8, 251–2
Sergeev, Mark 38, 39, 46
Sestra, river 178

Index

Shaginian, Marietta 9, 222–4, 227, 230, 235–7, 238, 239, 240
Shakhovskoi, A. A. 250, 252–5
Shalikov, P.I. 248, 250, 252
Shaman's Rock *see* Cape Burkhan
Shamanka *see* Cape Burkhan
shamanism 33, 35, 36, 38, 40, 42, 43, 45, 47
Sheidlin, A. 108–9, 111
Shepit'ko, Larisa 9, 10, 207–219
see also internal rhythm 209; exaggerated camera angles 214, 215; religious allusions 217
Sheridan, R.B. 245
Shishkov, A.S. 247–8
Socialist Realism 182, 222, 223, 224, 230, 235, 240
Sokolov, Sasha 7, 70, 72–6
Solov'ev, Vladimir 192
"Song of Volga", song 86
Sophia (Divine Sophia) 192
Soviet Armenia 222, 223, 224, 229, 231, 233, 237
Soviet film-making: in Stalin era 213, 230; during the Thaw 207, 208, 218
Soviet musicals 84, 86, 200, 213
Spa: comedy 245; culture 246; discourse 247, 255; Russian and European spas 245–7, 251, 252, 255–6
spirits 34–9, 40–7, 65, 67, 76
springs: as a source of drinking water 129, 130, 140, 146, 208, 210, healing 44, 53–5, 154, 245–6, and idioms 20–4, 25; sacred 7, 37, 42, 44, 51–5, 60–62; veneration of 7, 24, 52–62
Stalin, Joseph 177, 178, 182, 213, 230, 235
statues 153, 185, 201
superstition, 51, 53–7
Svetloyar, Lake 218
Symbolism 193, 194, 200; Symbolist art 191–4; Symbolist Correspondences 200
Symbolist poetry 195–6
synesthesia 193, 194, 195, 200, 202

tailgan 38, 40, 42
taste 152, 248, 249, 254
tea 8, 117–26, 128, 131–2, 134–5
Tegsh 40

territorialization 226–7, 235, 236, 238, 239
thirst 21, 117, 120, 129–34, 178, 210
TIME AS A FLOW OF LIQUID 198
Tolstoy, Aleksei K. 84
tourism 7, 38, 44, 68, 99, 101, 106–10, 111, 113, 184, 247
tractors 85, 209, 212, 213–5, 217
traditionalism 160, 163, 165
transcendence 191–4, 196
Trans-Siberian Railway 101
tundra 117, 120–2
Turgenev, Ivan 69, 193, 195–6, 200
Tver' region 147

Ukrainian famine 217
Urals, the 7, 98–110, 111, 113, 114
Uspenskii, Gleb 105
utopianism 9, 110, 191, 223, 225, 229–30, 232, 234–6, 239–40
Uvarov, S.S. 248, 251

Viazemskii, P.A. 248, 249, 253, 254–5, 256
Vechorka, Tat'iana 170, 171
Vesnovskii, Viktor 107
Virgin Lands Campaign 207, 210, 213
Voeikov, A.F. 256
Volga, river 3, 5, 7, 67, 69, 70, 72, 81, 84–93, 99, 175, 176–8, 182, 184
Volga-Don Canal 5, 176, 179, 181, 182, 185
"Volga River Flows", song 87
"Volga the Free" (*voliushka*) 92
"Volga-Volga", film 86
Vlasova, Elena 103
von Goethe, Johann Wolfgang 192

water delivery 126, 129, 131
water infrastructure 125, 127, 129
water symbolism 15–16, 20, 22, 23–7, 34–5, 66, 82, 89, 94, 168, 184, 250
water quality 122, 125, 127
Wings 209, 218
Wagner, Richard 200
washing 20, 47, 60, 128, 238 *see also* bathing
water pollution 42, 91, 126, 251
Weltseele ("the World Soul" or "anima mundi") 192
Weiner, Douglas 2–3
Westernization 10, 245, 256

White Sea 178, 179, 181, 184
wit 252, 253, 254
word play 27, 252
World War I 67
World War II 86, 90–91, 218

Yastrebov, Evgenii 101, 110–11
Yekaterinburg 101, 102, 110, 111
Yenisei river 38, 47, 99
"Yermak's Swans" 109

Yupiget people 118, 120, 124–5, 128, 131–3

Zagoskin, M.N. 253
Zamiatin, Evgenii 170, 171–2
Zenkevich, Mikhail 161, 164, 166, 169, 170
Zhukovskii, V.A. 192, 251, 252, 253
Zoshchenko, Mikhail 172
Zykina, Lyudmila 87

Helping you to choose the right eBooks for your Library

Add Routledge titles to your library's digital collection today. Taylor and Francis ebooks contains over 50,000 titles in the Humanities, Social Sciences, Behavioural Sciences, Built Environment and Law.

Choose from a range of subject packages or create your own!

Benefits for you
- Free MARC records
- COUNTER-compliant usage statistics
- Flexible purchase and pricing options
- All titles DRM-free.

REQUEST YOUR FREE INSTITUTIONAL TRIAL TODAY

Free Trials Available
We offer free trials to qualifying academic, corporate and government customers.

Benefits for your user
- Off-site, anytime access via Athens or referring URL
- Print or copy pages or chapters
- Full content search
- Bookmark, highlight and annotate text
- Access to thousands of pages of quality research at the click of a button.

eCollections – Choose from over 30 subject eCollections, including:

Archaeology	Language Learning
Architecture	Law
Asian Studies	Literature
Business & Management	Media & Communication
Classical Studies	Middle East Studies
Construction	Music
Creative & Media Arts	Philosophy
Criminology & Criminal Justice	Planning
Economics	Politics
Education	Psychology & Mental Health
Energy	Religion
Engineering	Security
English Language & Linguistics	Social Work
Environment & Sustainability	Sociology
Geography	Sport
Health Studies	Theatre & Performance
History	Tourism, Hospitality & Events

For more information, pricing enquiries or to order a free trial, please contact your local sales team: **www.tandfebooks.com/page/sales**

 | The home of Routledge books

www.tandfebooks.com